An Innocent
in Cuba

ALSO BY DAVID MCFADDEN

POETRY
Intense Pleasure, 1972
A Knight in Dried Plums, 1975
The Poet's Progress, 1977
On the Road Again, 1978
My Body Was Eaten by Dogs, 1981
The Art of Darkness, 1984
Gypsy Guitar, 1987
Anonymity Suite, 1992
The Death of Greg Curnoe, 1995
There'll Be Another, 1995
Five Star Planet, 2002
Cow Swims Lake Ontario, 2003

FICTION
The Great Canadian Sonnet, 1975, 2002
Animal Spirits, 1983
Canadian Sunset, 1986

NON-FICTION
A Trip Around Lake Erie, 1981
A Trip Around Lake Huron, 1981
A Trip Around Lake Ontario, 1988
An Innocent in Ireland, 1995
Great Lakes Suite, 1997
An Innocent in Scotland, 1999
An Innocent in Newfoundland, 2003

An Innocent in Cuba

FURTHER CURIOUS RAMBLES AND SINGULAR ENCOUNTERS

DAVID W. McFADDEN

M&S

Library and Archives Canada Cataloguing in Publication

McFadden, David
An innocent in Cuba : further curious rambles and singular
encounters / David McFadden.

ISBN 0-7710-5506-4

1. McFadden, David – Travel – Cuba.
2. Cuba – Description and travel. I. Title.

FI765.3.M33 2005   917.29104'64   C2005-901799-6

We acknowledge the financial support of the Government of Canada through the Book Publishing Industry Development Program and that of the Government of Ontario through the Ontario Media Development Corporation's Ontario Book Initiative. We further acknowledge the support of the Canada Council for the Arts and the Ontario Arts Council for our publishing program.

Author's note: The first names of several people in this book have been changed, and no full names have been used. No one requested their real name not be used, but it seemed like the right thing to do, just to be on the safe side. Also, population figures in the text are 2005 estimates from www.world-gazetteer.com.

Typeset in Goudy by M&S, Toronto
Printed and bound in Canada

This book is printed on acid-free paper that is 100% recycled, ancient-forest friendly (100% post-consumer recycled).

McClelland & Stewart Ltd.
The Canadian Publishers
481 University Avenue
Toronto, Ontario
M5G 2E9
www.mcclelland.com

1 2 3 4 5   09 08 07 06 05

For my father, my daughter, my brother
– and for Cachita too.

If there were only one truth, you couldn't
paint a hundred canvases on the same theme.

– Pablo Picasso

CONTENTS

SEA OF HAPPINESS

Saturday, February 14, 2004. From the nineteenth floor of the four-star Hotel Neptuno Tritón there's a wide-angle view of the western-most limits of suburban Havana, the parklike area south of Miramar Beach – lightly industrial, lightly residential, agricultural hardly at all. Clusters of palm trees dot the tops of green hills on the southern horizon. The sky is baby blue and speckled with swirling little galaxylike clouds of baby pink. The lights on tall metal poles around the front of the hotel switch off at precisely seven o'clock. It's a new day: two loud sharp clangs come from a tuneless bell way off in the distance and small groups of workers quicken their pace to the construction sites. Hotels are going up all around here, with fabulous neo–art deco lines and dazzling colour combinations.

On Cuban construction sites where workers are docked pay for being late or absent, there is much lateness and absenteeism. On jobs where one is not docked, workers will go out of their way to show up on time every day. That's why workers aren't getting docked these days. I've heard this twice already, so it must be true.

Ten years ago the view from the nineteenth floor would have been dominated by the neo-classical red-roof Iglesia Jesús de Miramar off in the distance, with its beautiful pearl-grey dome. It would have had a vast rural rolling landscape to itself, an opalescent island in a sea of emeralds. But now that church, still with all its attractions, has been rendered less significant, dwarfed by recently constructed hotels, the Havana Trade Center, and the beginnings of new residential neighbourhoods.

Traffic on the highway below seems light – a few speeding toy cars well spaced, now and then a toy lorry loaded with cement blocks. People will casually sidestep onto the sidewalk to avoid the occasional bus jammed with people. A former beauty queen from Venezuela is touting Reduce Fat Fast pills on the twenty-two-channel universe, and gives different numbers to call for different Latin American countries. Each country is listed on the screen, except for Cuba, where obesity is rare, beauty contests are considered moronic, and few people have credit cards.

Winter storms have paralyzed traffic in Istanbul, airports have been turned into dormitories in Athens, in Toronto it's fifteen below – but in Cuba it looks like another fine day with hot sunshine. The only snow is on an old man's beard and the only ice is in his first drink of the day.

The flight from Toronto was full of people from Detroit, Cleveland, Chicago, New York. They were a serious bunch, curious about Cuba rather than just wishing to sprawl mindlessly on the beach for a week. They were more interested in sizing up the island, sniffing out opportunities. A group of five had been corresponding with the Council of Cuban Churches and were now excitedly going over their maps and discussing their plans to visit every single one of the Protestant churches in Cuba – dispensing advice, no doubt. Nine out of ten such churches are said to be lacking pastors. Anti-abortion feeling is high among the faithful, and the more outspoken get thrown in jail. The non-Cuban world, including Amnesty International, calls these people dissenters. Most Cubans call them worse names. What seems clear is that there is a long-standing majority tradition in Cuba of considering a woman's desire for a safe abortion to be inviolable.

At the José Martí Airport last night, it was like being trapped inside an ant's eye. Every television monitor was showing a weary but passionate old Fidel giving yet another speech. We were in Toronto when he started and he's still at it, with no notes, no teleprompter, and no wire in his ear feeding him lines by his brother Raúl. The speech is being delivered to the people who love him and understand him, and anyone else who wants to tune in. Passengers disembarking stare at the TV screens with an unconscious look of disdain, as if at the shock of actually seeing Fidel on the tube speaking, instead of being the invisible subject of unfriendly one-sided roundtable discussions on the U.S. networks. [Note: This was the speech in which Fidel said that President George W. Bush couldn't debate a Cuban ninth grader, and that after four decades of economic block-ade the Cuban economy is in better shape, in certain important ways, than the U.S. economy, which is hanging by a thread. Also, he said once again that Bush was actively plotting to have him assassinated and planning to invade Cuba. Cubans should get ready to defend their country with guerrilla tactics. He may even have mentioned bomb shelters.]

A. lives in Toronto and doesn't travel much these days. She has been generous with her memories of her two-week urban ramble in Havana ten years ago, all the little details from beginning to end. For starters, she related how high-spirited schoolteachers from southern Ontario filled the plane with their crazed screams and sudden erup-tions of funny noises and silly remarks. The pilot was careful not to break the law by flying the more direct route over the United States, which would have saved an hour of corny jokes. After the teachers staggered off the plane in Varadero, A. was the sole passenger to continue to Havana. She said she felt like a shadow. The one person on duty in the dimly lit customs shack had no desire to look at her shadowy passport, her shadowy bag, or to ask where she planned to stay. There were no taxis or buses waiting.

In the tropical night, gawking up at the full moon among the tow-ering royal palms, she was approached by a friendly tall beanpole of an Afro-Cuban and his very short black wife, plump and with a sense of humour. They said they were driving into the city. They often drove out to the airport to watch the Canadians disembark, to see the joy on their faces as they feel their bones thawing, their allergies disappearing, their sex glands self-secreting. Did they actually say that about the sex glands? A. laughed and admitted she made that up. So, could they have the pleasure of her company? They would drive her into the city and help her find a hotel. Of course!

She booked into the Deauville, and if her friends got a commission for taking her there she didn't notice. Her friends, in fact, stayed outside. Then they all went for a long slow walk along the Malecón. They sat on the crumbling concrete seawall. They wanted to explain to her how the system works in Cuba, so that she would understand what she was looking at. In no way would they consider themselves even mildly anti-Fidel, but they assured A. that black people (A. is white), no matter how well educated, or how many languages they spoke, could not get a decent job in any branch of the government – not even in tourism. Picking up people at the airport was her new friends' idea of performing voluntary labour on an unsolicited basis for the good of the country, although many would call it running an unlicensed taxi even though they refused to accept any money for the ride. A. couldn't even buy them a drink. They assured her that they were not starving, they were not homeless, they even had this nice little old car, but they were unable to get the kind of job they were so obviously qualified for, and they saw themselves as marginalized and unfulfilled. They also said that many whites, especially if they were Catholics, had similar problems.

Then they told her about the *jinatera* situation. A. was about to discover that Havana was a sea of prostitutes day and night, and the *jinateras* with their cosmetics and pretty dresses and flowers in their hair were like exotic islands in the gloomy greyness that Cuba was in 1994. The Soviet Union collapse and the sudden withdrawal of Russian aid had been devastating. What Fidel dubbed the "Special Period" was at its most critical.

They told her that one *jinatera* represented a neighbourhood mini-industry – with extended family and friends chipping in for cute outfits, beauty aids, and sly suggestions – which was in turn rewarded when the money started coming in. If the girl was pretty enough she was commissioned shortly after her fifteenth birthday. There were many variations on this theme, but the general system, in this field as in others, still confuses them sometimes, they told her, even though they've grown up in the milieu. In fact, they didn't think anyone understands it.

Fidel's long-gone-to-Miami daughter, Alina Fernández, in her book, *Castro's Daughter*, writes that "in 1993, our main purpose in life was to choke down our anguish."

A. said that was exactly what seemed to be going on in March 1994. The mood was bad. There was no music in the air, no pleasure. Bitter resentment was everywhere. There was a lot of anguish being choked down. The only smiles were on the faces of the *jinateras*.

A.'s friends were not waiting for me. I knew the chance would be slim, but I did look around for a couple ten years older still answering their description. Instead I booked at the Neptuno, with the commission that would have gone to my travel agent going instead to the airport lady at the hotel table, who insisted that my first choices, the Deauville, the Inglaterra, the Valencia, and the Havana Libre (A.'s famous four from '94) were all "overbooked" – a term by which she meant "all booked up" rather than referring to a sleazy (but understandable) business practice ubiquitous in countries that may not be quite as advanced as Cuba.

My booking fee covered the taxi ride, but the driver was a very strange man who remained silent, refused to respond to any of my comments, but every mile or two he would turn to me and repeat, in tediously memorized English, "My boss make all the money, all I make is the tip." Do you think he was giving me a hint?

It's an interesting line, and although he sounded and looked anything but sincere, it could have been true, or simply an exaggeration for effect. Besides, in tourist-related enterprises such as cab driving the exchange rate between U.S. dollars and Cuban pesos can be very favourable, and U.S. dollars tend to be thrown around as if they were only a peso when in rough terms it would appear that they represent twenty-seven pesos in Cuban buying power, and often much more depending on whose hand they land in. In retrospect, I'm sure the cabbie's only income is the tips. I can't see him getting a penny of the rebate from the hotel.

There seem to be three kinds of Cuban attitudes surrounding the U.S. dollar: The first and most common would be that held by many associated, however peripherally, with tourism – the more they can get their hands on the better. The second would be the Revolutionaries, who are more relaxed about things and have to be talked into taking payment for services rendered. These are the people who can magically transform a generous tourist into a beggar, pleading with them to take a little monetary gift for their kindness. The third would be the truly dedicated Revolutionaries, the ultra-proud nationalists of this blood-soaked land, the incorruptible ones, who are maybe a bit puritanical because under no conditions would they be caught dead with a U.S. dollar in their pocket or purse, any more than a Presbyterian would dance a jig. In these groups, all of whom would be pretty well convinced of the necessity of massive investments in tourism, there would be much overlap, backsliding, and changes of position according to changing circumstances and different understandings. A. said that even in the bad times ten years ago there were people who refused to take money for things one would expect to have to pay for. To use a happy-hour metaphor, the three groups could be compared to the drunks, the social drinkers, and the teetotallers.

Ten years ago, in spite of the general gloom, the people of Havana would make a fuss over a single female tourist. Shy, curious A. was an event. They were eager to show off their command of the English language, and would ask to be corrected if they made a mistake. This seemed to be particularly true of the blacks. One of my duties here is to check out A.'s significant but strange observation that in Cuba the blacker your skin the more likely you were to speak excellent English.

But now there's a sense in the air, upon arrival, that interest in English is fading fast. Among Cubans, there is as little interest in learning English as there is among Albertans in learning French. Many Cubans who spoke excellent English ten years ago have forgotten a lot of it. English-language tourism is *numero uno* in Cuba, by far, but there is a tendency for Cubans today to fade out when they hear English spoken. They've lost their ear for English. English is no longer considered sexy in Cuba.

At first I thought it was a slow reaction to the cruelty of the forty-five-year economic blockade against Cuba, and the continuing insults from the White House, and the assassination attempts and/or threats, the harassment, the bombings. But maybe it's something less obvious. A more Cuban form of Spanish is evolving in Cuba. Creating a new language is more exciting than learning an old one. Cuba is becoming a country of serious linguistic nationalists. If evidence comes to me over the next month that this is not so, or that any of the observations I make or conclusions I draw this early on turn out to be on shaky ground, I shall consider it my duty to advise the reader.

It's time for breakfast in the vast dining hall behind the Neptuno lobby, with walls of windows allowing for grand views, between the exotic flowering trees and royal palms, of the deep dark shining blue Straits of Florida.

There aren't many people here, just a sprinkling of South American tourist couples, sometimes with children, and groups of business people who seem to know what they're here for. Everything is slow, quiet, calm, civilized. No elbows or low blows. We're all having scrambled eggs with fresh carrots and papaya plus numerous cafecitos. Úrsula is a large happy Afro-Cuban hostess mingling with the guests in a capacity that borders on does-she-work-here-or-is-she-just-friendly? She has no problem with shifting topics or waxing semi-philosophical. She maintains I was wrong to think the situation of black Cubans has improved all that much in the past ten years. She insists things have improved only minimally. "If you're black you have to be good," she says. And she doesn't mean morally good. She means really good in every way just to get a job, better than all the whites – brighter, more energetic, more competitive, better qualified, more enthusiastic, sexier, funnier, with a better grasp of the issues, and a lot better at dancing. Or maybe she means morally good as well. Or morally good period. As in, and this is probably it – politically good. In Cuba, politics and morality are one.

Her English is very advanced, she is well into the verb tenses – but she thinks that she is part of a dying breed. "People are getting tired of English," she says. "Even the kids, they prefer to learn French."

We get all serious in a long discussion of boring tourism statistics, of which all I can remember is that after all these years Canada is still the source of most Cuban tourism, with Latin America second, and Europe third. So Canada gets a gold medal for tourism.

Úrsula seems in no rush to leave. In fact, everyone in the cafeteria seems in a trance. Everyone is moving so slowly. People get up slowly and take their trays to the buffet for refill, then return to their tables slowly. People eat slowly, chew slowly, and stare into the distance forever before going for another mouthful. Even the children play with their food slowly. Cafeteria workers slowly wheel in new platters full of exotic breakfast fare, with eyes slightly lowered and steady, like Tibetan monks. If someone drops a fork, it falls slowly. And it makes no sound. There is perfect silence. Úrsula slips away.

An old white-skinned, white-haired cabbie with a new red Toyota parked in the hotel forecourt promises to get me and my bag to the Deauville and he didn't have to look at any map. I'm curious to see if these hotels really were "overbooked." And if they were all booked up, I'd for sure find something in that area just off the Prado. Havana looked wonderful coming in through Miramar – a dizzying display of neo-classical, Spanish baroque, and art deco palaces that were in a moribund state ten years ago – grey, windowless, empty – and are now spiffy as all get out, and home to numerous embassies, government agencies, and a multitude of *polyclinicos*.

The driver is Lázaro, and he is giving me a grand tour, with excellent commentary in slow Spanish, and feeling me out a bit as to who I am and what sort of dirty rotten business I am involved in, before offering me a splendid suggestion. He knows of a *casa particulare* in Centro Habana and he knows in his deepest heart, from chatting with me, that it'd be better for me than the Deauville. It's unlucky to say no on your first day in Havana, and the Deauville would still be there tomorrow. The *casa* is on the fifth or sixth floor – a long winding climb – of an old art deco Arab mosaic block of airy flats with balconies galore on the legendary Calle Zanja, in the west end of Centro Habana, in the centre of a vast maze of streets throbbing with life and death in all directions, and providing easy proximity to the Hotel Havana Libre, the Plaza de la Revoluçion, the Teatro Naçional, the Parque Coppelia with its famous ice cream, and many other interesting locales crying for my closer attention.

Lázaro has taken me to the spacious two-bedroom apartment of a mother and daughter, nothing resembling a commercial enterprise, and very proper but relaxed. They have a large back bedroom that looks cool and comfy. They go for long periods without anyone. I had the impression Lázaro was their only tout, and they didn't advertise, though they offered me a modest business card, as did Lázaro, who had delivered me into a quasi–Humbert Humbert situation when you think about it. Daughter, for instance, is a very attractive and charming young woman, but hardly a Lolita given that she is twice Lolita's age and a very dedicated well-trained physician to boot. Her name is Monica and she works at the Clínico Quirúrgico Freyre de Andrade. But she is just now dressed in white shorts and a white blouse and wet flip-flops as she wetwashes the floor with great energy. She is also wishing that Lázaro had arranged to give them a bit more warning.

Monica says she's working the night shift at the clinic this week, but could find herself switched at any moment with little warning. Her mother, Melba, always with the zaniest smile and often with a madcap laugh to match, is a doctor too, but now retired. The beautiful paintings throughout the house (except for the guest room, alas) are by Melba in her youth. She no longer takes an interest in painting, but she never tires of looking at her own. If nothing else her canvases are a testament to the fiery young woman she was thirty years ago – very Cuban in spirit, sophisticated, intellectual, meta-physical, angst-ridden. But now she seems more interested in watching a tele-novella: a stressed-out motorist on the lam from the Mob runs over a pedestrian, then jumps out of his car and starts pounding the roof and screaming. I offer M. and M. a bottle of Havana Club from the airport as *un obsequio*. They laugh and Monica says, "You must drink it yourself. We do not drink. We are doctors."

If I were Humbert Humbert I'd love Monica and hate Melba, both at first sight, but I'm not, so I love both of them the same.

The room is nicely cross-ventilated, two north windows, two west windows, and a small south window, all with wooden shutters thick with old paint. There's a double bed and a single, with a lovely dark-wood antique wardrobe and a cute little chest of four drawers bearing intricately carved and inlaid abstract patterns from the 1930s. Two oil paintings each show a seascape with the full-moon setting, or maybe one is setting and the other rising, or maybe both are rising. These are not Melba's style at all. They must have been specially selected for Canadian tourists.

The rest of the place is spacious for two people, there's a small dining room off the kitchen, with two large parlours, and a balcony with a great view of the street, which I shall notice will become very noisy and then very quiet at oddly unexpected times of the night and day. And there is a pair of parakeets chirping away in one cage, and a pair of canaries warbling away in another. The ladies let me know I have the run of the place. It's all mine. They are all smiles.

Monica is halfway through *Les Misérables*. I tell her it's my favourite big fat novel of all time. She shrugs, as if to say that's easy for someone from a capitalist country like Canada to say, but how could a gringo possibly relate to this book the way a Cuban could? She thinks I'm faking it, or being condescending, or trying to present myself in a bright light, or a bit puffed-up. As a trained scientist, she refuses to believe she just happens to be reading my favourite book.

Later she spoke of the "brain drain" of Cuban doctors to Venezuela (and Haiti too, working all through the recent coup), which is putting a lot of strain on the doctors who choose to remain in Cuba for now. And she smiles at her ironic use of the term "brain drain." She realizes she's using it differently than in non-socialist countries, and that the doctors are in Venezuela for compassionate reasons rather than fatter incomes. They're into areas where people live an entire life without knowing what a doctor looks like. President Hugo Chávez wants to establish medical care for the poor people of Venezuela, who haven't been able to afford it. So at least a thousand Cuban doctors volunteered. It's been a big success among the poor people, but the middle-class Venezuelans think the Cuban doctors are doing more indoctrination than doctoring. Same with the urban garden venture, transforming balcony and rooftop into little patches of fertile farmland, making the lives of the poor easier. This too is disliked by the middle class.

It seems odd that Chávez would refer to Cuba as a "sea of happiness." Other bright people have made similar remarks at different times. I'm interested in finding out what they mean.

TWO STEPS AHEAD
OF THE LAW

Sunday, February 15, 2004. On my first long stroll I stopped to listen to some high sweet trumpet notes drifting from the direction of the Teatro Naçional across the busy four-lane Avenida Carlos Manuel de Céspedes. There was a close-knit crowd of about thirty people surrounding a man tooting on a trumpet. The man seemed to be demonstrating the proper execution of long steady high notes, free of vibrato, and the open air is the best place for that.

"Yes, that is the professor of trumpet playing," said a thin dark-skinned fellow who had been trying to figure out what I was looking at across the wide avenue. "He is teaching the younger people." He tried not to seem eager to make my acquaintance, even while hustling me past the front entrance of the Plaza de la Revoluçion and under the giant two-dimensional steel sculpture of a ghostly black Che Guevara, who seemed a bit weary of having to wait around for the next massive anti-imperialist demonstration or five-hour speech by Fidel.

We were closing in on the theatre, and I casually asked my amigo if he liked baseball. He instantly came to a halt, stood very straight, and cocked his head back with a shocked look on his face. He said, "How could you ask such a question? What are you trying to insinuate? Of course I like baseball, there is no bigger baseball fan in the world than I."

He soon forgave my slur on his manhood and confessed that he played second "bass" for many years but didn't have what it took to get into the big leagues. Just then, as if by ESP, another man joined us, a friend of the first, taller, with darker skin and African features, except for his thin Irish lips. "He means 'base,'" he said. Each of the fourteen provinces has its own team, they told me. Some of the more heavily populated provinces have two teams, they told me. Thank God for our linguistic limitations. If we spoke the same language we'd have been talking about something much drearier no doubt. And less believable.

They wanted to know my taste in music. I liked Cuban classical music and Cuban jazz but hadn't consciously listened to a lot of it. I did not like nightclub jazz usually, and I wasn't interested in the *festivale folklórico* sort of thing. I preferred Pérez Prado to Desi Arnaz, and maybe even Arturo Sandoval to his one-time mentor, Dizzy Gillespie. They liked it that I liked Cuban jazz, and they took me to a cellar nightclub behind and below the 1950ish Teatro Naçional, which looks something like a three-quarter mockup of a domed stadium, even though it doesn't actually have a dome, and it's surrounded by serene parkland and clumps of magnificent royal palms so close together that the sun could hardly squeeze through. This nightclub was the darkly subterranean Café Cantanté Mi Habana, with its serpentine walnut bar long enough for any crowd, and it was a very famous place for jazz. The upstairs was famous for performances of the Danza Contemporánea and the National Symphony.

Although Fidel is pretty well the only one with a beard, the beatnik era is still strong in Cuba, and the aura lingers on here in El Café Cantanté like the glow after the lights go off. The long bar was closed for the afternoon. There were no musicians in evidence, and there wasn't even a CD player or radio to be found. But some people were lounging with their feet up on empty tables, and others were standing or wandering here and there, engaging in serious conversations, and most seemed to be long-term habitués of this threadbare club.

My friends were very insistent that I be here at ten this evening, for that was when the jazz started. I should have been thrilled, but oddly I wasn't. Maybe it was because they didn't seem to be thrilled either, just insistent. They couldn't tell me who'd be playing. The place lacked the sort of buzz one would expect if something really interesting was happening tonight. Missing a good performance is never as regrettable as having to sit through a bad one.

We three came up out of the dark bar into the bright day. We walked along the broad avenue. They complained pointedly about the heat, as if it were an old script they'd memorized. They asked if I had ever had a mojito Hemingway. I confessed that I had not, but I had heard that they were all the rage among the tourists this year. I knew someone in Toronto who flew all the way to Havana just to have one, but to their credit these bright guys knew I was testing their credibility. Soon we were sitting in a little no-name bar, one I vividly remember A. telling me looked ten years ago as if it had been bombed out. But it was now renovated, a nice little place, cool and breezy, neat and clean, surrounded by tall trees with great green fanlike fronds brushing the windows. The bartender kept looking at me with a sorrowful eye, as if to say, "If I were a tourist like you, buddy boy, I wouldn't be buying these bozos expensive drinks." I indicated that I had caught the message, and I understood his concern. I relaxed and waited for them to tell me exactly what was on their minds.

As we drank our mojitos it began to unravel. These fellows wanted to tell me about an exciting new way of getting rich fast, though they didn't put it quite that way. It was nice of them, and I appreci-ated it, and I didn't want them to think that I was crazy for not being interested in getting rich, and it wouldn't do to have them think that I distrusted them in any way. So I listened as they told of a certain local supermarket, the owners of which were a tad counter-revolutionary (they didn't actually use that term), and they liked to commute back and forth to the United States for special events like funerals, weddings, and the occasional picnic.

At the airport last night I was expecting to get U.S. cash from the bank machine, but instead I got crisp new three-peso notes, which were artificially pegged at the same value as the dollar, and were referred to as the convertible peso, or *chavito*. I'm not sure what it was I said, but my friends started snickering. Then they said that they wished to propose that in spite of the supposed one-to-one ratio of the Cuban peso and the U.S. dollar (they snickered some more), they would be interested in presenting any amount of U.S. dollars – any amount at all – to this supermarket in exchange for the same number of those fancy new convertible pesos. Then they got serious and put a great deal of time into explaining how simple this would be, and how I would be providing a great service to the poor people of Cuba by getting involved in this harmless little scheme. Any money I was willing to convert in this way, say a thousand U.S. dollars, they would gladly take the commission – it might have been 3 per cent – and split it between poor worthy Cubans such as these two and myself. When I finally understood this scheme (to the extent that I did), I had no choice but to tell them I could not get involved. I had heard many sad tales of life in a Cuban jail and had no desire to test their factuality. This would never happen, they exclaimed, as if they couldn't believe what they were hearing. Tourists enjoy complete impunity in Cuba, they insisted. Tourists are never thrown in jail. The worst that could happen, and it would be very unlikely, would be for you to be escorted to the airport.

It was my turn to snicker, and I told them that there are many Canadians who have believed such talk and who have nevertheless found themselves in a Cuban jail. They scoffingly demanded an example. The only one I could think of was the sad case of Perry King, of Edmonton. King worked for a Canadian oil company in Cuba, in the port city of Matanzas. In his off-hours he happened to "befriend" a fourteen-year-old girl and, when he found out how poor her family was, gave her a twenty-dollar bill "as a goodwill gesture."

The court in a very short trial sentenced him to a very long twenty-five years for corrupting a minor. He has been in jail a year and his sister says he is innocent, sick, depressed, and has lost fifty pounds. His Canadian lawyer said that King is innocent and was convicted on insufficient evidence presented in a one-day trial. This is based on information in two brief news reports.

The guys stared at me silently. My story was obviously a perfect justification for not wanting to mess with dirty currency tricks, no matter how innocent I might be. With great sincerity I told the fellows I'd get a second opinion on the legality of the scheme and then get back to them if I decided to dive in. They looked rather hurt, maybe even close to tears. They drifted away. It was sad.

On the Malecón I breathed the salt air as many have before me. Lovers strolled by locked in tender embraces. Even married couples, with their kids along, would be starry-eyed and in a high state of romance, as the waves licked the smooth igneous boulders at the foot of the seawall. A very young fellow and an older girl were walking in step with me. The fellow was about fourteen, but he had the cocky mannerisms of an experienced pimp twice his age. He had a horrible scar on his left shoulder, as if he had been trying unsuccessfully to burn off a small skull-and-bones tattoo. But he had just missed the tattoo, and it was even more noticeable now, and uglier. He spoke excellent English, but his girlfriend remained silent. She was much taller than he, and pretty, with dark skin and Spanish features. "Do you like her?" said the fellow. "Yes, but I'm too old for that kind of thing" – which is my usual reply in such situations. He protested, so I held my hand out with my index finger hanging down limply. This was usually all it took, but this young fellow was determined. I tried to tell him that as a single male Canadian in Cuba the only way I could avoid being stereotyped as a sex tourist was not to indulge. "But do you like her?" he said, as if my excuses might just be covering up the fact that I didn't find her to my taste. This was a sophisticated young guy, who could be ambiguous in both languages. "Yes, but does she like me?" I inquired, not wishing to offend them in any way, and knowing what the answer would be.

He repeated my question to her in Spanish. Her dull face lit up, she looked me deep in the eye, and said, "Oh, sí!" She said it so sweetly I almost succumbed. "She likes you," he said. It appeared that I was checkmated. But at that very moment, a shiny black 1958 Oldsmobile pulled over and, as I watched, the girl got in with only the slightest hesitation, if that, and the car raced away, west along the sea and into the setting sun, leaving me trying not to show my relief. The young fellow had a smug look on his face, as if mocking me for not jumping when I had the chance. The classy car made it perfectly obvious I'd been undervaluing the merchandise.

Night fell and the long legendary Calle Zanja was very dark, the only illumination from the open windows and doors of the bars and shops and houses that lined the street, with everything on ground level except for the roofs. The houses, open as they were to full public view, would be very neat and clean and tidy and well organized, and maybe a bit spartan, but with paintings on the wall, and bookshelves – well, books yes, but no bookshelves, not really. A small pile of books atop a chest of drawers maybe. Everybody reads, but people tend to keep books and magazines moving from hand to hand, in mutual exchange. A book on a shelf was a book not being read.

And did the people seem to mind being glanced at by gringos as they passed by? Most definitely not. People would be at the candlelit table in the back room dining frugally, maybe eight at a time, or maybe just drinking coffee, or simply talking with the table cleared and bare. The children would be playing in the front room, which would be darker, except for the glow from the television if it happened to be on. Usually there would be excellent Cuban jazz on the radio at very high volume, but definitely not blasting and not unpleasant. The kids would be dancing, and the adults would be sitting there with dreamy looks on their faces.

In one doorway two girls, about eleven years old, stood with their arms loosely hanging over the other's shoulders and each silently staring into the other's eyes. I walked down a side street to buy a cigar and watch the moon from the Malecón. On the way back the girls were still standing in the same position, giving each other the same deep silent look, with their arms around each other.

The Prado was every bit as gracious and soulful as A. had described it. Again and again I'd turn a corner off the Prado and find myself at some place she had told me about. But things had changed. All these shops that A. found closed then are now open both for tourists and Cubans. Occasionally I'd stop for an icy-cold Cristal and would have a dreamlike sense of seeing this bar through A.'s eyes, and it was as if the people sitting around were the same ones as were here when she was here, but ten years older. Impossible? *Sí.* Dreamlike? *Sí.*

I noticed him before he noticed me, and the innocent side of me called out, "¡Hola, amigo!" instead of letting him notice me if he wanted to. It was the second baseman, the first of the two guys I had met earlier. He seemed happy to have been remembered in such a friendly way, and when he noticed I was savouring a delicious cigar with bliss writ large on my physiognomy he said, "Wait here!" He returned five minutes later with five identical Relobas – and presented them to me with a bow, as if they were a little bouquet of flowers. Now, here's my logic: I'd paid a dollar for my cigar, he being a Cuban would have got these for a peso apiece, and furthermore I hadn't asked for them, and didn't know he was getting them for me. So I thought I was generous by giving him three dollars for the five. He made it very clear that he was disappointed and considered me just another cheapskate tourist.

But he continued with me along Calle Zanja. And so, during a lull in the chit-chat, when we were busy jumping over dark pits in the pavement and trying not to trip over a concrete block or some other impediment invisible in the shadows and so on, and puffing on our cigars like two little fireflies, he wanted to know about my smoking habits. He loved it when I told him the average Joe in Canada couldn't afford to smoke a Cuban cigar except on Christmas Eve. But he wanted to know if I smoked pot. I told him heavens no, it was illegal in Canada, and I told him that there is so much joy in Cuba it is obviously not needed, and yet I understand the penalties are even greater here. Besides, pot is famous for producing false hunger in a smoker, which is a cruel situation for a Cuban to be in. Not for the tourists, he countered, suavely. There he goes again, thinking that tourists can get away with murder. He said that tourists can smoke their heads off all they want, but the Cubans can suffer extreme penalties if they are caught. I instantly believed the latter assertion but was definitely concerned about the veracity of the first, as I had been about the same fellow's currency scam. But he insisted on taking me just a wee bit out of the way so that I could meet someone who would have some Jamaican pot and be willing to give me a little sample. I most definitely required nothing along those lines, but I had to go along with it for the sake of the book. One has to be a little adventurous now and then if one wishes to excel in travel writing. Not too adventurous though, because we must remember that writing itself is the number-one adventure.

Also, if one gets in the habit of saying "no" too often, or too emphatically, his or her face will turn into one big "no." One can spot at a glance the people who make a habit of saying no. Their faces are crabby and suspicious. They always grimace when in public. One senses that they could drop dead at any moment from an overdose of no's.

So he dragged me back the way we'd come, to a dark side street, and he introduced me to El Pinko, an albino with red hair and a mixture of Chinese and African features. We were to climb several flights of unlit stairs to a moonlit rooftop and he'd meet us there. It was a long wait. Some other men joined us. I was getting tired but tried not to insult these guys by yawning. One tall handsome fellow said he was the son of a famous Cuban baseball player, whose name I shan't mention, but who went to the United States and had a brilliant career there, then stayed on too long, and now he isn't playing, and things haven't been going all that well, and so on. But his son was proud of him. Then El Pinko came up, and he said everything was okay, the pot was being "prepared." Ten minutes later a Jamaican guy (to add some authenticity) appeared with three cute little joints. They'd been rolled in brown industrial-strength paper and the lack of gum was made up for by the elaborate bow-tie twist at each end. I wearily asked how much. He said smoke one first. I lit up. The first puff was without noticeable effect. I was suspicious, but if I was being conned why would they insist I smoke one first? Smoke more, they said. I kept smoking. They didn't want any. I tried to pass it to them. No, it's for you. So eventually I had it smoked down to nothing, and felt as if it might have been heavily cut with catnip and sawdust. The only effect I got was paranoia – a fear that if I refused to pay I might accidentally fall off the roof and break my neck.

So I didn't really feel as if I wanted to fight with them. It didn't seem to be pot, but I didn't want to tell them that. It just seemed that the prudent thing to do would be to give them the money and make my way down to street level, the safe way, via the staircase. I went back to Melba and Monica's, wondering what it was I smoked, and why were these cats following me and nipping at my pantcuffs.

VANILLA AND CHOCOLATE

Monday, February 16, 2004. I am sitting at the kitchen table drinking coffee and Mama Melba is standing in the doorway laughing. She laughs all the time. It's her nature. Monica must have got tired of all this gaiety at an early age because she is serious and her laughter is infrequent, awkward, a bit forced. I didn't catch what field of medicine she's in, but she has the air of a dedicated doctor, and a dedicated Fidelista as well.

Monica has never been anywhere much outside of Havana and its suburbs. She nevertheless speaks with pride and affection of Santiago de Cuba (she sighs and calls it "the second Havana") and Trinidad de Cuba ("the whole city is a museum"), both of which for her must be found only in the magic of books and dreams for now. Just knowing they are there is enough for her. And yet there's a sadness about her, a need that is not being fulfilled, one which she is trying in vain to ignore. Like many Cubans she wants to travel, but she wants it to be for a meaningful reason, something beyond self-indulgent tourism.

When Monica left for the suburbs to visit her father this afternoon, her mother relaxed. She lay for hours on top of her neatly made bed while enjoying a laughter-filled series of telephone chats. Then she sat on a comfy old sofa in her darkened parlour watching silly TV shows, laughing to herself, and taking a few more phone calls. Her English is non-existent. At one point, because she hadn't laughed for a bit, I dressed up in my winter things from home, including an absurdly long and heavy woollen scarf, three jackets, a heavy-duty Nepalese toque. I stood there at the entrance to the parlour, shivering, with arms folded tightly over my chest and teeth chattering. She glanced at me, then leapt to her feet. I told her, "This is me – on the way to the Toronto airport." She drew nearer, shaking with laughter, her eyes wide.

In the afternoon rain I'm wearing my Hamilton Tiger-Cats jacket, black and yellow, light as a nylon feather. A very exclusive, dollar-only restaurant, with keen-eyed doormen, where my friend A. had dined ten years ago, on Avenida de los Presidentes at Calle 23, is now a wreck. The sign has fallen off, but the place is still alive and selling coffee and sandwiches for pesos. Conversely, other places that would have been left derelict at that time are up and running now. For instance, the Coppelia, the famous Havana ice-cream parlour, was definitely having a bad time during A.'s visit. She remembered a fellow standing behind the counter in a white smock, but he looked sad and hopeless. There was no ice cream and it looked as if there hadn't been any for quite a while. A. thought the fellow had been asked to stay on because nobody knew when the ice cream would be delivered, it could be any time of the night or day, and he could double as a guard while waiting.

But today the ice cream had definitely arrived. I sat in the soft rain with a two-scooper in a silver dish, chocolate and vanilla. Heavenly ice cream, every bit as good as what used to be served in England, except with no chocolate wafer sticking out of it. Unfortunately you can't get it anywhere else, so I'm told, this is it, the Coppelia hasn't been franchised yet, and ice cream elsewhere in Cuba has little to recommend it.

An Afro-Cuban percussionist is standing amidst a crowd waiting for the bus while playing simple music with two sticks and two drums. In the light rain, almost a warm mist, and with such dreamy ice cream, I find myself listening more carefully to the percussionist, and in a flash the music transforms itself into something as all-absorbing and as complex as a Bach prelude.

I was spooning up a little sliver of the vanilla scoop, then a little sliver of the chocolate scoop, making it last on a humid day, with the rain ensuring the lineup will be short should I wish more. There was a girl about four years old, very dark-skinned with African features, and with a pair of red-ribboned pigtails. She was off in the distance to my right and was not keeping up with her parents because she insisted upon continuing her chat with a grey kitten rolling on its back on the rainy pavement. Her parents, who were behind me and to my left, halfway to the percussionist already, were stamping their feet and calling out, "Merédios, ¡vamos!, ¡vamos!" Finally Merédios said goodbye to the kitten and came running to her parents. But just as she passed me, for some reason she stopped, turned around, looked at me full in the face, then jumped up on my lap and gave me a big wet warm kiss on the lips. I was shocked and strangely pleased at the same time, while also a bit embarrassed, and thinking of the sad story of Perry King. So I didn't want to look at the parents. But I could sense they were laughing. And then I started laughing, and then I looked at them, and sure enough they were laughing, and then the little girl had bounced off my lap and was running toward them. She was laughing too.

Las Bulerías, on Calle L in the shadow of the Hotel Havana Libre, is a basement pizza patio by day, with a large dining room inside, which is cleared to make way for disco parties after hours. There's a bright yellow Cristal umbrella over my table, so I sit there in the sunken forecourt having a slice with a beer and watching people go by at an interesting angle in the gentle afternoon rain. I'm as thrilled as a cinematographer who has discovered the perfect angle. My eyes are about at knee level with the passing throngs, which would include skinny young handsome cops in brown or grey, some with batons, others with sidearms; the occasional garbage picker, operating with stealth in this tony area; bearded old men with friendly faces; and groups of fifteen-year-old girls in frilly long dresses, going to a birthday party.

The word used to be *jinatera*. In a speech a decade ago Fidel claimed that the Cuban *jinateras* are the healthiest women on the planet. But *jinatera* appears to have fallen from favour. The word is now the subtler and more ambiguous *chicas*, or, equally available night and day but less noticeable in the crowd, the *chicos*. One very attractive blonde, about twenty-five, struck up a chat with me under the broad yellow Cristal umbrella. "Gummo," she said, with the sincerest sigh she could dredge up, and placed a Chiclet on my tongue as if it were a sacramental wafer. "Gum," I answered, glumly. This woman's name was Aída. She had a gold chain around her neck with her name on it. She was studying Italian but had no use for English.

It used to be easy to spot the *jinateras* from blocks away, because they were dressed colourfully, and with flair, with pretty dresses, and makeup, and coiffures. Now the borders are blurred, and all the women dress that way, even older ones, or strive to. There is no longer much of a line separating the *chicas* from the non-*chicas*. The *jinateras* had a wonderful sensuality infused with intelligence and humour, and nothing seemed to bother them. They were the only ones with smiles on their faces. And it was a leisurely sort of occupation. If you don't wish to have sex, then let's put some money in the jukebox and dance. Or let's just have a beer and tell me stories about Canada.

At first glance the *chicas* of today seem more professional, more mature. There are fewer Lolitas on the prowl. They can be aggressive as well, as in not wanting to take no for an answer. They don't stand out so flagrantly. In fact, I'm beginning to think that behind every woman in today's Cuba, even those as old as Melba or older, there lurks a laughing *chica*.

Melba is about fifty. She's missing an upper incisor, which adds character to her sweet and happy smile, and to the giggling spirit of a slaphappy teenager at a sleepover. As soon as she hears that I have finished my shower and am returning to my room naked but for a large dark violet towel that I wear like a Dorothy Lamour sarong, she charges toward me with a book in her hand and, natch, a smile on her face. "Good morning," she says in perfect English, although I suspect she had just learned the term while I was showering. "English!" I exclaim, with a manic smile. "You can speak English!" She laughs all the harder.

I'm embarrassed by the rustiness of my Spanish. But not discouraged, for it occurs to me that my linguistic handicaps will allow my intuition to blossom, the same thought Che Guevara might have had in the last few weeks of his life, among the Bolivian Indians whose language he didn't know. I shall see everything more clearly and understand the basics more easily, without a lot of fuzzy rhetoric and distracting philosophies getting in the way. I may not be all that clear on what people are saying, but I see all the more clearly what people are thinking and feeling. And if I should die, my instructions are to bury me in El Cementerio Gringo.

If I had stopped to realize how badly my Spanish had deteriorated over the years, I'd have brushed up. But now that I'm already here, I refuse to be discouraged. It will make for a more interesting book. Could Herodotus speak Egyptian? Could Livingstone speak Swahili? Could Gertrude Stein speak French? Could Hemingway speak Italian? I bet Hemingway wasn't all that fluent in Spanish either. And in Hemingway's day, *los cubanos* almost all spoke excellent English.

The book Melba had in her hand when she gave me the brightest, cheeriest "Good morning!" of all time was a very passionate cheap Mexican *historia* about an *escritora* – a female writer who, it would appear, is continually falling into the arms of the wrong man. It's Melba's solemn duty to read these books so she can better advise Monica on the right step to take at any given time in the brave new world of computers (they don't have one yet) and bombs in the street (not for quite a while now). Yes, Melba is always reading, or talking on the phone, or watching TV in the dark. Besides the soaps, she also likes programs featuring hot Cuban music and dancing, and her birds get very excited when she turns the volume up.

In my room is a small Samsung fridge, which keeps my rum cold and my cigars fresh. The dark walnut wardrobe is very spacious and can be locked. The bed is part of a suite of five furnishings all from the same manufacturer – one bed, two night tables, a tall thin oval-shaped mirror, and a matching table below it for cosmetics. All these furnishings are made of wrought iron in very gracefully sensuous flowery swirls. It's by far the best example of erotic wrought-iron work I've seen in bedroom furnishings. Mounted on the wall is some kind of greasy fuzzy old electronic device either designed to prevent power surges from damaging the Russian air conditioner adjacent to it in the window, or maybe it's a kind of burglar alarm. There is unfortunately no bed lamp, the only illumination being an overly bright fluorescent rod on the ceiling. There are figurines and doodads, knick-knacks and ceramic vases, curious whatnots and happy ceramic pigs with artificial flowers stuck in their backs, and there are also numerous little china dogs and sombreros with "Cuba" written on them – souvenirs from the Batista era possibly.

The windows are innocent of the glazier's art and open for every breeze. The Venetian blinds are thick wooden slats assembled like a stack of small horizontal cricket bats, with the ones in the bottom half of each window fixed in place for privacy.

There are many excellent paintings hanging on Melba and Monica's walls, but the best paintings are Melba's. It's a pity she didn't put herself forward more vigorously way back in the days when painting was everything. But medicine called. Her work resembles the paintings of the Canadian Bill Bissett, more famous for the ultra-phonetic spelling of his amazing and fun-to-read poetry. But Melba's work lacks the pointillist element that is Bissett's trademark. Both Melba and Bissett highlight the naked human form, but Bissett's are straight ahead and deliberately simple, in brilliant primary dabs of colours, while Melba's are much curvier, more elaborate, intricate, and with a subtler and smoother palette. In one of her canvases a naked female is in agony while naked satanic hobgoblins try to pin her down with evil intent. In another a golden Blakean figure emerges from the sun, and in repeated forms becomes less and less a figure of light and more a figure of flesh and earth. *Muy metafísico*, I said, for the sake of saying something beyond *magnífico*. *Sí, sí*, she said, with shining eyes. She hasn't painted for decades, but she still looks at her work admiringly and loves to have guests notice it.

I managed to walk for miles without aggravating my blisters, but there was a stiff norther coming off the Straits of Florida and smacking against the Malecón with great explosions of foamy spray, then flooding over the road, so that a pedestrian can get sprayed from the waves hitting the seawall on one side and from automobile tires hitting the puddles on the other side.

How can I stuff myself with expensive dinners when people everywhere are on extremely strict rations? I can't and won't. A family of four, so I'm told, must make do with two hundred grams of coffee a month, and even then it's not the same coffee the tourist becomes so smugly and self-congratulatorially accustomed to. One hears that it gets cut with ground peas. Sometimes a tourist will be given ration-book coffee by mistake, and will soon be making highly vocal complaints, causing great sadness all around.

It's true that rations are much less strict than a decade ago, but fatsos are still a rare sight in Cuba. Even the police are skinny as a fencepost. And the famous Castro brothers, Fidel and his brother Raúl, are looking a bit slimmer these days. According to the late Arthur Miller, in an excellent piece in the *Observer* on his visit to Cuba, Fidel seems to live on nothing but spring water and lettuce.

The streets of Havana Vieja are thronged with tourists and are no longer grey and crumbling as they were in A.'s photos from ten years ago. It was to cry, and now it is to laugh. And maybe even to celebrate, cautiously. This is the anniversary of A.'s visit, and now her close friend has come to the island, armed with her memories.

There is a large congregation of English tourists standing in the lobby of the Hotel Ambos Mundos, with their luggage at their feet. They seem to be on their way home. Meanwhile a large congregation of French tourists has just arrived and is laying siege to the not-so-large dining room of the Hotel Valencia. My friend A. contracted a horrible bout of food poisoning in that very dining room, but that was then, this is now.

At the Ambos Mundos bar I order a strong gin and tonic, with Angostura bitters, no ice, no sugar, the way Hemingway liked it in *Islands in the Stream*. I take this symbolic drink up to the fifth floor to pay a visit to the room Hemingway usually stayed in, a small room but it's in the corner, with a north window and an east window to help keep things light and breezy. On the wall is a framed handwritten page from the manuscript of *For Whom the Bell Tolls*. Instead of a period at the end of a sentence, Hemingway would put an *x* in a circle, a sign of a highly self-conscious personality, and perhaps a reference to his days at the *Toronto Star*, where he spent some time editing other people's copy, using such symbols. There was also an alarmingly downward slope to his handwriting, but this might have been just on that one particular day. His handwriting was writ large and flowing, not in the cramped style of the scholar, but the pessimistic flow of a cynical big-game hunter. But still highly self-conscious.

The room is decorated with numerous photos of Hemingway, including one of him whispering something in the ear of young Fidel, the one and only time they met. The always magical Fidel was supposed to judge the fishing contest that day, but he somehow ended up catching the biggest fish, outdoing even old Papa. There were excellent photos taken of Papa and Fidel, one showing Fidel burdened down with a vast number of fishing trophies. In each photo they seem to be the same height – though Papa was said to have been six-foot-even, and Fidel six-foot-three. Someone's lying. They looked happy together. They obviously clicked.

On the same floor is the private office of a uniformed doorman who is trying to sell me a box of Cohibas for $70. I promise to be back on March 17 and make the purchase just before flying home. He puts on a very disappointed face, and is unable to believe that I'll show up on the date in question.

Someone tells me Cuban scientists have developed a new anti-cholesterol drug called PPG. It is also called Policosanol. Fidel is said to swear by it. It was developed in Cuba a decade ago with chemicals derived from sugar cane, and it is rumoured to have Viagra-like side effects – no extra charge for this extra charge, as Lady Sekhmet, Sacred Artist of the Internet, would say. Not to be believed at all, but the word around town is that Fidel doubles his dosage on nights when his girlfriend is visiting.

So, just as an experiment, I went into the handsome old *farmacía* on Calle Obispo and with no questions asked was given a three months' supply of PPG for a mere $25. I popped a tablet in my mouth on the way out of the pharmacy. This was all very innocent.

But an hour later, I was being guided by a beautiful woman named Mimi on a tour of a certain interesting old government building. She was definitely not young, but she had the deepest, darkest, keenest eyes, as she led me through the ancient rooms of this magnificent building. She was a very respectable black woman with somewhat Indian features, and I was rather stunned by the intensity of my reaction to her. I was smitten and she knew it. I have no idea if it was the PPG or the woman herself. Perhaps a combination. It was insane. I wanted to smother her with kisses. It was like being back in high school. It wasn't all that one-sided either, for there was a certain electricity emanating from her lovely self.

Ahem! She cautioned me that she had been on this job twenty years and it was imperative that we don't get carried away. We were alone in the seldom-visited recesses of the old building, but she was a Cuban government worker and I was a single male tourist. She did not wish to be caught in any kind of embarrassing position. It could be dangerous for her. Spies were everywhere. Who knows what hidden cameras there were in this building, which I am being careful not to identify. She could be accused, if only by certain of her more puritanical co-workers, of trying to romance foreigners in order to get out of Cuba, or otherwise personally enrich herself. She could lose her job, or be transferred to a job she didn't like in a part of town that wasn't to her taste.

At any rate she did agree to meet me tomorrow evening after work. And she introduced me to a fellow employee, a woman who understood these situations. She confirmed Mimi was wise to be cautious. I really didn't think all this had anything to do with the PPG, but not only will I be there tomorrow evening, I'll be popping in earlier to make sure she's not going to chicken out. And yes, like most Cuban women her age, she has been long divorced.

Perhaps I should be ashamed of my behaviour with Mimi. But it didn't bother her at all. What I *am* truly ashamed of happened a bit later when I was strolling along the treelined Prado. A young fellow with two stumps for legs wheeled his ancient wheelchair after me and said something about my long-visored red Team Canada baseball cap. I thought he wanted it and I said no. But he kept on smiling, and he said he just wanted to see what it said. Churlishly I turned to him so he could see it, then continued walking without any sign of friendliness. Now I feel very badly about that and if I see him tomorrow on the Prado, or anywhere, I will give him the hat. How shameful to be caught in one's own shadow like that. Any Habanero with stumps for legs on the Prado should be wearing a Team Canada cap, or any cap he wants, especially one with such a lengthy beak.

In Havana, at any given moment, a mood will sweep the city, a sort of psychic drift, and it will settle on an entire neighbourhood and drive all the other moods away. Tonight everything is quiet. No music, no hollering, no loud noises. Everyone is being pleasantly quiet, sitting on hard chairs tilted back a bit, smoking cigars, whispering, smiling at some old memory. Today was a good day and in the silence of the night I feel a beam of happiness from a distant star. Maybe I'm in love. But if Mimi doesn't show up for our date I promise not to fall to pieces. I will just be normal. I am too old for broken hearts. Thank God I'm all grown up! And why did it take so long?

THE GREAT FASCIST

Tuesday, February 17, 2004. It's 6:40 a.m. In my dream I had come to Cuba to manage the construction of a series of windmills for power generation. But something went askew, and the windmills turned the wrong way: instead of generating electrical power they were degenerating it, draining Cuba of power and sending it to other countries, although I was the only one who seemed to realize it. So I became very annoyed, made a big fuss, and blamed the whole thing on Fidel. On the front page of *Granma* (dream edition) was an editorial stating that I, an unnoted non-expert on just about everything, had the audacity to state publicly that windmills were an unreliable source of electric power. So it was embarrassing, a bad review and I haven't even written the book yet.

What woke me up was the thunderous screech and roar of a caravan of fifty huge trucks carrying heavy loads through narrow streets in first gear. The great trucks were inching their way through the neighbourhood, in a gear-grinding, ear-splitting manner, one big fat overloaded, underpowered lorry after another, so loud the hens had to strain like mad to hear the roosters crowing.

After what seemed like two hours but was probably only about one and a half, the roar of the last truck began to fade and the cocks resumed their crowing, the dogs barking, and the scooters a kind of whining and wailing not unlike a chainsaw at full throttle.

It's odd that Cubans aren't bothered by noise. Theirs is an unmuffled culture of spontaneity and they make noise whenever they feel like it, and they expect others to do the same, and nobody even notices the noise except the occasional irritable tourist. Noise, señor? What noise?

It was such a pleasure to see twenty kids playing football on the excellent marble surface of the Prado. *Arribe! Arribe!* they cried like excited exotic birds, hoping to get their hands on the ball, and the smaller the kid the louder the cry. As I walked by I glanced away from the game for a moment and just then the ball smashed into my shoulder. The kids went into freeze-frame mode, but when they saw the old man wasn't hurt they relaxed.

There's a billboard with a picture of Fidel saying, A better world is possible. I imagine Fidel motoring by, shaking his head and saying to his driver, "I don't remember saying that. Sounds more like Che."

"It'd be a better world already," says the driver, "if we weren't behind a billion dollars in oil payments to Venezuela."

"Just drive, okay?"

My blisters have hardened over without breaking. But last night I stumbled badly on a dark street and my big left toe has a deep nasty cut that has become infected. What an angry-looking toe that is. I shall look away. I shall call it my *dedo doloroso* (sore finger) rather than the more cumbersome *dedo del pie doloroso* (sore toe), and there are two red lines running out from it, like the forked tongue of a rattlesnake, as if trying to reach up my leg and bite into my heart, before the toe turns gangrenous and falls off.

The modernistic Museo Naçional de Bellas Artes (built in 1954 and recently reopened after a five-year spell of renovation and reorganization) is fairly crowded today, while ten years ago there was nobody, and my friend A. had the whole place to herself for the entire afternoon. The little bookstore where she bought some little books has since been incorporated into a much larger bookstore at the other Museo Naçional de Bellas Artes. There was only one then, but there are two now, with the one big collection having been divided into the International Collection and the Cuban Collection, with the international having been moved to another location, which I promise to visit and report on at a later date.

The most astonishing piece in the Cuban collection is *The Great Fascist* by Rafael Zarza. It shows a bull dressed up like a man, but with great long horns. Blood drips from his mouth. One can see this ugly figure as Mussolini, but there's more than a hint of Fidel in his stance, and Fidel's well-known air of meditative thoughtfulness is well captured, so much at odds with the blood, and the sense of fury and fear. The bull is standing on a balcony, with his right hoof in his jacket pocket, and his left hoof emphasizing some point he's making as he holds forth to the crowd below, a crowd of cattle of course, rather hysterical looking, each one trying to find a way out of this stockyard before it's too late.

Fidel is hardly a fascist, but this large painting was painted in 1973, still a bad time for the homosexuals of Cuba, and to many he must have seemed like a fascist. Zarza is apparently still alive at sixty, still living and working in Cuba, and he travels out of the country from time to time. He was in Nigeria last year, and has had solo exhibitions in Caracas, Damascus, and many in Cuba. His work is represented in the national galleries of Germany, Finland, Venezuela, and Spain, and he's been involved in group exhibitions in Uruguay, Mexico, Scotland, the Czech Republic, the United States, Slovenia, Puerto Rico, Egypt, and Finland. So he has definitely not been blacklisted for the audacity of calling Fidel a bloody fascist. Other works in the gallery are similarly aimed at Fidel in terms as critical, but not as obviously so.

What Fidel thinks of this painting I haven't heard. He'd have seen it as essentially a pro-Revolutionary work, I imagine, critical as can be but in a supportive way, and he would certainly admire

Zarza's courage. It's likely El Beardo took one look at it, saw a bit of himself in it, shuddered, and vowed to be as unlike that in the future as possible.

Another painting shows a woman, with one arm recently amputated, her left, and not healed yet, sitting calmly on a grey bull and wearing a simple black dress. Another, more colourful and joyful, called *La Virgen del Melón* (1973), shows a big slice of watermelon floating in the sky and a Cuban Virgin Mary ascending to heaven with the sexiest smile on her face, and the shortest skirt imaginable, and a yellow robe. She's floating above the watermelon and there are two little angels assisting her by holding up her skirt even higher. On the ground there are many people, some looking up, some not noticing anything odd, some merely noticing the melon, others seeing beyond the melon to the virgin. Also on the ground are several barn-yard animals, a dinosaur, and some palm trees. As in all truly great art, every stroke is pregnant with meaning. And as for the painter, whose name I have misplaced, you can tell he has a lusty appetite for watermelon.

Mariano was getting more information out of me than I was out of him. I kept asking this museum guide questions about the paintings and he kept asking questions about me and why I was asking such questions. I told him I didn't think I'd ever seen such an interesting collection of politically committed art, full of the subtlest ambiguities and ironies within ironies. For instance, there was one painting of a bouquet of flowers, in a very undistinguished amateurish style. But it redeemed itself with a banner bearing a Fidel quotation, "Art Too Is an Arm of the Struggle." Mariano agreed when I took it to mean that Fidel's quotation overshoots the mark, and maybe the artist was making fun of Fidel, accusing him of being superficial, and asking him how this painting of a bouquet of flowers can possibly be an arm of the struggle. Mariano said maybe too the bouquet can be an arm of the struggle if a naive tourist is deceived into buying a work of such banality with foreign currency. He also thought that the word "struggle" might be taken to mean struggle of a personal rather than Revolutionary nature.

There was an excellent action painting of a blond white American boxer with blood gushing from his nose getting knocked out by a tall handsome proud unscathed Afro-Cuban boxer. Mariano confessed he didn't like the work because that's not what things are really like. With Cuba and the United States, it's not a matter of a boxing match, it's not one system against the other, it's just two entirely different systems, and there's no need for them to fight, there's no need for one to prevail over the other, there is no reason for them to have any hostilities at all. I agreed, but he didn't quite understand my suggestion that this particular pugilistic painting was really about Cuban art versus U.S. art, rather than the Cuban system versus the U.S. system, and Cuban art winning out, which it really truly does if the wonderful collection in this museum is any example. He might have thought I didn't appreciate the ideal virtues of peaceful coexistence. But it does seem odd in retrospect that he took it to refer to politics and I took it to represent art. Nobody for a moment would think it was just a boxing match. Except, maybe, the artist.

Also, he might have been faking it, but he expressed great astonishment when I confessed that in Canada one very seldom any more sees any political engagement in the work of painters or poets. Well why not? Canada is a democratic country, he exclaimed. You have freedom to express yourself any way you want.

Was that a smirk on his face? I said political artists in Canada are just not taken seriously. Their canvases are piling up in their studios unsold. Nobody's interested. People who would have been excited about this work twenty years ago now get all the political art they need from the editorial cartoons in their favourite daily, and all the political poetry they need on the op-ed page. But then again artists who remain apolitical are losing their audience as well.

It's always a good time for art in Cuba. But there is also a sort of marketplace censorship here. It's the pretty pictures that the tourists buy, not the ones with political content; in other words, the political stuff is not to be taken seriously, except by the Cubans themselves. The pretty pictures are the new avant garde, more so if they are inventively pretty, with old cars in them, and other allusions to this lovely island, but not too inventive so that they could be confused with the political. It was a sadly inconclusive little chat. It left me feeling a bit debilitated. Things were beyond my capacity to deal with today. There's a horrible paralysis in the arts. Everybody's just hanging on to everybody else, but nobody wants to be hung on to.

Mariano is not an artist, not a painter, not a poet, but he reads a lot of poetry, and has tried his hand at poetry – in dealing with personal problems mostly. But he wouldn't call himself a poet until he had broken through into something beyond that. He is a fastidious little guy in a neat uniform of maroon jacket and white shirt, a dark narrow intelligent face with a long nose, and an aura of Revolutionary certainty about him.

Later I spent a couple of hours walking around the nighttime streets of Havana Vieja. Fidel's remark about art being an arm of the struggle struck me again and again as I wandered past one artist's studio after another, with painters actually inside each studio slaving over a hot easel, and the walls festooned with paintings bright and beautiful, with hypnotic colours, and unusual angles and twists. But these are mostly pleasant works for the tourist market, skilled souvenir paintings of little subtlety, with the more serious works shoved to one side, and often there will be one single solitary painting, with a biting political reference or two, or some oddly interesting metaphysical conceit, on the wall among a dozen touristy paintings, and the artist obviously is hoping that someone, anyone, will notice.

It's the subject matter that gives the game away. The tourist paintings, or souvenir art, will be geared to the soul of the tourist. For instance, here's one showing an old black guy with a white moustache standing next to a 1957 De Soto in front of a Cuban hacienda with a Cuban flag in the window. This is obviously a souvenir painting for the starry-eyed tourist who will gladly fork out sixty dollars for it, so that he can take it home and hang it on the wall. And feel warm and soulful in the middle of winter.

The one serious painting on the wall, by the same painter, with the same style and palette, shows a vast cemetery, with the skyline of Havana behind it, and black people are coming up out of their graves, with big smiles on their faces, and bright sparkling eyes, as if they are being reincarnated into a happy new world. But the happy new world is the New Cuba, and all you can see is their heads, like radiant coconuts, coming up like spring flowers. I love the strange mystery of that painting. It seems so simple but it's anything but; in fact it made me shiver to look at it and I'm shivering anew thinking of it.

Numerous *chicas* one after the other along the dimly lit Prado and the Malecón were accosting me later that evening. Finally I came up with the perfect rebuttal. A pair of scantily clad Lolitas tried to interest me in a two-for-one special. Sorry, I have to rush off to meet my wife, I lied. A stroke of genius! They immediately laughed at themselves for having read me wrongly, and then they went back into the shadows. Except that I have perhaps caused them to lose confidence in their ability to read a tourist. "He just didn't look the type to have a wife."

But it didn't work with one woman. It was turning cool. I had my hands in my pocket. A warm body came up behind me, put its arm in mine, and said, "Howdy, sailor, how ya doin'!" When I turned to look at her she burst out laughing. Aha! A whore with a sense of humour!

She was a long-legged, lightweight Afro-Cuban racehorse of a woman, very attractive, in her late twenties, chocolate brown. Smart as blazes. We walked and we talked and we stopped for a beer. Her name was Yamílet and she spoke of her life. She had red tresses woven into her black hair. She said her mother had done that. She lives with her mother and her baby brother. Her father left Cuba when she was ten years old. He is now teaching physical education at the University of California. He sends a card at Christmas. She can't visit him and he can't visit her.

Several days a week she goes to the University of Havana, where she studies English on the Internet. She also probably exchanges e-mail with friends from other countries, well-heeled tourists who might have befriended her in the past, and given her their e-mail address, and are now being asked to send money for food perhaps, although not in a crass way at all. I didn't suggest she try to get through to her father on the Internet. You'd think he'd send more than a card at Christmas. Maybe he should know that his darling daughter is now f**king foreigners on the Prado for U.S. dollars and English lessons. Maybe he thinks his wife and daughter are perfect little Revolutionaries, making do with the ration card.

So we were drinking beer and talking. She seemed to know a bit about Canada, that Canada was a friend of Cuba, and she was currently most upset about the unsurpassed nastiness of the United States in refusing a visa to several old-time jazz musicians from the Buena Vista Social Club who had won Grammies and had been expected to come to the United States for the Grammy ceremonies. She said it was yet another new offence against Cuba, and these astounding international insults never seem to get any easier to take.

All of a sudden I looked at her with more clarity. I liked her a lot. We were sitting at the bar and I smiled and looked deeply into her eyes in the friendliest fashion. In return, she gave me some very profound kisses, which had my barstool spinning, with the bartenders looking on with great amazement. "I've never seen a barstool spin like that," one said. I refused to go with her to one of those little *casas particulares* that is set up for girls to bring the tourists for sex, where the people who run the *casa* watch the action through peepholes, or gaze down from an unnoticed upper level. It was out of the question. So I just wanted to listen to her talk. She said it was very hard to get a good meal on pesos. She gets sixty dollars from a tourist when she scores but has to split that with her pimp.

It finally dawned on me that she might not have eaten today. You're not hungry, I said, are you? And she just rolled her eyes and sighed. She was very cheerful for someone half-starved.

So I said let's go and have something to eat. She happily chose her favourite restaurant in the neighbourhood, a dark little place, crowded with tables but not with people, just west of the Prado and south of the Malecón. We went in, were seated, and looked at the multilingual menu. She was happily showing off her German and Italian, which seemed right up there with her English, but her French was poor. Another lover, another language.

But then I realized I wasn't very hungry, it was too hot in there to eat. I had no appetite. So I suggested that instead of ordering something, I should give her thirty dollars, say, as a goodwill gesture, *à la* Perry King. It would be like scoring except she didn't have to perform the deed, and furthermore she didn't have to give half the dough to her pimp. I told her I just remembered I had to meet someone. She said okay. I suggested she get the restaurant cook to prepare a big box of food and take it home to her mother and her baby brother. I gave her the money. She solemnly promised she would do that. I think she meant it. Off I went.

Mimi was definitely not a *chica*, and definitely not in her twenties. But on the way to meet her I made a wrong turn, and I got there late, and I waited at her corner for half an hour, but she didn't show up. She would have been nervous anyway about being seen with foreigners socially. A. had told me about meeting a nuclear physicist, Moscow-educated, who lost his teaching position at the university because it was judged that he had "too many foreign friends." But that was ten years ago. It may not be so bad now, but it still exists, and there are self-appointed spies lurking in the shadows.

As I waited, a skinny Afro-Cuban, a bit old for chasing tourists, approached and beseeched me to go into a store with him and buy him some milk for his baby. It would be three dollars. I said why don't I just give you three dollars and you go in and get it. No, he said, they wouldn't sell it to me. He kept looking sideways into my eye to see if I believed him. So I thought, Aha, I'll just give him a dollar and say I have to go, so I did. [Note: This was only the first of many encounters with the very interesting "milk for my baby" scam. It seemed to be exclusively the property of Afro-Cuban Habaneros. The three dollars will become five dollars as we get further into the high season.]

On her first afternoon in Havana, A. met an ancient mariner, an old black sailor who spoke excellent English with a Brooklyn accent. He told her he was born and raised in Brooklyn, New York, and joined the United States navy in his youth. He fell in love with Havana one weekend in 1954 during a stopover, never returned to his ship, and he'd been here ever since. He hadn't been in touch with anyone from home. Didn't know who was dead, who was alive, and didn't seem to give a hoot. He was a funny old guy with deep-set eyes.

Immediately after his ship had departed he discovered Sentería, and became seriously religious, mystical, shamanistic perhaps, more Catholic than the Pope. He didn't want any money from A., or anything else, he just wanted to show her his apartment, and his collection of large plain wooden Sentería crosses, each sitting in its ritual glass of pure water, as if waiting to sprout into a Tree of Life. His room was on the third floor of a decidedly open-concept apartment building, a voyeur's paradise, with a view of pretty well everything that was going on in every apartment on every floor. A. pinpointed the place on the map for me, and I tried to find it, but it's all been transformed into offices now. A lot of dilapidated residences have become sparkling commercial enterprises over the past decade. I've heard that most of the Havana Vieja residents from ten years ago would have been relocated to a less favourable area west of Havana.

I was crossing the Prado over to the Hotel Inglaterra, thinking maybe I should go in there for an icy-cold Cristal, then hop in a cab back to Melba's for the night. And halfway across the street someone slipped her arm in mine – again! And said, "Howdy, sailor, how ya doin'?" – again! The look on Yamílet's face told me she was more than merely happy to see me. She was purring with pleasure. She pulled up her shirt to show off her dark-chocolate slightly rounded belly, not slightly rounded as in early pregnancy but rather slightly rounded as in full of the yummiest tender morsels, and with her navel sticking out cheekily, and a little forest of black hairs growing around her navel and in a narrow band disappearing into her skin-tight jeans.

And she said, smilingly, sighingly, "Here . . . feel . . . I'm full of food." As if it was the first time in years. And she took my hand and stroked her tummy with the tips of my fingers. And she said she got a big box full of chicken and all kinds of wonderful things for thirty dollars and she took it home and they stuffed themselves, she, and her mother, and her baby brother, and they had lots left over for tomorrow. The people in the restaurant were happy, but my mother was overjoyed, she said, and more so because it was not required that I have to have sex. And my mother said, You should marry that guy.

Let me think about that, I said. So then we locked eyes and smiled dreamily. As if I were her dad just returned from California. Then I kissed her on the forehead, hopped in a cab, and waved goodbye.

DEDO DOLOROSO

Wednesday, February 18, 2004. Can't get a cab this morning, every cab is occupied. The smart people are wearing quilted jackets with hoods. Some seem fairly comfortable in light jackets. People in T-shirts only have their arms crossed and are shivering as they walk. Another cool morning in Havana. Some would call it cold. The ones without jackets, for instance. It's somewhere between twenty-seven and twenty-six degrees Celsius. From my window I see that everyone who has a jacket is wearing one and everyone who doesn't have one is envious. And cold. I am very privileged. I have three jackets with me and three others at home. Disgusting! How the bourgeoisie gets a bad name. But all six are rather scruffy and from the early 1970s. Nobody will mistake me for Bret Easton Ellis.

My green fountain pen is even older, but not scruffy at all, like an old car from the 1950s that has been lovingly maintained, and it seems to love Cuba. Upon arrival, the pen immediately started producing a richer flow of ink and with a longer time between fill-ups. Even on a coolish day like today it's working more smoothly than when I bought it for two dollars at age seventeen.

All morning someone in a large block of flats across the street has been playing the drums, perhaps to keep warm. The drumming is good-natured, intricate, impossible to dislike.

Melba adores my T-shirt. It shows a pair of belugas, mother and baby, swimming together in a pristine sea with blissful smiles on their faces. She doesn't ask me to translate the caption – Wildlife at Risk – but she asks if I have any children, which makes sense, because it's the kind of T-shirt a daddy would wear. Melba has very thick hair, well brushed, with only a few streaks of grey, and close-cropped at the sides and back. She is small and with a mode of dress that is carefully chosen for a mature woman with flair. The jacket she is wearing this cool morning would seem a bit loud on a man, even a young man, with its multicoloured checks, but it looks perfectly fine on Melba.

Yesterday in Havana Vieja I came across numerous old Afro-Cuban grannies dressed up in floral hats and brilliant Aunt Jemima dresses, sitting here and there on concrete steps or little wooden boxes and puffing away on extra-long, extra-large Cuban cigars. Actually they're not really puffing, they're just holding those cigars cold for atmospheric effect, and as visual aids to amateur photographers with no time to spare. They probably have to give them back to the boss at the end of their shift.

One of these grannies had a medium-size brown dog, with short hair, and it was very well behaved, almost too well. The poor pup had also been decked out in a little Aunt Jemima junior dress, and with a floral cap on its head – and a pair of overlarge sunglasses with thick white plastic frames. When I spoke to this mutt, and tickled him behind the ears, he looked over his glasses at me very sadly with deep soulful eyes and not enough energy to move his neck or wag his tail.

Could these dogs have been sedated for the benefit of the tourists, to facilitate easier snapshots? Or perhaps because Cuban dogs have an instinctive dislike for tourists, and tend to be snappy with them? Now and then a Cuban will make a sudden unexpected move, but tourists do this constantly. Makes a dog kind of nervous and in need of a good doggy Demerol. Not a knockout drop, just a little something that will stop the average hound from giving a hoot about anything.

The numerous other elderly Aunt Jemimas, similarly attired, included skinny women with skin like leather, and others corpulent and shining, smiling like the tropical sun, and they may be sweeping the streets with brooms, or tending to the trees and flowers in the various parks that were apparently such an eyesore ten years ago but now are just so pretty and so dreamlike, as beautiful as they had been in all their ancient colonial splendour.

My *dedo doloroso* is killing me. At the Hotel Havana Libre I painfully wait in a long lineup at the front desk. When I finally get up to the cashier, she tells me they don't do cash advances any more, though they used to, when A. was here. I have to go outside, turn left, and go down the road a bit. So I hobble to the little bank, trying to keep my mind off my agony, and there are two long lineups in there, one for the cash machine and one for the counter. I get into the one for the counter as it seems slightly shorter, but after a minute or so a big serious-looking cop, in his fifties, shoulders me out of the one lineup and into another. I think he's trying to even up the lines, but he's doing a poor job of it. When I ask why he's taken me out of the short lineup and put me in the long one, he puts me back into the short one (except it's now longer than it has been but still not longer than the other lineup).

So now I just wait motionlessly while an exceedingly lengthy transaction is taking place. Then the cop brings in a pregnant woman and escorts her to the front of the queue. Then two women from a store with lots of cash to deposit come in the back door and are ushered likewise to the front of the queue. Then one of the cash machines breaks down, so that line is placed at the end of my line. But when the people complain about being put at the end, they are given a lineup of their own, parallel to my lineup, even though there is just one teller, so the teller has to make sure he takes one person from one line followed by one from the other.

When I finally get my cash I go out looking for a *polyclinico*. And now I'm sitting in a cool shady waiting room waiting for the doctors to see my *dedo doloroso*, which sounds more dignified and serious than "sore toe." I'm close to tears thinking of others somewhere in the world whose toe may be even sorer than mine.

There are two elderly ladies in the waiting room and they have lost something. They had been having a quiet chat and now they have the sofa upside down and are shaking it. It's the white woman's gold hoop earring that has been lost, but her black friend is looking for it every bit as hard. I have one shoe off for the pain, but am hopping around, lifting up the other sofas, then I get down on my hands and knees searching for the earring, which must have rolled somewhere. The black woman points to the white woman's ear, the one with the hoop in it, and says the one we're looking for is just like that one. Now they are giggling, so we give up, straighten the sofas out, and sit down. The white woman is trying to remember where she last noticed she had both hoops. Next thing I know they've decided my toe is more important than the lost earring. They get down on their knees and examine the damage. They ooh and aah and commiserate tenderly. They make me feel I've come to the right place already, and I haven't even seen the doctor yet. You can really tell you're not in Canada.

Dr. Melba and Dr. Monica, when I earlier showed them the state of my toe, were not at all impressed. They seemed to think it was nothing. So when I got in to see the *polyclinico* doctors on duty (two, both female and youngish), even they managed to give me the impression I was overreacting to a very minor wound. Lazily, between much chit-chat of a personal nature, both on the phone and off, they disinfected and bandaged the toe. Then they gave me a spool of medical tape to take with me. And a half-litre bottle of *cloruro de sodio* .9%, enough to last a lifetime of sore toes. And of course it was all on the state. They didn't even require my signature, or to fill out any forms. They didn't even want to see my passport. The only thing they forgot was the extra cotton batten to go with the extra tape and I was too shy to ask for it.

But it all seemed right somehow. I kept thinking this is truly ideal, there is no valid reason why it shouldn't be like this in Canada, and everywhere else. The only time I had more impressive medical treatment was in a tiny Fijian hospital in a remote village up in the hills where I went with dangerously infected sunburn sores on the tops of both feet. The very large and kind female Fijian doctors had to fight with the skinny little snobbish male Indian pharmacist who insisted they were treating me wrongly, I should be given drug A rather than drug B. "They want to put antibiotic eyedrops on your feet?" he said. But the doctors won out. "Don't worry," they merrily told me, "he doesn't know what he's talking about, we're doctors, he's just a pharmacist who thinks he's smart." And I was right as rain the next day. Cuba isn't the only country where the doctors seem more serious and well informed, and with a kind of boundless dedication to the sick and injured, rather than to their bank balance.

Meanwhile, back in Havana, I put my sock and shoe back on and feel a lot better. They give me the address of a larger *polyclinico* in Miramar that stocks walking sticks. I hobble up to the street and hail a cab. It's an old beat-up pale yellow Lada. You have to lift the door a few inches before it will open. It is a terrible wreck, but the driver is very proud of it, in a melancholy hangdog sort of way. We understand and instinctively like each other. His name is Carlo, but he likes it when the tourists call him Charlie. He is sixty-three, and he can't figure out how to get the car going faster than twenty miles per hour, which gives me the opportunity to observe certain aspects of Cuban traffic. Even the bicyclists are passing him. He keeps as far right as possible, to cut down on the horn-honking from the rear. Our route is lined with old Spanish palaces, which were empty and falling apart ten years ago but are now beautifully restored, sparkling in the sun, and housing embassies, cultural centres, government offices, medical labs, concert halls, lecture halls, art galleries, various non-government organizations, and so on.

When we get to the larger *polyclinico*, Charlie kindly comes in with me. There are three canes hanging from hooks on the wall behind the main counter. I choose the black one. It is twelve pesos. So I give the attendant the smallest I have, a twenty-peso bill. She looks very confused. Why doesn't she just give me eight pesos in return? Then I realize my twenty-peso bill was really the tourist pesos, fixed on the U.S. dollar, so then I am very embarrassed and don't know what to do. But Charlie, who has been having a little siesta on his feet, suddenly leaps to my rescue. He hands the woman eight pesos (thirty cents) from his own pocket and off we go.

This was definitely a poor person's cane. This wasn't the sort of cane you buy at Shoppers Drug Mart for twenty bucks. It wasn't black, it was dark green with a black rubber handle that was attached by a screw to the cane and was already coming loose. But it felt good in my hand, I felt ready for anything. I wouldn't be bothered by touts and hustlers any more, because the *chicas* would see I had a cane, a sign of aged impotence, and the *chicos* would be worried I might be a homophobe and hit them with it.

Charlie took me back to the Havana Libre, where I blew twenty dollars reading Canadian newspapers in the Cyber Café. Southern Ontario is warming up, it's now zero degrees Celsius, and Paul Martin's government seems to be going down the drain with a heavy burden of petty scandals. That twenty dollars was wasted because when I got back to the bar, I met two Torontonians, newlyweds who had decided on Varadero Beach for their honeymoon, but it's been too cold for swimming or sunning, so they signed up for a day trip to Havana. They were wearing identical Toronto Maple Leafs sweaters and black-and-white Canada ball caps. It turned out we live exactly two subway stations away. They filled me in on what I'd already been filled in on, but I didn't mind because news from home is always worth hearing twice. They also implored me to visit them at their favourite bar in Toronto when I get back, and described it in wonderful detail, but I forgot to write down the name of it.

Cuban bartenders don't fanatically measure their drinks, so tipping them liberally pays off very well, as does shaking their hand and introducing yourself, offering them a cigar, etc. I'm now nursing my toe, freshly bandaged and treated, at the main-floor circular bar at the Havana Libre, and I am also nursing my well-deserved gin and tonic with Angostura bitters and about three ounces of gin for the price of one. A waiter is taking three glasses of red wine to a table behind me, and the servings are widely disparate. There will be a bit of a squabble no doubt over who gets which glass. Hard not to love a country like this. Cuba *no problemo*, as they say, hereabouts, constantly.

The Restaurant El Barracón is also on the first floor. A. says the food here was wretched, so it better be better than it was ten years ago or it's no tip from me. The ancient limestone coral walls and pillars of the original building are exposed, for a pleasant multicolour effect, with numerous natural trailings of green and orange leeching through the thin whitewash, and with ancient rings for horses also exposed in the old walls, cut into place long before this early post-modern hotel (formerly known as the Havana Hilton) was dreamt of. There's an unusually good three-man mariachi band, with a singer who does "My Way" better than Frank Sinatra, followed by "Only You" better than the Platters. They even made that dull old chestnut "La Rumba" sound good. I had a bowl of lobster soup and a large serving of white rice and black beans.

They have me sitting behind a stout seventeenth-century pillar, so I can listen to the band without having to watch it. And when they finish "La Rumba," I get up from my table and step out from behind the pillar in order to applaud and be seen applauding. When I sit down, the singer, who looks about fifty, handsomer than Frank but not as rich, in spite of being a great singer, comes to my table and thanks me for my enthusiastic response, which was definitely deserved, he seems to be saying, but seldom forthcoming, because people are so cheesy, and can't tell good mariachi music from bad these days. The bad bands give the good ones a bad name. I didn't have any requests, but I had a dollar for him, a good handshake, and a lot of deep eye contact – three things that are still very much appreciated in Cuba.

Charlie told me today that all the different car-rental agencies are about the same price, the same value, etc. They're all standardized by the ministry responsible for car rentals. So I think I'll rent a car tomorrow and just get out of here in search of interesting informa-tion and excellent experiences. In the meantime, I'm up to page 232 of *Islands in the Stream*, where Hemingway says of a certain character: ". . . He was an excellent car handler with beautiful reflexes in the illogical and neurotic Cuban traffic."

Illogical and neurotic, eh? Could Hemingway have been project-ing his own death-wish demons onto the poor people of Cuba? I shall rent a car, hit the highways and rural routes, and find out for myself. Till then, my first impressions indicate the motorists aren't homicidal, or even mildly hostile, as is the norm in cities like Toronto, nor do they have that special resentment toward pedestri-ans Toronto drivers love to display. Give me neurotic and illogical over homicidal any day. But the more neurotic and illogical the driving is, if it is, the sooner I'll be back in Havana, returning the keys to the rental agent.

STOLEN NOTEBOOKS

Thursday, February 19, 2004. Woke up thinking about something actress Carrie Fisher said in some British paper I was reading at the Hotel Ambos Mundos bar: "Resentment is like drinking a cup of poison, then waiting for your enemy to die." She was supposedly referring to something from her unhappy Hollywood childhood, but it seemed at the moment to capture the essence of U.S. policy toward Cuba.

A. is still haunted by the memory of a little boy who approached her in a crowd in front of the Capitolio a decade ago. He looked ill, his complexion was deathly grey, he was shrunken and sad. In his belt his mother, supposedly, had securely fastened a transparent plastic envelope with a U.S. dollar inside, on display. Unsmilingly, silently, desperately, he caught A.'s eye, then pointed to the dollar bill, with his eyes glued to hers for signals. She handed him a dollar and he held out his hand for another. He was a walking-talking empty billfold seeking to be filled, a billboard promoting U.S. currency.

Even in *Islands in the Stream*, there's a reference to a man who gives a poor person a twenty-dollar bill out of simple compassion. And that was Perry King's sole defence, apparently – that he had given the money out of compassion and not for any ulterior motive. Wherever in Cuba there are foreigners, this kind of simple heartfelt gesture is repeated, so it's driving me nuts to know that Perry is nearby, in a Cuban jail somewhere, with lousy food and crowded cells. At least we know he's not being tortured, because torture in Cuba went out with Batista. There was before, there might well be again, but for the past forty-five years Cuba has been a torture-free zone. And maybe the food isn't that bad these days. And the cells not that crowded, if at all.

After breakfast I sat in my room reading *Islands in the Stream*. And trying to figure out why I had such a horrible nightmare. Who fills our minds with such dreadful apparitions? Why, when I'm peacefully sleeping, do I suddenly see two cars colliding head-on at high speed, and the occupants thrown out under the wheels of a speeding bus? In vivid detail, I watched as the wheels of the bus crushed heads and tore limbs off, with many replays, and each replay shown from a slightly different angle. As the bodies flew out of the cars, for the fourth or fifth time, in slow motion, their faces had the horrified look of the horse in Picasso's *Guernica*, or the screaming mother holding her dead baby in the same painting, or the silent scream of the dying man in the foreground, with bombs still falling from the sky.

Does this mean I should cancel my plans to rent a car? Or is it merely a warning that in my driving around Cuba I should be especially aware of the possibilities of such horror. Maybe it was a warning that Hemingway was right about Cuban drivers – or maybe the roads themselves are illogical and neurotic. This was some kind of dreamworld warning, from some deep part of me that I usually am not in contact with, and it definitely was not a pleasant way to start the day. The dream shook me; it was so powerful I was even thinking of cancelling my stay and flying home. What sort of fatality rates prevail on Cuban highways? The guidebooks don't speak well of the roads or the safety thereof. But for some reason this dream has given me a mad desire to prove them wrong.

That's it for the Canadian embassy. I won't call them again. At first they were out to lunch, then they were at a meeting, then they were out of town. This from three separate calls, each about an hour apart, after the Cuban receptionist took my name and forwarded it to the various secretaries. All I wanted was to chat informally, maybe arrange a meeting with Fidel, get filled in on the Perry King situation, and bring up the issue of the late Greg Curnoe's notebooks.

Curnoe was an important and much-loved painter on an official visit, invited by Cuba, along with other Canadian artists, and he was sympathetic with the Cuban government, and with Cuba, which is not to say he wouldn't have been critical. The visit occurred fifteen years ago. Greg's notebooks were full of watercolour sketches of beaches and palm trees, pen-and-ink drawings, and interesting little poems executed with rubber stamps and a ballpoint pen. He left them in his hotel room and when he returned a few hours later they were gone.

I've written about Curnoe's lost notebooks in the past and have called on the Canadian government to make an official request for their repatriation, but nothing has happened. Greg was killed a few years later in a cycling accident, on a quiet country road in southern Ontario. What a hero I'd be if I could return to Canada with his notebooks under my arm! Or at least return with some kind of plausible excuse for their disappearance. Greg would not have made much of a fuss, but the loss of those books was definitely a disappointment.

I'm tempted to think that the dream, and my inability to get ahold of anyone at the embassy, are dual omens. But for some reason I'm interpreting both to mean I should get out there on the big highway and explore the island as it's never been explored before. Slowly and carefully.

Like all great novels, *Islands in the Stream* is much better the second time. The minute I finished it I threw everything in my bag, said goodbye to Melba (Monica was on duty), and headed for the Hotel Havana Libre, where there is a row of five or six desks devoted to car-rental requests. Each desk represents a different agency, although they are all connected at the ministerial level. I flashed my passport and credit card and was soon off in a grey Peugeot 106 – pretty well the only object of that particular colour in all of Cuba these days. I didn't know where I was going, but I was determined to do all I could to avoid the fate of those little people in my sour and sobering dream last night. Somerset Maugham used to maintain that the wise traveller travels only in his imagination. But I hereby promise to prove the exception to that rule, if such a thing is in my power. It is true though, there is something unwise about travelling, and most of us do altogether too much of it. The truly wise stay at home, rent movies, and read the odd travel book.

EL CRISTO DE JILMA

Friday, February 20, 2004. Everybody was off to work. They were going into the fields and the warehouses of agriculture. Children and teachers were being dropped off at school. Medics were heading for the hospitals and *polyclinicos*. Pictures of Revolutionary heroes lined the road, with their names and mini-biographies. I had to stop the car because two skinny old men, who didn't seem to know what they were doing, had a cable stretched across the road. Instead of doing this the easy way, letting the cable down so I could drive over it and continue on, they insisted on pulling it as tight as they could, one at each end, with all their feeble strength, so that it would be high enough for me to drive under it. Which I managed to do, with a cheery smile, though it scraped the roof a bit. Maybe they thought I'd get a flat if I drove over it.

The sun was blazing and I was heading back to Santiago de Las Vegas, a bit south and west of Havana, near the José Martí Airport, to look for my glasses. I must have left them in the deep grass at the side of the rocky road where I had my flat tire last night. I also think I left the tire wrench there in the Cuban night. And my watch seems to be missing too.

I feel like an air-conditioned jerk driving through the centre of a vast number of busy agricultural communities, with everybody rushing off to work. They go on horseback. They go on horsedrawn wagons. They go on bicycles with wide baskets on each side and with sidecars. They go on motorcycles with sidecars and trailers. They go squashed nose to nose on the backs of trucks. They go in Fidel-type uniforms, they go in yellow-and-red school uniforms – and man, do I need a cafecito or two. It was very cold last night to be sleeping in the car. I had to drink a lot of rum to get warm enough to dose off.

It all started last night around Santiago de Las Vegas. Later when I told the story to Nelson at the car-rental agency, he said, "Oh don't go down there, that's where all the potholes are." He would say that though. Anyway, on a nice paved road with no potholes at all, all of a sudden one huge pothole opened up out of nowhere and – bang! The second I hit it a miserable hissing of air was followed by the bup-bup-bup of a deflated tire. So I pulled over, wrenched all the nuts off the wheel, then worked on that jack for an hour trying to get it to lift the right front corner of the car, but it would go up only so far and then it would stop, so that it was impossible to get the wheel off.

Out of the darkness came an old man, who told me straight off that he was sixty-three years old, and the big fat beautiful red sow he had on a leash weighed 325 pounds. It loves mashed-up sugar cane, he told me, and cigar butts. He was taking that porker for a walk as if it were a dog, or so it seemed: the real purpose would be more serious, either insemination or slaughter.

To meet a stranger on a lonely road in such darkness can be a bit disconcerting, but this was fine. The old fellow had just a moment earlier found a razor-sharp machete in the grass. He was testing its sharpness with his thumb. He said people shouldn't leave these lying around, schoolkids could pick them up and hurt each other. He handed it to me. I pretended to shave myself with it. You'd need a really steady hand, though, or else you'd be perforating a nostril or poking your eye out. So I handed it back to him. Switching the machete back and forth like that was a little ritual of trust, like shaking hands, except more suitable for the middle of the night when evil spirits fly abroad. Now I could trust him not to cut my throat and steal the car, and he could trust me not to cut his throat and steal the pig.

He started working on the jack and he had the same problem. It only went so far. He said, Wait a minute, don't go away, don't do anything, just wait here, I'll be right back.

He came back without the sow but with his son, a very tall man, handsome, serious, a strong agricultural worker, a believer in the Revolution and all the slogans. He was about twenty-eight, and he brought his own jack with him. In a flash he had the car all the way up, the wheel off the ground, the nuts had already been removed – but now there was a second problem. The wheel still wouldn't come off. We were almost blind in the darkness, but there seemed to be a large nut in the hub that had to be removed.

Without the slightest complaint, the selfless son, raised on the principle of helping out whenever possible without any thought of reward, went all the way back to the farm and returned with his big tool box. He found a monster wrench that fit that nut perfectly. But the nut, if nut it was, was still unbudgeable. We decided it just looked like a nut, it wasn't really a nut.

Since we didn't know what to do, we just stood there looking at each other. Finally the old fellow got another idea. He told me and his son to wait. He was going to get El Mecánico, the village mechanic. The son and I waited forty-five minutes, trading Spanish lessons for English in the dark. Then the old man returned with an even older man, a skinny little guy about seventy, with well-cared-for long white hair and sandals. He sported a white cardigan and a small white goatee. He seemed to be the village godfather, and he had a massive lead pipe over his shoulder – about five inches in diameter and six feet long.

With not a trace of excessive dignity, El Mecánico sat down on the grass right in front of the car and started whacking and whacking and whacking the wheel with his big lead pipe. This was insane! Nothing was going to happen! And he just kept whacking and whacking and whacking – and all of a sudden, like a burst of lightning after you've seeded the clouds from your biplane for the thirtieth time, the wheel fell off. Wow! All four of us started dancing a little jig around the car. Then I put on the spare and tightened the nuts, while the young fellow lowered the car. Everybody laughingly shook hands and said goodbye. I gave ten dollars each to the old man and his son, and I gave them each a huge hug, and multitudinous *muchas graçias*, etc. They could buy another pig or two with that money.

The dapper godfather with the sandals, he wouldn't take a cent, he just absolutely refused, it was against his socialist principles, even if I was a rich tourist, practically on my knees begging him to take my money. He didn't mind the other guys pocketing the dough if that's what they wanted, but he didn't want any part of it. He must have had the wisdom to know that money always leads to trouble, for nobody knows when enough is enough. Maybe he had some money once and didn't like it. It's a strange feeling when a poor person won't take money after they've done you a big favour. You feel so helpless. Especially if you're just passing through. You know you'll be in this man's debt forever.

So it was still pitch dark, and there were some wonderful Cuban stars up there, but their light wasn't reaching the ground. Venus was looking a bit sleepy, quite high in the west, when I first got the flat, but by the time the flat was fixed she had dropped below the horizon. Exhausted, I drove into a church parking lot and slept there, even though I knew I'd left some of my important belongings behind. There was a school with an alabaster bust of José Martí out front keeping watch over me. At first, while having a pee, I thought it was a ghost watching me, and was so startled I peed on my foot. But it was just a bust. Real ghosts aren't quite that gleamingly white. Not even an albino ghost could be.

Most of the morning I spent trying to find the same spot again. And finally I found it, after driving through much scenic beauty, but the glasses could not be found. I hoped someone found them who could use them. Lucky I had this old pair, but they didn't work so well. Also my watch must have fallen off my wrist as I was trying to get the wheel off, but I gave up searching for it in the tall grass. In retrospect I may have mistaken the spot.

So I had no choice but to drive back into Havana, to get a spare. I had to keep giving Nelson more details about what happened to the tire in order to convince him that I shouldn't have to pay the damages, and that he shouldn't charge me for the tire, which was shot. He understood perfectly what I was saying, all these things that were no fault of my own, including the problem with removing the wheel, which is not common but does happen, and everything worked out okay.

My powers of persuasion succeeded with Nelson. I told him when my friends come to Cuba I will now have no choice but to tell them not to go to Panautos for their automotive needs because I had a terrible problem with that agency. Nelson was rubbing his chin and thinking hard. I would do it, he said, if it were my company, but I am not the boss. I told him the boss would be proud of him for making such a decision on his own. Also I told him that I had heard that in the matter of car rentals anything that goes wrong is automatically assumed to be the tourists' fault. But this malfunctioning jack was most definitely not. Et cetera. My nerves are shot. I've had a whole day of my precious time in this beautiful country *stolen* from me. He twitched when I said "stolen."

And so he bit the bullet and offered me an extra day free. I took it. And gave him a cigar. And shook his hand warmly. And called him *compañero*. I told him about my dream of the traffic accident and with his Cuban wisdom he said, "That's good luck!"

When I gave him the cigar, he refused it. I don't smoke, he said. Then give it to a friend, I said. Well, he just beamed, he thought that was a nice idea, and he took it from me. But then he thought of an even better idea, he wouldn't give it to a friend, he would keep it forever on a little shelf in his parlour, and he would put a little sign on it saying, David W. McFadden of Toronto, Ontario, gave me this cigar. I bet he does too. He seemed like the type to enjoy having a commemorative cigar on his shelf. Nelson had a dark, handsome, round face, with a widow's peak, and he had that applelike Lorca look about him. And he had quiet eyes with no bottom to them.

The west window at Melba and Monica's had provided me with many lingering looks at the Plaza de la Revoluçion, the fabulous Hotel Naçional, and a soaring bronze statue of the Virgin Mary holding the Baby Jesus with his arms outstretched and eyes closed, as if saying, "Like it or not, here I am." The statue is twenty-five feet tall and stands atop the high tower of the Convent and Church of Our Lady of Carmen, so that Mary's halo is about 225 feet above the Calzada de Infanta, which separates Centro Habana from Vedado. Wherever you stroll in those two neighbourhoods, the Virgin seems to sail along in the sky, accompanying you, like a guardian angel holding her baby out front and centre.

But I left there yesterday and am now here, on the far side of Havana Bay, standing high on a cliff leaning my head against the base of a massive white marble statue of El Cristo de la Habana. El Cristo is sixty-five feet high, overlooking the city to the west, his empty eyes peering into every window, and he stands on a height of land a hundred feet above the harbour below. Just as the Virgin sails along with you as you walk through Vedado, Christ will play pecka-boo with you as you wander the streets of Havana Vieja. From this distance, the Virgin seems about the size of a fingernail clipping. El Cristo is facing her way. Unfortunately, she is not returning his gaze because she too is looking westwards. If someone were to climb up there and somehow manage to turn the Virgin and Child around to look eastwards, she and El Cristo would be gazing into each other's eyes across half the city and the harbour. That couldn't hurt.

This is a physically powerful Jesus with a lantern jaw and the great strongly veined hands of an agricultural worker. He looks as if he could reach up and pull King Kong down from that skyscraper without missing a breath, and with hands so huge he could squeeze the breath out of a *Tyrannosaurus rex*. He is a King Arthur without a sword, an Alexander without an army, a superhero without a comic book. This fearsome Christ is also known as El Cristo de Jilma, after the sculptress, Jilma Madera, from Pinar del Rio, who happened to have finished the work just as Fidel Castro and Che Guevara were advancing on Havana, and Batista was getting his suitcase packed. A miracle! No way she could have planned it like that. The statue was erected in the final days of December 1958. It's billed as "the largest sculpture of white Carrara marble ever made by a woman." It's not quite as famous as the Christ the Redeemer atop the Corcovado in Rio de Janeiro, and it must be said that the latter, which dates from 1931, is more spectacular, almost twice as tall, and stands on a summit two thousand feet above the sea.

But when El Cristo was consecrated, Jilma Madera told the crowd, "I made it for you to remember him, not to adore him: it's marble." She described herself, ironically, as an atheist, an early follower of José Martí, and an admirer of Fidel. But she sympathized with Christ's politics, and his concern for the poor in spirit. You can see this attitude very clearly in the statue itself. Christ looks down on Havana not as if he wants people to pray to him, or to accept him as their saviour, as much as he just wants people to know that he's watching, like a celestial police chief, a United Nations peacekeeper, whatever your beliefs may be, and he's also conferring blessings on anyone who thinks of looking his way.

And even though Jilma's Christ is almost blindingly white, he's not just for the white people of Cuba. With his Asian eyes and African lips, he's for everyone. Jilma also is said to have left Christ's eyes empty, to symbolize that he is there to watch over all the people, everywhere, not just in Havana, not just in Cuba.

There's an artist sitting on a folding chair behind the statue. He's having a little nap. No, he's just listening to music on his tape player with his head down. He's done some watercolours of El Cristo for people to take home as souvenirs. Also still lifes with oranges, views from a window, etc. A portrait or two of Che, a moonlit lagoon. These are bright and colourful, minimal and untutored, not laboured at all, but executed with grace and enthusiasm.

He and his girlfriend started guessing where I was from. "Los

Angeles! New York! Florida!" No no no. "England?" No. I'll give you a hint, it's on my hat. They look. "Ohhh! Canadá," they exclaim with great pleasure. Then they keep repeating it, "Canadá! Canadá!" A man goes by with a long stick and four brown goats. In the beautiful countryside there are little buildings in the least likely places, and here comes a very fat short woman about fifty wearing a T-shirt showing a dinosaur riding a bicycle. The T-shirt says, Cyclosaurs.

In Cuba One Can Grow Old with Dignity and Security, says a billboard in Guanabacoa showing a smiling elderly couple. And in Regla I spot my first 1947 Studebaker, my favourite car from child-hood, the first streamlined family car, equally pointy at the front and the back, like a Buck Rogers spaceship. And the big kids would say, "You can't tell if it's coming or going," which sounded dangerous and ambiguous. This one is original sky blue, not rusty at all but very shabby and dull, and the front and back points seem to be sagging like a bankrupt Concordia. Before getting out of town I spot two more. They used to have a lean and hungry look, now they have a hangdog look front and back.

Hemingway should have called the Cuban police the "illogical and neurotic" ones, rather than the motorists. I've just been flagged down and stopped, at full highway speed, in the fast lane, by two cops, one on either side of the road. One pointed at me to pull over into the slow lane and the other pointed at me to pull over into the fast lane. I told them they were going to get somebody killed this way. But they misinterpreted me and thought I was complaining about them committing the horrible sin of stopping a tourist.

"We are the police and we can stop anybody we want," said one. The other said, "We wanted to give you a small inspection, but because you are a tourist, you can go – so keep going." Just as I went to take off they stopped me again and wanted to know where I was going – just to see if they had guessed right and I was really a tourist and not a terrorist. I said San Francisco de Paolo. They'd never heard of it. It was world famous as the site of Hemingway's Finca Vigía and it was right in the area, but these skinny bozos had never heard of it.

So I got off the highway and onto a secondary road, got out of the car, and found another cop. I was going to keep pestering the police till I found one who knew where San Francisco de Paolo was. There were no signs, but I knew it was very close. So the next cop glared at me and said, "Where's your car?" He came over and gave it a small inspection, then said, "Just go down there and turn right." I caught him smirking at another cop, in such a way that I got the impression that's what they always say when tourists ask directions, down there and turn right.

Then at a stoplight a woman came running up and asked for a lift. I said I was only going as far as San Francisco de Paolo. She said, "Oh, all right, no problem," and walked away. Wait, I said. Did she know where it is? She said, "Just go down there and turn right."

Yesterday, before my rendezvous with the pothole and the pig, I managed to find the Finca Vigía, but that was by coming up the other way. Coming this way it seems impossible to find. I will have to go to where I started yesterday, and then I will find it. But when I found it yesterday I was a bit late. It closed exactly at 5 p.m. and even when I got down on my hands and knees and begged them, the two handsome Afro-Cuban teens guarding the gate laughingly said, No can do.

So now I'm trying to get there again, but nobody has ever even heard of San Francisco de Paolo, it's not on the map, and it's not signposted. I spoke to an old man with a bright red T-shirt with this cutting slogan: Mr. Imperialist, you are causing genocide on the Cuban people.

He said go down there and turn right.

Finally things started to look familiar, and I found the place, but again it's after five o'clock and I'm snookered two days in a row. True, there's nobody guarding the gates this time, but the gates are closed and heavily padlocked.

This four-lane divided highway is called the Circuito Norte, and while cruising along you can look out over the Straits of Florida and down at a string of hotels along the coast. A police officer and a blonde in a miniskirt are sitting under a bridge eating strawberry ice-cream cones. A young man has brought two cows to graze along the side of the road, and another fellow a bit farther has thirty-seven goats grazing on the thick green grass. The sea is bright deep blue with patches of green closer to shore, and some choppy foam as the waves hit the breakwater. The water is cold. The only person I've seen swimming was one fellow whose fishing line got snagged and he dove in to free it. A very tall industrial chimney with red-and-white stripes is emitting a great cloud of black smoke that will fly southwest over the island of Cuba. Let's hope it's dispersed before it reaches Honduras, which is where it seems to be heading.

In *Islands in the Stream*, Hemingway tells a story about a Cuban fellow in the San Francisco de Paolo area who cut his girlfriend up in six parts, wrapped them in paper, and dropped them off at different spots along the road. So Mr. Hemingway the writer, in his role as Mr. Hudson the painter, used that as an excuse not to go jogging. Not because he was afraid of slipping on a body part, but because of not wishing to be shot. People would say, Oh look, somebody running (highly unusual in Cuba), it must be he who did it – where's that rifle?

There are some soul-stirring mountains over there, beyond the coastal plain. They're the magic mountains Hemingway would have seen from the *Pilar*, weaving among the islands off the north shore looking for German U-boats, and he would observe that these mountains looked exactly as if they were topped with snow. They become very steep at the top and the vegetation falls away to expose vast patches of limestone as white as the Carrara marble of El Cristo, or the chalk-white cliffs of Dover, or the glaciers of Greenland under the midnight sun. But the actual tops of the mountains are capped with thick green grass and palm trees.

Two black children are taking wicker birdcages home with them. A skinny white *campesino* standing in the middle of the highway under a hot sun with no sombrero is hoping to sell a couple of bunches of the most delicious bananas, those little ones Hemingway thought looked like fingers on a hand. The smallest bananas are the sweetest, as mother used to say. I gave him three dollars for two bunches. Put them on your cereal, he advised. Another fellow appeared with a heavy tray laden with a bright yellow mountain of nicely cut cubes of butter for sale.

There's a guy with flare. His car broke down on the road, and his entire family is with him, so in order to protect them as he tries to repair the engine he gets a large dead leafless branch from a tree and places it about forty feet behind the car to make sure nobody will plough into him. Clever fellow!

This is still the province of La Habana – and behold the wondrous landscape. I'm looking at the landscape of Cuban painters – they've been painting these rolling hills forever, with lots and lots of little palmettos, and rivers lined with a wild array of deciduous trees, many in blossom, and giant royal palms. But we're out of Hemingway's transcendent area of seemingly snow-capped mountains already. The limestone here is yellow, tending to brown. You see trucks loaded with pulverized yellow limestone, for all your construction needs.

And now here's the great old Cuban city of Matanzas, on its lengthy and magnificently curved seafront, a vast half-moon bay with a seawall spiffier than Havana's (perhaps because marginally more pro-tected from storms). I didn't know that Matanzas meant "slaughter," and that it was in former times the site of the stockyards, the Chicago of Cuba.

Two little girls about eleven or twelve, black girls with pigtails and wearing shorts, are shamelessly strutting their stuff along the highway, and they glance over their shoulder to see if anyone's noticing them. Coincidentally, Matanzas was where Perry King had been working. Can't get my mind off that poor guy. I hope Perry's cell isn't crowded and he has a bit of room to stretch out. Not that I have any way of ascertaining his guilt or innocence.

There's an attractive but modest three-storey hotel and restaurant from about 1952 on the beach a bit east of Matanzas. I am now driving back to this hotel after making a U-turn halfway to Boca de Camarioca. Too tired, plus I just want to go back where everybody's so happy. The happiest person of all is a bright skinny woman in her fifties with lots of pep and lots of lovely laugh lines on her face. The hotel was fully occupied, but she said if I don't find anything suitable in Boca de Camarioca to come back and we'll take you to our *casa particulare* and we'll feed you and you can stay the night, etc. I don't even know why I left after that except that I was a bit tired of *casa particulares* and was hoping for a hotel. It would be wonderful to spend the night in this hotel, you'd be able to see the sun coming up over the sea, and I was hoping for another one just like it but with a vacancy, but there was nothing so I turned back.

This woman is very funny. She doesn't laugh as much as Melba, but her laughter is more contagious and makes me feel happy. She doesn't speak a word of English and her Spanish requires more concentration than I can muster, but she definitely wants to take me home with her and her husband, Pepé, who is busy pacing the floor waiting for her and who is always bugging her to bring amusing people home for the night when the hotel is full. The weird thing is, it's not a real *casa particulare* because they won't take any money for it. It's just for the friendship, and the laughs, and seeing what I think of their lifestyle.

Manacas Clara. This is my favourite Cuban beer so far, with its festive label of a red ribbon around a white egg on a green background, brewed in the town of Manacas in Villa Clara province, a light India Pale Ale sort of beer, but it's hard to find. At this point I wrote in my notebook, "In Cuba everything is politics" – but I can't remember the context. It is true, though: politics as in the art of being polite and civilized and with a feeling of being connected with people no matter who they are, what their politics are, or where they're from: simply a matter of caring for the world.

Josefa of the laugh lines comes down to tell me she's on bartending duty upstairs and to come up when I've finished my meal.

Everybody who works here changes jobs constantly. A cook one day, waiter the next, bartender the next, floorsweeper, washroom attendant, chambermaid, then back to cook.

The dining room boasts a vast window facing the sea, but the sopa de polo is nothing short of inedible. The frijoles negros are fine except they have a slight taste of something they shouldn't have: a bit of dish soap maybe. But the rice is okay. And the Manacas is excellent. The waitress noticed I had abandoned the soup, wondered if there was something wrong with it. I told her, mildly, that it was fine, it just wasn't to my taste, no problem. She seemed to agree that the soup was no good. So she very *unkindly* told another waitress that I didn't like the soup, and this waitress promptly stormed over to my table, brokenhearted, in tears, waving her arms around, because apparently it was her very own recipe, and she can't believe I don't like the soup. The soup is fine, I tell her, excellent in fact, very well made soup – it's just not to my taste at this particular moment. Any other moment, I'm sure I'd love it. I can't stand to see a woman upset. I stood up and gave her a consoling hug. The first waitress, still on my side, stood in the background rolling her eyes and pretending she was vomiting in the sink. Everybody in the dining room hushed up and stopped eating to watch the fun. Finally the second waitress calmed down and I helped wipe her tears away. But she still had the look on her face of a very hurt pussycat who is smiling through her pain. She still senses in her heart that I didn't like her wretched soup, no matter what I say. If I liked it I'd be eating it. That's all there is to it.

So now in order to make her feel better and to get rid of my guilty conscience about being so fussy about food in such a poor country I decide to eat the soup, all 340 grams of it ($2.20). Both waitresses eagerly lean forward as I work up my courage for a second spoonful. Excellent, I declare (even though I wish I could spit it out), but it needs a touch of salsa piquante. They look at each other. No salsa piquante. I suggest maybe some . . . salsa inglese? They look at each other again and shake their heads sadly. I'm about to ask for ketchup when the second waitress disappears and comes back proudly holding a little bottle of Tabasco sauce made in Louisiana. She cautions me it's very hot, much hotter than salsa piquante. I very cautiously and obediently put one tiny drop in the soup, then smilingly shake out a dozen more. She was shocked, but the soup was transformed. I took a few spoonfuls and then with great gusto picked it up and began drinking it straight from the bowl and smacking my lips. Her sadness turned to happiness, with just a touch of embarrassment for having shed tears prematurely, and she said she'd add Tabasco sauce to her recipe for sure. I pointed to the tiny "made in U.S.A." and said I was just doing my bit to mend fences. She said the fences are indeed in need of mending.

I got talking to an Italian-speaking Israeli at the next table, who had no problem claiming to be in Cuba solely for the *chicas*, and he wanted to know what I thought of the menu. There was a whole page of drinks that start with the word *Ciego*. He thought it must mean "gin." I thought it meant "blind," but that didn't make sense. Blind soft drinks? Drink this and go blind? Oh wait, maybe it's pop, soda pop, and the plant is probably in the city of Ciego de Ávila, commonly known as Ciego. I'm thinking out loud and the Israeli isn't missing a word. Oops, I'm wrong again: it's not Ciego de Ávila, it's the famous mineral water known as Ciego Montero, and it's from a spring – a blind spring? – in the city of Cienfuegos on the south coast, and it's a mineral water you can get doctored, as on this menu, with different flavours such as pineapple, lemon, orange, cola, maté – in 40-cent, 45-cent, $1.20, or the giant two-litre size for $1.45.

And under the heading Platos Principales, the affluent can gnaw on the 120-gram "steack de jamón viking" for $15, the 348-gram grilled chicken for $9.60, or the 315-gram fried chicken for the same price, while a 232-gram bowl of moros y cristianos (moors and christians, or black beans and white rice) will be $2 with or without Tabasco sauce.

So this is a hilariously lovely hotel/restaurant right on the edge of the sea, you can even see the twinkling lights of Varadero Beach on the distant horizon, and on my table is a very nice pot containing a daisy and a rose, both artificial. And the bartender wants to take me home with her! Her deeply lined face is as ready to laugh as a tiger ready to pounce. She looks as if she was born skinny as a rail and stayed that way. She's got almost no lips at all, she's got a skinny face, and a skinny body, and she's about five-foot-six, and funny.

One of the members of tonight's three-man mariachi band must have got sick of the soup, so to speak, and sailed off to the States, and they haven't found a replacement yet. So it's a fifty-year-old man on guitar and a twenty-year-old man on bongos. They've been murdering everything in their repertoire tonight. The Israeli and I encouraged them in their pathetic version of "La Rumba" by playing air bongos and air piano, then we each gave them a dollar, which inspired the other diners to cough up some tips for them as well if only to save face.

My infusione arrives (30 millilitres, 40 cents) and it's cold. There's only one dessert on the menu and it's marmalade with rum in cream cheese (145 grams for $2).

When we got to the *casa*, Josefa and Pepé turned out to be newlyweds in spite of their advanced age. Pepé enjoyed drinking glasses of clear cheap dry Havana Club rum, with no mix, no ice, no chaser, and so did I (on occasion), and in their spacious, very clean and orderly second-floor apartment in Boca de Camarioca on the road between Matanzas and Varadero, closer to the former than the latter, this little vice we shared created an instant bond, as shared vices often do. There was a balcony on the south side overlooking the starlight-strewn sea, and a balcony on the north side overlooking vast stretches of agricultural land and hills farther back. If I'd been thinking right I'd have brought a bottle for Pepé. He is now telling me the stories behind all his prized possessions, but there weren't that many and they weren't that prized. There was a framed photo of Che and Fidel walking side by side in the mountains and seemingly gazing into each other's eyes as if they were lovers, which I'm certain they weren't, except platonically perhaps. But Pepé just smiled, he hadn't taken it, he didn't know who had. It looked like a photo I should know, because it was a great shot. But I knew I'd never seen it before.

VARADERO BEACH AND THE BATTLE OF IDEAS

Saturday, February 21, 2004. Last night, when I first saw handsome Pepé, who was also very skinny, and medium height, about an inch taller than Josefa, he was just getting up from a sound sleep. He had stopped pacing the floor some time ago, and had fallen asleep with the TV on. They could only get one channel, and very bad reception, but they still watched it. They had no phone and he hadn't been expecting company. He looked dazed, with his droopy Jockey shorts and his slightly receding jaw. He didn't like it at first that I was there, but Josefa with her womanly ways soon had him smiling. Revolutionaries never know when they're going to have to leap out of bed and look sharp. You don't see Fidel snoring away when he should be up.

They gave me a pair of lightweight, ultracool baggy khaki shorts to wear. And a pair of Zico flip-flops. I felt transformed; over the next hour or two Pepé and Josefa stood in the kitchen, pouring out glasses of rum for the three of us, with powerfully uplifting cafecito chasers, waving their hands around and laughing. Both were born in 1950, she was married before, he was never married. We married in old age, said Josefa, and we're very happy together, for sure, no doubt, seeking confirmation from Pepé. They smiled fondly at each other. They were both of the same type somehow. They had a movie-star quality about them. Pepé could have been the Scarecrow in *The Wizard of*

Oz. And Josefa could have been the Cuban Auntie Mame. Her teeth when she smiles are excellent, but they are black in places, and you can see fillings here and there. And she's actually nicer than Mame.

Pepé was very youthful and amiable for an old soldier. He was the only Cuban to show me his little red card, the one proclaiming him a member of the Communist Party of Cuba. He had amusing stories about his two years in Angola in the mid-1970s, with the Cuban army successfully defending the government against the invaders from South Africa and the United States, and causing Henry Kissinger to rail against the effrontery of a small Third World country like Cuba daring to change world history. Pepé was definitely in the thick of it, for two years, firing madly in the heat of battle on occasion, "shooting imperialists." He makes a funny but fierce face, starts firing an imaginary rifle, and goes "pop-pop-pop-pop," then he makes a peaceful saintly face and pretends to be injecting drugs into his arm, then shaking his head emphatically, then pretending he is smoking pot, then shaking his head and saying no no no. What he was saying was that he could understand, and maybe even be involved in, drug use in other countries – Africa maybe, or Iraq. Particularly in time of armed struggle. But not in Cuba, because – he spun around ecstatically with arms outstretched – everything's so beautiful here, no need to get high.

He had no pension. Nobody gets a pension from the African wars. They weren't paid a peso for their courageous and noble service abroad. But any job that they left in order to serve in Angola, when they got home they would get their entire wages from all the time they were away. That was a vast amount of money, he suggested, but I wasn't quite sure what his job was that he resigned from in order to go to war. It was hard to imagine what either of them would do with a vast amount of money, or any money at all for that matter. People are poor, but their needs seem pretty well as few as their options. And their primary needs are twofold: freedom from the fear of another invasion and the end of the sanctions.

Pepé showed me an intricate gadget that looked like some arcane instrument of torture. But it turned out to be an oil heater. Very economical, he said proudly. And then there was his monster oil tank that magically never goes empty, as if Venezuelan elves sneak in and top it up in the middle of the night. Josefa put the strange little antique oil heater in the sink. It was like a Russian samovar from the Chekhov era. Then she filled a can with water and put it on the heater. When the water boiled she poured it in a pail, and then topped the pail up with cold water. She placed it on the floor of the shower for me and said that since I had been travelling all day I would require a shower before sleeping.

In the morning, all three of us got up at the same time. After breakfast, it was time to go. But they refused to take any money from me. So I went downstairs to talk to Yandys, Josefa's son-in-law, who works for a hotel at Varadero and whose English is perfect. He says he never knows which hotel he'll be working that day when he gets up in the morning. He is a very soft-spoken gentleman in his mid-thirties, a totally unlined face, handsome and serious, loves to fish. And he's modest for a fisherman. He catches a certain fish that is about a yard long, the wahoo, and he will catch twenty or thirty wahoos in a day if he works at it. But he has never been able to hook into one of those big marlins Hemingway specialized in. He not only takes tourists out for the wahoo and maybe the sea bass, but he also goes out on his own. Anything he catches this afternoon will be on the tourist's plate tonight. "Very good fishing off Varadero," he says.

There's a large rapt audience for this little chit-chat – his three kids, his wife, his mother, his mother-in-law – and I'm not sure what happened to Pepé. Oh yes, and an older very sad, quiet woman. *Mi madre*, said Josefa with a worried smile. Yandys says the Canadians pay $250 for a day's fishing. He thought they wouldn't enjoy it as much if it was free.

Should I continue pressing the money on Josefa or would she be insulted? Oh no, he said, she'll take it probably if you keep working at it. So I went back up and told her that Yandys had given her permission to take the twenty dollars. Her face beamed. Then I gave her an extra ten and said it was for Pepé. I looked around. He seemed to have disappeared. She seemed very happy, but I had the sense she was going to keep the ten to herself. Something in her eye told me Pepé and that ten would not get to know each other. But that wouldn't bother me at all. I also gave her all my little baby bananas. And a big jar of vitamin C tablets.

Varadero is a magnificent imitation of a working-class paradise, with perfect pointy-roofed thatched Polynesian cottages and various extravagantly ultrapostmodern hotels painted in wild combinations of primary colours and pastel hues. The only problem is, they're going through a bad patch weatherwise: the sun is too hot and the water is too cold. I'm walking along the beach, with the sea just as faded as my jeans, a startlingly placid other-worldly white with a single drop of blue tincture for the entire sea out to the horizon, like a freshly laundered sheet of faded denim. As for the horizon you can almost reach out and run your finger along it, as if we've accidentally stepped into a different universe where different rules of the horizon apply. And just to put a focal point into this strangely captivating and dreamlike scene, a fellow comes flying by in a little one-person sea-plane, with just a surfboard on the bottom and a smaller surfboard on top, and a ten-horsepower outboard motor. The fearless pilot is sandwiched between the two surfboards, and this surfboard seaplane is climbing beautifully. The pilot, as if he knows that he will meet his fate somewhere among the clouds above, can cut the engine and float down to land on the flat surface of the sea, but he'd prefer to continue climbing just now, in his flat-out passion, flying eastwards parallel to the beach, about fifty yards off shore and fifty yards off ground, climbing steadily at about two o'clock, striving always to dwell in that quivering little penumbra that separates life from death.

I won't bother you with my banal thoughts about Varadero, except that although the hotels lack the sublimity of an ancient Zen temple, they are pleasant to look at, to be in, to wander through, and the silence and serenity can be transformative. Some of the hotels may be a bit flashy, but they're super-friendly, airy, spacious, and full of transparent colour. The architecture is reminiscent of the pavilions at Expo 67, though more solidly built, and they provide for an interesting interface between the workers of the capitalist countries and the Cuban hotel workers, musicians, artists, construction workers, and so on. People are getting together, comparing mythologies, punching holes in each other's propaganda systems, hearing the other side of the story first-hand, until there's nothing left but unlimited peace on earth. They even have information kiosks where news-starved Canadians can find out all about Volverán! – Los Cinqos Innocentes.

But the happy holidayers do of course look terribly silly riding along in their off-track choo-choo train, and gawking at the palm trees, and pretending not to feel too obviously uncomfortable when they pass gangs of Cuban construction workers slaving shirtless and shining with sweat under the hot sun – building hotels, roadways, golf courses, information kiosks, and shopping malls.

But when you work year-round at some mind-numbing job in a capitalist state you have to go somewhere for your vacation. Somewhere you can relax and forget all your miseries, and where whatever it costs will go to the benefit, more or less, of the long-suffering Cubans. The five-star Maritime Varadero Beach Resort would be perfect, if I can say so after such a short afternoon visit. The devout have their temples, the secular masses have their beach resorts. It would be a very boring two weeks, but boredom can be nice. You could bring along your copy of *The Tale of Genji* to help you slow time down even more.

News alert! On the flat sea there are three beach balls half-heartedly racing each other toward the horizon. People in shameless bodies lie on blankets and coat each other with cream. Now there are three people reading books on chaises longues under palm trees, while three others swim slowly in the sea. Also, why is it that everything associated with paradise has to be boring? It looks so benign, so timeless. Maybe the swimmers are looking for their beach balls that have disappeared over the horizon. Also there is a gigantic, bright blue-and-yellow inner tube, which could hold about thirty people on its pretty canvas deck, and it is anchored and being ignored by the guests for now, the sun being too hot.

Everybody here seems to be either Canadian guests or Cuban hosts. Six Canadians were standing in the lobby chatting as I strolled by. Somebody made some reference to "home" – and a very short, stout lady about forty said, irritably, almost panicky, and a little too loudly, "Oh, I wish I was home – now!" The tone of her utterance was so anguished and heartfelt, I automatically turned to look at her, and my jaw innocently dropped, and I knew that this utterance of despair came from the deepest level of her soul. But when she saw me gaping at her, the shallower level kicked in. "Oh, I didn't mean that," she said. "I was just joking of course."

In the central part of Cárdenas (est. pop. 98,500), the Museo Oscar María de Rojas contains, among thousands of items on display, three that I will remember as long as memory lasts. First there was the garotte, the instrument of slow execution used in Cuba during the colonial repressions and wars of the nineteenth century, between 1830 and 1880. I actually tried it on for size and it was dead scary.

Second, there was a collection of fabulous seashells – including many polymites, astonishingly bright, small, red and orange and yellow concentric seashells that look like shining little eyes warning predators to lay off. Third, the stuffed lioness, of which something must be done – it's very sad. It appears to have been shot twice in the head and once in the side. The bullet holes have been corked and painted over with red nail polish. She's such a gentle beast, the wimpiest lion imaginable, a harmless creature who didn't deserve to die.

There is a handsome black fellow named Pérez who speaks flawless English, has just graduated from the University of Matanzas, is working as a guide here, and he seems to be resented by the other guides, who are white, speak no English, and take little interest in anything except tips from tourists. Pérez tells me that the lion was spending a life sentence in the Cárdenas Zoo, and in 1922 escaped and was shot to death by a police officer, afraid it was going to attack someone. What an injustice! She just happened to wander away from the zoo because someone had forgotten to lock the gate. She began to wander around town, innocently going to see the homes of the very people who were always coming to see her in her home.

Now here was her chance to repay the visit. Then suddenly a loud bang followed by searing pain and death!

"In those days, you know," said Pérez, "they didn't have tranquilizer guns. The officer didn't know what else to do, probably. He didn't want the lion to attack anyone, and so as a cautionary measure he shot her several times."

Pérez's English was so precise and eloquent, perfectly intonated and modulated, with a fine choice of words and expressions. He was pleased, but he'd heard it all before, and he modestly said he was very "interested in languages" and studied very hard. His skin colour was closer to caffe con leche than espresso. He seemed to think black people weren't usually "capable" of the hard work needed to learn a language, and it would have been foolish for me to argue with him. He thought his father, who was French and spoke excellent English and Spanish, would have been the source for his linguistic preoccupations. I was disappointed that Pérez hadn't been on tap to be my guide when I arrived, and I had to endure the much older Antonio, who wouldn't stop talking in a screechy voice an inch from my ear as he rushed me from room to room in spite of my protests. Oh, how I tried to get rid of him. I even told him, in many different ways, that I would like to continue the tour by myself now, but he refused to stop mouthing a memorized spiel about the various collections.

Now, as I chat with Pérez, Antonio is sitting on a chair in the corner glaring at us. I asked the young fellow for his favourite thing in the museum. He said it might be the garotte, but he wasn't sure. That would certainly be the item one would be most likely to have a nightmare about.

He decided it was the butterflies he liked the best. I could appreciate that, but for me it was the polymites, the ones from the waters around Cuba. I hoped my dreams tonight would be more about polymites than garottes.

In Cárdenas I've just seen the kindest human gesture imaginable. An older gentleman in a blue jumpsuit is watering the grassy Parque

Colón with a long black hose. He's lost his nozzle, he's just control-
ling the flow with his thumb. He was watering patches of flowers
rather than the lawns, or where there are young trees growing, but
now he's giving special emphasis to the fully mature trees. They have
red flowers and green leaves at the same time.

There are two boys on the street playing catch with a yellow ball
about the size of a golf ball. It has quite a bounce to it, but it's lighter
than a golf ball. One boy misses it and the ball bounces through the
iron fence and comes to rest at the foot of the man in the blue suit.
The man has his back turned, and he doesn't notice the ball. The
boys say to him, "Excuse me, señor, my ball!" And the man turns
around, looks at the boy, finds the yellow ball in the wet green grass,
and picks it up. But before he throws it back to the boys he wipes it
off on his trouser leg, then tosses it to them. That automatic gesture
was so touching. It would have been bad manners, at least in his
mind, for him to have thrown the ball in such a way that the boy
might get his nice clean school outfit spattered with mud. Or some
muddy water might splatter on his face.

And then the ball came flying back again. He picked it up, and
this time he didn't dry it off on his trouser leg, he just washed it off
with his hose, then threw it to them. Then along came a fellow on
an old beat-up Chinese bicycle wearing a T-shirt that said, Canada
Beef Export Federation, and he was looking very serious, scratching
his head, and adjusting his eyeglasses.

Cárdenas's predominant style for girls between twelve and sixteen
is flat sandals, with cross-hatching of very long thin yellow shoelaces
all the way up to the knee, then nicely tied in front of and immediately above the knee. Also it helps to be wearing a pair of cut-off jean
shorts, and a very sheer, transparent black blouse with a solid black
brassiere under it and clearly showing through. And I was not to see
this particular style elsewhere in Cuba though it's ubiquitous in
Cárdenas. All the males, from age twelve to ninety, ogle these young
girls with great glee, and sometimes they will even sneak up behind
them and pat them on the behind, causing the girl to squeal and
scream with great joyful anger.

In addition to the sexy young fashion models, there are many serious-looking young people around Cárdenas today. They wear reddish-maroon silk scarves, white blouses, blue miniskirts – and the boys wear white shirts and blue trousers with red scarves. Would these be the José Martí people – youthful scholars devoted to Martí's teachings?

Dressed in that manner was the woman who guided me around a beautiful old fire hall that has been transformed into The Battle of Ideas Museum. She spoke personally, and told me about a Canadian friend of hers, from Montreal, whom she misses terribly, and who is the godmother of her child. She allowed me to tape her:

Dave: How did you get to meet her?

Dania: Well I used to work as an entertainer in Varadero. So I met her there when I was pregnant and I wasn't working. And she is a person who cannot have children, she is not allowed to have children.

Dave: She was a Canadian on vacation?

Dania: Yes. And we met each other. And I made her to participate with us in the carnival time we had in Varadero. And she become very close to me, you know. She called me every time she wanted to go somewhere or those kind of things.

Dave: What was her age?

Dania: A little bit older than me, maybe two or three years, but not that much. We were very close. And then in the second time she was in Cuba she went to meet me at the hotel and she saw me pregnant. And she was so happy! And she wanted to be my baby's godmother. And I said to her if you will be that, it will be the biggest present of my life.

Dave: I'm getting goosebumps.

Dania: Yeah!

Dave: Where does she live?

Dania: She's from Quebec. She speak French. But she's very fluent in English. She's a hairdresser. And she works a lot in many different things, you know. But she's such a good person. I like her very very much. Her name is Linda Rochefort. I was with my daughter here today. She's six years old. I've been writing to Linda and she is crazy to come back to Cuba. But she fell down, and she was having an operation because of that. And it's been three years that she hasn't been to Cuba, and she's very sad because of that. She send me pictures and letters but she's crazy to see her daughter, that's the way she call her, her daughter.

Dania showed me some precious documents of early Cuban history, relating to the rivalries between the United States and Spain for possession of Cuba. And she showed me some old photos dealing with various atrocities committed upon the civilian population of Cuba down through the years. For some reason she brought up the subject of Isla de Pinos and I asked if she had by chance ever been there. She seemed to be trying not to show her sadness at being unable to travel freely. "Unfortunately, I have not had the pleasure to be there yet," she said. And I, in a moment of extreme insensitivity, said I was thinking I might head down there next week, and I could sense a flash of envy added to the sorrow. And yet she is, obviously, a very dedicated Cuban socialist and profound admirer of Fidel.

"Lucky us!" she said. "The store were closed at this moment, and they were counting all the currencies and other kinds of things – and there were not too much people in there. Lucky us!" She was remarking on the photos of the wreckage of Havana's largest department store, El Encanto, blown up by U.S.-sponsored terrorists in April 1961. Eighteen people were injured, one killed. By "us," she didn't mean herself among them, it was her way of identifying herself with the people who were in the store.

Another photo: "This one, it was a plane that came from Florida to put a bomb in the sugar factory here in Perico [a few miles southeast of Cárdenas]. But the plane exploded in mid-air. Those things over there are part of the airplane, the fragments they could get back after the explosion. And on the other side there is a big picture of Playa Girón [Bay of Pigs]. Maybe you've heard something about that? We won this battle in only three days.

"And this was a big ship that brought some armaments to Cuba, and the United States put in there two bombs set for separate times.

They had a spy in the ship, so when they arrive here, he leave the ship, and the two bombs were planted already in the ship. So when the first one explodes, some people die, and the other ones run there to help those people who were in the ship, the second bomb explodes, and so, many more people die in that action."

There was also an exhibit devoted to the life of a young volunteer teacher who was hanged by a counter-revolutionary band. Many young literacy advocates in the early days of the Revolution were harassed and murdered for trying to teach people to read and write, inspired by Fidel's stirring command: "If you don't know, learn. If you know, teach."

"He was teaching the Cuban people to write and read, and this is the piece of wood where the young teacher, Conrado Benitez García, how can I say, was hung up, you know?" "He was hanged?" "Yes, on January 5, 1961. And they also killed another one younger than this one, he was only fifteen years old. Terrible!"

There is a large three-part exhibit, colour co-ordinated, and devoted to the Elián González story. "You can see three different colours. Blue is the time when he was found on the sea. Red is all the actions that we were doing to bring back the boy to Cuba. And the white area is about the boy when he comes back finally, with his family, to Cuba. Here you can see a T-shirt that the fisherman was wearing the day he found Elián on the sea."

Dave: Ah, Elián González was from Cárdenas?

Dania: Yesss!

Dave: Is he still here?

Dania: Yes. Well, he used to live near here, I don't know where he's living now. Because they moved. If you want [to talk to him] we can try. He study near here. Next block on the corner you will find the school where he study. He's big now, more or less. And he's very happy. He's been here because he belongs to the computer club here in the museum. He come here sometimes to practise and learn something about computers and all that kind of things.

Dave: Does he realize how famous he is?

Dania [laughing]: Yesss! He knows!

Dave: Does he strut around?

Dania: No. He's normal. He has another two brothers, younger both than him, and the three of them, they're on fire, they're moving all the time, running around – terribles. [She laughs.]

Dave: But not really bad.

Dania: No, I mean it in the best way. You don't have to be pushing them to do something, like some kids in their homes. They are not that kind of kids, they are active. They are always running, laughing, making noises.

Dave: What is the uniform you are wearing? There are many young people in Cárdenas wearing that uniform.

Dania: This is just the uniform the people who work at the museum wear. So all the workers here should dress in this way. But we have here many associations, you can belongs to José Martí Association or Nicholas Guillén Association, it depend on your inclinations.

Dania said if kids show interest in writing, for instance, they are invited to join associations devoted to journalism and poetry. "But it doesn't matter what association you belong to. It's more or less all the same, because they all fight for the same thing – Cuban freedom."

She showed me a photo of the chubby-faced José Antonio Echevarría, the anti-Batista student who was shot in the back at the age of twenty-five in 1957.

Dania: He was from this town. He was shot, but not in this town. In Havana. He died in Havana.

Dave: What a waste! José probably had three times the IQ of the man who shot him.

Dania: You're right! You're right! You're right! Human beings! You're right. I don't know how I can explain that. But they have no sense.

Dave: It's pretty hard to understand.

Dania: Yes, it is.

Dave: It's as if they have no control over their own blood lust. Nobody with a mind could be that senseless.

Dania: They don't think about it. They just took this decision and never realized how hard it is for us. They have the power so they do it, that's all.

I was admiring the photo of Camillo Cienfuegos, who was very close to Che and Fidel. He was killed at age twenty-seven. "He died in a plane" – she paused for effect – "accident. He was missing in the sea – and no, we never found the plane or anything. So every twenty-eighth of October all the Cuban people go to sea and we throw flowers to him. Because we never found him. But he was a very popular leader here in Cuba, and very brave."

We keep wandering. There are guitarists, at first they were playing classical guitar music, now they are playing popular songs. People come in and out of this bright and beautifully restored and renovated fire hall. I seem to be the only non-Cuban on the entire island, population eleven million, land area 42,803 square miles, or 110,860 square kilometres, for a population density of 256 Cubans per square mile, or 99 Cubans per square kilometre.

We stop at the foot of a larger-than-life statue of José Martí with his arm around a young boy.

"So," said Dania, "José Martí, he used to say that kids were the heart of the world, you know? And that's why José Martí is hugging the boy against his chest, and with his other hand he is pointing in the direction of the embassy of the United States, and his attitude is, well, he is accusing the *imperialismo* for all the things that is happening here, and in the world, with the kids, and the poor persons in the world. And here is a picture of Fidel, on the day that we opened this museum. Yes, Fidel Castro was here, and he wrote these letters for the workers here."

She showed me Fidel's letters, in a hand reminiscent of a famous letter he wrote at age twelve to President Franklin D. Roosevelt, asking for a ten-dollar bill: a very distinguished handwriting style, then and now, with many artistic curlicues.

"He says something about this being the first museum of its kind in the world, but there must be many other ones like this one in the future. He is referring to the concept of a museum devoted to the 'Battle of Ideas.'"

"He is no stranger to ideas," I said.

Dania said, "He was born with ideas. And he says in the letter that the Battle of Ideas cannot die, because the humankind depends on that – on our ideas, what we think about the world, and what we think we can do to make it better."

I asked if she could translate the final paragraph from the letter. She read, "The first in Cuba and in the world. There will be another ones but this one is the first one. The idea, it will be like in a school an example for the rest. The Battle of Ideas will lose but it won't be lost. The humankind depend on them. Honour and gratitude to all the persons who created this historical museum. July 14, 2001. And he sign it Fidel Castro Ruiz."

Dania is fighting back a tear or two after such a feat of spontaneous translation and remembrance. She is very proud to be part of the Battle of Ideas. And in a photograph on display you can see Fidel busy writing the very same letter that we now have in our hand.

Did she meet him?

"Yesss," she breathed. "It was very impressive. You don't know what to say, you don't know how to move. It's, it's incredible."

"Did he look into your eyes?"

"That's the worst part, because you are sh-sh-shaking! Yeah, he did. And also he touched some persons with his hand on their shoulders. And you didn't know what to do."

"And he's so tall and intimidating."

"Yes he is six-foot-three more or less, he's tall, and yes it is intimidating, believe me it is."

"Yet there's nothing to be intimidated about, really."

"That's right. That's the problem. And he speak to you so kindly, you know. Later on you can go and relax in yourself, but in the beginning you don't know what to do."

We move on to a display devoted to the Volverán issue, the plight of the five men known all over Cuba and elsewhere as Los Cinqos Innocentes. They have been given lengthy sentences in U.S. prisons on espionage charges. While working in the United States they got word to Fidel that they had evidence an attempt was about to be made on his life. There are billboards all over Cuba with pictures of the men and with the single word *Volverán*, which literally means "They will return."

"Now this is the part of the museum dedicated to the five heroes, maybe you heard about this, that they are in the United States in five different prisons."

I confessed to being slow on picking up on this issue and still didn't have the full picture.

"Well, they work in the United States for our government. They give us information about what the United States is planning to do against our president, against Cuba, and all that kind of things. But they weren't doing anything against the United States people, not at all. It was to try to avoid, how can I say, to try that they don't do anything against our people, you know. Like killing our president, and all that kind of things. That was all they were doing. They couldn't demonstrate in the trial anything against them, but anyway."

"Were they all working in the same place?"

"All different places. And the United States couldn't show any evidence against them."

"But they couldn't be sentenced to life for trying to prevent the assassination of the leader of a sovereign nation?"

"But they have." She reads out the names and sentences: Gerardo Hernández, two life sentences. Antonio Guerrero, life sentence. Ramón Labañino, life sentence. Fernando González, nineteen years. René González, fifteen years.

"Two life sentences, this is crazy," said Dania. "There's not life enough to have that. They have problem with the family to visit them in the United States. Kids, wives, mothers. The United States government doesn't give them any visas to get into the United States. So we are having many problems with all this kind of things. Also, the lawyers, they have some problems, with the new trial that is about to begin. We want that that trial will be out of Florida, out of Miami, to be an impartial trial. René González, he send this letter to Fidel, because they have birth on the same day. And when Fidel get this letter, he wrote back, and all the Cuban people could be happy about that, because he was reading it on the TV. And then he sent another letter to Fidel to thank him for giving back that answer. It was a big help for him being in prison."

She spoke of Elisabet Palmeiro, wife of Ramón Labañino. "They had two girls together, and then she was pregnant when he was arrested, and he has never met his new daughter. In this letter, he talks about how he loves her very much even when he doesn't know her very well, just by pictures. And her mother and him, they did have a lot of love, that's why he love her, as much as he loves the other two girls that he has, even though he hasn't met her. So they are three girls."

I said, "And the mother has been trying for five years to get a visa so he can meet his daughter."

"Yeah," she said. "The mothers did some visits, but every time they tried to go with the whole family it was impossible, they don't give a visa to all of them."

"They look like good guys," I muttered half to myself. "Would I have had their courage?"

"Their families has come here many times," she said, meaning to the museum, "and we have talked to them. It's like a crime, you know. You see them, they are strong, but they need the people to tell them thanks for what you're doing, because it make them stronger, you know, and you have to be a very strong person to know that you cannot see your son, your husband, just because someone doesn't allow you to."

"It's very cruel punishment," I said. "Especially putting them in all separate prisons so that they can't even see each other."

"Yes. And we have this museum so that people will know what is happening. After what happened with Elián, all the things that we see they are doing with these five heroes that we have here, and all the things they are doing, or has done, historically, against our country, all the persons they have killed here, all the Cuban people that has died on the sea trying to get to the United States – that hurt us, very deep. And so we are persons who knows every time more, because they teach us. We are culturally prepared, so we understand better the things that are happening.

"And that is why we follow Fidel. It doesn't matter if we don't have a lot of material things, spiritually we are rich, richer probably than anyone in the world, and that's important. Maybe materially you have too much things. We have little things, and we share it between a lot of people. So, we don't have too much – but spiritually! Ten years ago people were saying that many many people spoke badly about Fidel. They were saying that only about 10 per cent of the people were behind Fidel, that's what everybody was saying, and it seemed true. And things have changed a lot in ten years."

I told her my friend A. had been in Cuba at that time and reported that the vast majority of people were very opposed to Fidel.

"You know what happened, at that time we were also with Russia, and then they pulled out and we were alone."

"It was very bad economically," I said. "Fidel called it the Special Period."

"Yeah, and that's why many people were thinking like that. But at this time, things are getting a little bit better, and people can think and see what is happening, and it brings us happiness. You wanna go upstairs?"

She lead me up a winding staircase to the roof. This is where the *bomberos* (firefighters) would formerly hang out, playing chess or dominoes, catching a cool breeze while waiting for the next fire. Dania and I not only had cool breezes up there we had a spectacular view over all of Cárdenas. It was much larger than I thought. It stretched to the horizon in all directions, except north where it stretched to the sea, then the sea stretched to the horizon.

Dave: But many people were saying in those days, ten years ago, "I'm Catholic and so I can't get a job."

Dania: That's not true, not at all.

Dave: And the black people, they were saying I can't get a job because I'm black.

Dania: That's not true. You know what happened? People don't like to work too much. That's why. People here in Cuba, we talk too much and we hate to work. Normally, I'm telling you, white people, black people, they would prefer parties, dancing, walking on the street, and all that kind of things. That's the truth. So maybe your friend saw the people who don't really like to work at all.

Dave: That's a pretty good answer, I guess.

Dania: So they use that as an excuse.

We both laughed. It was unspoken but true that both of us felt on shaky ground. Just for a moment, I felt that my ground was less shaky than hers, and I wondered what Fidel would say if he were here at the Battle of Ideas Museum. Everybody knows that when times are tough certain racial groups or religious groups get marginalized, if not worse. But when times are good, jobs, money, and love are in abundance.

Dave: But, you don't see very many black people in the government, or many black people in tourism even.

Dania: Yeah, but if you go to our sports clubs, and our dancing clubs, and all that kind of things, you will find a lot of black people. That's what they like – sports, dancing, music, and that kind of things – in my opinion. They don't really like to think too much.

That was a zinger. To the Canadian ear that would sound like racism. If, say, a Canadian Member of Parliament said that, he or she would be thrown out of the party. But to me, it's all a matter of tone, and to me it was as if she was actually praising the blacks for having the wisdom not to work too much, not to think too much, to enjoy life, sports, music, dancing. She was definitely dealing in racial stereotypes, but with no evil intent.

Dania: But here we have our leader in the museum, he is a black person. And the second one is black too. And they are beautiful persons.

Dave: And the governor of La Habana province?

Dania: Yeah, he's black too!

We stood quietly looking out over the city. "So this is the view of my town," she said.

"It's beautiful!"

"It is, right?"

"And what's the domed building over there?"

"That's the marketplace, where you can buy fruit and all that kind of things."

"It looks like the Capitolio in Havana."

"Yeah, it looks like it."

"I know the outskirts of the city are very depressed, but it looks very beautiful from up here, and the outskirts of all cities tend to be depressing if not depressed."

"That's it. And this one is from the nineteenth century and so it is a very old town."

"I came along from Varadero, and I saw all this messy part of Cárdenas, by the bay and the train station and the zoo, and I wanted to get out of here, I almost didn't come downtown."

"Yeah, it was terrible. The government here in this town is working hard, trying to clean up all the places. But it takes time, because you have to educate also the people not to throw things on the street and all that." I laughed. "No, it's true," she said. "And that" – she pointed into the distance – "is our principal Catolico church here in our town. And maybe you can see there, the flag? Well, this place was where for the first time in Cuba our national flag was, how can I say? Raised?"

"Yes. What year would that have been?"

"At the beginning of the nineteenth century, I can't remember exactly what year."

"That's okay. You know the people of the United States say you copied it off their flag."

She hadn't heard that. She was momentarily stunned. It was true that both flags featured stars and stripes, and both were in red, white, and blue – but the arrangement was much different. "They can say whatever they want," she said. "I don't care." We both laughed. And we relaxed and enjoyed the cool breezes.

I wanted to make sure I had her name right. Dania Hernández Monti. There's a vague tradition of an Italian ancestor, but she has never taken an interest. I said maybe it's a Canadian ancestor – you've heard of the Royal Canadian Monti Police.

"Who knows?" she said, laughingly. "Who knows? I never been looking for it in the book, so I have to look for my ancestors, to see where I come from. . . ."

"But you're Cuban!"

"Totally! From my heart to my toes. Completely. I love my country."

I told her I was very impressed. Ten years ago Cubans were not saying such things, or if they did they spoke in ambiguous terms, with no enthusiasm. But now all the Cubans seem to be speaking like that. And yet in Canada, if you spoke like that about Canada, then or now, people would shy away, they would think there's something the matter with you psychologically.

"They don't think they belong to any place," she said. "Not only in Canada, but in Cuba, and in many places in the world it's the same way. They don't belong to any place, and they don't care. It doesn't matter. But I am from here and I am proud of that."

"Oh, you gotta be, you gotta be, Cuba's the best. It seems to be on an upward spiral. I mean, Cuba is going places. In every way."

"Something has to happen," she said. "People have to wake up and see what is really happening. We don't say we have all the truth. But we are not that far away from the truth. We are closer. Every time."

She got a bit choked up. We leaned against the railing and looked out across Cárdenas, and across the sea. Silently. We shared a quiet little tear or two. It was winter in Cuba, and night was falling fast.

SANTA CLARA 10, HOLGUÍN 2

Sunday, February 22, 2004. In the middle of a dark road about seven miles west of Coliseo, near the villages of Sumidero and Castellano, lies the twisted wreck of a bicycle. A large agricultural stake truck has swerved off the road in the dark night, flown over a gully, demolished a fence, climbed a hill, and smashed into a barn, losing its stakes and spilling its contents all the way but remaining upright. The body of the cyclist has been taken away by a motorist, as it would be a while before an ambulance could get to this remote locale.

Traffic was crawling, volunteers waving motorists on, trying to keep the accident scene intact until the police could arrive. Even a mile farther along people were out of their houses and standing in the road trying to figure out what had happened.

I was getting back up to modest highway speed, and a great green fireball appeared in the sky, falling almost horizontally over the Straits of Florida and disappearing behind a low hill a few miles east of Cárdenas. There were no sparks coming from it that I could see, but it must have disintegrated just a moment before it would have hit the ground. I'd never seen anything like it.

The appearance of this green fireball somehow gave me permission to overcome my numbness at the accident, and produced in me a sense of grief for whomever had been killed. It may have been a mother and her child cycling along, or a pair of star-crossed lovers, or an old married couple. Who knows who would have been on that now-twisted mess of bicycle parts? Wherever they were from, there would be great sadness. One often sees three people on a bicycle serenely sailing along the highways of Cuba late at night, bicycle lamps seem unobtainable, and even simple little reflectors in short supply.

Of course there was no connection between the sudden accident and the sudden appearance of that vivid green teardrop in the sky moments later, but I can't convince my heart of that. Who can explain such things? It was just a one-two punch, very strange. The first punch was devastating and left me numb, and moments later the second softened me up and allowed me to grieve at the death of someone unknown.

A hotel called Los Brizes was marked on the map, but it was a poor map and the spot could not be found, so for the second time I slept in the back seat, this time twenty miles this side of Santa Clara, a half-mile off the road, at the edge of a vast sugar plantation. The stars in the tropical sky were suitably twinkly, and a giant question mark of a constellation was floating high above the island of Cuba, taking up an entire quadrant (almost) of the southern sky. The dot star twinkled in the warm air, at times threatening to disappear entirely and at other times expanding to become almost as bright as Venus. That question mark seemed to be saying that even the heavens have no idea what is going to be the fate of Cuba.

In the morning I was awakened by a *campesino* on horseback wearing a droopy straw sombrero. He just happened to be galloping by and stopped to give me a cheery hello and to make sure I wasn't dead. Then some agricultural workers on bicycles stopped to ask if I had a good night's sleep. There was a semi-abandoned filling station on the north side of the highway. It seemed like a good place to clean out my car and get things organized. The station obviously hadn't been in full operation in eons, and it had been stripped clean of everything but its basic whitewashed structure: two empty service bays, an empty office. The pumps had long gone, but the concrete base on which they stood was still there.

It was great to see that people were still bringing their cars here for communal repairs. There were no lifts, no parts, no gas, no oil, no tools, no mechanics – but it still was a magnet for people needing to do repairs, to search through each other's tool boxes for the perfect wrench for some strange nut, to exchange spare parts, or to swap tips on fixing a car in such a way it will stay fixed at least until the next time it breaks. Most of these repairs could be done at home almost as well, but tradition dies hard.

Also, keeping these old cars on the road would basically be a full-time job. Repairs would be something one had to be performing almost every day. So let's make a social thing out of it. It'll make everything so much more pleasant.

One big fellow hastened over to see what I was up to. After finding out I was a Canadian and had slept in the sugar fields all night, he insisted on taking me home for some coffee. He wanted me to see his place, and his family. His name was Orestes, but his friends called him El Capitano. He was tall and heavy-set, beefy, very much in the Fidel Castro mode, but no whiskers, and not quite serious enough to be intimidating, although maybe a bit stern at times, seemingly, and he even wore a plain olive-green cap, with no logo, though it was not exactly the Fidel style. He had a very youthful manner and was light on his feet, though he was sixty.

He had completed some little tune-up on his bright blue shiny 1954 Chevrolet, and now he wanted to go home. He insisted I get in his car so he could drive me to his *casa* in a tiny community just off the highway, and I could come back and get my car later. His place was a perfect little Cuban paradise, a tiny perfect *finca*, in fact. Just by the big highway tower saying CUBA, a tower about a hundred feet high, and a billboard with a map of Cuba proclaiming, A Better World Is Possible – an inspiration to those of us who are beginning to think the world will continue to be this cheesy forever.

El Capitano has a one-storey house, fairly spacious by rural Cuban standards, and a two-car garage, a very kind wife, two tall skinny handsome bright sons – twins, about twenty-four, named Ernesto (after Che Guevara) and Alfredo (after Alfredo Maceo). There was the sweetest little screened veranda at the side of the house, and it was set up as a breakfast nook, so one can sit and watch the road out front and the wilderness out back at the same time, and the place is surrounded by a modest but beautiful plantation.

So we have here a good number of chickens darting around, one dog, several orange trees all in fruit, a few mango trees, two coffee trees, and some other kinds of trees, both beautiful and useful. Orestes picks his own coffee beans from his own tree, puts them in the oven, and when he gets them roasted black he grinds them and makes his own coffee.

There was some problem in Canada. The Captain's wife was telling me she has a daughter recently married to a Canadian and moved to Montreal. The husband has fallen ill and is having major abdominal surgery today. So she's been phoning Canada to find out how the surgery has been going. They're trying hard to hide their preoccupation, and she seemed perfectly pleased I was there, as if having another Canadian show up on such a day was a good omen for a successful recovery. And maybe that was why Orestes invited me to come home with him.

They squeeze the juice out of the freshly picked mangos and pour it into beer bottles. They have a simple old-fashioned capping machine. They cap each bottle and stack them in the freezer to get frozen. When a guest arrives, they study the pleasure on his face when they hand him a bottle of fresh-frozen mango juice. It was like pounding stubborn ketchup at first, but it soon starts to melt on a hot day in Cuba. When it's fully melted it's still almost ketchup-thick. I also could not resist accepting three tall cold glasses of ultra-fresh orange juice in a row, and I also had a couple of right-off-the-tree peel-and-eat oranges, all devoured in an aura of heavenly bliss. Plus they kept feeding me numerous dizzying cafecitos. And a pair of perfectly fried eggs from free-range chickens on a farm that has never heard of chemicals. And a chunk of fresh baked bread.

A couple of hours later when Orestes took me back to get my car, a little guy who was doing some repairs to his own car came running over with a terribly agitated expression on his face. He had urgent news. I had left the car unlocked. Luckily I had put all my junk in the trunk. But even the trunk was unlocked – and there were many adolescent louts hanging about, trying to look tough and all that. Shocking, but I think the reason they didn't touch the car, besides the fact that they were too well bred, was because I had on the dashboard a booklet about the Miami Five called *La Incredible Historia de Cinco Innocentes* – plus Fidel's book about Che and the current English-language edition of *Granma* were also on display. The little guy said he had kept close watch over the car for me, so I gave him a dollar.

We say goodbye, Orestes takes off for home, and I'm dashing off to Santa Clara. But halfway there a brilliant idea causes me to slam on the brakes, turn around, zoom back to the Captain's compound, and ask him if he wants to come with me to the big city (pop. 175,000). Maybe we could catch a baseball game. He jumps at the chance, he thinks it's a fantastic idea. Within about three seconds he's in the car, without even asking his wife's permission. He left her home to worry about her son-in-law's surgery all on her own.

> "Che was one of those people who is liked immediately, for his simplicity, his character, his naturalness, his comradely attitude, his personality, his originality, even when one had not yet learned of his other characteristic and unique virtues."
> – Fidel Castro, October 18, 1967

The bright and beautiful city of Santa Clara serves as a perfect little microcosm of all of Cuba, if for no other reason than that's the way it feels on this lovely day, with many birds singing sweetly in every leafy tree. Maybe it has to do with Che's remains being interred here, in 1988, twenty years after his death, along with the ashes of all the other famous fighters who died with him in Bolivia. Also, ten years later, in 1998, the late Pope John Paul II visited and no doubt enjoyed Santa Clara's pleasant atmosphere. He would have known that the city was named after the first Abbess of San Damiano, Saint Clare, who was the great spiritually intimate friend of no less than Francis of Assisi, penniless patron saint of animals and the environment, and founder of the Franciscan order.

First stop was Che's mausoleum. Interred here besides Che are twenty Bolivianos, fifteen Cubanos, and three Péruamos. There were no slogans, everything was very solemn, and there was the sacred eternal flame. No way could I hold back the tears. Orestes looked at me shyly. I blubbered something about how over and over again the best are killed by the worst, and how is the world ever going to get anywhere this way, with my brain extremely embarrassed and trying to get my heart to shut up. The mausoleum was beautifully designed, and Che's marker was the same style and size as those of the other thirty-eight. Even the bricklayers and carpenters seemed to have been caught up with the solemnity of what they were doing. But I felt suffocated, as if an asthma attack was coming on, and couldn't wait to get out.

We're all of course admirers of Che Guevara, a seriously handi-capped asthmatic of supernatural courage. And you'd have to be pretty thick not to be stirred by a man who could say, "If you tremble with indignation at every injustice then you are a comrade of mine." But I've never cared for the Bolivian escapade, and not just because it was a lost cause. The low ceiling was contributing to the gloom, and Orestes didn't care to linger long either. I also didn't like the big statue of Che outside the mausoleum. It was all wrong, and it made him look like the Michelin man with a rifle. The Che museum adjoining the mausoleum was closed for repairs.

We had some time before the baseball game so we went to Parque Vidal, the city square, where in December 1958 Che and his men took positions and fired up at the ultra-romantic art deco Hotel Santa Clara, where numerous disheartened and demoralized Batista soldiers were occupying rooms all the way to the tenth floor. The handsome facade is still bespattered with bullet holes, but they give the hotel a certain cachet. A cinema takes up most of the first floor, leaving only room for a cramped front lobby. The hotel is now just as it was then, except there are no Batista supporters staying here, as far as we know.

Orestes showed me the exact spots where Che and his men had been positioned, down on one knee and firing away. I looked up at the hotel, tall, slender, beautifully proportioned, painted in two shades of green, alternating vertically. About thirty baseball players in their Holguín uniforms were spilling out of the lobby onto the street. They were handsome, youthful, happy to be in Santa Clara, so bright they looked as if they might be movie stars dressed up as ball players. If the Santa Clara team is as sharp as these guys, it would be a good game.

Then the two of us went to the railroad tracks, where several hundred Batista soldiers forty-five years ago had steamed in on a freight train from Havana to reinforce the handful in the hotel. They were shaking in their boots because they knew a madman named Che was on the scene.

El Capitano explained how Che's men were firing at the train and tossing Molotov cocktails at it, causing the engineer to lose his cool and open the throttle to full speed. This was a fatal mistake, for he did not realize that the clever Che was busy knocking out the tracks with the sharp black blade of a heavy-duty yellow bulldozer. The train hit the damaged tracks while still accelerating, and was promptly derailed in the most spectacular fashion. Four of the boxcars, riddled with bullet holes, still lie there today in a quaintly haphazard manner, the way they landed so long ago.

Batista's soldiers came running out with their arms up, throwing their rifles away, calling out, "Don't shoot!" This moment marked the fall of Batista. He was out of the country in twenty-four hours, never to return as far as is known.

The spot is now a memorial park, with the boxcars lying where they fell. The bulldozer looks very impressive on its stone platform. It still looks new. It's a U.S.-made Caterpillar – without this overgrown snowplough Batista might still be running Cuba. But how did Che and the others know that the Caterpillar would have enough power to rip up the railroad tracks? They didn't know for sure, but Che took a chance and it worked.

Fidel Castro delivered a magnificent outdoors speech attended by close to a million Cubans in Havana's Plaza de la Revoluçion in 1967 a few days after it was confirmed that Che Guevara was dead. He said that Che had made an "audacious" attack on Santa Clara with three hundred guerrillas, and Santa Clara was defended by tanks, artillery, and several thousand infantry soldiers. These and other battles stamped Che as an "extraordinarily capable leader, as a master, as an artist of Revolutionary war. Many times it was necessary to take steps to keep him from losing his life in actions of minor significance."

He also said, "If Che had an Achilles heel, it was his excessive aggressiveness, his absolute contempt for danger." And he suggests in the same speech that Che had "meagre self-regard." Had Che realized how valuable he was alive he wouldn't have been so eager to be forever courting death.

Orestes and I had box seats on the third-base line at Estadio Sandino. There were maybe four thousand people in the stands. Even without knowing that Holguín was way down in the standings and Santa Clara way up, we could tell during the warmup that the Holguín players had somehow lost the confidence they radiated as they came out of the hotel. Now they seemed unprepared, out of their league perhaps, and Santa Clara looked ready for the World Series. The Santa Clara team was all smiles and high-fives. Holguín looked despondent.

Amusing moment: There was a Santa Clara player on first. A ball was hit hard into extreme right field and the fielder had to run like mad to get it. But he got it and he threw it very well, but I'm not sure who he was throwing it to. The centre fielder missed it, and the second baseman missed it, and the shortstop missed it, and the third baseman missed it – so the guy who hit it ran all the way home to score two runs. Can you imagine? You don't see plays like that at SkyDome. The centre fielder was so miffed he threw himself on the ground and kicked his feet in the air.

That was in the first inning, and the player who racked up those two lucky runs batted in when he hit that ball, I can't remember his name, but he was from Holguín even though he was playing for Santa Clara, and there was a full-page profile of him in *Granma* last week. As he was warming up before the game Orestes called him over, and he shook hands with both of us. We figured our luck had rubbed off on him – or maybe the other way around.

The manager of the Santa Clara team, I forget his name also, but apparently he's a great Cuban hero for turning down a huge contract to play in the United States. When the pitcher began to lose control in the fifth, the manager came out and openly lambasted him. I think he was angry because the pitcher had drunk too much last night.

You express your feelings in Cuban baseball. Elsewhere when the pitcher delivers four straight walks the manager goes out and politely asks him if anything's bothering him, and did he remember to have his bowel movement this morning. In Cuba, the manager goes out and starts screaming before he gets there. And everybody can see him waving his arms around and throwing things. He doesn't even care if the player's mom and dad are in the stands.

The score was lopsided, but it was an exciting game. Everybody in the stands was on to every pitch right to the end. Even the beautiful women wearing wild orchids and other tropical flowers in their hair were very concentrated on the game, as they sent out exotic messages like multicoloured parrots in undiscovered forests. Even the police were very intent on the game. Even the kids who had arrived with cardboard boxes, painted to look like TV cameras, and who were running around pretending to be cameramen, even they were intent on the game. The only ones not to be were the sixteen-year-old girls sexily dressed and armed with their photograph albums in case any of the younger players wished to see what they looked like in evening gowns, at coming-of-age parties, with palm trees painted on the moonlit backdrop.

The Pope performed mass at this stadium in 1998. He only spent four days in Cuba, but his face looks lobster red in the Santa Clara photos. The crowd is said to have been much quieter here than in Havana, but they let out a thunderous roar when the Pope called for a "free and independent" Cuba.

I AM YOURS FOREVER

Monday, February 23, 2004. I'm lying flat out in the biggest bedroom at Orestes's place, with my mind "just saying no" to the drug of sleep. It's one-thirty. Last night about this time, before pulling into the sugar plantation, I stopped off at a little town but I forgot the name of it and had a coffee at a little coffee place whose name I also forgot, and it was served by a fellow whose name I've forgotten, and I forget what we talked about. Just kidding. His name was Juan, he was tall, skinny, with a closely shaved head, and he was very alarmed when I told him about the accident I came across earlier. He excused himself and made some phone calls. All his closest friends seemed accounted for.

At yesterday's game there were two black guys sharing a bottle of cheap, powerful aguadiente in a labelless bottle, with no lemon, and they were standing up rather than sitting down. A police officer, also black, came by and told them to sit down, don't stand up. And they said no no, you sit down, we stand up. They refused the cop's orders, so the cop backed off.

There were two kinds of police officers in attendance: the ones from the Ministry of the Interior (MININT) in green and from the Ministry of the Revolutionary Armed Forces (MINFAR) in grey. But there weren't very many of them, and they didn't seem to be armed at all, except for the shiny black batons in their belts, and they were more interested in the ball game than anything else. They weren't about to blow a gasket because someone wouldn't sit down.

When we got home from the game, it was time to eat – the missus had been cooking her head off. All the little thoughtful touches were just so amazing. They not only didn't want me to drink tap-water, they didn't want me to drink the bottled spring water for fear it would give me tourist tummy. I've been drinking bottled water all along, and it hasn't bothered me. But instead they presented me with a huge pitcher of fresh orange juice from their backyard trees. And there was spaghetti with tomato sauce and chunks of sweet pork, and she even cooked a separate plate of meat for me, cooked in soya, and plates of meat for the others all cooked in something she didn't think I'd care for, or which she had heard might not appeal to tourists.

And there was cup after cup of thick black coffee. One of the sons came in with his girlfriend and their little girl, four years old. And when I asked for news about the son-in-law's state of health, the Captain's wife leapt to her feet, went running into the kitchen, and brought out some pills for me. She thought I wasn't feeling well. I had a look of sympathy for the son-in-law, which made me look ill, and I was pointing to my stomach – so she misinterpreted me. She thought I meant my stomach needs some sympathy. The son under-stood exactly what had happened, and he succeeded in calming his mother down. He's okay, he's not sick, he told her, following her into the kitchen and back again. He understood the situation before I had. Orestes just kept wolfing down great amounts of food.

So here I am at two in the morning with lots of time to kill. Very strange, I went to the washroom, and just as I was returning, Orestes came out and asked if I wanted some coffee – at two in the morning! No, I said, very kind of you, but I must go back to sleep.

I have all the windows open, and a big Russian fan going full blast, the fan labelled INPUD. But it turns out I was wrong. I would find out later that it wasn't Russian, it was an excellent Cuban fan, and

INPUD stood for Industria Productora de Utensilios Domésticos, an all-Cuban firm inaugurated by Che Guevara in Santa Clara in 1964 and still going strong. Its big forte is refrigerators. On its Web site is one of those comical poll questions. The question is very strange and hard to translate, but people are asked if they would be in favour of petitioning President Bush to allow three thousand poverty-stricken people from the United States to be invited to Cuba for a lengthy stay, and put them in a Cuban educational program that would make them self-sufficient, and lead to productive work, perhaps in the INPUD plant. The number three thousand would be an attempt to make a positive response to the three thousand who lost their lives in the tragedy of 9/11. Voting results were very much in favour: 369 to 58.

The generosity of the Cubans is unsurpassed. It seems that everywhere you go in the world the poorer the people the more generous they are. Even in Toronto, the panhandlers will tell you that they almost never get spare change from well-heeled people, they only get help from people who can't afford it. Orestes and family are treating me as if I were the Pope, as if I were José Martí come back to life. What do I have to offer them? Nothing. What have they asked of me? Nothing. I'm even in the biggest bed in the biggest bedroom. Maybe they want me to tell everyone Cubans are the best people in the world. I just might do that.

In the morning I woke up to find my car shining. The Captain had completely washed it, with help from his handsome sons. Breakfast was a tall glass of icy-cold mango juice and two excellent fried eggs. The minute I got up, it was ready for me. Sounds like another day in paradise, but Orestes's sons had discovered that my two front doors can be opened by any key or a nail file, or even a toothpick. And all along I've had no protection at all when I've carefully locked the car with my notebooks and tapes inside.

Orestes's phone wasn't working this morning, so I couldn't inquire about getting a new car. He took me to another place much like his, a spacious house, plenty of fruit trees and coffee trees. This place was full of dark-skinned women in their late forties or early fifties who were all very sad because their children had grown up and moved to Toronto where they are working as Spanish teachers. All their men seemed to have gone away too, except for their youngest son, who was about twenty, and who told me that his sister was working in Toronto for the Cuban Tourist Board.

These people very kindly let me make numerous phone calls, but things got so complicated I chilled out and decided to stick with the car I had. And to be extra vigilant about my belongings. Let's look at the odds: who would try to get into my car using a nail file? I should have checked that myself because you could tell by the look of both locks that they had been forced sometime in the past.

El Capitano definitely did not request any compensation for his hospitality, for paying for the baseball tickets and incidentals such as pizza and coffee, and for the tour of the town and the country. Also for the excellent book of Cuban maps (1:300,000 or 1cm=3km) he insisted I take with me, for all the wonderful food, the friendship, the patience with my lousy Spanish, the best bed, and so on. He even wanted me to take the flip-flops he'd loaned me.

But when I flashed forty dollars in front of his eyes, he didn't say no. What a deal! He accepted the money with a wonderful look of surprise and a huge hug, as if it was the last thing he expected, needed, or was hoping for, but he appreciated it anyway. He hadn't wanted the Santa Clara people to have even a sniff of my U.S. money, but he didn't mind taking it himself when offered. Isn't that odd? Not really.

An old *campesino* with a straw sombrero is walking along the side of the *autopista* on the far side of Santa Clara with a pair of yoked oxen lugging a twisted hunk of scrap metal. He has stumbled on this find, and has been lugging it along the highway under his own steam. But now – good luck! – he has spotted the oxen going his way, I suspect, and at about the same speed, and so he has tied the rope to them. So they can lug it along. They won't know the difference, but it's like night and day for him. Thing is, he doesn't know where these oxen are going or where they're coming from. Or if there is someone along the road waiting for them. All he knows is who they belong to. They belong to El Beardo! They belong to everyone!

This area southeast of Santa Clara is very cowboyish, with lots of horses and horsedrawn wagons. The homes are elegantly designed, no two alike, but very cheap – concrete blocks, wood fronts, sagging eaves, and brightly painted. Everywhere you look you see a scene from something you might remember from an old picturebook from childhood, showing a benign sort of Third World, with a family-of-man spirit of solidarity. Here's the local bus driver driving a tractor pulling a trailer with about eighty children in it, and a couple of kids on bicycles hanging on to the rear end of it so they don't have to pedal, though they could pedal a lot faster than the tractor was going, since it's not a highly powerful tractor, and you have to be careful with those precious children.

The filling station on the *autopista* sells cigarettes but no matches or lighters, and it sells toothpaste but no toothbrushes. The young fellow behind the counter tells me he has a degree in industrial engineering from the University of Santa Clara, but pumping petrol is the only job he can get just now. He hasn't quite found his bearings yet. Like many of us. And sometimes we think we have found our bearings, and a brick will fall on our head, or we will come down with stomach cancer. Which reminds me that when I dropped Orestes off at home, his wife happily told us that their son-in-law had come out of the surgery with excellent chances for a complete recovery.

There are always people hitching rides on the roads in Cuba, and one should pick up as many as possible. You never know who the person you pick up is going to be. It might be Jesus, just testing your compassion for the poor, as mother used to say. But right now my car is too messy, I'm trying to take notes, and talk into my tape recorder, and flip through my book of maps, and watch out for cyclists and cattle on the road, etc. Please don't be angry with me, Jesus. I promise to pick up two hitchhikers tomorrow, okay? It's just that the hitchhikers – particularly the females – look so profoundly sorrowful when you sail by without stopping. I realize they're just putting it on, at least to an extent, but it still hurts. And there's a billboard saying, Siempre Con Fidel. Fidel Forever.

But I've been drawn back to Santa Clara, and have taken a room at the Hotel Santa Clara Libre. And now it's midnight and I'm under the covers but not very sleepy.

Those girls with the photo albums at the ball game yesterday reminded me of a few days ago in Havana Vieja, when a pretty young girl in a black evening gown got out of a spiffy car while tourists gaped. She would have been fifteen, this would have been her coming-of-age party, her *quinze*, black would have been the colour she chose. A good choice! Black is a fiery colour. With black you never know whether the fire is out or still dangerously hot. This girl in black, however, did not have a very happy or even fiery look on her face. She looked bored and depressed. She looked as if she considered the *quinze* ritual a waste of time. Maybe she chose black to represent her dislike of anything frivolous.

Even old Orestes was remembering to admire the pretty young girls at the game – from a distance, of course. "Look at that one, Dave!"

Advice to English-language guests at the Hotel Santa Clara Libre on the subject of "What to Do Before, During and After Hurricanes."
1. Do not drink alcoholic beverages or pills.
2. Keep your five senses alert.
3. Remain calm, a very well-trained team will take care of you.

Men bled and died in this very room plus others, Batista's men, many of whom probably wished, belatedly, that they were fighting on Che's side. They took bloody hits from Che's ragtag beatnik bearded rebels in El Parque Vidal several storeys below. The official religion of the Cuban Revolution may be atheism, but they always seem to have God on their side. The bullet holes are all around my window. I can stick my head out and turn my neck and see them. And through it all (it's now five-thirty) the view is heavenly. Two little stars are peeking out from behind the cloud cover. An old man in white shoes, a white shirt, and black trousers is sweeping the street. The park is paved and there is a slight partition, easy not to notice, all the way around, dividing the pavement into two circumambient sections. According to the history books, in the colonial era the European people walked along the inside section, and there would have been a fence separating the inside section from the outer section, where the African people walked around. Also, the Africans weren't allowed to take mass, but they would stand outside, listening to the music and stretching their necks to catch glimpses of whatever could be seen through the open doors. Even today you still see groups of ordinary Cubans, from whitest white to blackest black, standing outside dollar stores, restaurants, bars, hotels – looking in, but unable to get in because they don't have the right kind of currency, or not enough of the wrong kind.

Directly across the square from my window is the grand marble library I strolled through late yesterday afternoon. Each book has been read a thousand times, each time more carefully than the time before. Nobody has scribbled in these books. To put any kind of ink mark in a library book is to insult the next reader, though some of these books are badly soiled, from much earnest reading. And if you accidentally tear a page, you take it to the librarian for repairs. Cuban libraries seem short of books. They have plenty, but nothing at all current. Suddenly I feel like one of the Nigerian anthropologists touring southern Ontario and grossly misinterpreting absolutely everything they see, as in André Alexis's hilarious play, *Lambton Kent*.

The library was very quiet, with numerous scholars in deep concentration. A short nondescript woman in her late forties was studiously taking notes from what appeared to be a highly advanced textbook on metallurgy, or maybe climatology, from the glance of the charts and diagrams as I passed and repassed her table. Also many kids in school uniforms are studying intensely. I didn't see anybody in this grand old library who wasn't deep in silent concentration.

More silence. From my hotel window I can see all the way out beyond the city to the *autopista*. If any traffic goes by on the *autopista*,

I will see the lights. I saw something go by about ten minutes ago. I can also see the baseball stadium from here, everything bathed in silence.

Of the old colonial palaces surrounding El Parque Vidal, I've already mentioned the library, and to my right here's a massive ancient stone colonnaded building now used as a secondary school. And to my left is the Decorative Art Museum, which I visited a mere twelve hours ago. I was the only visitor. My first guide and I couldn't communicate, and unlike in Cárdenas, she told me she had a better idea. She presented me with the prettiest, smartest, cutest, most studious, smallest, and most serious eighteen-year-old girl imaginable, and her English was excellent. It was no fault of her own, but she was a fair-skinned Cuban angel, with the power to turn the toughest hombre into a rank sentimentalist.

She was very shy, but she had trained herself well and had a head full of all kinds of interesting information about the Limoges china, the Tiffany lamps, the seventeenth-century armoire desk with thousands of tiny drawers inlaid with ivory, the paintings and the prints, and so on. When we came to the nineteenth-century French photos of naked women in unusual poses, and she blushed, it gave my heart an odd twist. And each time I would try to get a closer look at these barenaked ladies, she would blush a little more.

There were many romantic paintings from classical mythology. Some were faded and cracked. Cuba needs serious help in the art-restoration department. But there was one romantic painting that I was taken with. My little friend said, "The title of the painting is *I Am Yours Forever*." She looked deeply into my eyes as she said it, and I just stared back at her, dumbfounded.

And then she said, "How would you say that in French?"

I looked into her eyes and said, "Je suis à vous pour toujours."

And she blushed again!

The annual Spanish literary festival is being held all over Cuba. So far I've seen it in Havana Vieja, Cárdenas, and here in Santa Clara. And in every stop there will be a table with hundreds of copies of the newly published green-covered novel called *Celia*. It looks like an interesting read, but for some reason it doesn't have the author's name on the cover. You have to look inside to find out who the author was. And then you forget.

There was a heavily attended literary event, with presentations and readings, in an old auditorium at the side of the park, but I was late getting there, didn't make it till 5:30 (the sign said 5). I got stopped at the door and they didn't want me to go in. It couldn't have been invitation only, or they would have said so on the sign. Could it have been because of my linguistic shortcomings? Or did they think I just wouldn't like it? But I rather rudely insisted and they relented.

It was a beautiful old circular auditorium with fabulous acoustics and the place was jampacked, standing room only – there must have been more than a thousand people. So I stood, while a woman onstage read something, it sounded like a lengthy biography of the prize-winning author she was introducing. It was very flat and boring. The entire audience seemed to agree with me. But then when the author got up and started to talk about his early development as an author, the boredom increased until the audience was breathing oddly, looking around, and shuffling their feet.

So I left after ten minutes, and the very stern man and woman at the front door smirked as I went by. A little gloating look that said, "See? Didn't we tell you?" At first glance they knew this was not my sort of thing. The only people in the audience were people who had to be there, or felt they did.

Discovery Channel episodes have been featured all night long on the telly. This time they're proving that the Battle of Agincourt was such a disaster for the French not because of Henry V's superior military genius or English superiority in the archery department, but because of a simple fluke of topography that neither side understood in the least at the time. I'm told that these Discovery programs are bootlegged through the rooftop antenna at the Hotel Havana Libre, dubbed into Spanish, then rebroadcast all over Cuba on the educational channel. Fidel, you're a genius!

Everywhere you go in Cuba you see kids in uniforms, different colours for different schools, or for different scholarly specialties, etc. There may be forty kids walking down the street wearing a blue shirt with white checks, and green trousers, or green skirts. It seems as if the uniforms are chosen at random, and then everyone in that particular school dresses that way. Or maybe different colour combinations are nominated by the students, and an election is held to choose the most popular one. The colour combinations aren't that numerous though, to be truthful, and they never get very wild. It's mostly red, blue, white, mustard, and occasional pink. It's neither fascist nor in any way militaristic, as is sometimes charged. It's just an extra way of forging a bond between the kids who go to the same school. A feeling of solidarity. Imagine forty kids walking through the Parque Vidal all wearing mustard trousers and a pink shirt. It's beautiful, it's a sight to behold! It's like a field of flowers – which is not original, some famous poet used that line in connection with Cuban schoolkids, I think it was the Nicaraguan priest-poet, Ernesto Cardenal. If you see one kid wearing mustard-coloured trousers and a pink shirt, it's no big deal. But when you see twelve all dressed the same it's very pleasing to the eye, and calming to the mind. All flowers on the same bush wear the same colour petals, and they do okay – why can't all kids in the same school do the same?

I heard one young boy having some kind of an argument with another, they were dressed identically, they were about nine years old, and one of them glanced at me as we passed, figured I was a gringo, and switched to English. Then he said to the other kid, very loudly, in English, "What the f**k do you know about Vietnam?"

Okay, it's 6 a.m. I'm not a great drinker, but have put away almost a half-litre of Havana Club over the past eight hours and that's a real lot for me, and I still can't sleep. Let me check the checkout time. The bedside card says, "Guests must be out at two o'clock and if they're not out by two-fifteen an additional charge will be made."

Blame it on the rum, but suddenly it occurs to me that the dead can fly through walls. If I tried to fly through the wall I might bump my head so severely I'd die, and then I'd be able to fly through walls. When you die, your spirit comes out of your body and enters a different dimension and it can fly through any wall anywhere, even the Great Wall of China; in fact, there could be spirits of the dead looking at me right now, like cats, naked and furry, knowing I'm thinking about them, and trying to figure out if I will maybe stay another night here at the Hotel Santa Clara Libre, given my sleeplessness and probability of falling asleep at the wheel if I try to venture on into the unknown.

But I certainly feel more wide awake than Alina Fernández, of *Castro's Daughter* fame, who writes at one point, "Not even amphetamines or a cup of bitter, thick black coffee could dispel my narcolepsy." She's a good writer, really, she's almost embarrassingly up front with her own sexuality, and even though she employs an overly self-revealing tone, far beyond my feeble attempts, she makes it all terribly interesting, and not just because of who she is. You can't help like her wild spirit. She's reminiscent at times, in his critical attitudes toward Cuba, of novelist Reinaldo Arenas, that other member (deceased) of the Cuban community in exile (formerly known contemptuously as *los gusanos*). It would be hard to decide who was the more sarcastic, for they're both over the top. She's very sarcastic when it comes to her father, but Fidel gets off lightly compared to what she has to say about her daughter ("meringue face"/"troll"/ "delivered to the wrong address"), her brothers ("The Five Vegetables"), and what she has to say about the Union of Writers and Artists of Cuba (UNEAC) ("fallen into mediocrity"). Her visits with Fidel are engrossing, and it's easy to forgive her for perhaps at times thinking she understands him more than she really does. You have to leave some slack with your parents. You can't know everything about anyone, not even your own dad. End of lecture.

My favourite scene is when she's recovering in the hospital from some illness or other, and Fidel shows up with two crates of hydroponic cauliflower for her. He shows the staff exactly how to cook and season it, then spoils everything by telling Alina he bought it with his own money.

She also says Fidel told her that he has been studying medicine and is convinced that in order to keep children's food from contamination, they should have their own little refrigerators, separate from adults.

Vive Fidel!

No sleepless sonnets tonight, but I did write what I consider a clerihew (the poet Kildare Dobbs says it's not a true clerihew) about the events of yesterday, the visit to the mausoleum followed by the baseball game:

Baseball's the best, and any old day
It beats sitting around sniffing the ashes of Che.
Yes, going to the game is a whole lot better
Than watching the dead getting deader and deader.

By the way, the Holguín team is staying at the hotel again tonight. They are very subdued, wearing their casual uniforms, black trousers, black shoes, and white shirts with a big H on them. A silent H.

HOW THE UNIVERSE WORKS

Tuesday, February 24, 2004. Near Santa Clara there was a small medium-security prison. Forty men, middle-aged, dressed in grey, and with hangdog looks on their grey faces, were milling around behind a chainlink fence. It was remarkably like the animal enclosure at the zoo, especially since it was exposed to people passing along the main highway, like myself, and rudely gawking in at them.

Some of the men were pacing, others were sitting, and there was a large old tree of great circumference in the middle of the enclosure, with men sitting around that. Some men were silent and alone, some were in groups of two or three talking quietly, and there was a row of wooden cells that looked like an old unpainted motel from 1948. I didn't notice any bars on the windows or doors. The men looked educated, intelligent, handsome, rather peaceful, and very normal, but sad and resigned. One would expect to sense anger, or that they would appear to be certain they were right and Fidel was wrong. But it wasn't like that at all.

I stopped and was shyly looking at them, and debating whether to go over and have a chat with them. Then a little green three-wheeled truck went by with the back loaded down with a ton of great blocks of pure ice, each perfectly cut and fresh from the freezer. All the prisoners, plus me, looked up to watch it go by. That ice would soon be in the freezers of various hotels and restaurants around town.

That little three-wheeler was going as fast as it could, naturally, which wasn't very fast, and the ice hadn't noticeably started melting yet. I was smiling and so were the prisoners.

Placetas is a country-and-western sort of town liberated from Batista's forces by Che's forces the day before the latter's assault on Santa Clara. South of Placetas one enters an area of very pointy hills, some of them resembling pyramids covered in vegetation right to the top, with the occasional palm tree growing on the sides or sometimes two or three growing out of the pointy summit. This would be the Sierra Escambray. On my left is a perfect ancient pyramid of a mountain. I'm sure it's been excavated, and they know it's a natural formation, but it doesn't look natural. It looks like a pyramid to me. Too symmetrical for anything else.

A big black pig is snuffling along the road, then she starts climbing up a steep pathway. A mother and a little boy approach me as I look at my map. I thought they were going to ask for a ride, but they just wanted to see if they could help with directions. Then they ran over to the other side of the highway and started following the pig as it snuffled its way up the steep laneway to some farmhouse atop the hill. The little boy, who was about five years old, ran after the pig, and his mother ran after him. But the faster the kid ran, the faster the pig tried to get away from him, and the more slowly the mother ran.

The Cuban countryside doesn't seem all that dry, but apparently it is dry, so dry there is worry about fires. In a few more days without rain, fire is expected to be breaking out all over the eastern provinces, destroying crops and maybe worse. I've just spotted the first little fire, along the side of the road here. A couple of roadside acres have been blackened, seemingly from a carelessly discarded cigarette. It seems to be cooling off now. But in the blackened part that is still warm there are about twenty beautiful white egrets, perched precariously on long skinny legs, picking away in the black steaming soil, searching for and feasting on barbecued bugs, roasted roaches, warmed-over worms, and other tasty treats straight from nature's oven. I've never eaten a roasted insect of any kind knowingly, but friends who have done so tell me they taste terrible. It must be a great treat for the birds, though. They occasionally lift their feet to cool off.

A Jesus-loving Afro-Cuban hitchhiker showed me a photo of her and her little boy, obviously taken a long time ago, when she was young and beautiful. Now that she's forty-three I wouldn't have been shocked if she'd said she was fifty-three or maybe even sixty-three. But you cannot say she hasn't aged well because although she's lost her youthful beauty she hasn't lost her spirit and charming manner.

She showed me a book about Jesus, and she was very nice about it. I showed her the silver cross around my neck, which I wear to hedge my bets in dicey situations, and told her it hasn't failed me yet – touch wood! She had this big happy smile on her face and it seemed permanent. Occasionally you could see her try to turn down the intensity of her happiness a bit, but it didn't last long.

It's unrealistic to ask hitchhikers for directions, especially the younger ones whose sense of personal morality and interconnectedness is still incompletely formed. They'll only tell you where they want to go, not where you want to go. I was like that myself in my student days: when a car would stop and ask for directions but not offer me a ride, even though I was going to the same place, I'd take great delight in giving them really wrong directions.

The first person I picked up, just out of Santa Clara, was a teenage student who had forgotten that classes had been cancelled today, and so she was heading back home. I told her I was trying to get to Cienfuegos and she told me I was on the right route. But I later found out I was definitely on the wrong route, and she would have known it, and she took me way out of the way because she wanted to go to Placetas. So after I dropped her off there I had to double-back and was losing a lot of time on that, so I made a bad decision and took a more direct route on lesser roads, soon becoming badly messed up.

Something had been bothering me over the past few days and it might have been the fact that I had been passing mobs of hitchhikers without stopping, even though I had three empty seats in the car.

I kept rationalizing that being a tourist, and not knowing the roads very well, and not overly familiar with Cuban driving habits, I can't be expected to risk a hitchhiker's life by stopping for them. So at least I'm stopping now. I've seen the light.

But now as I sailed through the small Sierra Escambray foothill village of Güinia de Miranda, a man sitting on a chair at the side of the road shook his head at me and pointed back the way I'd come. He seemed to think I was going the wrong way; but I, being a tourist, knew better, and kept going. The road had been badly pitted but now seemed to be improving. Several miles south of Güinia, I passed an old man who was giving his mule a little break from the task of drag-ging two large dead trees God knows how far. Then a younger man who had been talking at the side of the road with a large group of *campesinos* jumped in front of the car like a rabbit and forced me to stop. He insisted I was going the wrong way. This road goes nowhere, he was saying – but when I got out my map and asked if he would be kind enough to show me where we were he squinted and turned the map every which way but couldn't find the spot. This must be a road that is not on the map. Could that be possible? No way. Not with a new, highly detailed book of maps like the one Orestes had pre-sented me with, and which I was following slavishly.

The two of us were standing in the middle of this unmapped route to nowhere, a road innocent of motorized traffic of any form, although it was quite wide and covered with loose gravel. We were waving the maps around, while his friends stood by watching our confusion and frustration with great fellow-feeling. We all had solemn looks on our faces. It wouldn't do for Cubans to be laugh-ing at a tourist's distress. Fidel would not be very pleased to hear about that.

It was obvious I had to return to Güinia de Miranda, about half an hour back. My new friend said he would accompany me and if I would consent to drive to the *escuelo secondario* just outside that town, he would introduce me to the English teacher, who spoke fluent English and would be able to explain everything in words I could easily under-stand. Soon I would be on the right road to Cienfuegos. The school was exactly where he wanted to go as well, as it happened.

We both burst out laughing at that moment, laughing with relief – and suddenly all his friends also burst out laughing, in the most pleasant fashion, as if to show solidarity with us, and to show pleasure that our differences of opinion had been resolved, and because they'd been wanting to laugh for quite some time but were waiting until the best moment, or until we laughed first.

His name was Pablo. As we drove back the way I'd come, he proudly pointed out his fine house high in the hills back quite a stretch from the road, but clearly visible. He said he was a teacher of "physic." Did he mean physical education? No, he said, he meant "physic," as in "Galileo and Einstein and how the universe works." "Physics," I said. Yes, he replied, "Physic." We may seem very backward here, he said, with our sombreros, and horses, and cowboy boots, but we are very intelligent, at least as much so as are los Habaneros and possibly as much so even as your people are in Canada.

"How *does* the universe work, Pablo?" I said. "I've always wanted to know."

"That's a big question," said Pablo. "You'll have to register for my class."

Then he slowly and dramatically got out his glasses, a sign of high intellectual attainment up here in the hills, polished them with a bit of red chamois, and put them on, as he smilingly watched me out of the corner of his eye. They were excellent glasses, with a gaily multicoloured thick string on them so they would not fall to the ground if they slipped from his nose. He was immensely proud of them.

"I have never harboured the slightest doubt," I said, "that the Cubans – even ones in the most remote areas such as this – were on an intellectual par with every other nationality in the world."

"In other words," said Pablo, "you knew even before I put my glasses on that there was nothing stupid about me."

"If I'd thought you were stupid, I'd have ignored your advice and continued driving, eventually falling off a cliff."

"You wanted to ignore my advice, but I wouldn't let you."

When we got to the school, Pablo asked me to wait, and he went in for ten minutes, then brought the teacher out to meet me. She did not look very happy to be disturbed in the middle of a class by a mere tourist, especially of the single-male variety. Her name was Kenya, and she was very much a black Afro-Cuban, a very short, heavy-set, and powerfully serious *campañera*, and in no mood for frivolity. She didn't care for that friendly imperialist smile on my face. The Saxon smile, as the Irish call it.

"How may I help you?" she said unsmilingly.

I told her that I wanted to get to Trinidad de Cuba, and found the signs a bit confusing – misleading at times but most often simply missing. She said I should just proceed along the road that runs by the school where we were standing. It would take me there. Not far, only thirty-five miles. I was very happy and asked, cautiously, if she'd been there lately.

Not in several years, she said sternly, as if she felt that was a frivolous question and didn't enjoy having to answer it. I'm not sure if she was angry with me for wasting her time, or with Pablo for bringing me here when he could have told me just as easily to continue along this road, which branches off from the first road, at the point where the latter passes through Guinia de Miranda.

I think that the strict *compañeros* (male comrades) and *compañeras* (female comrades), of whom many of the best are also *campesinos* (male agricultural workers) or *campesinas* (female agricultural workers), have a rather ambiguous attitude toward Trinidad de Cuba. It was the notorious tyrant Fulgencio Batista who decided way back to restore the old part of Trinidad de Cuba as a magnet for tourism, and perhaps because he loved the era of Spanish control and hated to see its relics disintegrating. If it had been Fidel who got the bright idea, that would be fine. But Batista? Even the most bloodthirsty tyrants sometimes do good things, theoretically, but for a solid *compañero* to visit Trinidad de Cuba would be akin to an Italian socialist trying to find it in his heart to admire some of those impregnable and massive train stations built in the 1930s by Mussolini. Theoretically.

And even though Trinidad de Cuba has been declared by UNESCO a World Heritage Site, it is said to practise a form of apartheid, in terms of the inhabitants not caring to see blacks and whites together at a table, or walking arm in arm, especially if the black is a local one and the white is a tourist. This is stated with great authority by Christopher P. Baker, in *Moon Handbooks: Cuba*.

In fact, it's possible that Kenya had me pegged for some kind of imperialist stooge, a single-male sex-tourist ignoramus on the loose in a rented car. When she said she had not been to Trinidad in several years I merrily blurted out an invite to come with me if she wished. The look on her face was one of extraordinarily stern disapproval. So I countered by saying that it would of course be impossible for her to go because she had classes to teach, but I couldn't quite find the words to atone for the insensitivity of my invitation. She was as huffy as she would have been if I'd asked her to become my sex slave.

And so I left Kenya to her charges, and Pablo as well, she obviously angry at being taken from her duties, and he itching to get in there and teach the kids more about how the universe works.

After a few miles the Trinidad road became very bad. It would stay bad all the way. I passed a chilling sign saying, Perigrosa. There had been a similar sign at Manicuaga, at the start of the previous road, but for some reason I thought the sign was the name of a village coming up. I'd forgotten that *perigrosa* meant "danger." And I realized that the thirty-five-mile trip to Trinidad was about to become a huge nightmare. I felt fated to drive this bone-jarring high-mountain road for all eternity, alternating from first to second gear, never getting over twenty miles an hour maximum. I'd have turned around and gone back to the *autopista*, but every time I was about to do so, I'd see the gleam of some fresh pavement up ahead and so continued on. But time and again the alluringly fresh pavement would deceive me and turn out to be even more full of dangerous potholes than the unpaved patches. Some of the potholes contained rainwater, so it was impossible to determine their depth.

The only moment of respite was when a man on horseback offered me a big bunch of bananas. He even invited me to his home for dinner, but that would only have prolonged my agony. I had to get off this road or I'd go nuts. Besides, I now had all these bananas to eat.

A large Afro-Cuban woman came running down to the road. I
didn't want to pick her up because she looked so heavy and I didn't
want to put any more rubber on these sharp stones. But how could I
refuse to pick up a single hitchhiker on a such a dreary and lonely road?

She had appeared out of nowhere in shorts, very tight, and very
short, and she had the hairiest and fattest thighs of any woman anywhere. And for the rest of the way to Trinidad de Cuba – with my
every nerve end focused on checking the depth of the next crater in
the road, one after another, scattered randomly like brown spots on
the skin of an overripe banana – she kept poking me sharply in the
ribs. I hear that Fidel has the same irritating habit, in fact you see it
a lot in Cuba. Every time she thought of something more to tell me
about her wonderfully cute little *niña*, and her handsome and caring
novidad who happened to be on a "special mission" to Venezuela at
the moment, she would jab me in the ribs to get my attention. Her
husband was not a doctor, she said. He was involved in the urban
gardening venture there, so that the poor city dwellers could have
more to eat, without being at the mercy of the great food conglom-
erates. She couldn't remember how long he'd been away and wasn't
sure when he'd be back.

We finally arrived in Trinidad de Cuba. I drove her to her lovely
little house on a cobblestone street at the edge of the old part of town,
the part the tourists come from all over the world to see. She seemed
to check out the street a bit too carefully for my comfort before deciding to hop out of the car at great speed and rush into her house
without even a look over her shoulder, or a whispered *muchas graçias,
señor*. She must have known this was rude, but she had very dark skin
and mine was very bright pink, so her rude departure may have had
something to do with the unofficial apartheid policy Christopher
Baker claims still lingers in this rich old colonial town.

But I was only in Trinidad an hour and didn't get up to the area of
colonial splendour, with great old palaces turned into state museums,
and where tourists wander from museum to museum taking photos.
It just didn't appeal to me on this particular day. I could see the

tourist buses parked all over the place and didn't want to go any farther. There must be something wrong with the shocks on this car, because I'm taking a beating even from these cobblestones, no matter how slowly I drive. And every time I get out of the car I'm surrounded by schoolkids in uniform, with sly looks on their faces, demanding U.S. dollars.

An hour later I found myself at the most peaceful spot on the seashore, a very quiet and relaxed beach bar and restaurant, and I sat watching the sun go down on a dreadful day, and watching myself calming down – with the help of a relaxing tablet. The red snapper, freshly caught, perfectly cooked, looked a bit like an old Cuban automobile from the tail-finned 1950s. My table was on a nicely constructed stone elevation overlooking the beach and the sea, with its milky green and blue horizontal stripes. I was the sole (as opposed to snapper) diner, in La Boca, a newly opened bar/restaurant with only a bit of straw overhead on sticks to deflect the sun. Sometimes my gaze would shift from the sea and sky to the shapely vectors of the glorious Topes de Collantes mountains, part of the Sierra Excambray, mildly precipitous hills grassy green to the top and with dense palm forests from the deepest valleys all the way up the sweet steep slopes to the impossibly highest peak (slightly rounded) of the highest mountains, and there were many.

But there were no rooms at La Boca. They hadn't finished building the overnight quarters. Also all the *casas particulares* along this stretch had become booked, owing to tourists wanting a cheaper place to stay within a short distance from Trinidad de Cuba. And the ugly barracklike hotels, so I was told, were only for the Cubans. But I was also told that if a foreigner goes into the lobby of a Cuban hotel they just might be happy to take him in, depending on the liberality of the person on the desk, and how busy they are, or whatever.

And so I had to hit the road again, this time a bit smoother, but still a problem because I was exhausted from too much tense driving, induced relaxation, and recent bouts of insomnia. Also night had fallen. But shortly a perfectly nice hotel and bar/restaurant presented itself, at Playa Yaguanabo, situated on a rocky little cove – and I promptly booked in, showered, then threw myself in bed and fell asleep until the phone rang an hour or so later.

ONE SHORT SAD STORY
AFTER ANOTHER

Wednesday, February 25, 2004. *Jesús querido*, if you need me for anything it's 12:33 a.m. and I'm in room 116 at Playa Yaguanabo on the Caribbean coast halfway between Cienfuegos and Trinidad de Cuba. I fell asleep at 10:30 to the sound of rocks splashing against the waves – or was it the other way around? – and became involved in nightmares about being humiliated, beaten, tortured, shot by firing squads, and hanged over and over again. I'd been captured by counter-revolutionaries and charged with being a Fidelista spy. My only hope was to be saved by El Beardo himself, in person, but he refused to get out of bed.

Then the phone rang – three very loud rings. My heart pounded. I couldn't answer. When I calmed down I called the front desk and sarcastically asked the young woman not to call me so late, call me in the morning. To her, my abrupt manner would be a greater sin than a midnight phone call. She simply and sadly said, "Okay."

I unplugged the phone, but imagined the woman bursting into tears, so I got dressed and went over to the front office to apologize in person for my rudeness.

The young woman apologized right back. She was a timid, serious, sensitive, and pretty little soul about twenty-five – all alone on the night desk. Not a pleasant job for such a person. She decided it was probably someone in one room trying to call a friend in another room and my room got called by mistake. Of course, why didn't I think of that? A tourist bus full of Canadians had arrived shortly after I booked in.

The large bar and dining room was closed already, but a woman and two men were drinking Havana Club, straight, in little glasses. They immediately called me over, and poured me a stiff one on the house. They were the waitress, the bartender, and the manager. I told them about the midnight phone call, and that less than half an hour ago I was in bed dreaming that I was being hanged.

"Many people have been hanged in Cuba," said the woman.

"But not lately," said the bartender.

"And there has not been one instance of torture since Batista fled the country," said the manager.

The sewage exploded in the shower at 8:30, when I was lying in bed with a map trying to figure out my route for today. All this raw sewage, from an overloaded bilge tank being fed by too many toilets, is bursting like a geyser at great pressure out of the blowhole of my shower stall, then dripping from the curtains and slithering out like sludge all over the floor of the bathroom and into the bedroom. And it just keeps coming. I know it will eventually die down and stop, but I don't know when. It seems to be slowing down a bit. The stench isn't as unbearable as one would think. But it's strange that such a thing would happen in such a nice, modern, newly built hotel.

The same desk clerk from last night picked up the phone. I told her what was happening and held the phone toward the bathroom door so she could hear the powerful volcanic activity originating therein – great sucking sounds followed by great blowing sounds. She did not get flustered in any way, she just became more saddened, more resigned. She said she would take care of it, but she didn't know what more she could say about it right now. I had the sense that this had happened before, and they had put in a request for a larger holding tank, but there had been no word about when or if there would be one available for them. After all, they're a bit out of the way, and they would only have a few busy nights a year, so it wouldn't be considered that crucial.

So I threw my bag in the car and headed to the office to settle up. The pretty young woman was distressed about the sewage eruption. She had catnapped on the sofa overnight. She had no makeup on, but she did have some gold speckles on her eyelids, and she seemed not overly tired, maybe even fresher and more attractive than she seemed last night, with such sadness in her countenance.

Among other things, she told me that it was very sad that all the tourists come to Cuba but the Cubans can't go to other countries. It's not a matter of human rights as much as it is of dollars and cents. "We cannot afford it, it's very expensive."

I'd been paying in cash and not bothering all that much with receipts. I was sure she had told me last night that I could pay in the morning. But when I got out my wallet she told me in no uncertain terms that I actually had paid last night. I looked at her and said, Are you sure? She looked at me and said, Are you crazy? I thought she had a point there, and I put my wallet away, and thanked her profusely for her honesty by giving her a very large tip. She refused to take it, but I kept insisting. I finally wore her down, and she gave in and thanked me with such sincerity I had to fight back a tear or two. It obviously meant a tremendous amount to her. It would have represented more than her wages, exclusive of tips, for the entire month.

As I was leaving I gave her a heartfelt smile and tried to inject a bit of humour by saying, in a rueful tone, "So keep on building that socialist paradise now." It sounded glib and shallow.

She gave me a very modest smile, a classic rueful smile to be exact. "Did you understand what I said?"

"Sí."

We looked sadly at each other for a while. She realized the tip was larger because I didn't want her to think I was blaming her (or anyone) for the raw sewage or the late-night call. Also I still couldn't remember paying last night. She was obviously a born stranger in a strange land. She didn't fit in, she was not one of those with any tolerance for shortages, hardships, or Fidel's vision of creating a new improved human being. She can't be blamed if she wants to be like young women in all the other countries. And having to deal with explosions of raw sewage at breakfast time did not make her feel any happier about her existence.

I wouldn't forget her in a hurry. She seemed very quiet and retiring, refined, cultivated, maybe a strong Catholic, or Baptist. She was dressed very conservatively in a blouse that was a bit on the sheer side, and it showed off her nice lacy brassiere (trust my demon to notice that!), and a plain dark skirt.

Later, on the road, thinking about everything, I gradually felt more and more certain I had not paid her the night before. She had just said that because she felt so badly about the midnight phone call and the early-morning sewage storm. She didn't care what the boss thought, she decided I shouldn't have to pay for my room after all that.

The Circuito Sur that runs between Cienfuegos and Trinidad then continues on to Sancti Spíritus beckons me eastward. I'm no longer drawn to Cienfuegos, for now my primary desire is to get farther down into the Oriente section of Cuba, where I can pay my symbolic respects to the poor people imprisoned at Guantánamo Bay, if only by getting as close to the base as I am permitted to get, perhaps to get a glimpse of it from a hill, or something like that. And other reasons as well. Santiago de Cuba beckons.

On a bridge over the mighty Río Cabagán, which broadly and swirlingly flows down from the mountains and into the Caribbean, forming the border between Cienfuegos and Sancti Spíritus Provinces, a fellow holds up a sign in big letters saying, in English, STOP, and then, amusingly, in smaller caps, OFFICIAL. He's trolling for tourists, but what he's going to say? He tells me if I turn right over the bridge I'll come to a very nice restaurant. I tell him thank you very much, and take off, but then I hear him yelling, "No no no, stop stop stop!" So I stop again, thinking he will want to come with me, so that he can make sure I find the place, and so that he will get his commission, and I'm all ready to tell him that I'm not hungry just now owing to an explosion of raw sewage at breakfast time.

But that wasn't what he wanted to know. And he said, "Sir, my house is . . . ," and then he stalled, became tongue-tied, and I became impatient. "I'm sorry, but I must go," I said.

One feels badly about such rudeness, but what can one do? The word for a tourist chaser in Cuba is *mosca*, and when you see a tourist exiting stage left pursued by *moscas*, it's a bit like seeing someone being chased by a cloud of flies, and the tourist slapping at the bites, and bleeding a bit too.

On the seashore an oddly cinematic little scene shows in a glance the sadness of poverty and the absurdity of wealth: three men are busy trying to keep out of the blazing sun while they build themselves a ladder out of fresh-cut timber. They seem to be doing a good job of it. In the background there is a van taking up the whole road so you have to squeeze by. This van belongs to eight German tourists dressed up in wetsuits and ready to go snorkelling. For the rent of one snorkel for one hour one could purchase a beautiful aluminum ladder that would last forever and never need repairs. And have change left over for a good meal. And these Germans are spending thousands of euros to see fish underwater.

It's amazing how dignified and polite the Cubans are, in the face of all this horrible inequality between native and tourist, and helpful even when they don't need to be. At the tip of the Ancon Peninsula, some men on bicycles came by, and they regarded me with the kindest looks on their faces and shook their heads and pointed to their mouths. If you want to eat, don't go there, they seemed to be warning. Either they have no food there, or the restaurant is closed. So they do wish to be helpful.

The restaurant was closed. And on the way back, when I came to a fork in the road with no directions posted, and looked a bit confused, another guy on a bicycle pointed to the road a tourist fellow like me would be most likely to take. It was the right one.

Back on the Circuito Sur, a mile or two past Trinidad de Cuba, I stopped for a hitchhiker. He was a scholarly and dignified older man in an ill-fitting threadbare suit carrying a briefcase that looked as if it had been with Che in Bolivia. This was the drama teacher and producer of theatrical events, Adolfo, of Sancti Spíritus, whom I would spend several hours with today. After I picked him up, and even before we had introduced ourselves, we passed a rental car, just like mine, except it was lying upside down totalled in a gully at the side of the road. The tourists, a man and a woman in their thirties, Germans, were standing by the car shaking and pale. They had been travelling west, and seemed to have lost control on a gentle curve. They might have swerved to avoid something and went out of control, but the car was finished. They were dazed, looking around nervously, feeling guilty for being alive, maybe not sure they were alive, as if in a state of near hysteria. It hadn't registered on them what had happened yet. It soon will though, because the police have arrived and will explain everything.

Adolfo was a distinguished gentleman of advancing years, in a grey suit and white shirt, his English at the level of my Spanish, so we chatted non-stop all the way to Sancti Spíritus, and he would correct my Spanish and I would correct his English. During periods of silence each knew the other was trying to figure out the simplest possible way of saying something so the other would get it, with the fewest number of syllables in each word. And we'd be thinking to ourselves, Will I be the next to say something or will he? So finally I would say something, and he would think about it for a while, then he would say something back to show that he understood, and vice versa.

He told me he produced and directed plays in Trinidad, that was his job. And he lived in Sancti Spíritus. He hitchhiked back and forth, from home to Trinidad, and back again. He said he almost always gets rides right away, he can be in a huge crowd of people waiting for a ride, and someone will stop and point at him, and leave all the others behind. He has no idea why. He tends to stand out from the crowd, maybe because he looks more intellectual, and somehow more important, with that grey suit and old beat-up briefcase.

Trinidad is a prime tourist magnet, so I asked if his plays were for the tourists. Oh no, just little plays, he said mysteriously. But as the story unwound, somewhat reluctantly, it turned out that he taught a drama course in Sancti Spíritus a couple of days a week, and he put on plays in Trinidad on alternate days. He said he was the director, but when I asked if he hired his own cast and crew, he said oh no, he just uses his students. So it made me wonder how the students got back and forth, and why he didn't put on the plays in Sancti Spíritus. So it was as if he was keeping something from me.

He had a wife who was in the hospital, and he was worried sick about her. He would touch his stomach with a woeful look on his face. He said she had an *estómago enfermo*, which sounded truly dreadful, as if she was definitely in agony and on the way out. And he confessed that he was praying for her as we spoke.

It turns out there are three hundred Baptists in Sancti Spíritus (est. pop. 127,000), and Adolfo is one of them. They have a minister, and they study the Bible. They read contemporary books about things like the true meaning of the Cross, and mystical books about El Diablo, who tries to trap us, to get us to turn away from the light, the light being Jesus, the light of the world, which Adolfo somehow identifies with the entire universe, that is somehow connected to every single individual in it, every bird, cow, insect, microbe, chimpanzee, parrot, even trees, they all have extensions that encompass the whole universe somehow, all connected in this vast field of light that exists even in the darkness. There were two large trees, one on each side of the road, and they had formed a bit of a canopy, with their fine upper branches commingling, and he said, "Look, lovers! They are falling in love."

I told him I was a believer and a non-believer at the same time, it was a paradox, and he understood perfectly. So we talked on and on like that. I asked if he knew about Shakespeare. He said oh sure, he's read all of Shakespeare's plays, and several Dickens novels as well, but in translation of course. Shakespeare and Dickens didn't wear their religion on their sleeve, but they certainly dealt in a big way with the issues of good and evil, light and darkness, and that seemed to be the main interest of Adolfo's Baptist fraternity in Sancti Spíritus.

When we passed Embalse Zaza, a large shining lake surrounded by trees, there was one single solitary melancholy meditative Cuban out there all alone in a little kayak, getting away from everything and everybody, almost motionless in such a placid lake. It was surprising to see, without any warning, a Cuban in such a solitary pursuit. This was Cuba's largest lake, artificially created by the damming of two rivers. It's surrounded by a pristine patch of protected "wetlands" (if you're a conservationist) or "swamplands" (if you're a developer).

We also passed some fellows building a structure out of concrete blocks deep into the earth just off the road. They're building a bomb shelter, said Adolfo. Really? Yes, we never know when the United States will launch another attack.

I asked if he wanted to stop for coffee, but he said no, he was anxious to see his wife in the hospital. He expected me to drop him off on the highway outside of town, but I said no, I'm taking you right to the hospital. So he directed me all through the city till we got to the hospital, then he asked me to wait for him, he'd be right back. He went in and was out again five minutes later, and said his wife has been discharged, and she is now at their daughter's house in another part of town, and if I still wanted some coffee he would take me there and I could meet his wife and his daughter and have some coffee. But, he said, first come into the hospital, I want to show you the hospital. And I want you to meet someone, a man who is recovering from a very serious head injury. So we went in, and we walked along many corridors, with a lot of activity going on, medical staff in white uniforms running from room to room, every bed occupied, and with extended families in jeans and T-shirts clustered around many of the beds, and other beds with patients looking lonely, wishing someone would visit them. Unlike more modern hospitals, there was neither fluorescent lighting nor air conditioning, just lots of bright windows and well-designed cross breezes, and a beautiful inner courtyard with an impressive grove of royal palms and many flowering trees and bushes.

We found his friend's room and we went in. Adolfo introduced me to a fellow lying flat out with a heavily bandaged head. He had been walking down the street, Adolfo said, and a brick fell off the top of a building and bonked him right on his bald spot. It had happened a few months back, he had to wait for his surgery owing to a backlog, though that was hard to believe. He was lying completely still, and it looked as if he had just come out of the anaesthetic, though he seemed fully conscious.

His eyes were wide open, and I'll never forget them. He didn't seem to be in pain, but he was very deeply worried. Terrified in fact. He was looking anxiously into my eyes, and he could see my concern, even though we didn't know each other. He seemed to think that I was on the medical staff, and perhaps had come to give him some bad news, that the brain damage was much worse than previously thought. So I put my hand lightly on his shoulder and told him that the operation had gone well, everything was going to be fine, you'll be out of here in no time. But his terribly worried look didn't relax. It was as if he was worried that the painkillers would wear off and he was about to have one helluva headache, or that he would never be able to provide for his family, or he would be watching the cartoon channel for the rest of his life.

Adolfo took me to another part of town, on the right bank of a large river, the Río Yayabo, which flows through town and into Embalse Zaza. Adolfo's house sat on a high bank overlooking this beautiful steep-banked river, a very pretty site for a house, bucolic but close to all the amenities.

Unfortunately the house was all wrecked. It was just a shell of a house. He had told me his house was in a terrible state, but I had no idea it would be this bad. The roof had been blown away, and several walls had collapsed. Had it been bombed? No, because there were no indications of the kind of charring that would be involved with an incendiary bomb. It looked almost as if it had been struck by a tornado, but there was no damage to any other houses on the street. I tried to get him to explain what had happened, but he didn't want to get into it. He did say he had a friend who was restoring it for him. And outside the front door there was a large stack of terra-cotta tiles for the new roof, and within the ruined walls was a small mountain of old recycled bricks from some building that had been torn down, or maybe the bricks were from this house, and they were going to be used to rebuild the walls.

The place was an incredible mess, it was hard to see how anyone could live in it. There must have been some living space at the back. I could see into a bedroom, there was a bed there, and a lopsided clock on the wall. It all seemed very odd. Adolfo wanted me to see, but he didn't want to talk about it.

Adolfo was a very nice man, I couldn't imagine him having enemies. But maybe he had said or done something that had annoyed somebody. He didn't want to burden me with that. He seemed as if he wouldn't have an enemy in the world, but still I wondered. Baptists can be puritanical and judgmental, and therefore have enemies. Also if you are deemed too outspoken on the subject of human rights, or particularly on the subject of abortion, then you could be jailed. Or if not jailed, according to Amnesty International, in a 2004 report, "[Cuban] authorities continued to try to discourage dissent by harassing suspected critics of the government. Suspected dissidents were subjected to short-term detention, frequent summonses, threats, eviction, loss of employment and restrictions on movement." Could wrecking someone's house be considered a form of eviction? Or would hitting someone on the head with a brick be considered a threat? Adolfo seemed like a very mild-mannered fellow, but being a Baptist perhaps he was a bit too outspoken on the subject of abortion, for instance, or maybe certain Sentería practices, and so his house was wrecked as a warning. Whatever, he didn't wish to talk about it. He just wanted me to witness it. He wanted me to figure it out on my own. He wanted me to witness the work of El Diablo perhaps.

He had already told me that he didn't care for atheists, agnostics, Catholics, and he had only one word for the Sentería people – evil! A man like that would have enemies. And when I asked if the plays he put on were religious, he said not overtly, but there were some religious elements in them.

Then we went to Adolfo's daughter's place, to meet his wife, and his daughter, Ana, who is a dentist, and her little boy. It was a very spa-cious apartment taking up the entire top floor of a two-storey build-ing, like a big fat box sitting atop a slightly larger flat box, so that the apartment, with numerous open windows and doors, was surrounded by a kind of patio. But there was no railing on the patio, and it would be so easy to take a false step and suffer a very nasty fall. It's only a one-storey drop, but it would be a hard drop.

Ana's place was in a poor part of town, but it was fortunately on the highest hill in town, just high enough to catch the breeze. Every breeze comes first to those who live on the hill. It was a family-oriented neighbourhood, and in fact the whole city had an aura of calm and quiet about it today. It was okay to leave the car unlocked.

Adolfo kept asking where I was going next. He wouldn't take "I don't know" for an answer. Orestes had been like that too. I told Adolfo that I can't make plans, because when I do then El Diablo steps in and screws everything up. When I don't make plans, then El Signor steps in and guides me in the paths of righteousness and keeps me out of trouble. We also talked about the Will of God and all that sort of thing, and he told me that he had no problems understand-ing the concept of God's Will. I told him the Canadian poet Leonard Cohen has problems with the word "repent" and the Canadian poet Susan Musgrave claims not to understand the word "soul." Many times have I asked to have the term "Will of God" explained to me, but the explanations never seem to make sense. Sometimes I seem to understand it, but not for long. All I have is a sense that as long as I don't plan ahead too much, everything's going to be fine. And I love that old saying, "Man proposes, God disposes."

Adolfo's wife came out from the bedroom where she had been resting. She was the prettiest little granny imaginable, about sixty years old. She was just glowing with health. I jumped out of my chair, I couldn't believe it, I said I thought you were sick. She said,

Oh no, I feel much better now. She was radiant, I gave her a kiss on each cheek, and I told her it was obvious she had many more years of life. She was only about five-foot-two, but she was standing quite erect, like a teenage footsoldier being inspected by Fidel. Adolfo, very portly with his little white moustache, said he was fifty-eight and his wife was two years older. And there was a small metal plaque on his old briefcase saying,

THE JET SET
LONDON * PARIS * TOKYO

I asked if he'd been out of the country and he said no. Had he been to Havana? Yes, but just on business, and apparently just once. He was a religious man, but it was as if in his heart of hearts there is only black and white, there are no greys, no pinks and blues. The universe is one big faceoff between a zillion hockey teams in white sweaters and a similar number in black, each player seeing which can outstare the other, or outfox the other, and score the most goals. And if Adolfo seemed like a religious man, his wife seemed like a saint. She glowed, and so did their daughter the dentist. She seemed like a veritable daughter of God, somebody who had really seen the light. Adolfo didn't glow. Not on this particular day at any rate. Not with his house all wrecked.

The parlour here was very spacious, clean as a whistle and sparsely furnished in a very pleasant way, with the small console TV set having a very nice silk Indian print cloth, with a red border, hanging over the screen when the TV was not on, because it's kind of ugly to have a screen there with the telly turned off, like a dead man with one eye open. When you were finished watching, you turned off the TV and then pulled the silk cloth over the tube like closing the eyes of the dead. It seemed very civilized. Maybe a bit too civilized.

Ana was about twenty-eight, short and rotund. And when she found out my name started with an Mc, she got out a whole collection of books, all very new and with pristine dust jackets, seemingly unread, by a fellow whose name also started with an Mc. These books were beautifully printed and produced Spanish editions of books by a Baptist Scotchman inspirational preacher, telling people how to get on God's side and take pre-emptive action against Satan. The books had memorable titles, but El Diablo has caused me to forget every single title and the full name of the author. She had about twenty of them all by the same guy. Each had a circle on the front cover, divided in half, with the word BUENO in the top half and MAL on the bottom half.

Adolfo presented me with a little blue breastpocket book called *Nuevo Testamento*, by a guy named Salmos Proverbios. It's published by Este Libro No Sera Vendido. I'm joking of course, it was the New Testament in Spanish, including the Psalms and the Proverbs, and it is not to be sold. Adolfo wrote my name in it, followed by "Hermano de Canadá" – and then he wrote his name and address. I flipped it open at random and read, "Bienaventurados los pobres en espíritu, porque de ellos es el reino de los cielos." Whew! It gave me the shivers and I told him I was going to read it front to back and every word I didn't understand I'd look up. By the time I was finished I'd be ready to come back to Cuba and see if he had his house fixed up yet.

And then Ana's little boy came in, having woken from his nap – a plump darling about seven years old. He walked straight to where I was sitting and gave me a very serious kiss on each cheek. Then he went over to the television, undraped the screen, and began watching a cartoon from the 1940s, with Tom and Jerry chasing each other around in black and white.

So Adolfo let me witness certain things, but wisely left me to make my own interpretations. I think his young friend in the hospital was trying to stop some anti-Baptists from wrecking Adolfo's house, and accidentally or not a brick landed on his head. On both sides of the equation the passions are beyond my ken, as they would be for the vast majority of Cubans, no doubt.

In the very busy ground-floor dining room of the Hotel Santiago, in Ciego de Ávila, I'm the only non-Cuban. My waitress is a young woman named Gina who looks as if she has the lost blood of the extinct Taíno Indians of Cuba flowing through her veins. She is short, thin, and her skin is very pale with a slight golden glow.

By now I was getting hooked on Cuban cigarettes. I hadn't smoked for years, but at some bar somewhere along the line, I bought a pack of Populars (fifty cents), because everyone else was smoking, and then promptly got semi-addicted. Unlike Canadian cigarettes, one puff of which can cause me to have chest pains, they seemed very rich, delicious, harmless. Pure black Cuban tobacco, but mild, benign, and very fine. Each puff seemed to be adding another day to my life.

Gina is working the other side of the dining room, but she notices my unconsciously admiring gaze from a distance and insists on serving me. I have an unlit Popular in my hand and she offers me a light. But I look at the flame in her eye rather than in her hand and accidentally blow her match out. She snatches the cigarette from my hand in mock impatience, puts it between her thin but charmingly curved lips, and lights it herself. She takes one puff, then hands the cigarette back to me. I burst out laughing, and so does she, and so do several of her co-workers who happen to be watching, and a whole family at the next table. In a rather provocative tone, she asks if I would like anything else. Hah, I told her, I'd like you!

When she went back to her work station, her co-workers wanted to know what I'd said. Then they all started laughing and looking at me very fondly for having told her I wanted her, especially since they knew it was just a flirty joke. What a sexy country!

CHICA CHICA?
CHICA CHICA CHICA?

Thursday, February 26, 2004. The windows in my room on the second floor were shuttered, with nothing between me and the noise from the street, causing me to lie awake for hours listening to a wild cacophony of frenzied yelling back and forth, ambulance sirens, kids kicking cans, and a tourist car that got stuck in a gutter that took three or four men thirty minutes to push back onto the road, with the engine gunning and squealing with a decibel rating far above the recommended level. If this was Ciego de Ávila, what must Baghdad be like?

In Cuba if one sees a toilet with a lid on it he or she must be sure to use it, if possible, because it may be a long time before another shows up. They do tend to get stolen. In fact so many have been stolen they're practically extinct.

If the United States really wished to impress the Cubans, it would immediately send them totally gratis a small gift of five million unbreakable plastic toilet seat lids. It wouldn't cost much, but every time a Cuban went to the toilet he'd send a little song of loving gratitude to the United States of America. Bombs create enemies, toilet lids create friends.

And light bulbs too. This is one of the few Cuban hotels I've been in where there are reading lamps, one on each side of the bed.

But there were no bulbs in them. The bulbs weren't burnt out, they were AWOL.

I paid six dollars for the all-you-can-eat special last night and when I took my plate to the food table there was nothing that tempted me, not even the salads. So, in spite of the noise, and the bad food, the people were nice, and they were quite aware their service was, in general, lousy. The chef went into the kitchen and whipped up a "chicken supremo" plate just for me, but even that was tough going. The staff wasn't apologetic, but they kept glancing into my eyes for signs of displeasure. I insisted that everything was fine.

The menu for the free breakfast has all sorts of wonderful things on it, but when you go to place an order in the morning all the inter-esting items are unavailable – no eggs, no this, no that. But the coffee's hot. So I managed to have four cafecitos and some bread. Gina handed me a little slip of paper on the way out, all it said on it was orange juice, and she asked me to sign it. Why? I didn't even have orange juice. But then I woke up and realized it was just so that I couldn't come back and order another free breakfast. You never know what some scoundrels will try. But not this one.

As I was gobbling up the chicken supremo last night, in came a blind man who had his hand on the shoulder of his friend guiding him. The blind man was a medium-height middle-aged white man, very sloppily dressed and with hair sticking out all over, and his seeing-eye human was a tall and very happy-looking well-groomed black man. Neither carried a white cane. They both took a table next to the piano, and after they got settled and had some coffee, the black man got up and helped the blind man to the piano, sat him down, and placed his hands on the keys.

This happy black man probably worked full-time for the pianist, and they seemed to appreciate each other a lot. As the blind man played numerous romantic songs from the 1940s, mostly of Cuban origin, his friend would bounce in his chair, keep time with his hand, smile, close his eyes with spasms of pleasure, then leap to his feat and lead the applause at the end of each song. About eleven o'clock he took his first break, and his friend lead him to the bathroom. Everybody was hoping he'd come back and play some more, but when they reappeared his friend lead him outside and they disappeared into the darkness.

Ciego de Ávila and Sancti Spíritus are both interesting little ciudads. Peaceful, family-oriented, but Ciego is deafeningly noisy all night long. Sure, I was only there one night. But you could tell this was an every-night sort of thing. And I will probably be returning to prove it.

It did quieten up a bit around one o'clock. I went out. There were people milling around on the street, but pretty well everything was locked up. There was a dance club playing loud disco music, but there were no dancers and the bar was closed. When I got back, most of the hotel staff were sleeping on sofas or soft armchairs, waiting for the morning shift. I spotted Gina snoring away, but very sweetly, of course, almost completely drowned out by the heavy-duty snorers. It was amazing how her skinny yellow arms were covered with fine black hairs, that with all the snoring going on would rustle like little leaves in the wind.

In El Parque Agramonte, in the light of the impressive Catedral Santa Iglesias of Camagüey (est. pop. 348,000), a man sits on a bench playing very quietly on his guitar with his case open, even though tourists are few. In strolling around the park, feasting on the faces of the people and the facades of the surrounding edifices, only one tout, a man with a very silly smile, came up to me. He was dancing and circling me, crouching over while keeping his distance, snapping his fingers, and saying, "*Chica chica? Chica chica chica?*" repeatedly. And behind him, sitting on the base of a stone wall next to an antique cream-coloured roadster, were two skinny twin girls about sixteen very nicely dressed and as cute as buttons with bright red lips and huge white-toothed smiles on their dark black faces, hoping that I would say yes. I apologetically declined, claiming to be on important business.

There was a barbershop adjacent to the park, with three tall black barbers sitting there in their white smocks waiting for business. I've never had a shave from a barber, and I haven't come across any decent blades or shaving soap in Cuba so far. So here's my chance. I kept walking all the way around the park, psyching myself up for my first big shave administered by a professional, and in passing I said hello to a guy smiling behind the wheel of a 1928 Model A Ford with the top nicely cut off so that it looked like a hot rod from old Archie comics. When I got back to the barbershop, just a few minutes later, all three barbers had become wide awake and busy with customers, and there were three more customers waiting. There's a moral here somewhere. Don't walk around the park till you've had a good shave.

So I head back to find the guy with the old Ford, see if he'll give me a tour of the town, but he's disappeared. He probably would have loved to give me a tour. He was otherwise occupied, like the three barbers, except that with them I knew where they were and what they were doing, but as for this guy with the Model A, I think he went for a little tour all on his own. I'd forgotten that you have to be able to strike like a rattler if you want to be a good travel writer.

Two Canadian guys were sitting on an Agramonte park bench. I'd walked right past them, unnoticing, in a tropical daze, although I did vaguely notice English being spoken. A pot-bellied red-haired fellow yelled out, "Hey, Eaton's Centre." He was referring to the silver logo on my black shoulder bag, which happened to be over my shoulder at the time. So I turned and looked at him with my Team Canada logo on my bright red baseball cap, and they said, "Team Canada! Eaton's Centre! You must be a Canadian."

So I sat down with them. The skinny fellow, maybe a bit older, stood up all the time his friend and I were sitting on the bench. He was from Sault Ste. Marie. "See, I'm a steamfitter, eh?" he said. "So I make a lot of money, eh?" But then he lost 150 grand in the Nortel disaster. It was his life savings, and the loss changed his life. So now he works at his trade, and when he's accumulated enough money he comes down to Cuba for a few months. He usually comes to Camagüey, in fact he married a woman here and they had a child together. But then he became increasingly disaffected with his wife, because she was basically a *chica*, a street hooker, and he thought he'd saved her from that, and given her a whole new life of respectability and freedom from hunger. But now she was slipping back into it. She missed the old life, working the streets, hustling tourists.

"Heartbreaker," I said, full of sympathy. It doesn't take long for a young woman to get bored with an old guy, even if he is a generous Canadian. "There's a lot of heartbreakers around here, man," he said.

The red-haired fellow was a chubby real-estate agent, from Hamilton, and he too works part of the year and spends the rest of the time here. Both were about fifty. The real-estate guy knew a cousin of mine. When I told them I love to pick up hitchhikers, then put on the air conditioning full blast to see the looks on their faces, they said, "Cubans hate the cold. When the air conditioning is on they hate it and beg us to turn it off." But in my experience, they are overjoyed when I switch it on full blast in the car, and when I ask if it's too cold they say, No, no, we love it!

The guy from Hamilton was an opinionated person in the disparaging redneck style made famous by Don Cherry in sports or the various right-wing columnists in Canadian tabloids. He wanted an update on Canadian news, so I went over all the new scandals I could think of. When I mentioned the Governor General, Adrienne Clarkson, was having her expenses checked, he said, "I hate that broad." When I mentioned that former cabinet minister Sheila Copps had lost her riding, he said, "I hate that broad too." And so on. But he was okay. When I told him about the old Model A Ford I'd seen a few minutes ago, he told me he knew that guy and he had a little Suzuki engine under the hood: "You never know what you're going to find under the hood of a Cuban car, except that you can be pretty sure it won't be what you would expect there to be. Good old Cuban know-how. Engine-uity."

It seemed odd that he spoke well of the Cubans in general, but his attitude toward Canadian politics, except for the most right-wing party, was intolerant, and he also hated unions, except for the police union. He hated environmentalists period, and he wasn't very happy about Canada's unwillingness to join President Bush in his various invasions of little countries. But he had much sympathy for Cubans, although he insisted that anyone wearing shiny black-leather shoes was a spy. He and the steamfitter had met Christopher P. Baker, the author of *Moon Handbooks: Cuba,* and had a few drinks with him. They hadn't seen the book so I showed them my copy and they were very impressed. The chubby chap said Baker knew a lot about Cuba, and he was a very interesting guy to drink with, but there was one thing about Baker that he found disturbing: his ponytail. "I don't know what to say," he said, "about a guy who is sixty years old and has a ponytail." He looked as if he was going to spit. I said I'd love to meet him, he seems to know every square inch of Cuba, he'd be a spellbinder over a beer or two. "For sure, but that ponytail's gotta go." Why? "A guy sixty years old with a ponytail? You gotta wonder about a guy like that." I didn't care how he wore his hair, my only beef about the book is that he seems to interpret certain things in as negative a way as possible, but he never goes overboard with his positive statements about things he likes, and he emphasizes too much the dangers of being mugged and otherwise cheated and robbed. He stops short of referring to Cuba as a "communist hell-hole," however.

The chubby fellow said he used to go to Santiago de Cuba every year, but he switched to Camagüey because Santiago was "too poor, you can't do anything with the people, you just have to be saying no all the time, and that's no fun, you can't help everybody, you just can't." They'd be waiting at his front door when he woke up in the morning. So he had to get out. Soon he'd be getting out of Camagüey probably, though so far he hasn't had such problems. When I mentioned Havana, he adopted a contemptuous look and said he had no time for that place. But he wouldn't say why. I figured it would be because a foreigner can't spend pesos in Havana as easily as he can in the smaller cities, and maybe the people there are too sophisticated for his tastes.

But he had brains. For instance, he was studying Spanish very diligently, and showed me his textbooks and notebooks to prove it. When they wanted to know what I was doing, I told them I was gathering material for a book of poetic impressions of Cuba. It dawned on them right away that I might be counted on to give them a bit of free publicity in the book, and they didn't require any free publicity just now. So first the skinny guy said he had to go. He said he'd look up my books for sure, but he didn't ask my name or the titles. He was supposed to meet his new girlfriend half an hour ago. After he left, the chubby fellow said of him, admiringly, that even though his wife ran out on him he still gives her two hundred dollars a month in child support. He also maintained he has no problem with Cuban summers. You acclimatize quickly, he said, you adapt to it, you know how to find a cool spot and stay there when the sun is blazing. He said the saving grace for most Cubans who are under-employed, or completely unemployed, is to belong to some kind of cultural/political/historical association, where you can get out of the house, which may or may not be comfortable and cool. You're always welcome at the club hall, and you can just sit there, watch TV, chat with people just like yourself, and play chess or dominoes, and feel somehow important. He said time goes more slowly here winter or summer. When I went to jot something in my notebook, he skit-tishly scurried away, saying he was late for his Spanish lesson.

Heading east out of Camagüey, I had an interesting group of three people in the car. First stop was to pick up an Afro-Cuban about thirty, a very shy woman with chubby cheeks. She indicated that she spoke no English and couldn't understand my wretched Spanish. But before we could take off, a happy married couple in their mid-twenties tapped on the window, and they got in the back seat. The couple spoke excellent English, and we chatted away about all the little things that were happening in their lives. It turned out the man was an ardent sports fisherman, like Yandys, and worked as a cook in a large glamorous new hotel just outside Camagüey. He told me if I were to get there about two o'clock he'd personally cook me a really good pescado fresh from the sea.

He also said he'd take me fishing if I were interested. It seems the only people who get to go fishing work in the hotels. Boats of any kind seem in short supply. I told him I very much appreciated the offer, but I'm an unlucky fisherman, I never catch anything. Ever since I was a kid, it's been the same story: everybody in the boat will be catching fish left and right except for me. I glanced at the black woman and she was trying to suppress a laugh.

"Aha!" I said. "You speak English! I caught you in a lie!" She smiled guiltily and confessed. I don't know if she really needed to get out at that point, or she was just making a stop request out of acute embarrassment. But as I pulled over, and she was getting out, I asked what she did for a living. "I'm a policewoman," she said in perfect English, blushing through her black skin.

In a large electronics store just off El Parque Céspedes, in the beautiful sixteenth-century city of Bayamo (est. pop. 192,600), I tried to buy a new tape recorder. This simple transaction involved three salespeople and the manager, much running up and down stairs, and at least three phone calls to head office in Santiago de Cuba. When the transaction was finally complete, it turned out they had inadvertently charged me the wrong price, and we had to start all over again, with another three phone calls, and the manager, and numerous Cubans were leaning against the counter and watching with glee the fuss over this cheap tape recorder. When I got back to the car and put on my glasses it turned out it wasn't a tape recorder, it was just a tape player. I had to take it back again. Turned out they didn't have any actual tape recorders in stock, so another conglomeration of paperwork was required to give me a refund. I had to present my passport for the third time.

But then I spotted a box of ten blank tapes on the shelf, and the price was almost as much as the tape player, so we just made a simple switch. No paperwork at all, except for that involved in cancelling the transaction.

It was mid-afternoon, and I made a deal with myself. If the ice cream at the crowded Tropicrema is as good as it looks, I'll spend the night at Bayamo. If not, I'll move on. So I stood in line, the only gringo among hundreds of Cubans, each of whom was buying two ice-cream cones and putting them together head to head, and licking them as they twirl the pointy ends of the cones. With Cubans, ice-cream cones are like shoes, they only come in pairs.

But when I finally was about to be served it turned out it was pesos only. Like a fool, I flashed a dollar bill and pleaded, but they just shook their heads solemnly. So I zipped around the corner to the bank to buy some pesos, and just as I got there the bank closed.

Since I still didn't know if the ice cream was any good, I decided to stay overnight in Bayamo if there happened to be a front balcony room available at the gorgeous and attractively restored Hotel Royalton, overlooking the *parque*. The desk clerk, a friendly fellow who hasn't had a word from his brother in Toronto for a decade, said there were plenty of vacancies but unfortunately none at the front. I told him about my deal with myself, and he smilingly sympathized, but couldn't do anything about it.

So I decided to stay if there was an Etesca office where I could check my e-mail and see if everything was fine at home. But there wasn't one.

On the way out of Bayamo I passed a little hospital for people seeking treatment for the kind of eye diseases often caused by poor nutrition. It was a restful little place, with about six or seven men sitting outside on hard chairs and quietly squinting at passersby.

Everybody in town has ice cream – except for me and these poor fellows.

Farther out on the highway there was a penal institute way back from the road, and two handsome bright young well-dressed fellows in handcuffs were being marched along the highway toward it. These kids didn't seem like bad guys at all. They seemed full of confidence, giving no hint that they were frightened, depressed, or even slightly worried about their fate. They may have been "dissidents" – overly vociferous anti-abortionists who might have been pleased that they got a light sentence, that they will be able to spend some time praying in their cell, and also spreading the word to the other prisoners about the evils of abortion. Farther on, a green military truck was stalled on the road, and some soldiers were trying to push it to get it started.

Those two Canadian guys in Camagüey told me a schoolteacher makes ten pesos a day. They were dead-on. I picked up a charming, happy, uncomplaining hitchhiker, a schoolteacher, twenty-three, who says she makes the equivalent of ten U.S. dollars a month, which is exactly ten pesos times twenty-seven days. She teaches eight hours a day, five and a half days a week, and has to hitchhike fifteen miles back and forth six days a week. "The bus is so uncomfortable," she said.

Life is cruel. If she only knew how much cash I had on me – US $637, plus a card with a line of credit which, though modest by Canadian standards, would have dazzled her. And what do I do for it? Yet she lives rent-free, while I'm often on the verge of being unable to pay my rent. Isn't that odd?

We were passing through sugar-cane country. We passed a billboard saying, The struggle is day by day, but the victory will be eternal. We exchanged quick glances, silent but meaningful. I decided it was impossible to decide who was the more fortunate child, the one born in Cuba or the one in Canada, though Canada's infant mortality rate is slightly higher.

After the teacher got out, I stopped for a large group of schoolgirls waiting for a bus, accompanied by a couple of teachers. Three happy eight-year-olds hopped in the back seat. I hopped out and ran around to open the back door, helped one of the kids out, and put her in the front seat. Then I thought I better do up their seat belts, an accident would ruin our day. All the other kids, and the teachers, were sitting there watching this with great glee.

These kids had obviously never seen a seat belt in their lives. They tried wrapping them around their necks, but couldn't get them fastened. So I had to get out again and run around and clip the seat belts for them with even greater laughter from the rapt crowd. The girls in the car were giggling like maniacs, and so were the rest of the gang, watching from the little pickup station. Then I hopped in the car, did my own belt up, and took off.

Their uniforms were white blouses and short maroon skirts. The girls were eight, no more than nine. As I took off I noticed the male teacher had been among the crowd of kids laughing. He seemed pleased about my seat-belt concern, even though he deemed it unnecessary because nobody uses seat belts in Cuba. Only rental cars have seat belts. Adding to the unnecessariness was the fact that the girls were only going about three miles. And had hitched hundreds of miles already in their young lives. They were so pretty – and they knew a bit of English.

At another point I picked up two older schoolgirls, about fourteen at a guess, also pretty. They were in the back seat, and in the front was a gap-toothed unsavoury-looking character who smelled as if he hadn't changed his clothes since the Papal Visit in 1998. With a big evil smile, this slob looked at me and said loud enough for the kids to hear, "You and I and those two in the back, we could do the f**ky f**ky." I was embarrassed as all get out, but when I glanced in the rear-view mirror, the girls definitely were not embarrassed: they looked and sounded so cute with their heads close together in mock fear, saying, "No, no, por favor, señors, no!" Giggle giggle!

EL UVERO, EL COBRE,
AND THE BLACK VIRGIN

Friday, February 27, 2004. This morning's grapefruit juice tasted the way it did in childhood. In the street, Cubans cross their arms under their T-shirts, then pull their T-shirts down over their arms. When the temperature dips below twenty-eight Celsius, people go home for their sweaters. But the hitchhikers love to have the air conditioner full blast. Isn't that odd?

This is the Hotel Niquero, in the town of Niquero, on the Gulf of Guacanayabo, at the extreme southeastern tip of Cuba. Niquero is where a big cruiser named the *Granma* intended to land in 1956, after a three-day sail from Mexico, but things didn't go smoothly: it landed a few miles farther south, at Belic, in a mangrove swamp, after a seven-day sail, and after being strafed by machine-gun fire from planes tipped off by a spy, still not identified, who was thought to be among the eighty-two aboard the *Granma*, according to the Mexican novelist and biographer Paco I. Taibo II. If the spy was indeed aboard, that would explain why the enemy neglected to sink the boat. It was not a pleasant trip for Che, who was suffering so badly from asthma that his fellow *guerrilleros*, most of whom were seasick, thought he was dead and were on the verge of throwing him overboard. Fidel and his brother Raúl were the only healthy ones.

In Niquero today, all the boys and girls on their way to school are dressed in light denim uniforms, trousers, and shirts. While standing on the curb bending over to open my car door, I see in the rear-view mirror that one of the girls has stopped and is brazenly checking me out, giving me a visual appraisal from head to toe. So I suddenly turn around and smile at her. She is astonished. She can't figure out how I could have seen her, plus she is probably shocked that my face was so pink, so lined, so grizzled. She is thinking to herself, Some of these old gringos must have an eye in the back of their head. She catches up with her classmates, whispers to them, and they look back and giggle.

Hotel Niquero has a nice write-up in Christopher P. Baker's book. I showed it to the two women at the night desk. They squealed with delight. Nobody had told them that they were so famous! There was a big hotel in Manzanillo (est. pop. 128,200), but A.'s spirit whispered in my ear that I should continue south along the shore. She was sure I'd find a romantic moonlit seaside hotel that would be nicer than that monster. But there were no signs. Whenever it was a toss-up over which was the main road, I would choose the wrong one. I found myself in an enclosed barrio with a vast maze of wretched roads, and the way in and the way out seemed to have closed up on me. People would give me precise directions for an exit strategy, but time and again it wouldn't pan out. Kids would have to break up their ball game to let me pass, then ten minutes later they'd have to do it all over again for the same guy. Many times I passed the same father throwing the same blistering baseball at the same young son. The boy was only about ten but was doing a good job of catching these speedballs, with no glove, and trying to laugh off the pain.

Soon the sun had sunk into the Caribbean and the night was profound. The nightmare continued. A short, heavy-set, scowling Afro-Cuban guard with an extraordinarily unpleasant personality was standing at the gate of a military camp. He had twice already given me directions to the main road, the second time in a much less cordial manner. The third time, he was about to strangle me. He calmed down and said he'd hop in the car and direct me to the exit road. I asked him to get in the back seat because I had all my stuff in the front seat, but he insisted on sitting in the front. He got in, very stiffly, humourlessly, and with great self-importance. I offered him a Popular, he said no, he directed me down the same barrio road that I had taken twice before according to his directions, and there was something I hadn't noticed before: a narrow unmarked pony trail of a dirt road disappearing into the bush. Nobody would ever have taken it to be the main road leading from the barrio to the highway. He got out of the car and told me that's the road that will lead to where I want to go.

I thanked him and, since I didn't think I should tip a soldier, I offered to drive him the mile or so back to where he was serving guard duty. But he refused. He just wanted money. And then he gently caressed his left hip where a loaded pistol hung from his belt, and reminded me that this was a dark and desolate area. I smilingly pulled a dollar out of my pocket and handed it to him with a flourish, hoping that would be enough and pretending I hadn't noticed the threatening gesture. He grabbed the dollar, grunted, got out of the car, and walked back to his post. [I was to see the same guy in a couple of days, miraculously, at Guantánamo Bay – or maybe it was his twin brother.]

But that was yesterday, this is today. I've left Niquero behind, passed through the town of Pilón, and for the next few hours the highway takes me along the geometrically straight southern coast, to Santiago de Cuba, with the Caribbean on the right and on the left the tall green mountains of the largest and most famous range in Cuba, the world-famous Sierra Maestra, including the highest mountain in Cuba, Pico Turquino (6,476 feet). Fidel took an altimeter when he climbed this mountain, we're told, just to make sure Turquino was the same height the geographers claimed it was.

At the battlefield memorial at El Uvero, the stunning main monument is surrounded by royal palms, concrete benches, and stone walkways. It's a short walk up from the highway, with the vivid

Caribbean shining through the trees, stretching out like the empty space between planets, and unconsciously displaying an ecstatic *voluptuosidad* of its rarest and most exotic milky greens and shining dark blues, with Haiti to the right and Jamaica to the left, and both just over the horizon. El Uvero was a Batista garrison, attacked by Fidel on May 28, 1957. The battle took place right here, and it was over in three hours with the rebels triumphant. A great all-weather map shows the positions of each man at the beginning of the fight. Six of the eighty rebels were killed and nine wounded, and of the fifty-three Batista soldiers, fourteen were killed, nineteen wounded, and fourteen taken prisoner. Fidel refused on principle to execute any of the prisoners, which is not surprising since four years earlier in a courthouse in Santiago he had accused Batista's soldiers of killing seventy of Fidel's men after they had already been captured and dis-armed, following the ill-favoured attack on the Moncada Barracks in that city. Some of these soldiers were in the courtroom, squirming with embarrassment as Fidel spoke, since they were wearing watches, rings, and crosses they had removed from the bodies.

It's quiet here now, with numerous bushes bearing unusual flowers – purple-red azalealike blossoms with vivid yellow multipetalled centres, for instance. A baby donkey is quietly nibbling away at the lush grass and trying to ignore the cries of a nasty rooster. I should have a vast choice of Haitian, Jamaican, and Cuban music at this point, but the radio in my car seems to have died. I can't get a thing.

The long narrow town of Uvero has a sleepy atmosphere even though it's more commercial than residential, sort of a farming centre, with a handsome baseball park, a cinema, a school, and an awesome number of repair shops, machine shops, oddly shaped buildings, hexagonal huts, circular structures with thatched roofs, and several tae kwan do studios along the main street, with every-thing freshly painted and nicely colour-coordinated. Don't let anyone tell you the martial arts aren't big in little Uvero – even if the most internationally prominent of the Cuban tae kwan do prac-titioners, Olympic star Urbia Meléndez who took the silver in Sydney in 2000, lives in distant Holguín. Interesting facts: From the

1900 Olympics in Paris to the 2004 in Athens, Cuba has copped sixty-five gold medals, fifty-three silver, and fifty-two bronze. Its best year was Barcelona in 1992 when it won fourteen golds, twice Canada's total for that year, and with only one-third the population.

No signs! This isn't tourist country. Everybody is supposed to know how to get where they want to go. Maybe signs are for sissies, and Santiago de Cuba isn't called the City of Heroes for nothing. Fidel had no signs when he drove all the way from Havana to Santiago in 1953 in order to launch his assault on the Moncado Barracks. For that stunt he spent a year or two in jail in Santiago, in solitary, reading books and composing his essential essay, "History Will Absolve Me."

One could theoretically get to know Santiago (est. pop. 556,000) in about one-quarter the time it takes to get to know Havana. But sometimes larger cities are easier to get to know than smaller cities. Maybe all cities, and even all towns, take about the same amount of time to get to know – i.e, forever. Santiago is a city where one could spend his life contentedly, where motorists obey crosswalk signs, and pedestrians can hold out a forefinger and walk across the street confident that all traffic will stop, and won't start again till you're safely across, a slow-moving town, where even the motorcycles just putter along content to get there when they get there.

It's an interesting town atmospherically, people have time to gawk at strangers, walk with friends, and talk with tourists. There's something terribly benign about it, a pleasantly sweet town that seems to run on – I don't know what – sex, yes sex would be number one, and music, music would be number two. The two engines that drive the Santiago de Cuba economy: sex and music! Don't like to see happy people having fun? Don't come to Santiago de Cuba. Coincidentally, it's said to be the most African of Cuban cities.

I left the city knowing the longer I stayed the harder it would be to leave, and wishing I had the rest of my life to explore it. It seemed to be more mysteriously attractive than most cities, even Cuban ones, and everybody seems to have interesting things going on in their lives.

When you come over the mountains from the west and get your first glimpse of Santiago de Cuba, you're probably mistaken, what you're actually seeing is El Cobre, a three-spired cathedral with three prominent red domes and a vibrantly pale yellow exterior, a graceful vision perched atop a high hill on the coast twenty miles west of Santiago, in the town of El Cobre, visible from much farther down the coast, and dedicated to the Patron Saint of Cuba (as those who are mystified by her call her), the Black Virgin (as those who respect her call her), Cachita (as those who adore her call her), or La Virgen de la Caridad de El Cobre (as she is officially called).

When I left Santiago I was planning to head east to Guantánamo province, but the Black Virgin seemed to be drawing me, pulling me toward her, and by her distant presence calming the tossing waves of my heart. So I drove straight to the church.

Cachita's colour is amarillo, and her saint's day is September 8, when a giant effigy of her is paraded around town. The Sentería people identify her with Yoruba, the goddess of love and dance, a sort of sanctified Aphrodite. She is usually depicted with darkish skin, and sometimes more African in appearance than in others. The church was very full, and the children were making a lot of noise. In Canada, the churches are always silent and the libraries noisy. In Cuba, it's the opposite. This cathedral is dedicated to Cachita, and she is one of the small circle of patron saints who never really existed on earth, except in one single solitary vision way back at the beginning of the seventeenth century.

One of the three boys whose life she saved, in the year before Shakespeare had probably even begun to think about writing The Tempest, was a slave boy, and the other two were the sons of prosperous slave owners. When you see a small boat in a wildly tempestuous sea, with three people in it, with a young white man at either end and a young black man in the middle, desperately praying, it will refer to this event. The three were out in the boat, a major storm came up, they became frightened, the Black Virgin appeared as a vision in the sky, the storm calmed itself, or rather she calmed it, and the boys were saved. She appeared with her feet just grazing the waves, and with a baby at her breast, a crown on her head, and wearing a yellow robe. She said, "I am the Virgin of Charity," and the sea became calm. In hearing for the first time about this blessed vision it must be difficult to avoid taking it seriously, at some level, no matter how skeptical one may be.

In the fascinating vestibule of the cathedral hangs a framed Amnesty International map of Cuba giving the names of all the prisoners of conscience and showing where they were being held as of June 10, 2003. Displayed in glass cupboards are numerous odd little items that people have donated not because of their material value but because of their magical value. There are photographs of people who were saved through the miraculous intervention of the Black Virgin, and several paintings of the church by amateur artists whose lives have been touched in some way by her. There are numerous medals and pins associated with La Virgen, a crushed orange motorcycle helmet worn by a fellow who was in a serious accident and survived, about thirty baseballs and one soccer ball signed by famous players who won important games, flags and sweaters of various teams, and a record album signed by Juan Carlos Alfonso, the leader of the famed Cuban band Dan Den. But the most famous gift came from Ernest Hemingway, when he won the Nobel Prize for *The Old Man and the Sea*. I don't think he hesitated for a split second before heading for El Cobre and donating his gold medal to the Virgin of Charity who calms the waters just when you think you are heading for the bottom of the sea.

It was 1954, about the time Fidel was thinking of attacking the Moncada Barracks. At the press reception for Hemingway at the Hotel Naçional in Havana, he's pictured wearing a *guayabera*, and he has his eyes closed just at the moment of this photograph, and he has shaved his beard. He's in his early fifties, and looks ten years older. He is announcing that his Nobel Prize medal will be donated to the church at El Cobre, in honour of the Patron Saint of Cuba. The medal was sitting here in one of the display cases among all the other donations until 1988, when somebody stole it. The loss was a big story around Cuba for a while. But they finally collared the crook and retrieved the medal. I like to think he was caught trying to sell the medal to tourists at the Finca Vigía. It must have seemed like a good idea at the time. But some things even tourists won't buy.

Meanwhile there's a little service going on in the church. Four aged nuns in white are in the first row, and in the second row an ordinary, middle-aged laywoman is reciting lines from scripture, while the four old nuns do the responses. Even though the nuns have been doing this all their lives, you get the sense that they are deeply into it even today, just as a baseball player or a poet, who may have been at it for decades, can still get deeply into each game or into each sonnet.

I pretended to be shocked and astonished to see that my car hadn't been stolen, and vigorously shook the hand of the fellow to whom I'd given a dollar to watch it. I was Fidel and he was a Revolutionary hero who had performed a great service to humanity, and he seemed very pleased to have had a medal pinned to his shirt even if it was an imaginary medal. The other guys were all watching and laughing. This is the kind of humour Cubans like. Maybe I'll get a nomination by the El Cobre Car Watching Society for tourist of the week.

Behind the cathedral, on the other side of the parking lot, there's an ancient convent, highly colonnaded, beautifully constructed, in a perfect state of repair, and going back to the early eighteenth century, though it has never been restored. The wide corridors, porticos, and dazzling marble staircases, baroque columns, and rococo railings are as they always were, festooned with faded religious paintings, engravings, prints, and reproductions. It's in good shape and well cross-ventilated. It's cool and breezy up here in the higher foothills of the Sierra Maestra, and the breezes blow right through the building. I'm sitting wrapped in a blanket on the spacious second-floor porch, watching the stars. I thought about Fidel having stayed here for a week prior to the Moncada Barracks affair, and also about Lina Ruiz, who donated a small golden statue of a guerilla fighter to El Cobre, to provide some spiritual protection for her son, Fidel, when he was up in the mountains engaging the Batista boys in deadly combat.

When I asked for a room for the night, the large Afro-Cuban woman on the night desk said yes, that will be eight pesos. I asked if eight dollars would do. She looked at me as if I was crazy. Eight pesos is thirty cents, eight dollars is 216 pesos. Do you wish to pay 216 pesos for something that is only worth eight pesos?

When you put it like that, I guess not.

She had her chance to fleece a tourist but resisted. You won't find her in hell with the demons when she dies.

But maybe not, because when I first got there she had been having some kind of a squabble with a nun. Everybody was in a bad mood, and angry about something. It seemed more than a squabble, more like a long-standing grudge.

A room for the night?

Sí, sí, sí. Un minuto, por favor. We have to keep fighting for another minute if that's okay with you.

So I wandered away and looked at some paintings, and drank in some views of the cathedral, and the mountains, and the parking lot, from various windows. When I came back a middle-aged Cuban couple was there; they were booking a room, and they took forever. I had that left-out feeling. When they got straightened out, the registrar, not knowing what to do about the peso problem, had to call her rival over again. The nun scolded her for not waiting on me first because I was way ahead of that couple from Santiago. And as for my eight dollars, just give him 216 pesos in exchange, and then take eight pesos for his room. Could anything be simpler? So now I have pockets full of pesos. If nothing else I can give them out to the *moscas*.

Speaking of which, my car watcher has gone home. He has a dollar bill now. He could blow it all tonight on a big Saturday night party in the town of El Cobre or he could be a tightwad and make it last till Wednesday.

So then I was free. I went into the dining room and had an excellent meal consisting of a hard-boiled egg cut in half and smothered in red-hot chile sauce. Everybody gets the same thing. And just when I thought that was it, along came a big plate of white rice, with some rather sweet salsa on another plate, to pour over the rice. Plus a bowl of highly salted spaghetti soup. Plus a pitcher full of freshly drawn well water. Trouble was, the water came late, and before I could finish my first little glass of it, the dining room was closed down, everything was picked up and taken away, and the diners all got shooed out.

So that left me terribly thirsty. I didn't know what to do. There was no bar, of course. I didn't want to go downtown. I just wanted to go to my room and have a contemplative evening, in a cloistered room with no distractions, do some good thinking inspired by the spiritual presence of La Virgen, and the spiritual absence of television, revved-up motorcycles, and squealing brats.

Turns out there is a lot of noise, but it's just the kids running along the marble colonnades. It would appear that some families have moved in for the night, and even though there are signs saying SILENCIO, that just encourages the locals to be anything but. Oriente Province, as this part of Cuba used to be called, is famed for its rebels.

So although I keep telling myself it doesn't matter, it doesn't matter, the kids keep up their relentless screaming as they run in stockinged feet along the polished marble floors of this wonderful second-floor colonnade. Doesn't matter, doesn't matter. If a kid can't scream, what can he do? We all have to be free to scream when we have the need to scream. Even kids, one of whom is screaming to his papa to hurry up and get off the toilet. One does untold harm to a future adult when one stops a kid from screaming or laughing or doing anything that's loud.

Yet one can't help but try to imagine what this old palace would be like if there were nothing but SILENCIO. I imagine it would be even more beautiful than it is now, in the clear clean cool moonlight and the breezes. I'm on the second floor, in Room 18, and there are faded water-stained ecclesiastical prints on all the walls. Colours may fade, like the joyful screaming of children, but the blacks and whites remain, and a bit of the greys. Here's a picture of Baby Jesus lying on the ground, looking up at Mary, who is deep in prayer, standing over

him, with an oversized halo around her head. The look on Baby Jesus'
face is priceless. He has his hand over his heart as if he is in deep
prayer as well, but he also seems to be staring rather crossly at Mary,
as if he's saying, "What the heck are you doing?" That's the look on
his face. "Can't you see I want to be picked up and cuddled?"

It's a cool night. There are only two guys left to watch four or five
cars. These two are really desperate, one more than the other. The
less desperate had small items to sell, little plastic icons, portable
offerings, a bag full of El Cobre souvenirs. The other had nothing to
offer, and had long given up the fakery of the car-watching scheme.
Besides, a scheme like that would take more brain power than this
fellow seems to have on tap at present. Every time he catches my eye
he scrunches up his face and goes over and over till I turn away, "Mi
mi mi mi mi! Gimme money!" And to add emphasis, he points at
himself. All this stuff was really getting on my nerves. I told him to
stop washing my windshield with that dirty dry rag. I told him to
calm down. When I asked him if he was hungry, he just fell apart. He
burst into tears and fell against the car. I told him I would go in and
see about some food.

I got shunted back and forth between three different nuns, and
then all four of us got together. They decided they couldn't provide
a meal for this fellow, even though I had offered to pay for it. They
wanted to be kind, but food was scarce and there were things about
this situation it wouldn't be proper to discuss. They agreed with me
that it was the duty of the church to feed the poor when they knock
on the door. But they wanted to assure me that they do practise
plenty of charity toward these poor destitute lads, some more destitute than others.

I didn't know what to do. I didn't want to give him money because
he seemed so crazy and in so much pain he might wind up in worse
shape with money in his pocket. It seemed as if he had run out of
charity, he'd gone too reliant on it over the years. I don't know.

So I gave him the big fat tomato and big fat red onion I had on the
dashboard. He accepted them, but he had a curiously expressionless

look on his face as he stared in my eyes. Any gratitude he felt was cancelled out by something else, just for a moment. What would it be? I can't say. I went for a walk, and when I came back he had gone home. I guess he went home and ate the tomato and onion. For all I know he shared the food with his wife and six kids. Or maybe he invited a neighbour or two over, and they brought some carrots and, as a special surprise, some Tabasco sauce, and maybe a bit of rum left over from the last time something nice happened.

And then I acquainted myself with skinny old white-haired José, a very amusing coffee-coloured Afro-Cuban. He was fifty-six, and was the night clerk. By now everybody else had gone home. He loved my impressions of sexy women on the streets of Santiago, and he started doing some of his own. The way they eye you with maximum voltage. The kind of sexy stride these señoritas adopt, or the kind of eye contact, and sometimes they make funny little fishlike motions with their mouths.

So there we were strutting around like cheap whores, and flirting outrageously with each other. But one of us, I forget which, put his forefinger in his mouth, and that did it. All of a sudden we both stopped and looked kind of embarrassed and started talking about the weather. A special kind of divinely sexual magic is everywhere in Cuba, it will reach right into the convent, and it can even turn the sexual preference of a man or a woman around in a flash.

José confirmed that the nuns from the convent are in the habit of being charitable to these car-watching guys. I can't help wondering why people are hungry when there is food everywhere. On the surface, with numerous goats prancing about in your front yard what's to stop you from grabbing one, slitting its throat, and inviting all your friends over for dinner? It's a tough one. I did see a guy walking along the highway with a dead unplucked chicken under his jacket. He'd grabbed the chicken, twisted its neck, and was taking it home. Let's hope that this sort of thing is overlooked nine times out of ten, except when perhaps the same person does it too often.

One fellow I picked up hitchhiking insisted that when things get that desperate you can borrow someone's car and run over a chicken or a goat or whatever, then take it home and eat it with impunity. He said, "If you run over one of those lambs, it's lamb fricassee right away."

I'm still terribly thirsty and ask José where I can get some of that delicious well water. He takes me behind the counter in the dining room, furnished in pretty well exactly the same way it would have been a hundred years ago. He shows me a great silver coffee and tea machine. He tells me it's been in continuous use on this counter for 120 years. One spout's for tea, one spout's for coffee. Next to it, breaking the mood of ancient times, there's a sky-blue plastic five-gallon picnic container for fruit juice.

Here, have some Cuban water, says José. And he fills a glass for me, right up to the brim, and it looks like thick muddy water. He smiles slyly. Yech! What is this? So I take a very cautious sip, and by golly it's really good! Fresh mango juice! Every bit as good as at the Captain's place, maybe better. It goes down fast and I ask for more.

THE ROAD TO BARACOA

Saturday, February 28, 2004. It's five o'clock in the morning at the old convent at El Cobre. The kids are still running and screaming in the halls, cars in the parking lot are still gunning their engines, and the cocks are crowing with a passion as foolish as it is admirable. It's cold in here. I have one winter blanket, but it seems very thin. I could ask for an extra blanket, but I don't want to disturb José at this hour, he's already been so kind, and so generous with the mango juice.

Cuban roosters in the middle of the night scream like men who can't take it any more and have snapped and gone insane, or like the man in the famous Fellini film *Amarcord* who climbs a great tree in a beautiful meadow and proceeds to scream out, "I want a woman," over and over so loudly that women from all over the countryside start climbing the tree to present themselves to him. But even that man didn't scream with the intensity of an El Cobre rooster at five in the morning.

The roosters are off in the distance, but they have the convent surrounded. There are so many of them it sounds like the screams at a ball game when the home team is behind four runs but has the bases loaded in the bottom of the ninth. I've taken a relaxing pill, and am about to drift off back to sleep, and the roosters have changed their tune. They now sound as if the umpire has made a bad call against the home team. "He was out by a mile, ya bum," they scream over and over. It's amazing what you hear when you lie awake listening to the animals.

"The umpire is senseless," screams out a rooster who seems to have been misreading a Kathy Acker novel. "Quit pushing, you stupid bastard," a short-tempered rooster calls out. The roosters are screaming because they want to have sex. The fans at a ball game are screaming because they want to have runs. Not much difference really.

In such a sad land as Cuba it's thrilling to see the bright intelligence of the children. One very serene and lovely nun about fifty was around till late last night. She oozed kindness and saintliness, in every fibre of her body there was no sense of selfishness, everything she did was for others. One of the families visiting from Santiago de Cuba had two little boys, one about eight, with glasses, and the other about three, without. And the nun and the two little boys were sitting together on the wide flat marble balustrade at the grand main entrance. The younger boy sat with his legs crossed and his spine erect for long periods of time without being uncomfortable. His brother seemed already the family intellectual: they were talking about José Martí and the Beatitudes. It was their first visit to the convent, and their first meeting with a nun. The nun took to them with great warmth and they were responding beautifully. They were fascinated; she was the most interesting person they had ever met.

And it got me thinking of poor Fernando, yesterday, the twelve-year-old I picked up hitchhiking, and he got sent home by suspicious Ministry of the Interior officers at a checkpoint, in the shadow of Pico Turquino, and there was nothing I could do about it. The boy was in the back seat of an air-conditioned car having a friendly chat with me as I drove along, and he was genuinely interested in practising his English, and helping me with my Spanish, and telling me jokes, and laughing at mine. The police imagined the worst; man and boy, just met, in a car together, not a good thing. They had a stern talk with him, maybe caught him in a lie, found out that he wasn't really going anywhere, and so they told him to go back home.

I suppose he just stuck his thumb out because he liked the look of the shiny new car. And there he goes, walking away sadly without even looking back at me. Just a few minutes earlier we were going to be amigos forever. It seems wrong of the police, but checkpoints are where questions get asked, and they probably asked him where he was going, and he had no idea, and that would have been their reason for sending him home. It's all perfectly understandable. Obviously when the police questioned him he told them he lived farther south, and he was hitchhiking home, but the car was so nice, and the air conditioning was so nice, and the Canadian was so nice, that he wanted to stay in the car, and talk with me, and figure out how to get home later.

I turned around, and there he was, walking home, back the way we'd come, staring at the ground in front of him. And there was nothing I could do about it, because the police still had my passport, and I was guilty of forgetting that Christopher P. Baker at one point in his book says one should never let the police walk away with one's passport. You can let him see it, but if he tries to walk away with it one should scream blue murder. And now I'm drifting off, the cries of the roosters are getting softer and less annoying, like in the final scenes of a bad movie, and I am mumbling into the tape recorder, and then silence . . . except for the occasional little snore.

That relaxing tablet took effect and I went into the deepest loveliest sleep. All of a sudden there was a lot of noise outside, and it kept getting louder and louder until I woke up. And it was José, outside my door, yelling in at me, and then he started hammering on the door, louder and louder. Did I make the mistake of telling him I was in Room 18? No, he probably found out in the ledger book. I opened the door a crack, and he said he had to go home to sleep now. All right, José. Thanks for letting me know. Good night. And he didn't want me to forget to give Carlo the money for watching my car. Okay, I won't forget. And then when I went to close the door, he said, "Money for me, money for me."

So I woke up a bit more and said omigod, this is terrible. I'd offered him money last night for all that mango juice but he refused. Could this be the same guy? I looked at him. It looked like his evil twin. He seemed as desperate as the guy who'd been scratching my windshield with a dry rag and cried when I asked if he was hungry. And I'm sure the personality switcheroo José had engineered was perfectly logical in his mind. So I gave him a dollar bill, and the old José smile returned to his face, though his eyes were bulging out more than might be good for them. "Ohoho!" he said. "Oh *whoa* ho!" A whole slide show of things he could do with that money flashed through his mind. And off he went. But not before pushing the door all the way open and giving me a nice big hug, even though I was starkers.

He knew I'd be asleep at 5:30 in the morning. Why couldn't he have taken the money for the mango juice last night when I offered it to him, begged him to take it, in fact? It may be more complex than this, but I think I have it figured out. If he had taken the money at the time he gave me the juice, he might find himself duty bound to turn it over to the convent. By going for it now, when he was about to leave, he could keep it. If the nuns later noticed the shortfall in the juice department, they might very well have questions. If he told them that he had taken money for it, he would have been required to turn the money over to them. But if he had told them he didn't take any money for the juice, which was true, they might have been a bit annoyed, and they would have suggested he not be so generous with the juice of others.

But I shouldn't worry about José, a family man, with one wife and two kids, and they'll be so happy to see the dollar bill when he gets home this morning. My only wish is that he'd called a bit earlier, when I was wide awake, rather than spiralling downward into dreamland. May the Virgin of El Cobre forgive this fellow his sins. And José's as well while she's at it.

"Money for Me." Sounds like a hip-hop album. Bound to be a big hit. Soon you'll be able to download it for seventy-nine cents. And if you ever decide to stay over at this convent, whatever you do make sure José has all the money he needs before you retire for the night.

It's 10:21 a.m. Had a very bad night's sleep, and I'm lying here trying to translate a poem about Santiago de Cuba, by García Lorca, which is printed in the tourist guide. I'm having problems. It doesn't sound right in English. Maybe my friend A., who enjoys this sort of thing, can try her hand at it upon my return to snowbound Toronto. I give up. Federico García Lorca spent almost two months in Cuba in 1930, from March 7 to the end of April 30, visiting churches and giving lectures all over the island. He visited Santiago toward the end of his visit, and he must have been very much impressed because he wrote this ecstatic poem just before heading back to Spain. Some people didn't like García Lorca. Jorge Louis Borges, for example, sneeringly referred to him as a "professional Andalusian." García Lorca was cruelly assassinated in Spain eight years after his trip to Cuba (and New York), a greased pistol was stuck up his anus and fired, at the beginning of the Spanish Civil War, shortly after he had announced on Spanish radio that he was gay.

When I got downstairs at eleven, breakfast was over. I asked the nun if I might at least have a cafecito. No no no, she said grumblingly, in a foul mood. But then it seemed as if the Virgin of Charity whispered something in her ear, you could see a change come over her face, her eyes became merciful, and she said yes yes yes. The cafecito really hit the spot, and so did the tip I gave the nun. Her face lit up like a beam when I handed her twenty-five pesos in gratitude.

But then another man, a harried and flustered sort of guy, noticed me drinking my cafecito. He went running up to the counter and loudly demanded one for himself as well, pointing at me in a rather rude fashion. No no no, said the nun. He stayed here overnight and didn't get any sleep because of the noise. So the poor fellow got very unhappy and stormed out, glaring at me as he passed.

Things change fast in Cuba. Shortages one day, surpluses the next. Yesterday young men lined the route to El Cobre holding up large bouquets of artificial yellow flowers for sale as votive offerings to the Black Saint. But today it's real sunflowers they're holding up. Who knows what it will be tomorrow? So now there is a long row of

Cuban males receding in the distance, each one holding up a freshly harvested sunflower and with a hopeful look on his face. All because of three sixteen-year-old boys who four hundred years ago almost drowned at sea. "I Am the Virgin of Charity!" said the saint, floating above the waves with her baby in her arm, the waves became calm and the boys were saved. Funny how as we age we learn to be believers and non-believers at the same time.

I decide to make a dash for Guantánamo, and get a hotel there. I want to see the U.S. base. I've heard there's a hilltop restaurant where Cubans and tourists can dine and gaze down at the camp through coin-operated telescopes like at Niagara Falls or the rooftop of the long-gone World Trade Center. I'm told Guantánamo Bay is built to resemble an idyllic midwestern U.S. small town of the 1940s, with a cinema showing old Ronald Reagan movies on the main street, and husbands and wives lining up for tickets when they're not busy guarding the many inmates who have not been charged with any crime, and where nobody would know habeas corpus from a hole in the ground.

There is a huge statue of Antonio Maceo in Santiago de Cuba, in the Revolutionary Square, and right across from it is a little service station. There is only one attendant and he has his head on the desk and is sleeping. I just need air for my tires, but there is a big lineup of cyclists at the pump. The guy just keeps on sleeping. But as soon as it came my time to put air in my tires, he woke up, came running over, and insisted on doing it for me. So I smilingly asked him why he didn't offer to help the others, but he's eager to help me. He drew open the breast pocket on his shirt to show me he had lots of money and didn't need mine. He did the air on all four tires. He explained that if he didn't do that for me, I might leave without getting any gas. But I had to inform him, sadly, that I had a full tank already, so I had no choice but to leave him without a sale.

In the suburbs of Santiago, there are numerous old colonial build-ings with signs indicating what each was now used for, such as the home of the Italian-Cuban Friendship Society, the Jewish Society of Eastern Cuba, the National Institute of Sugar Cane Research, and so on. But no signs pointing to the highway. I'm lost in another barrio, a very posh barrio this time, with stately old homes in terrific shape. There was a car just like mine, with an almost identical licence plate, obviously a tourist car, and a red-haired Dutch fellow about fifty had pulled over to buy some bananas from a roadside stand. He had two extremely elegant and beautiful black-skinned Afro-Cuban women in his car. Plus a very pretty fair-skinned slightly mulatto blond girl about four years old, possibly his daughter. He put the bananas in the car, then went across the road for a dozen eggs. He spoke perfect English with a slight Dutch accent. At first he thought I wanted a ride, but then he saw I had a car just like his, and he understood exactly what my problem was. He too has had a hard time learning to navigate around Cuba in the absence of good maps and directional signs. So he gave me some superb directions, and very patiently asked me to repeat what he had told me to make sure I had it right, while his three ladies sat patiently in the car. He said in the four years he's been in Cuba he has never had even a fender bender. But he's had many close calls.

I have to continue along the road I'm on till I get to the *punta control*. Do you know what a *punta control* is? Yes, a checkpoint? Right! And then about a kilometre past the *punta* take the road to the right, and it will lead me to La Maya, and then along to Guantánamo. And then he said, "It's true, there are many signs for many places, but there are no signs for Guantánamo." He cautioned me to beware of the Sunday drivers tomorrow. He said there is a tra-dition among truck drivers to do a lot of drinking on Sunday. Sunday in fact has become the big drinking day for Cubans, whether they drive or not. There are a lot of inebriated drivers on the roads on Sunday, and many of them are driving big trucks.

All the time we were talking, the two black ladies and the little girl were sitting in the car watching us, with very sweet looks on their faces. When the conversation was finished, and he turned to get back into his car, they were still looking at me, all three of them, and so I told them they had *un bueno hombre* there, and they smiled and said they knew.

After I passed the checkpoint and was heading toward La Maya, en route to Guantánamo, there was a red-haired man tilling a field for spring planting. He was with his son, who was much darker. In this area there seem to be many red-haired natives, or blondes, with fair skin, and they would be referred to as *los ingleses*, the descendants of the English copper miners who settled in Santiago in the nineteenth century. Most of them apparently speak no English, couldn't even find England on the map, but they vaguely know that they are fairer of skin than the others and are distinguished also by being called the *ingleses*.

There's a good-sized town not on the map, and not at all signposted, and the houses seem dumpy and uncared-for, though lived in. There is a tiny rather unkempt park with a small Russian tank sitting in it rusting and rotting. Three nasty-looking boys are walking down the main street with gleaming machetes in their hands. It's not just that humanity is the same all over the world. That's to be expected. But also men are men all over the world, and women are women. It seems odd that as I pass through these towns, which I've never seen before, I have the sense I have been here before. I will pass through a town, and say, Holy cow, what's going on here, I know I've never been here before but I've seen this town before. The feeling is so strong I'm racking my brains trying to figure out why I think I've seen before something so seemingly identical to this place. Maybe it stems from dimly remembered visits to rural old Florida and Georgia in my childhood. And the chubby Canadian from the park in Camagüey was complaining that the Santiago area was, for him, too reminiscent of the poor U.S. "deep south."

Along these roads, and even in Santiago de Cuba, there are a lot of what seem to be U.S. military vehicles. They look like a lot of fun to drive, and the people driving them seem to be young males having a lot of fun. It's a bit alarming really. The people in the vehicles are well-dressed and bright-eyed young men and I'm certain they must be somehow connected with the base at Guantánamo Bay. Which is not to say they are from the United States, because numerous Cuban nationals are hired for support-staff positions on the base, much more cheaply than bringing support staff from the United States would be, so I'm informed.

It would appear that these young men are Cubans who are working on the base, and who are very well trusted, and who are allowed to borrow these U.S. military vehicles on the weekends. The vehicles have blue Cuban licence plates, and they always start with the letters US, followed by one other letter, and then three numbers. I've seen a USE and a USF, but I've never seen a USA. The drivers are immaculately dressed and groomed. They tend to be slow, careful drivers, and they tend to pick up hitchhikers. And the vehicles are sparklingly brand new, although one that just passed by had a rear left wheel that was wobbly, and the driver is going slow, and has a worried look on his face. He is a large black man with a shaved head.

Everything seems to be going well in the pleasant town of La Maya. They even have a cinema. Nicely painted houses, no two colours the same – except for two houses that have been just recently painted bright red. They are not side by side, but merely separated by two other houses less flamboyantly hued. The sign says fifty miles to Guantánamo, but I don't know if that's to the border of Guantánamo Province or actually to the centre of Guantánamo City. My copy of the *World Reference Atlas* has Cuba as being European African (formerly mulatto) 51%, white 37%, black 11%, Chinese 1%. (In the same atlas, it would appear that the United States recognizes neither European African nor mulatto as ethnic categories, for that country is listed as being white 84%, black 12%, other 4%). So in the black sweepstakes the United States is beating Cuba 12-11, if one adopts the U.S. categories, or Cuba is beating the United States 62-12 if the Cuban categories are used. The busy little town of La Maya, however, would probably be, at a guess, about 60% black, 30% European African, and 10% white. If that seems high in the black proportion, it may have something to do with the proximity to Haiti, Santo Domingo, and Jamaica.

At Mirador de Malones where the Guantánamo Lookout is located, the gate is locked. Next to the gate is a little military checkpoint, with a Cuban flag flying, and out comes a fellow with an extremely nasty look on his face, a twin of the fellow who helped me out of the barrio two nights ago. Instead of a pistol on his hip this fellow has a machine gun in his hand. He said that I can't go up there, the restaurant is closed, and even if it were open I couldn't go up there with my car, and furthermore I can't walk up there, he can't take me himself, I can't hitchhike up there. But I can come back tomorrow, he said, and if I do I have to come in a taxi, or on some kind of a guided tour, I can't bring my car in.

But again he wasn't sure if it would be open tomorrow. Yesterday, for instance, he didn't know if it would be open today. It seemed to me that I should head for Baracoa today and forget about taking a chance of being able to get to the lookout tomorrow.

In the small coastal village of Tortuguilla, a dry area where turtles are plentiful and the newly hatched often get crushed under the wheels of motor vehicles or snatched up by birds as they make their way from egg to sea, the Caribbean looks different today. It's speckled with whitecaps all the way to the horizon. For an island nation it's amazing how few boats are out there. I can't remember seeing any fishing boats in my travels over the past while. Maybe the boats have all been taken by fed-up folks fleeing to Florida, and simply haven't been replaced, because the replacements will likely meet a similar fate.

This is still the flat-tailed southern end of Cuba, it's actually the eastern end of Cuba, but because of Cuba's crescent curve it is also the south end. And the mountains plunge straight into the sparkling emptiness of the sea, through its radiant hypnotic facade, and they keep on plunging dramatically down to the great silt mines at the unimaginable bottom of the deepest watery gully, where explorers claim to have found the ruins of cities fourteen thousand years old.

Along this south-shore route, between Tortuguilla and San Antonio del Sur, one encounters a beautiful low-slung wall of stone. This wall seems to be of Aboriginal construction, is composed of pale yellowish stones, and follows the straight line of the sea. It's pleasant to look at, with the sea on one side and a stretch of dry grassland on the other, before the high rocky hills start springing up. It's hard to imagine the reason for this wall. What is it supposed to be keeping out or keeping in? Nothing. It's something like the cold grey two-thousand-year-old Pictish Walls one sees all over the highlands and islands of Scotland. But in these walls (the Guantánamo Walls?), the stones, though all alike, are placed more haphazardly, and with less finesse and patience than the Pictish Walls. So it may not be that the Aboriginal Guantánamoans lacked the technical skills of the Picts, but that they were more in a hurry, and there were fewer of them. But it's a pretty damn good wall. Also, behind the walls, at the foot of steep rockfaces, can be found occasional caves, with windows and benches that suggest human occupation in the remote past.

Past the villages of Macambo and Yacabo Abajo, I stopped for a cold bottle of mineral water, and someone must have overheard me saying I was on my way to Baracoa, where Columbus landed uninvited on October 13, 1492, and straightaway started raising hell. When I got back to my car, just as I turned on the ignition someone whipped the back door open and said, "You going to Baracoa?" And before I could answer a battle broke out, with about six people trying to get in the car.

The strongest man managed to get in, followed by the second strongest, who very roughly pushed the first man's wife out of the way, and the two guys managed to get the door closed, and sat there with pursed lips and an air of total innocence. Others were beseeching me to unlock the front door, but I refused for any number of reasons.

The woman who had been separated from her husband was crying and pleading not to be left behind. So I asked the man if that was his wife. He said yes. But when I asked him how he could leave her out in the cold (so to speak) like that, there was no answer.

At the same moment a well-dressed black man, who might have been a minister of the Baptist church, motioned me to roll down my window. When I did so he stuck his head in and said, with the elegant manners of the elderly, "Excuse me, sir. Are you taking these riders for money?" He was the only black person, everyone else in the crowd was white.

"No, no money at all. Free."

And he said, "Well that's not right. Because it's necessary for you to pay for your gas and everything."

He obviously understood my problem and was very kindly trying to encourage me to attempt to negotiate a way out, also he was subtextually informing me that these guys were sort of ignorant, illiterate louts, and I shouldn't be bothered with them. But I said, "Thank you, sir, but please don't worry about it." I was afraid they would leap out of the car and physically abuse him. He walked away.

I looked back at the husband, straight in the eye, and said, "Your wife's there crying. Wouldn't you rather be with her!" He looked straight ahead with his lips tightly closed.

So I turned to the other guy and said, "Do you want to separate this man from his wife?"

"Sí!" he said brightly.

I had a lot of important but messy junk on the front passenger seat, and could have put it in the trunk and let the woman into the car, but if I did that I'd be allowing other people to fight their way in. Some people are just born to be pushed out of the way, and many of them would do anything for a ride to Baracoa. They've been living all their lives in Yacabo Abajo and had often heard fabulous stories about Baracoa and who could resist the chance to visit it?

And then everybody who wasn't in my car went flying toward a bus that had just pulled up, including the wife who was still sobbing. Everything seemed to be happening at once. No idea where the bus might be going, but it was pointed in the same direction I was going, and maybe it was eventually going all the way to Baracoa.

So I drove off with the two guys, and it was very unpleasant. I felt more and more bummed out, their silent weight was dragging me down, and I knew the climb up through the spectacular eastern-most mountains of the Sierra Maestra would be spoiled with these astronomical anomalies in the back seat. I just did not want to be with them one minute longer. One can be a good socialist without wanting to have uninvited people in his car, his house, or his bed.

Soon I found my window of opportunity and crashed right through it. There was an artless hangdog little sign indicating a beachfront motel and restaurant, down a long lane from the main road. It was just for Cubans, but sometimes you can get lucky, particularly if there's not much going on. So I stopped and told my uninvited guests that I had to go down this road because I was very tired and required a little nap. Which was true. It's not easy to get to sleep in a noisy convent.

So I got out and opened the back door, but they wouldn't get out. Not even when I told them I would return after having my nap and pick them up unless they had taken another ride by then. They just sat there looking straight ahead. So I finally shouted at them, "¡¡¡¡VAMOS!!!!" Then they got out in a hurry, and they immediately sat down under a shade tree, looking forlorn and sheepish, and expecting they'd never see me again, and they'd have to walk back home, and what would the one guy's wife say? He'd be in the *casa de perro* for weeks over this escapade.

So I offered them an almost full litre bottle of fizzy mineral water, and they refused to take it. They were miffed because I'd shouted at them..

There were a lot of peso people down there at the beach motel, so it wouldn't be cool to provide a room for a tourist. It's almost like a matter of not knowing how to deal with something like a tourist wanting to have a nap, or feeling shy about having a tourist hanging around, and maybe I was a motel inspector from the government, or a Talahassee terrorist. They seemed about as happy to see me as I had been to see the two bozos in my back seat. To them, I spelled trouble somehow. Besides, everyone was drinking rum. And there was no coffee available. Cuba is a nation of Sunday drinkers, and they were getting warmed up for the big day.

So I had no choice but to drive back to the highway, and there were the two guys still sitting under the tree. But I cleverly avoided looking at them, and willed myself to forget about them. I pretended that I had forgotten about them or that I was assuming they had got a ride already. I looked to the left for traffic instead of to the right for them, didn't even glance their way, although peripherally I could sense them jumping to their feet and waving their arms.

And almost immediately there was a billboard bearing an excellent suggestion: Abolish the Genocidal Blockade.

The scenic road that crooks its perilous way up into the mountains is lined with elegantly dressed *campesinas*, tall and black, who have heard the car chugging up the long incline. These beautiful women are holding out great bunches of bananas, coconuts, papayas, or whatever is on hand, plus beautiful cucuruchos, which are coconut puddings, mixed with papaya and orange and various nuts and spices, intricately and ingeniously wrapped in dried palm leaves, with a palm-leaf loop for carrying them over your wrist like a fashionable Parisian handbag.

The villages along this climb through the mountains to Baracoa are solidly African. People are washing clothes, carrying wood, and working on little repairs to their little thatched-roof houses, often without walls, just four poles with a thatched roof, or sometimes a hammered tin roof, surrounded by dense palm forests. When they hear a car coming, men-women-children all grab strings of fruit and cucuruchos and run down to the road hoping (and fully expecting) to make a sale. A very handsome black man about thirty is walking along the road wearing a green singlet, a pair of khaki shorts, and flip-flops, and he's holding on to about twenty ropes in his hand, and each rope on the other end is tied around the neck of a goat.

Steep hills, lush valleys pulsing with botanical splendour, amazing flowering trees I've never seen before and couldn't begin to identify. The clouds are a shiny gold colour in the late blue afternoon, and it looks like rain. And a veritable phantasmagoric fiesta of mountains whichever way you look.

This is the kind of landscape that can be seen, in dramatic black and white, and shot from a helicopter, in the Kalatozov/ Yevtushenko movie, *I Am Cuba*. This is what all of Cuba must have looked like when Columbus arrived. What a profusion of nature's wealth, and beautiful jagged mountains way off in the distance. And so clement is the weather that trees go straight to the very peaks of the tallest mountains, and sometimes right at the peak of a tall mountain you'll see a proud royal palm standing there like a cross after Jesus has been taken down, while the thousands of palm trees along the slopes more closely resemble strange little green windmills from another planet.

A young woman had her thumb out with a sweet smile on her face. As I selfishly passed her by, wrapped in my own thoughtlessness, I looked in the rear-view mirror and saw her look turn to one of absolute hatred. She was standing outside a very nice Baptist church with an ochre roof and saffron walls.

We're almost down to sea level, and the people around here, healthy looking, beautiful, with a full spectrum of skin colours from black to brown, brown to white, pink to yellow – and everybody gets along the way God intends people to get along, if God's alleged goodness is not an illusion.

And there's a tall white-pink guy with a red handlebar moustache sitting on his bicycle and picking his teeth with a toothpick. Another man is yanking at his horse, who is attached to a milk wagon, and who will not budge no matter how angry the boss gets. A fellow on a bicycle whispers something a bit indecent to the girl sitting on his crossbar as he pedals, so she turns, aims, and slaps him hard across the face. He laughs and keeps pedalling. What a dream this place is, with Revolutionary slogans everywhere, and everyone is doing their bit for the ozone layer by getting around on horseback and bicycles.

It occurs to me that the woman who was pushed away from my car in Yacabo Abajo, maybe that bus she hopped into was going to Baracoa and she's here by now, or soon will be. She'll be waiting for her husband, with forgiveness in her heart perhaps, but she'll be waiting for a long time because he is probably still sitting under that shade tree by the old seaside motel, wondering what to do. Maybe at my hotel in the morning that woman will be cleaning my room or serving me breakfast. Then too, maybe her husband will be serving me breakfast. All made up. Forgive and forget. I hope they don't recognize me.

This is a dreamlike unspoiled area of flowers and fruits, colour and beauty. It's like living in a government botanical garden or a nature preserve. Usually such beautiful surroundings are saved for the rich. Everything is so perfect, nothing is out of place, there's no garbage anywhere.

This is where those brightly coloured polymites are found. *Polymita pictas*: a species of tiny snails native to the Baracoa region. Christopher P. Baker relates a pre-Columbian legend: The snails' shells were originally colourless. One lonesome traveller of a snail climbed a hill (slowly, slowly) and was so taken with what he saw he asked the mountains for some of their green, he asked the sky for some of its blue, he asked the sands for some of their yellow, and the sea for some of its jade and turquoise. "And that's how the polymites get their colours, which are as unique to each individual polymite as fingerprints are to humans."

Che Guevara spent a night or two in room 203 of the romantic little seaside Hotel La Rusa in Baracoa some time in the early 1960s. He was here to inaugurate a sugar refinery or something. A handcrafted picture of Che, in leather and black ink, hangs on the wall, and a white tassel hangs from it, and the tassel continues on all around the picture, so it forms a frame. El Yunque is the unusually bare, flat-topped mountain behind the town, which Columbus is said to have seen from far out at sea, and which drew him to land here. This was his second landing in the New World, the first being in the Bahamas. It's not known which hotel Columbus stayed in, but he raved about the beauty of this area in 1492, and nothing much has changed.

Máximo is watching my car, which is sitting on the street at the main entrance to the hotel. He wanted two dollars. I said I'd give him one now and one in the morning, but he outsmarted me and wanted the two now. When I came down later to have a look around, three guys were sitting on the roof of my car, and one of them was fooling around with the windshield wipers and had one of them pulled right out but not broken. As soon as they saw me, they jumped off the car and pretended to be whistling happily, nonchalantly. I told them that was a funny way to watch a car, and they started laughing and looking embarrassed. Máximo is twenty-five years old, and he makes a good living watching cars, if he gets two bucks every time somebody wants their car watched. Mind you, there are only two cars out there tonight and we're getting close to the high tourist season.

One fellow in the pint-sized bar seems to be from Italy, and even though he's well into his sixties, he has two hot-blooded young bosomy black women, one under each arm, and he's bought them dinner, and they finished their dinners off real fast, then got up and left him sitting there looking glum. There might have been some kind of language problem, and he was mumbling to himself, if I heard correctly, "Oh my God, I spent all that money on those women and now they've gone home and they're not even going to stay over in my room tonight and keep me warm and cozy. What a fool I am. Mama mia!" But then they came back and he brightened up considerably.

So there are lots of people down here, and the manager is a jolly fat young fellow named Enrique. It's unusual to see a fat man in Cuba; he's not all that fat by Canadian standards, just sort of pleasingly chubby. But he's short so it makes him look more like a basketball than a basketball player, and he's also very white. The waitress has the most soulful eyes, she's about forty, and I'm trying not to show how attractive I find her to be. There comes a time when we older folk try to recapture the rapture of youth, but it's just not recapturable if you ask me. Best to just turn your back on it, and move forward on the lookout for deeper raptures, like the rapture of not giving a damn about rapture any more.

So imagine little old Dave staying in the same room Che Guevara stayed in. Wowie! Not much of a room. Pretty small. Two single beds. Window looking out over the sea and overlooking the Baracoa Malecón (just like Havana but smaller). It's nicely cross-ventilated, a north window and a west window both facing the sea, because the shore takes a curve past the hotel, and the waves are smashing over the mini-Malecón tonight, and the wind is whistling like a thousand Whistler's mothers. The wind is more worrying than the waves.

Downstairs, couples continue to come and go, mostly old guys with young women. One of the women, I think she's a Brit, I've seen her in several different places, each time with a different male tourist. She's not wildly attractive, she just likes to pick up men I guess, and go places with them, and have long conversations about Bertrand Russell or maybe even George Sand.

But it's mostly Cubans in here. Enrique told me about an old man who lives down the street a bit, who might give me some background about the place, which he's known intimately for fifty years. Máximo comes in and shows me a scar on his arm, he does a lot of fishing, mostly from the shore, and for reasons that will become clear as I continue, he can't afford a boat. This is a young man and the sea story.

He pulled in a fish one day, and it was bigger than he was. He was trying to land it, for his three kids (each from a different woman), and it pulled so hard on the line it cut him all down the arm. So he now has a long straight white welted scar on his dark brown arm. And he tries to spend one-third of his time with each woman, and each kid. So that's a good story, and he's a very handsome young guy, skinny, with fine features, and he's ambitious to learn languages and other things. It was important for him to know that I could understand every word of English he spoke, with the exception of one word – he kept confusing the word "song" and the word "son." But even better, whenever I tried to speak Spanish, he got it right away. He understood my Spanish better than anyone has so far. He always understood exactly what I was trying to say.

As for Enrique, it's as if he owns the hotel, and it's very important that he keeps everybody happy. He's a bit too anxious about things. It's as if he's under pressure from the government to start turning a bigger profit from this place. Both Enrique and Máximo work in three or four different hotels in town, and they move, independent of each other, from one hotel to another, as needed, just as Máximo goes from one wife and child to another. We're as far as can be from Havana, but it seems to be a good loyal Fidelista area around here. Just like any country, the more you favour the government in power, the more the government in power favours you. There is still pressure to create profits, of course, except that they're not called profits, they're called cost under-runs, or income over-runs, or black ink, something like that. Even Cuba needs all the liquidity it can get, in a cruel world of blockades and bad will.

I hold my tape recorder out the window like a mouse, and on replay later the waves sound like a cat in heat: "Meooooww, pshhh. Meooooww, pshhh. Meooooww, pshhh." Also the wind at times sounds exactly like thunder, but thunder that just keeps on thundering for five minutes at a time. In Havana, when the waves hit the seawall they will flood out over the entire wide road, but here there is no road separating the sea from the hotel, the hotel is right on the seawall, so the waves hit the little seawall here, and then explode all over the hotel. It's amazing the hotel is still standing after all the hurricanes it has had to withstand over the past seventy years or so.

FROM BARACOA ACROSS
THE RÍO TOA TO MOA

Sunday, February 29, 2004. At 1:33 a.m. I'm sitting in Che's room on the second floor, listening to the waves smack the mini-Malecón and splash against the walls of the Hotel La Rusa. Someone seems to be pounding at the door – but it's only the effect of the hot-blooded wind. I have to drag the refrigerator up against the door to stop it from banging. The storm is bringing warm air up from the lower Caribbean, and pushing the cool air back up to Canada where it belongs. On a midnight tour of inspection, I discovered that my door is the only one that is banging. The bar downstairs is closed tight, I can't get a beer, and I'd go for a late-night walk around town but if I open the front door it'll disturb the bartender snoring on the lobby sofa.

Back in my room, the film version of Jorge Amado's *Tieta the Goat Girl* is playing on television, with Sonia Braga as Tieta. My two windows have bright red curtains and the two beds bright red bedspreads. Both the curtains and the spreads have little wallpaperlike windmill motifs, with images of bells and flowers and mountains all over the place.

The wailing wind keeps my brain spinning. At first sight of this hotel I imagined how pleasant to be lulled to sleep by the pounding waves. But there's nothing lulling about this storm. Cachita, Virgin of Charity, let your storm abate a bit, so that I will be fully rested in the morning and less likely to be in a bad mood when people start fighting each other to get into my car. Men and women flee their spouses from time to time, but excuse me if I don't want to be involved. It wasn't as if I'd abandoned those guys in the middle of nowhere. It was a shady spot by the sea, and there was a cheap resort for Cubans just down the walk. They both had backpacks, and I'm sure they had a few pesos in their pockets. It's unlikely I'll ever find out what happened to them, but who can predict? I'll imagine them having a great day at the resort, then spending the night there as well, with luck.

It's odd that as I lie here in a room where Che once spent a night, I spend hours trying to improve it, pushing the bed against the wall so the pillows won't slip to the floor, trying to devise a way of keeping windows with the latches broken off from blowing open in the stiff winds, and pushing a fridge against the door in order to stop it from banging. It took Che longer to improve Cuba, but I'm trying to do the same thing, one room at a time. Everything's perfect here for now.

Hours later, after a leisurely breakfast, I visited the studio of the old painter René Frómeta, who, as a child, born in Baracoa to unlettered *campesinos*, was adopted by a fabulously wealthy Russian opera singer. It's a Cinderella story with the genders reversed. Her name was Magdalena Rovenskaia Manacer, but most were content to call her La Rusa, or sometimes La Mina, or La Mina of the Hotel La Rusa. She had as many names as Cachita. Amazing that after spending all those years with the polyglot La Mina and her foreign friends, René still only speaks Spanish. But he understands my English a bit now and then, as I do his Spanish, and somehow he never fails to laugh at my little jokes. Maybe he's like Fidel, he understands English perfectly but prefers not to speak it.

Old René sat there watching intently as I studied the thirty or forty various-sized watercolours and oils on his studio wall. He modestly called himself a *primitivo*, but seemed pleased when I insisted he was more of a *realistico*. His subject matter was the bright beautiful colours, shapes, textures, and history of Baracoa, which is suspected

. of having been an inspiration for Gabriel García Marquez's *One Hundred Years of Solitude.*

He said that La Rusa was *muy artistico*, an opera singer in fact, and she fled the Bolshevik Revolution when her whole family was killed. But she eventually embraced the Cuban Revolution. Some suggest it might not have been successful without her embrace. Accompanied by her husband, Albert, she spent several years giving concerts all over the free world, but one night she arrived in Havana and gave a concert there. It was 1930, the economy was in terrible shape, and somehow she stumbled upon Baracoa, which was isolated from the rest of Cuba, no communication, no roads, a little country all on its own. Except that it was owned by the United Fruit Company.

She apparently didn't get along with the United Fruit Company, nor did she care for Batista and his friends. Fidel and Che were another story. When they arrived on the scene she jumped at the chance to have clandestine meetings with them, and she made numerous large deposits to their bank. She also bought the hotel, and René showed me pictures of what the place looked like at the time, before she added a bar, a restaurant, and a third floor, transforming a seedy seaside villa into a romantic seaside hotel. One woman, two revolutions. Fidel visited the hotel twice, Che three times. They all came to Baracoa to meet with La Rusa. She gave them $25 million in gold to help finance the Revolution, according to René.

La Mina died of cancer in 1978. Not sure how old she was, but René, who was a keen photographer in those days, was a mere fifty-two. He gets out the albums and shows photos of her, some by him. The camera loved her, even in old age. He showed me her well-preserved lighter. "Too much smoke and coffee too," he said. He also showed me a bound photocopy of the manuscript of *La Consagraçion de la Primavera*, by the late Cuban novelist Alejo Carpentier, and said that Vera is the name of the character based on La Mina.

Everybody's beautiful here. René shows me a photo of La Mina's long-dead mama, and even she was beautiful. And the photo of himself at age twenty-three was extremely handsome, in the García Lorca mould, with slicked-back hair.

René was not inspired to paint by La Mina, but much earlier, by his real mother, rather than his adopted one. He has a painting of Columbus coming into Baracoa, plus a lot of paintings of Baracoa from odd angles, including from great heights, perhaps remembered from airplane rides. He is very much a slave of the town he has lived in all his life. He paints the town more often than Picasso painted his mistresses. He is more interested in the town as a whole, and as seen from different angles, and the people in his paintings seem to play a secondary role.

He met and spoke with Che in the hotel in 1959, and the year that he was killed, 1967. What was he like? He shook his head frowningly and said, "Too intelligent." The Baracoa area is famous in Europe and Japan for its "ecological coffee," grown without chemicals. About 2,500 tons of it are exported each year. But it was the cocoa plant in Baracoa that Che inaugurated, and it is still going strong. Maybe that's what he was doing at the Hotel La Rusa. But according to René, Che was there for two nights and all he did was drink, eat, and sleep. He was probably recovering from a period of strenuous labour, or maybe from an asthma attack. It's hard to imagine Che doing nothing unless it was for health reasons. René had no memory of Che and Fidel being here together.

As for the late great Errol Flynn, it was "drink drink drink, too much drink." He would come in on his yacht, along with six or seven beautiful young women. Of the poet Nicholas Guillén, "I don't remember too much." René seemed to think there was nothing memorable about him, even though he's the Cuban poet today you most often hear about.

"La Rusa was a member of one of the richest families in Russia," said René. She would have been a White Russian, the rough equivalent of the Batista gang who gathered up their cash and jewellery and got out of the country when Fidel rolled into town. When René met her, she was forty-one, and a great beauty. "She became very special to me. She opened my eyes to art, and poetry, and fine music, and culture. I am the son of poor farmers. Everybody admired La Mina in Baracoa. She could speak eight languages. English, Italian,

French, Portuguese, Spanish, Russian, and two more. Albert had a heart attack and died in Santiago de Cuba in 1956. She lived another twenty-two years."

René said he likes to paint the ghosts of long ago. He claimed to be "a painter naturale, no academico. I poeta too. Oh yes, maybe twenty libros."

He showed me some of his books of poems, he showed me stacks of letters to La Mina bearing stamps from different countries, he showed me old first-aid manuals from before the Great Depression, also some dazzling polymites. I started reading some of his poems aloud. I told him this is real poetry, because I have no problem understanding it even in Spanish. He repaid my compliment by saying, "Your pronunciation is very good!" Whenever I tried to praise his poems he would tell me I was mistaken. Many of his poems were composed of eight rhyming quatrains. But he even denied that, and he said no, it's merely sentimental free verse.

I protested. Not sentimental, impassioned! The poetry of a man who is deliriously happy about living in Baracoa. Yes, he sighed. He asked if I were a poet of the academies. No, I said, I'm just like you, except that I am not deliriously happy about where I live.

When I said farewell and got back to the hotel I remembered I hadn't given him any money. He'd shown no concern. Enrique and others told me it would have been better to give him a little token of my appreciation, everyone else does, so I went back. From the street his eyes were closed and his head slumped down slumberingly. I said, Señor? René? He snapped to consciousness, and I passed five dollars to him through the window. He was very happy about that. And I told him I'd try to translate his poem into English and send it to him.

At the bank the teller said he wasn't allowed to change dollars to pesos, but he wrote down the address of a bank where it would be possible. I hopped on a bicycle taxi, and just as we were about to take off a lovely young lady put her face very close to mine and told me in impeccable English that I shouldn't park right in front of the bank, I should pull ahead about twenty feet. So I did, and just then the armoured car pulled up right in the spot where I had been parked. Guards jumped out brandishing pistols with very long barrels, and started toting bags of money back and forth from their armoured car to the bank.

"If you think I speak good English," said the lovely lady, "it is because I teach English at the language school. You would be welcome to come and see what we do there." She smiled very sincerely and I made some lame excuse. This will be a big regret, I realize it even before we've said goodbye. But for some damn reason I thanked her and said I wouldn't be able to. Some other time maybe. And I don't know why I didn't do it. It would have been really interesting.

The bicycle taxi guy waited faithfully for me in the second bank, then he took me back to the bank where I had parked my car. It was a long ride, from one end of this big town (est. pop. 48,300) to the other, and I was pretending to help him. Whenever he had to pump hard to get up to speed or to get up a little incline, I'd be grunting and groaning right along with him, and pretending I was desperately rowing a boat to help speed him along, as if by magic. Other cyclists would catch up with us and have a little chat with the driver, and to get a good look at the crazy gringo. English-speaking tourists in Cuba are not noted for their sense of humour, and even the most pathetic joke goes a long way. When we got back to the first bank, and when I considered how he had sweated his heart out on my behalf, I gave him, tentatively, a twenty-peso note, and he was absolutely blown away. Was he being facetious? No, he was genuinely in a state bordering on shock; he was, in a word, astonished. He must be used to getting one peso max for such a trip. In Havana twenty pesos for all that work would have been received with an air of contempt.

Apparently the language school is just a little place where the lovely lady teaches English to the locals. Maybe she's the reason so many Baracoans do speak English. She seemed to be a very fine person, about thirty-five, and I still do not know why I instinctively turned down her invitation. The mature freshness of her face, the wide-open friendly intelligence of her eyes – maybe in my subconscious heart I knew if I spent an hour or two with her I'd be unable to leave. Could that be it? Good enough reason, I suppose. That's my story and I'm sticking to it.

On the way out of town I became disoriented and stopped to ask a cop for directions. Big mistake! I asked how to get to the airport, because I could see on the map the airport was on the way I wanted to go, and if I could get to the airport it would be clear sailing. He ignored my request for directions and said I'd driven the wrong way on a one-way street. It's not a huge crime, there's very little traffic, and the street I turned down had many parked cars facing the wrong way. At first the officer shook my hand, which was a good sign. But then I noticed he hadn't removed his black leather glove, which was a bad sign. I thanked him for pointing out the tiny one-way sign that I had overlooked. So everything was fine. I was about to take off, without having received any help with directions, when he came back and asked to see my passport.

He was a handsome tall slender black guy on a motorcycle. He asked me many questions about my passport, and wrote everything down. Then he asked to see the lease agreement for the car, so I took my passport back to the car, left it in the car, and took the lease back to him. He scrutinized the lease, and scribbled on it a note to the effect that I had been looking for the airport and went down a one-way street. Then he wanted to see my passport again, so I went to the car and retrieved it. Then he wanted to see my driver's licence. So I went back to the car, put my lease and passport in the glove compartment, and came back with my driver's licence. Then he wanted to see my passport again, and so on.

By this time several locals and even some tourists had gathered around, biting their lips and wondering when I was going to lose my cool. Finally the blood started draining from my face, and I told him, in very slow, precise, frigid, and unfriendly terms, "No matter how long I live and no matter how hopelessly lost I may be in the future, I shall never again ask a Cuban cop for directions." He heard what I said, it definitely registered, especially when I turned, hopped in the car, and without asking permission took off real fast, leaving him to eat my dust.

He had the class and intelligence not to hop on his motorcycle and chase me down, or pull his gun on me. I think he was basically innocent, just a guy hoping to get some dirt on a single male tourist, who could very well have been heading for the airport to pick up a shipment of drugs or explosives. He was looking for that big promotion that makes all the difference in life. Everyone knows single male tourists are slimy bastards up to no good. Even Errol Flynn, when he sailed to Baracoa, had an entourage, perhaps to avoid suspicion.

Speaking of innocence, there on the main street of busy Baracoa stood a young boy about five years old proudly having a powerful piss, with people walking around him with little smiles on their faces, and he had a little smile on his face too. A few blocks later I saw a full-grown man having a pee on the side of the road. I shall keep my eyes peeled and report any other examples of outdoor urination.

For the next few hours I drove, slowly and calmly, absorbing impressions and soaking up the biodiversity, along the coastal highway running north and west from Baracoa to Moa. The broad and rhyming Río Toa was studded with pretty islands, and people were standing in the water up to their waist and doing their laundry. Now and then there would be a brilliant bay, and when I stopped and looked out to where the bay opened up into the sea, the waves would be breaking like dazzling white eyebrows on a bright green face. At one point several men from young to old had set up tables and chairs and were having a domino tournament in the cool shady mouth of a massive limestone cave. One guy spotted me coming and ran like mad to the side of the road, trying to wave me down, and pointing in the direction I was going. But I just wanted to be alone, and I suspected he just wanted to ride with a tourist in an air-conditioned car and maybe get dropped off at the next village where he could visit with his cousin. The situation makes me feel a bit like God, deciding who gets picked up and who doesn't. Not a pleasant feeling.

The sea is very chocolatey in toward the shore, as if someone has dumped a thousand tons of cocoa into the bay, with its little lakelike ripples, protected from the ocean waves by a reef that causes them to break prematurely. This is near the town of Punta Gorda, where the Río Cayo Guam flows into the sea, and there is a small-bore pipeline that starts up here and runs along the shore for ten miles. It appears to be a cocoa pipeline. It runs along the side of the road, and it is painted green, very expertly constructed, and with no signs of leakage. In fact there are two pipelines, side by side, like a two-lane highway, and each one is about two feet in diameter. Whenever there is a road leading down to the sea, as there is every mile or so, the twin pipelines take a dip and run underground for the width of the road, then pop up on the other side. And whenever I catch a glimpse of the sea, there is what appears to be cocoa sludge hugging the shore, like a benign oil spill.

Then along comes a sign saying that it is prohibited to take photos of the pipeline. I can see why, because any pipeline, even if it is just for cocoa, would be an inviting target for the enemy. No wonder the pipeline is painted green, it's harder to see from the air. Imagine how proud you'd be if you were to score a direct hit on a cocoa pipeline in a poverty-stricken country. You could gloat for the rest of your life.

Closer to the big town of Moa (est. pop. 93,000), the pipeline divides into four or five smaller pipelines. There are numerous billboards, but most of them simply bear stirring Revolutionary slogans, and none indicates what commodity is being refined, manufactured, exported, or imported. There's a Cuban flag blowing in the breeze, and immediately below it a Canadian flag similarly all a-flutter, and behind it is a picture of Che about twenty by thirty feet, with the slogan: Hasta la Victoria Siempre. Somewhere around here there is a well-known Canadian-Cuban nickel-cobalt mining venture (Cuban-owned, Canadian-operated, formerly owned and operated by Freeport of Louisiana but expropriated in 1959), but surely raw nickel couldn't be mistaken for cocoa. There's a huge reservoir full of something, and several others in the background, with green pipelines leading out from them. The soil around the vats is a chocolate colour. But there is no chocolate smell in the air, no matter how hard I sniff.

A security guard with a gun in his holster looks as if he's going to give me the business. He calms down and smiles when I tell him I'm a Canadian, but he still wants to know where I'm coming from and where I'm going. When I tell him – from Baracoa and to Holguín – he says this is not a thoroughfare, go back to the port and turn left. You came a little too far up, he adds. And then, charmingly, he apologizes – perhaps for not having the road properly signposted, perhaps for thinking I was a terrorist sniffing out places to bomb.

But then as I took off I did get a strong sudden whiff of chocolate in the air. And I could see that only one of the vats contained a cocoalike substance, the others seemed to contain clear water. One doesn't think of a cocoa-refining plant being that large, but this one is.

Where do the U.S. chocolate bar manufacturers get their cocoa from. From Mars? I wouldn't be surprised if they get it from countries that have imported it from Cuba. No wonder the United States is in financial trouble. All it has to do is accept one of Fidel's numerous olive branches, then it can start trading straight with Cuba again. But big countries tend to carry big grudges for long periods of time, while little countries, though they may have a bit of a (chocolate) chip on their shoulder, tend to be very forgiving. Fidel could be won over in a flash. Everybody knows that. But winning Fidel over is not on the U.S. agenda. All they want to do is murder him over and over again. In Estela Bravo's documentary film, *Fidel*, a reporter asks El Beardo how many attempts on his life have been made. Fidel looks very thoughtful for a long minute, as if counting, then gives up and says, "I'll tell you when I get to heaven."

Now it's late afternoon. How long will it take to reach Holguín? Shadows are starting to obscure the potholes in the road, so that they become like sharks in the water. This could be a problem. So one must be ever vigilant regarding shadows on the road. That shadow could be concealing a deadly pothole. And is it true they're called potholes because hippies used to hide their marijuana in them? Maybe not, but these potholes are so deep you could grow marijuana in them. And in Cuba, everywhere you turn it's some magnificent new tree or flower you've never seen before. Just passed a group of five or six tall trees with huge white flowers, interspersed with a group of equally tall trees with bright orange flowers. And, towering over them all, a single royal palm.

I stop to stretch my legs and along comes a group of teens. They see me and start pointing to a sixteen-year-old girl in a white dress with a big smile on her dark brown face, with her big bright red lips. And they're calling me over, as a stereotypical single male tourist, and saying, Here here here, she's all yours. Take her! So I'm rubbing my hands together and licking my lips, pretending I want to take her away with me, and they don't mind at all, and neither does she. I can take her wherever I want and it's no disgrace to anyone. As long as she's willing and has passed her fifteenth birthday. If they want to f**k foreigners to finance their future, they're free to do so. Then along comes an Afro-Cuban daddy, his wife, his brother, an old horse, and two very handsome Afro-Cuban boys, identical twins, about eight years old. The boys were quietly listening as we grown-ups chatted. A couple of times I said "yes" rather than "sí." One of the boys said "yes" out of the blue, just as an experiment in sound. Then he kept saying it over and over again, just because he liked the sound. Finally I laughed and called him "El Inglese!" Everyone laughed, so I pointed at his brother and said, "El Cubano!" Again more laughter, but this time the laughter was more serious, more hesitant, as if this might prove to be some kind of omen, some eerie precognition that foretold something that was going to happen to the two little guys when they grew up. Suddenly we all felt a bit spooked.

Holguín is a big city – population 200,000 people and a garbage truck, according to the tragically brilliant counter-revolutionary novelist Reinaldo Arenas. But in recent years the estimated population has leaped to 319,100. It's very quiet in the suburbs this late at night. First impression was of a clean and well-maintained city of broad main streets and interesting art deco buildings. Arenas also

referred to Holguín as "a town totally lacking in spiritual or architectural beauty." But he felt that way about pretty well everything to
do with Cuba.

I parked my car at the main square named after the nineteenth-
century general Calixto García. Everything was open, with lots of
music – but actual people seemed to have gone to bed early and all
the main hotels were fully occupied. I was referred to the Hotel
Turquino farther from the square, but there were no vacancies
there either. A young woman with a warm smile earned a nice tip
by walking me several blocks to a *casa particulare*. She told me
Holguín was an extraordinarily difficult city to find your way
around in. She couldn't explain why, but even people who have
lived here all their lives still get lost on a daily basis. It was like an
ancient curse come true.

But the *casa* seemed just right and I decided to take it for two days.
Then I went back to the main square to get my car and park it in
their garage, as per their kind offer. But even though it was only a
few blocks, I couldn't find my way. I hailed a bicycle taxi and he got
lost. He was a good cyclist, but he didn't know his city well. Finally
he got me to my car and I took off in it only to get lost myself almost
immediately, in spite of my seemingly excellent map of the town.
The *casa* was marked on the map to ensure I wouldn't get lost, and I
knew exactly where I was on the map at just about any given time.
But somehow I couldn't manage to get from where I was on the map
to where the *casa* was on the map.

It was after midnight and I was so tired I hired a young fellow on
a bicycle to guide me. He said he knew exactly where the place was.
He asked if his *chica* could ride with me in my car and he would
bicycle ahead and we could follow. He cycled very fast, like the wind,
all over town, with his *chica* chatting amiably with me. She was
twenty-three, very pretty, and with a shy look many young Cuban
women adopt. She had very bad halitosis as if she had been eating
something she had found at the side of the road.

Her friend soon had taken us from one end of town to the other
several times, so I told him I'd find the place on my own if I could.
He had no idea where the address was, even though I could see

clearly on the map it was just a few blocks from the main square. So the *chica* got out, I paid him and continued searching on my own – without success. My hosts, who were keeping the light on for me, would be getting very tired, as was I.

After ten minutes I ran into the cyclist and his *chica* again. They were frantically flagging me down. The *chica*, who had been propositioning me in the car, apparently on orders from her boyfriend, who frankly didn't seem smart enough to be a pimp, had left her keys in my car. She was overjoyed to get them back in her possession.

And then I found the place, all on my own. My hostess, Yoelkís, and her husband, a couple in their sixties, were standing outside, suspecting I was lost, and hoping to flag me down even though they had no idea what kind of car it would be, except probably a tourist rental car with TO on the licence plate.

AN AFTERNOON
IN HOLGUÍN

Monday, March 1, 2004. El Parque Calixto García is paved with marble tiles about four feet by four feet. Some of them are coming up a bit, creating dangerous conditions for the roller skaters. Dozens of laughing children, in ordinary running shoes but with rollers attached, are zooming around and around the statue at top speed, but they seem to know the location of every loose tile, and they do an excellent job of negotiating disaster. I don't know if the Cuban people get their fearlessness from Fidel or he gets it from them, but it's everywhere.

The park is very crowded. A feeble older fellow walks by wearing a T-shirt saying, Old Men Marry Nurses. Excellent advice. Young men too. You never know when you're going to need a little nursing, young or old. I never knew a man who regretted having married a nurse. There must be a hundred schoolkids in the park, some wearing mustard trousers or skirts, some in red trousers or skirts, with matching scarves and white blouses – and they are all randomly intermingled. But as soon as the teachers blow their whistles, all the mustards go to one teacher and all the reds go to another.

An Afro-Cuban woman is sitting next to me on a shady part of the long bench that goes all the way around the park. She starts talking about her hair. She says, "See, my hair is African," and she has these long strings with beads on them that must consume at least an hour a day in maintenance time. "Most people just comb their hair, but I have to do this. I don't know why, I just have to do it." I told her it looked lovely and she was pleased. And I was pleased because something about me aroused her curiosity, and she wanted to know everything about me, seriously asking me personal questions in a very gentle and non-threatening way. She was trying to figure out what a guy from Toronto was doing in Holguín. So I told her I was on a tour, gathering impressions for a little poetic travelogue.

It turned out she'd seen me walking around the park and talking into my tape recorder, and she said, "You better watch out, the police will think you might be a spy, and will be interested in listening to your tapes." I suddenly felt a bit foolish, and quickly put the tape recorder away. But I convinced her easily enough about my innocence, and so I felt I'd have no problem convincing the police likewise.

Three other Afro-Cuban women joined us, one close to nine months' pregnant. When they found out how friendly I was, and that I had wheels, they suggested all four of us go up to Playa Guardalavaca – one of the more famous beaches on the north shore – for an afternoon swim in Bahía Naranjo. All four were making swimming motions to make sure I knew exactly what they meant. I told them I didn't bring my bathing suit. They laughed and said don't worry, they could find something for me. I can't remember how I managed to get out of that without being too rude, but I managed somehow. It was tempting, they were very nice, I could pay for everything and it would still be a cheap date, and I was sure it would be a ton of fun, but I had visions of disaster. And so I declined. I liked these women a lot, they were beautiful, *muy simpatico*, full of joy, but for reasons I don't understand I told them I was on a tight schedule and had to move on.

Among the numerous schoolchildren, with their teachers shepherding them around, many seem to have eye problems. In one class of about fourteen kids, four of them had bandages over their eyes – freshly applied medical patches. And there were several such groups

of kids milling around with their teachers. And one girl was completely blind: she didn't have any patches over her eyes, was staring
off into nothingness, and the teacher was escorting her by hand. It's
a cool breezy day and even though she was blind, whenever she felt
her skirt was going to fly up with the breeze she made sure her hand
was there to keep herself from becoming overly exposed to the sight
of others. She was about twelve, but close to six feet tall and with
pure white hair and pale skin.

The wind did blow the skirt of an older woman in her mid-
twenties way up, and she "forgot" to hold it down. Before I could
avert my eyes I saw all the way to her belly button, and she looked
very astonished, and I looked very astonished, then she turned away
with the cutest little smile. A sexy moment. She was quite happy
about it happening, and you could tell she was only pretending to be
shocked and surprised.

There are at least three large two-storey departmentlike peso
stores around this park. I was looking for a string for my eyeglasses
but couldn't find one. The saleswomen just shook their heads no.
One woman wearing glasses with a string on them gave me a very
conscious smug look when she refused to sell me her string, as if she
was pleased that she had one and I didn't; furthermore, I must be the
cheesiest tourist of the day for even asking, and what kind of a
cheapskate is this guy for trying such a trick in a peso store. But I did
take my belt off and had a fresh hole punched in it by a young leather
worker who refused to take my money. It's hard to beat the security
of knowing that your pants won't fall down as you walk down the
street. For those with U.S. dollars there is no real shortage of food in
Cuba, but with the heat and all, I've been abstemious in the extreme
on this trip, and the flab from head to toe has been melting off me.
I'm skinnier than I've been since I bought this belt ten years ago, and
it feels good. The less blubber we have to carry around the happier
we have to be. Also it can't be good for the soul to gorge yourself on
three-course meals when all around you are people who can only
afford to nosh.

The kids in this park are full of unalloyed joy, delightful spontaneity, and unsurpassed innocence – even the ones with eye problems.

Anything that moves in the wind, from a tissue to a cola can, the boys have to stop it with their feet and play soccer with it. Two kids right now, believe it or not, are playing soccer with a stiff little leaf that has fallen from a laurel tree, although they prefer to play with an unsquashed can if they can find one, but these seem to be in short supply, so they will settle for a squashed one. But now and then a plastic beer cup, unsquashed, will appear out of nowhere and a new game of soccer will ensue.

A grungy old lonesome guy came by, and he was going along the perimeter benches, stopping at every person and asking for a handout. The entire park is ringed with benches, as with most of the central squares in the larger towns and cities sprinkled here and there randomly around Cuba. He was getting the occasional handout. I churlishly told him no, so he very cutely pretended he was going to hang himself with some of the Sentería artifacts on an old leather cord around his neck. Oh all right, I said, and gave him a little brown coin, with a picture of Che on one side and a five-pointed star on the other. The guy next to me, a male sex tourist from Italy, gave him substantially more, maybe to impress his beautiful Afro-Cuban amiga. And the supplicant then tried to throw his unwashed arms around him and give him a big wet kiss, causing the Italian to squirm out of the way, saying, "No, no, no. ¡Vamos!"

A white kid and a black kid, both wearing sleeveless T-shirts with number 10 on the front and SATISFACTION on the back, were kickboxing for a while, but now they have reverted to ordinary boxing. The white kid is much smaller, but he's lightning fast. Now they've stopped boxing and are reviewing the few strategic moves they've picked up so far, such as how to know when to bob and when to weave. Soccer and the martial arts are the perfect sports for the poor countries of the world: no sports require less equipment. Parents invest obscene amounts of money in outfitting their kids for hockey in Canada.

"Boxing is well suited to the Cuban character: we are brave, resolute, selfless," says Alcides Sagarra, a coach at Cuba's National Boxing School in Havana. There was an interview with him in a recent report from Reuters. "We have strong convictions and clear definition. We are pugnacious and we like to fight, to win. We are training to take all eleven gold medals in Athens. Thinking small doesn't give results."

Alcides must have received a huge jolt of inspiration in 2002, when Cuba's wrestling team won all seven gold medals at the Pan-American Games in Santo Domingo, restricting the U.S. team to four silvers.

The statue of General Calixto is dated 1912. He looks a bit like Teddy Roosevelt, leaning on his sword, and with a long moustache. But strangely, from this distance, it looks as if he's wet his pants – his crotch area is all dark and greasy while the rest of him is white as chalk. The plaque on the side has been torn off, also a plaque on the other side has gone the way of all plaques. But the one on the front is still there for now.

I've been walking around the park, being pestered by touts who want to sell me cigars, and trying to avoid the extremely beautiful, well-dressed, bright-as-blazes street hookers who are just trying to make ends meet, so to speak. They snuggle right up to you, and touch you intimately, and tell you about a little *casa particulare* that wasn't very particular, and where the two of you could go, and they ask what sort of things you like. I asked one very comely and intelligent young woman: Where is your boyfriend? Is he watching us right now? She said nothing but shyly looked over to a handsome young fellow sitting on a bench watching us with a big smile on his face.

Then she became very nervous and abruptly walked away for about ten paces, then turned around and beckoned me to follow her, at a safe distance. Apparently she saw a police officer heading toward us, looking as if he was going to tear the heart out of our budding relationship. She said that kind of thing happens all the time. Personal enrichment is what the charge is called, and it seems that the less well off you are the more you are likely to get punished for it. But it's not nearly as bad as it was ten years ago, when it was common to be thrown in jail for operating a restaurant out of your home (called a *paladare*), even on the most occasional basis. Fidel still doesn't approve of that kind of home cooking, so it's said, but at least he's been convinced it has to be allowed, and although Fidel has often been called a Stalinist by his enemies, I don't think it was possible to get Stalin to change his mind about anything. Fidel is constantly changing his mind as his thoughts evolve, and the thoughts of the Cuban people evolve.

So we wandered some more. I told her I'd like to meet her boyfriend, so she said wait here and she disappeared. Ten minutes later and no word from them. So I went back to the bench and sat there in the moonlight for a while. Yes, it's night already and the moon is shining off the alabaster head of the long-dead Calixto García, who was born in this city in 1840, and died in Washington in 1898, after fighting many battles against Spanish tyranny, arm in arm with José Martí, Antonio Maceo, and Máximo Gómez.

One fellow kept coming around and wanted a dollar for a mouldy old cigar he'd been carrying in his pocket for a week. Failing that, he could get me a *chica* or two. It's so embarrassing. He won't take no for an answer. He was like the cat who came back, and maybe because of some kind of impairment of the part of the brain that remembers faces, he keeps asking me, as if for the first time, if I want a *chica*. For instance, the first time he said where you from, I said Canada, and he said, *Canadá, mucho bueno*. The second and third time it was the same thing. The fourth time he asked where I was from I said Saskatoon, Saskatchewan, and he was rather startled. He looked at my face to see if I was Tibetan or Mongolian or maybe from a distant galaxy. *Chica?* Mouldy cigar? "Deseo nada," I told him for the fifth or sixth time, and he would understand, but not for long.

The seventh and final time he accosted me in a crowd surrounding a peanut vendor, and very quietly offered to get me a *chica*. So I lost my cool. I screeched angrily, at the top of my lungs, "NO CHICA!" About a hundred people immediately turned to look at him. I didn't think he'd be capable of embarrassment, but this was his town, and he was extremely embarrassed. He disappeared instantly and I didn't see him again.

So, there's no need to run when you're being pestered by *moscas*. If someone is really pestering you persistently, just hold your ground, and whatever it is they're trying to sell you, just yell out, "NO CHICA!" It's more effective than fly spray. And remember, Fidel is on your side. He likes to see the tourists happy.

The tallest building on the main square of Holguín is the public library. It's a near twin of the Hotel Santa Clara Libre, although it doesn't have any bullet holes, and it is badly in need of a paint job. But it has those vertical art deco alternating forest-green and sea-green stripes from the pavement to the roof, and it's a handsome building, though squatter and less tall and slenderly elegant than the hotel. From the front of the library, a large bank of speakers was rolled out into the park and Cuban music filled the plaza, causing everybody to be completely incapable of resisting dancing. Even a certain stodgy old Canadian was tapping his feet a bit. The speakers were set up to fill the square with a grand landscape of music, but a short block or two away and you don't hear it at all. Ground zero is right in front of the library, and readers will be glad to know that it was not until the library was closed before the volume was cranked up.

The old San José church from 1820, rebuilt in the 1950s, is located in Plaza San José, a few blocks north of Parque Calixto García. In wandering around the interior, I was suddenly very taken with one station of the cross, where Jesus has stumbled under the weight of his burden, and you can see he's suffering intensely, all the suffering a solitary human being is capable of suffering. But the artist has somehow managed to make his eyes look radiant, they are on a superior plane entirely, above and beyond all suffering, and there is the most peaceful look on his face, as if he is understanding all, accepting all, forgiving all. It's a very sturdy grey stone church, with a rather unusual and eye-pleasing exterior, you might call it neo-Romanesque, and it's odd the way that whatever church one visits somehow tends to become the most beautiful church in the world, at least for the duration.

Also in the church was a tiny old lady with a terribly worried look on her face, she was doing the stations of the cross and crossing herself and praying desperately at each station. The only other person in here was stretched out on the back pew, and although he wasn't snoring all that much, he was definitely deeply in dreamland. Outside in the plaza there is a kiosk selling beer, and someone has set up a music system over which Beethoven's *Piano Sonata No. 14* is playing. The speakers weren't excellent, they didn't have the clarity of the speakers in the main square, but in these surroundings, somehow, there's a harmony, and a warmth, and a friendliness, even among the desperate people praying for their children, or the desperate people trying to sell you cigars and *chicas*, there's something about the city that melds everyone together, even the tourists. Everybody looks kindly upon each other, and even the police seemed to be charmed by the beautiful music. It was a special version of the *Moonlight Sonata* with a choir in the background. Sounds as if it would be hokey, but it almost had me in tears as I sat there drinking my icy-cold Cristal. The Beethoven was followed by *Rhapsody in Blue*, with the same pianist and the same chorus in the background.

I was chatting with Enmo, a beautiful woman close to thirty, and definitely no *chica*. She was with her mother, Mirian, a very proud, blond, curly-haired woman who claims to be fifty-two years old, and has a very interesting way of walking, with shoulders pinned back, and swaying side to side, very proud of her sexuality, and nicely pleased with herself. Enmo is much more conservative, and refuses to strut her stuff like her mama does. Enmo says she has an evangelistic sister in Florida who goes around collecting money for the church in Cuba. She hasn't been back to Cuba in years.

It all started with this well-dressed guy with extremely angular features and a sharp chin and nose and a brand-new white cotton peaked cap of the sort that Cuban motorists wore in the 1920s. He was an artisan, and had carved two whales out of very fine and smoothly sanded and shellacked wood, in dark brown and pale yellow, and was trying to sell them in the park to tourists for five dollars each. Each whale had a little hole in the bottom, where a dowel was inserted, to form a stand for display purposes. A lot of patient work went into these artifacts, and everybody in the park was admiring them but nobody was buying them.

Enmo and Mirian spotted me as a tourist and called me over to have a look at these whales. Tourists were in short supply and they were trying to help the guy make a sale. Enmo knew him and said he was an Italian who came to Cuba for a holiday one winter and just never went home. He's been here for five years now. Funny the way we sheep will sometimes hop the fence and never return to the old meadow, no matter how lushly it may loom in our memory. Nothing bothers him, he seems very happy, he's not desperate, he's just one with all the poor people, doing his whales and being apparently unable to sell them, at least in this park and on this day.

Enmo seemed very impressed with my pathetic Spanish, and positively beamed with pleasure when I said that I admired the whales but had no desire to own one. She told me she works in the tourist resorts on the beaches just north of here, but even though she desperately wants a full-time gig she only gets short terms of two or three weeks, so she spends most of her time near the phone waiting for the "agency" to call. Even though she has the perfect personality and appearance for such a job and her English is good, they haven't phoned in months.

Canadian tourists often come home complaining about the lack of news available in Cuba. But Enmo said that besides *Granma* Cubans get an hour's worth of world news every night at 8:30 on channel 3, and they know all about the problems in the United States since George W. Bush took power, they know about the 9/11 disaster and the disastrous invasions of Afghanistan and Iraq. Many have their own computers, which they share freely with others, and Internet access as well. She told me exactly what she knew and it seemed pretty solid to me. She also told me that the Cubans, when they see the news from Iraq, are very solemn, maybe even bitter, and they know that Cuba could be next. And she confirmed that there are people who are building bomb shelters here and there around the country. People are getting very weary of the cruelty of the blockade, after more than forty years of suffering under it. They do not understand why it is they can't have a slightly alternate system all their own. Oh, it's just hopeless. But she said every Cuban senses clearly that the United States is capable of doing to Cuba what they've done to Iraq. It's like trying to raise your little family in a little house when next door there is a huge house full of numerous homicidal maniacs who despise them, and all the other little houses on the street as well.

We talked about Holguín, and the husband and father who hasn't been heard from in ages. I invited the ladies into the coffee shop. I had a beer and they had canned fruit juice that didn't look very appetizing. Enmo and I were merrily chatting away, but Mirian was bored, though she'd give us a smile from time to time.

At the next table there was a young Japanese man, looking very much alone, a sort of awkward solitude you sensed in him. He had a backpack, and was obviously a lonesome traveller, and he had a Cuba guide in Japanese, so I was identifying with him, and hoping that I didn't look so glum and awkward when I was sitting alone in Cuban cafés. He went up to pay for the cheese sandwich and beer he had. It was a nice cool place to drink beer just off Parque Calixto. I said, "Should we call him over? He looks so lonesome." Enmo said "Yes, that's a great idea." So we called him over. He got telling us that he was an economist with a special interest in Cuba because Cuban music is currently very popular in Japan, and people in Japan are very concerned about Cuba, and so he just wanted to visit Cuba to see what it was like, and he said he was having a fabulous time. As soon as we invited him to sit down, his demeanour changed, and he became happy and cheery. He spoke excellent English but was having terrible problems with Spanish, and maybe that was why he looked so glum. He was so happy to be able to speak English to at least two of us. Enmo had been asking many questions about my writing, she was very inquisitive about my book. So she told the Japanese guy, "David is a famous Canadian writer." To which I added, "One of many thousands." And I told him I'm a great fan of Japanese food, fiction, and poetry and had read a great number of famous writers from his country, both past and present, in translation.

He of course wanted to know which writers. And this has to be the most embarrassing moment of my life. My mind went blank. I couldn't remember the names of any one of the Japanese writers I'd spent so many delicious hours reading over the years. I could remember reading *The Tale of Genji* but could remember neither title nor author. I could remember reading numerous books by Kawabata and Mishima down through the years, but I couldn't remember their names. I couldn't even remember my love affairs with Basho, Issa, Lady Murasaki, Natsume Soseki (*Kokoro*), Osamu Dazai (*Self Portraits*), and Ogai Mori (*Vita Sexualis*). And I couldn't remember Masuji Ibuse (*Black Rain*), Abe Kobo (*Woman in the Dunes*), Junichiro Tanizaki (*Makioka Sisters*), and so on, all of whom had altered my life at various stages. I felt as if I was trapped in a whirlpool, my brain refused to yield up a name to save my life. So I just looked helpless and unhappy, which caused him to snort derisively.

With Enmo and Mirian waiting patiently for me to remember the names of all the Japanese authors I claimed to have read, the Japanese guy became utterly astonished and asked if I was crazy. In fact, he looked right into my sad eyes and said, "Are you crazy?" But Enmo didn't like that. And so he left.

Still, I was impressed by his seventeen-hour flight (not including a stopover in Cancun) from Tokyo to a country he wanted to see just because the music of that country was currently hot in Japan. But it would have been more impressive if he'd said he came to Cuba because he himself liked Cuban culture, rather than because it's the current craze. Sounds like he's trying to cash in on a trend rather than set a trend or follow his heart. But maybe his job is to chase trends. Maybe he's a journalist for some financial paper.

So here I am with my new friend Enmo, who is hanging on my every word, and her mother who is more my age but is not hanging on anything of mine. I couldn't resist suggesting we do a day trip tomorrow. Enmo went for it immediately. She suggested the three of us go to the place where the donkey drinks the beer. Tourists buy a beer, and the donkey drinks it. When there are a lot of tourists the donkey soon starts staggering, making funny noises, then lies down for a nap. So then they trot out another donkey. I counter-suggested Fidel Castro's birthplace, which was nearby, but Enmo had already seen that on a school trip. Then she thought she'd like to visit her own birthplace, a certain town where she was born and raised and hasn't seen in ages.

So I walked the two of them home. Her mother wasn't sure if she'd come. She'd sleep on it. Enmo was very sure. It was late, and as we walked through the city square, bereft of children now but with lots of adults enjoying the night air, someone sitting on the bench had a little marker flashlight, and was flicking a little red dot on the ground in front of us as we walked. I pretended I thought it was a firefly and was running around trying to step on it. Just to amuse Enmo and her mom. They seemed amused. In fact I got laughs all around the park doing that. It's so easy to get a laugh in Cuba.

I hopped on a bicycle taxi, a relatively lightweight Chinese bicycle with a sidecar. The driver got lost. I had my map of the city, trying to help him find the casa where I was staying, and it was just a few short blocks away, and on the map it looked easy to find. The driver was a bright kid born and raised in Holguín. It was very mysterious. Even Christopher P. Baker talks about this phenomenon, which is unique to Holguín. Just when you think you're almost there, the place you are looking for has disappeared. We would stop and ask directions, and the people would be sincerely interested in helping us, but the directions didn't work.

The bicycle taxi had no lights, not even a rear fender reflector, and the streets of Cuban cities are very dim at night – but for some reason I felt very relaxed, in good hands, completely unconcerned about an accident. A car or bus or truck would barrel by, and neither of us would blink. Something in the Cuban air turns a wimp into a hero. My driver was thirty-three years old, and he had a wife, and a little baby, and he spoke fairly good English, but when I asked him how he had learned English he couldn't somehow find the words to tell me, just as I couldn't remember those Japanese authors. I vowed to give him a huge tip if we ever got to our destination, and maybe even if we didn't. When he was going up a hill, I'd hop off the bike and help push. I gave him little pro-Cuba speeches, told him the whole world is very worried about Cuba, and everybody hopes that the United States is going to back off. He was definitely drinking it all in, and he said that he had lived in Holguín all his life and he didn't really know "anything about anything outside Holguín." And I'm sure he knew a lot about Holguín, but not how to get to my *casa*, which was in Central Holguín, at the corner of Aricoches and Avenida de los Liberadores.

Maybe Holguín has never been properly mapped. The maps we find in guidebooks and tourist kiosks look perfectly reliable but are copies of some fundamentally sloppy and bogus map drawn up in 1914. Apparently this is the only Cuban city that has this problem.

At one point while wheeling through these dark deserted streets he took off his hat, handed it to me, and said, "Look, look at what is on this hat." I looked, and all that was on the hat was the single word SIKKENS. "It's a very good company," he said, "and it's a trademark for your country." I had no idea what he was talking about, but pretended I did, since he was already working too hard to have to explain any further.

On a lonely dark side street we encountered a little old guy who was sitting there next to a rickety card table on which he had stacked about fifteen Cuban-style empanadas, which are not that much different from Scottish meat pies, but flatter, and about five inches in diameter. He also had another stack of pies that had been cut in four slices, for people who were only a quarter hungry. It was a very dreamlike scene, hugely cinematic, for it was past midnight, the street was empty, he was in a very poor location for commerce, but he was patiently waiting, like an elderly Lili Marlene, under the dim lamplight, to sell his pies while they were still fresh. Why didn't he set up his table on a busier street? Maybe he was too old to lug his table and pies that far, or maybe he didn't have a licence and so the police asked him to restrict his business to the barrios.

So I bought one for my driver, and he gobbled it up lickety-split, then gave me a big smile. To me it was like giving a bale of hay to a hard-working horse, but the old fellow got all emotional, leapt out of his chair, threw his arms around me in the warmest embrace, and said, "You're a good man!" He wasn't being ironic at all, he genuinely seemed to consider this the greatest act of generosity since a repentant St. Francis, in a fit of ecstasy, took off his clothes in the Assisi town square and gave them to the poor. In this life we get appreciated for the unlikeliest things, and never for the things we expect to be appreciated for. In 1968, in closing down the last vestiges of private business enterprise in Cuba, Fidel argued that among street vendors and hot-dog sellers, there is a high percentage of people who are planning to leave the country. But thirty-five years later I don't think this empanada seller is going anywhere.

The pieman said the *casa* we were looking for was right there. He pointed across the street and down a bit. And there it was! What a thrill! I bought my driver another pie, paid him handsomely, and we said goodbye.

It was well after midnight when I tapped on the door. My host didn't say a word, he just glowered at me as I offered my abject apologies and explanations.

AN AFTERNOON
AT THE BEACH

Tuesday, March 2, 2004. No spy would walk around the civic square whispering into his tape recorder. Only a totally innocent person, with nothing to hide, would be that stupid. And no terrorist or drug smuggler would drive the wrong way on a one-way street, then stop to ask a cop for directions to the nearest airport. So what's to worry about?

One nice thing about my *casa* in Holguín – it has an actual reading lamp. The lamp sits on an elaborate cabinet formation constructed to fit snugly around the head of the bed, and there is a matching chest of drawers with a large mirror. Everything is coordinated in pale cream and brown, or, in ice-cream terms, vanilla and chocolate, or, in arts-and-crafts terms, like the carved whales Enmo and I were admiring yesterday. The reading lamp is an old Tiffany, and if you give it the slightest little touch it comes on, if you touch it again it becomes brighter, and it keeps on getting brighter as you touch it and then it goes out. The only problem – it sometimes goes on all by itself in the middle of the night, as if a moth might have landed on it. Also, on the average of three times out of ten, it will give you an electrical shock when you touch it. A big-enough buzz to kill a bug and startle a human.

Yoelkís and her husband have two sons. One is an engineer who develops air-conditioning systems, and the other is a professor of engineering at the local university in Holguín. They each earn about $20 a month.

On the front door, as you're about to knock, there's a picture of a family walking down the street, mama, papa, and two little kids, and standing between mommy and daddy is Jesus. You can see right through him but he's there. And then on their dining-room wall, over the dinner table, is a large reproduction of the Last Supper. Below that is a small framed reproduction of the same painting, as if they couldn't bear to get rid of the small one when they came into possession of the large one. Also there's a ceramic piece about fourteen inches high, which depicts a drunken black man all dressed in a black tuxedo with bow tie askew, and a bottle in his hand, and leaning against a lamppost. And many plastic flowers, such as a splendid bouquet of orange roses with little artificial drops of dew, unnaturally tiny, on each and every petal.

Not to be forgotten is that last night at the *parque*: with the great Máximo Calixto looking down at them with no amusement on his face at all, there were three men sitting together on a bench, talking, laughing. Suddenly one man got up and he started to strut like a stripper on stage, then he pulled a black brassiere out of his pocket and put it on over his shirt, while his friends got up and started laughing helplessly. He stuffed some rags into the brassiere to make it look as if he had big fat breasts. So the other men started to molest him, shaping the breasts until they became smaller and firmer, and then caressed them till they came to a point. All this time the cross-dresser squealed happily. They were having a wonderful time.

In the sky, the moon and all the stars were speeding way beyond the speed limit. Oh oh, it's the end of the world, Velikovsky was right, the earth is spinning out of control. But no, it was an optical illusion caused by the fact that the clouds were moving so fast. It was very still down here, but up there the wind could have knocked a U2 out of the sky the way it was blowing.

This morning I settled up with my hosts and called Enmo to tell her to meet me at Parque Calixto. Then I paid up the ten dollars for two breakfasts (I thought it was included), plus two dollars for the use of the garage (they didn't tell me there'd be a charge for that), their unfriendly manner leading me to wonder if I might have inadvertently said or done something to annoy them.

I picked up Enmo and off we went on our great adventure. I told her she could be the navigator and I'd take her wherever she wanted to go. She wanted to go to Puerta Padre, where she was born and grew up. It was very tiny, and several miles northwest of Holguín. But first she wanted to go to two beach areas for foreigners several miles northeast of Holguín. On the way there she cautiously asked me if I had given her phone number to anyone. I said no, of course not, it was in my notebook and I hadn't mentioned her or her number to a single solitary soul. She said about two minutes – no more – after I called her this morning from my *casa*, someone phoned her place. Her mother picked up the phone, and a voice she didn't recognize asked if she ran a *casa particulare*. Mirian said no and the woman politely said thank you and hung up. It seemed peculiar, particularly coming so soon after my call. They'd never had such a call before, ever.

I remembered that two minutes after I called her I was out in the garage putting my bags in the car. Yoelkís had seemed annoyed that I was leaving, even though I hadn't knowingly said anything about staying a third night. So it was almost certainly Yoelkís who had called just to find out if the call I had made two minutes earlier was to another *casa particulare*. I had asked permission to make the call and assured her it was a local number. So even hard-core Christians can be a tad paranoid, it seems, and she had wanted to know if I was booking another *casa* in another part of town, but feared to ask me. It gave me the creeps.

Enmo wanted to know how Yoelkís got the number. I said she probably had a redial button on her telephone. Also, if it turned out that it *was* another *casa* I had called, perhaps she would have wanted to ask me if perhaps there was something wrong with her service, and she could do some quality control. Or maybe she could offer me a lower rate for the third night. But then again she could have asked me if there was something wrong anyway, or if the service was up to snuff, it wouldn't have hurt. And of course the service was fine, except for the unexpected cost add-ons, though that didn't bother me really. I was disappointed, but I didn't resent their enterprise, and it didn't bother me that they got a few more dollars out of me.

So it would have been after she had made the call, presumably, that she came out to the garage and hit me up for twelve more dollars. That, she said, was for the people at the Hotel Turquino, which had been all booked up, and who had referred me to her place.

Enmo and I stopped at a roadside stand and bought one pineapple, four oranges, and eleven bananas. Now we are at Playa Pesquero on the Bahía de Naranjo, where there are some beautiful people walking back and forth along the beach. The sea is deep dark blue, blue as the finely layered feathers on a peacock's neck. But when the waves bump into the reef, which is about two hundred yards off-shore, that slows them down, and they become turquoise, then green, then almost a pale yellow until the final waves break onto the white granulated sand, so refined and so sugary you almost wish to try it in your coffee.

I have no bathing suit, nor does Enmo, but she says it's just enough to be at the beach because it's so healthy, it's just enough to be sitting on the beach, watching the antics of the people who do have bathing suits, and let the sea breezes intoxicate us. She said the winds coming in off the sea are very good for the nasal membranes, the lungs, and the immune system in general. Some Italian tourists are playing bocce on the beach with silver balls, under some shady trees, and now and then they have to take out a tape measure to see which ball is closer to the main ball.

The hotels around here maybe aren't quite as posh as the Varadero ones, but they are painted in bright colours, with some of them just a massive splash of brilliant primary colours. Such hotels would seem out of place on the shore of Lough Gur in Ireland, Loch Ness in Scotland, or Conception Bay in Newfoundland, but they look great here. The water is still too cold for swimming, it seems, and there are more tourists riding horses than bobbing in the waves.

The Occidental Grand Playa Turquesa is the hotel where Enmo wished to come to see her colleague Neil, to remind him that she needs some work from the agency. Neil wasn't there, which caused some disappointment, but they will tell him tomorrow when he comes in that Enmo was here, hoping that she has not been forgotten. He will be pleasantly surprised, no doubt. And she'll get a call from the agency and be working very soon, I predict. She insisted I come in with her, and so I did, but maybe I should have said no, because being seen with a foreigner could under certain circumstances hurt someone's chances for advancement. And who knows, maybe she does not get hired full-time because they know about her sister in Florida collecting money for the churches, and thereby financing the anti-abortionists who will stage local protests from time to time in which they can be heard chanting counter-revolutionary slogans such as, "Down with the Castro-Communist dictatorship." Which would be at odds with Fidel's oft-expressed opinion that everybody in Cuba is a dictator, and he is their slave.

At a little seaside restaurant at Playa Guardalavaca, we each had a bowl of fresh seafood soup with tomato broth, rice, a bottle of agua minerale con gas each, and helado with raisins for dessert. The bill came to $10.10. And both of us were very full.

But, at the other table, just for the sake of contrast, were four couples from Sudbury, Ontario, who had just arrived yesterday, and you should have seen the food they wolfed down. It was awesome. And they were so fat and so short, Enmo whisperingly pointed out, that you could hardly tell the women from the men. Also they looked so tired and irritable after twenty-four hours in Cuba, which might have been inspiring them to keep shovelling the food in, hoping it will correct their bad moods. They each had the $20 blue sea special, which came to $160, plus they each drank two or three colas in the course of the meal. And each had an ice cream. They gobbled up all that food with amazing speed. Then one of the ladies went to the bathroom and was dismayed to find there was no toilet paper. She was rolling her eyes as if to say how stupid can these Cubans be! Oh my! What to do! No toilet paper! Why did we come to such a place? They complained to the waiter.

The waiter brought out a roll of toilet paper on a silver platter for the lady at the same time as one of her friends, back at the table, pitched a little package of tissue at her. She looked confused and didn't know which to use, the tissue or the toilet paper, so she took both back into the washroom. "Nice catch!" someone said, and we all smiled, even the restaurant staff. And when she came out, because she was wearing shorts, you could see an angry red toilet seat ring around her thighs. Then each of the other seven blubber addicts had to go through the same routine.

The men went out for a smoke and decided they wanted to stay outside, because it was very warm indoors. It was a small but sparkling new cakebox of a restaurant at the top of the beach – floor-to-ceiling glass windows and doors all around on three sides, and all the windows and doors hermetically sealed. It was big enough for about six or seven tables for four. They couldn't open the windows and have the breezes come through, because if they did there would soon be deposits of fine sand in the diners' food, and maybe even little insects.

When the Canadians were leaving, I asked one of them if Paul Martin was still prime minister. She said, "Yes, as of yesterday, when we left. We just arrived last night, and he was still hanging in there." Enmo said she thought they were profoundly unhappy people in spite of their huge wads of cash and credit cards, and they had spent on this meal at least one month's salary for a whole team of dedicated Cuban teachers or doctors.

Enmo is quiet today. She is enjoying the trip, but she is not as talkative as yesterday. Perhaps she is bothered by something that happened at the hotel, some subtextual matter I missed. Or maybe she had an argument with Mirian this morning. Our chit-chat is only on the simplest level. She said last night she would be honoured to be part of my book, but now that we're committed to a day together she's not so sure. She's very happy, her eyes are shining, but she's become shy and perhaps afraid of saying something she could later be criticized for. Also her English skills seem to have petered out overnight, while my Spanish skills have not improved. She insists I speak in English, but she's not tuning into it very well.

Enmo thought I should have a sombrero to protect my face from turning any pinker than it already is. To the Cubans, a pink face looks as if it has been singed with a blowtorch, and they tend to cringe with sympathetic pain. So we went to a little crafts fair near the parking lot. The straw hats looked a bit stodgy, as if specially fashioned for the tourists, and not the sloppy but authentic ones the *campesinos* wear as they walk along the side of the highway carrying their machetes or come galloping by on their steeds. I was attracted to a hat that was in the shape of Fidel's famous one (similar to Charles de Gaulle's), except that it was straw, woven very expertly. But they were all too stiff, and even though they might be the right size for one's head, they still didn't fit right. The vendor grabbed one hat off my head and started pulling it vigorously to loosen up the fibres and make it fit properly, but much to his disappointment it fit a bit better but still didn't have that "right" feel.

We're driving along a badly potholed seaside road, and every now and then excited little children will come running from their little houses and wave their little arms like little windmills. Everywhere chickens are pecking away at the ground. We drove along the Atlantic shore for miles and miles, trying to get to Enmo's birth- place, so she could talk to all her old friends, if any are still around.

We managed to get to Gibara (est. pop. 27,600) along a very bad road, with Enmo stopping and asking directions of the locals, who came running when they saw her flashing eyes and pretty face. One fellow was carrying a dead dog by the tail out to the goat pasture presumably to bury it, although he had no shovel. When Enmo went yoohoo, he tossed the dog as far as he could and came running back to the road. Gibara was beautiful, a smaller version of Baracoa, and the beautiful Bahía de Gibara was filled with boats anchored and bobbing in the waves, putting to rest my theory about the lack of boats. There were more boats here than I'd seen in my entire tour so far.

But the road kept getting rockier and narrower and we soon found ourselves driving by a desolate row of derelict houses along the sea. It was as if some kind of relocation program was going on, perhaps to create more international fun zones for foreigners. But some people were holding out, living in much desolation. Maybe these were towns abandoned by people who had given up on Cuba and sailed to Florida. Enmo wasn't saying anything. She seemed to be more in the dark than I was. Or maybe she was just pretending to be.

Finally the road got so bad, and the sun was setting, so we turned around and headed back the way we came without having visited Enmo's hometown. The road is very well marked in thick red on the map, but if we had looked more closely we'd have seen that at Playa las Bocas the road abruptly ended at a river with no bridge.

Then Enmo shyly broke the news that she had an appointment for next Tuesday with the head of the hiring agency for all the hotels in the area. She thinks he may have a job for her. And if he does she will be paid somewhere between four and five hundred pesos a month, depending on how well the hotel is doing, but she will also get tips, and that is where the real money is. On a busy day she could earn the equivalent of her monthly salary in tips, which always come in U.S. dollars these days; although according to *Granma*, Cuba is thinking of changing to euros at the end of the year.

Soon night had fallen and Enmo effortlessly navigated me back to her home in Holguín. I promised to call her tomorrow. I said I'd book into the posh Hotel Pernik, but they were fully booked, and I somehow ended up heading south, as I suspected I would, to the intriguing small city of Bayamo, and booked into the beautiful Hotel Royalton on the main square. The night clerk, the same handsome young fellow I chatted with when I was last here inquiring about a room, works a twenty-four-hour shift followed by twenty-four hours off, which is the norm for hotel workers in Cuba. But he was finding things difficult. He only made 188 pesos a month, less than half what the hotel workers on the beaches made, if he and Enmo are to be believed. He seemed healthy and bright, but his economic future was on life support. He had a brother in Florida and another in Toronto, but they seemed to have forgotten the family back home. He also stated that he knew for sure he could increase his salary tremendously by getting a job as a police officer with the Ministry of the Interior. They make eight hundred pesos a month, as much as a university professor. But the nature of the work wasn't to his liking.

IT'S PALMA DAY
IN BAYAMO LIBRE!

Wednesday, March 3, 2004. Last night I confided to the desk clerk that I'd be willing to give some needy soul two dollars to wash my car. Oh, if only I'd forked over the two bucks right then and there! At 5:30 this morning, like a few mornings ago at the convent at El Cobre, there was a tremendous pounding on my door. This time the sweetest, shyest young man was standing there. He very politely asked for his money for washing the car. I felt very small when I punched the wall and heard myself saying, "Couldn't you wait till I woke up?" How petty of me! He was probably more tired than I was and wanted to take some money home to his family in their tiny crowded apartment somewhere. I gave him the two dollars in anger and slammed the door in his face. Now I feel wretched. Now I definitely feel part of the problem. I hate myself!

But misunderstandings abound; in fact they outnumber understandings, whether one travels the world or never strays from home. Maybe Yoelkís really thought I had said I'd be staying three days instead of two. Maybe . . . oh why go on? You have to add the sour with the sweet when you write a travel book, or it will lack flavour. People do make mistakes, and people do go through periods of self-hatred when they contemplate the general inadequacy of their minds.

But there's a big celebration in Bayamo this morning. And I'm glad I had my car washed because it's sitting there gleaming, right at the front entrance of the hotel, right next to the speaker's platform, where everyone can see it. All the schools are out, all the banks, stores, and businesses are closed, and Parque Céspedes is thronged with students, teachers, and swarms of ordinary citizens. There are bands and speakers. Is it the anniversary of a famous battle? No, it's a great celebration commemorating the 128th anniversary of the wonderful day when Tomás Estrada Palma, a native son of Bayamo, became president of Cuba at the age of forty-four. Like Fidel, he was a lawyer, and was also a general in the vicious Ten Years War. He was a great hero. And he spent a lot of time in prison, both in Cuba and in Spain.

Anyway, it's a holiday, and the *parque* is thronged with what appears to be the entire population of Bayamo (est. 192,600). Yes, it's Palma Day in Bayamo and *todo los Bayameses* are shouting with joy! One wonderfully impassioned speech after another goes echoing around the *parque*, with many elected representatives taking their turn (and their time!) at the microphone, trying their best to emulate Fidel in the oratory department, and maybe even surpass him now and then. One fellow is at the mike, introducing all the visiting councillors and various elected representatives from such places as Santo Domingo and Santa Clara, and each time that he pauses, drumrolls break out from all around the square, along with multitudinous cries from the multitudes, yelling out "Vive Fidel," "Vive Cuba Libre," "Cuba Sí," etc. People squeal with joy and the drumrolls continue until the speaker starts up again. There's nothing like this in Canadian politics. Except maybe for Saint-Jean-Baptiste Day.

But I get tired of it and for contrast slip into the silence of the Catedral del Santísimo Salvador. Behind and above the altar is a larger-than-life statue of Jesus on a transfigured cross, with white and gold beaming out from it on all sides. Not to be disrespectful, but Jesus has his forearms lifted and his head tilted back, and he's standing on his right foot with his left foot kinda kicked back, and it looks as if he's doing the mambo. Maybe that's the Cuban idea of heaven – eternal mambo.

The church is brighter and airier than many, sparrows are flitting around, chirping away and pooping on the pews. It's off the main square and in a small square to the side. It's pale yellow, with a beautifully designed Italian campanile and a red terra-cotta roof. There's a large mural showing the unfolding for the first time of the new Cuban flag, which took place here in Bayamo on October 20, 1868, and right in this church a choir of twelve women sang Cuba's fiery Revolutionary anthem of independence for the very first time, with a shocked and horrified colonial governor in attendance. The anthem was composed by a local musician and poet named Perucho Figueredo, whose statue today adorns the beautiful Parque Céspedes, standing high on a base on which is inscribed not only the heroic words – "Do not fear a glorious death / To die for the Fatherland is to live," etc. – but the score as well, with all the little sharps and flats, semiquavers and demiquavers, clefs and staffs engraved in stone. The original church was built in 1516, rebuilt in 1733, and again after the fire of 1869. There is a huge old mural in the church that shows an independence-day gathering in the civic square in the mid-nineteenth century. It's definitely Bayamo, and the crowd fills the square shoulder to shoulder, much as it did today, with the only difference being that many of the men in the mural have rifles over their shoulders, and many are on horseback. There are no goat carts pulling the children around as there are today, but everybody, blacks, whites, and in-betweens, is very excited about independence, every woman is wearing her best dress and carrying great bouquets of flowers, and every man has doffed his hat for his first glimpse of the new flag. And in the sky over all, up there in the golden clouds, Jesus is looking down and bestowing his blessings. It's odd being all alone in this church, and hearing the speeches to the crowd drifting in from outside, while gazing up at this great mural, and knowing that outside, in the same place, history's themes are repeating themselves, with only the slightest variations.

There are several stalls all around, many of them selling books for schoolkids, plus the occasional big fat novel. Much food is being sold, a couple of stalls have large roasted pigs on the table, and the ice-cream shop, where I couldn't get ice cream last time I was here, is now so crowded because of the holiday that it looks as if I'm not going to be able to get helado even now that I have pesos. The ice-cream crowd looks very disorderly, but in fact nobody's pushing anybody. This is the Cuba of my dreams, fully integrated, everybody equal, everyone acting as an individual and simultaneously as a member of the most famous little country in the world.

The festivities are over, but the crowd isn't ready to disperse yet. An energetic man about forty is wielding two giant brooms, each about four feet wide, and he's cutting a huge rapid-fire swath through the litter, and people are lifting their feet as he goes by, and giving a little hop from in front of the brooms to behind them.

And now a parade has formed; numerous people are following a wild percussion band into the square and around and around, picking up a longer tail of shouting, laughing, overjoyed people as it goes, throwing their arms up and down with gleeful abandon, celebrating independence, sovereignty, and I don't think President Bush would have a chance here. Everybody here would fight to the death. It's all so unimaginable. The entire world would turn on Bush if he attacked this country with his ever bigger and better bombs. This is a great country, severely wounded by the boring blockade, and these constant death threats, but still dancing, and still full of joy, maybe more now than ever. The United States promised to end the blockade when the Russians were gone, but the Russians have been gone for twelve years now and still it continues.

Meanwhile, gently and carefully through the boisterous crowds, three men are pulling a cart on which are sitting about twenty-five oversized ceremonial cakes slathered with brilliant pink icing, the same colour as the ice cream that is being dished out. The cakes are perfectly square, about fourteen inches by fourteen. And then the cart gets wheeled into a dental office (bearing a happy-tooth, sad-tooth sign out front), and through the office to a smaller office at the back, where people learn how to use computers. Odd place to take twenty-five fresh-baked birthday cakes, but I'm sure the Cubans know what they're doing. And one of the fellows pulling the cake cart is wearing a T-shirt that says, No I Do Not Speak English But I Promise Not to Laugh at Your Spanish. Oddly enough, I seem to be the only non-Cuban in this entire throng of people.

When things returned to normal, I sat in the park studying my Spanish dictionary and then a woman a bit farther along on the perimeter bench started chatting me up. She asked if it was poetry I was reading. No, I was just brushing up on some verb conjugations. She went over a few with me. She appeared to be a teacher, and the handsome younger Afro-Cubano beside her was a serious student, writing in a big notebook. He was very concentrated on his work. Nothing else existed. The woman was very pretty, maybe thirty years old. The young man, who was about twenty, his pen ran out. She asked if he could borrow mine. Of course, I handed him my green fountain pen full of black ink and we continued our chat about the Spanish language. She said she worked in a small *tienda*, selling stuff to Cubans such as cigarettes and spools of thread. She said the best Cuban cigarettes were Hollywood and I shouldn't smoke Popular because they were too strong.

With the young student still writing away and consulting his book with enviable concentration, this seemingly pedagogical woman, who was small and cute in a light-skinned feline and slightly African way, suggested we repair to the Hotel Royalton for a coffee. So we crossed the narrow street and she dragged us into the bar of the Royalton rather than the coffee shop and ordered three icy-cold Bucaneros. But I just wanted a coffee and her student wanted a cola. So the waiter brought my coffee, his cola, and her beer. And I soon realized I'd made a fundamental mistake of the innocent variety. She was, whether accidentally or on purpose, touching me under the table. Oops, that was definitely not accidental. Whatever else she was – a teacher, a *tienda* saleswoman – she was a *chica*. Her young friend was her brother, she said. *Hermano y hermana*, she said, with pride – but I didn't believe it. They looked nothing alike in any way. No way did they come from the same mother or the same father.

The book our *hermano* kept referring to, studiously writing away and ignoring our talk, as if he'd heard it all before, or as if he'd been warned to butt out, was a Spanish-French dictionary. He's learning French! Yes, she said, Quebec French, not that fake French the people of France speak, the real French of Quebec.

When I recovered from that zinger, I asked if she was teaching him French. I still somehow had the notion she was a teacher.

Yes, she said. Quebec French. So I thought, Aha, my French is better than my Spanish so I started speaking French, but she didn't understand a word. This left me terribly confused. I guess she wasn't the first teacher to be teaching a language she didn't know.

Meanwhile, she handed me a postcard showing a semi-abstract and highly imaginative painting of a woman with her head turned to one side, her breasts a pair of bright swirling polymites, her legs and a hint of a long tail very reptilian, little eyelike loops all over her face and body, and a bright blue iridescent butterfly covering her genitalia. Under it was an unsigned, unattributed poem, which in my amateurish fashion I would translate as:

> *Your eyes are as profound as the place where the night beats its wings,*
> *with arms of fresh flowers and a flaming aura of rose.*
> *Your breasts are like families of white snails*
> *which fall asleep in the nest of your abdomen like the butterfly of a*
>   *dream.*

I told her the card was very beautiful and handed it back to her. Then she wrote her name and address out on it and, with her "brother" still concentrating on the books, in place of a message she drew a cartoonish set of five neatly executed images with the equivalent name in Spanish alongside each: *pinga, bollo, culo, tetas, nolgas*. These words and images were very simply obscene, but they were too cute and well drawn to be offensive. There was a deft innocence about them. There was no doubt she had written and drawn these words and pictures many times. I was astonished and very amused that a person I took to be a teacher, an intellectual, and she certainly looked the part, and with a hard-working student following her around, could be a woman of the streets, a *chica*. But she was and she was not at all ashamed of it. There was nothing wrong with it as long as one did it in the proper spirit and visited the *polyclinico* every chance one got. Meanwhile I continued to try to speak intelligently to her while she was running her fingers along my thigh, under the table, but not so surreptitiously that the bartender didn't know what she was doing, and the members of the hotel staff who came in from time to time didn't need to be nudged to see what she was doing. Everyone seemed to know her well and seemed dismayed to see me with her. This could be bad for business. And whatever reputation I had established in Bayamo was swirling down the drain.

Meanwhile, her "brother" finished what he had been writing and began to copy a name and address onto a stamped envelope, in which he had folded and inserted several pages. Then Marisolita (for that was her name) showed me the name and address of the man this was going to. It was a Mr. J—— H—— Pierre, such and such a number and street, and then the name of the town: Fonds, Quebec. No, there is no Fonds, Quebec, I said. Then I realized she had merely misplaced the Pierre. I took the envelope and asked permission to correct it. I crossed out the name Pierre and inserted it before Fonds, as it was, correctly, Pierrefonds, and the fellow's name would be Mr. J—— H——. And then, from a slip of paper I took from Marisolita, I added the correct postal code, which our serious young man – Chichi, she called him – hadn't written on the envelope because it seemed nonsensical. Now it will get to him, I said.

Earlier she had asked me to guess her age. I thought I'd give her the benefit of the doubt and said thirty-one. She gasped and said, Oh no, I'm only twenty-five. I was embarrassed but covered up with a little lie by saying I was only joking, she didn't look a day over twenty-five. When in fact she was probably thirty-five. I asked how old Chichi was. He had stopped writing but was still paying absolutely no attention to us. He was in a very serious world of his own, while she was engrossed in plying her trade. He is a baby, she said. Only twenty. He likes to suckle my breast – and she squeezed one of her little breasts and made wetly obscene sucking noises. I turned to the bartender, who was watching us non-judgmentally, and put my hand on my head and said, Oy vey! He smiled knowingly and averted his gaze. I seemed to have wandered far from my state of religious adoration in the cathedral an hour or two ago.

No, I said, he is no baby. He's a full-grown man – with a moustache and an air of great dignity.

No, she said. He is a baby.

Like all men at heart, you mean, I said.

No, even more than that, she said.

Then I became fully convinced that he was not her brother but her pimp, and what he had been doing all this time was not studying French with his Spanish-French dictionary but was busy translating a letter that she had written, in Spanish, to a former patron of hers, Mr. J—— H—— of Pierrefonds, Quebec. The note with his name and address was rather faded and crumpled so it had been a while since his visit to Bayamo. Imagine his astonishment at receiving the letter, which he undoubtedly would receive now that it had the town's name and the postal code corrected. Maybe he'd been dying to hear from her, and was imagining all kinds of cruel things. He would note that his address on the envelope had been edited and corrected by another hand, but he would not imagine that the other hand had been that of an actual fellow Canadian! Also I was confident that the letter as translated by Chichi the pimp would contain tender reminiscences of their time together, plus hints of great poverty, and a not-so-subtle request for him to reply along with some U.S. dollars, the more the better. I of course felt trapped. I wanted to say adios but felt it would be rude of me and I was waiting for the perfect moment. No wonder Chichi had been concentrating so hard. It's not easy to translate a letter from Spanish to French when you know no French except what you can look up in the French-Spanish dictionary. Also he was concentrating because this was a scheme – if things worked out there could be good money in the return mail.

She invited me to come to her *casa*. She said it would be just she and I there, it would be entirely private. This seemed odd to my ears because I was still in a state of detachment from my moment in the church, and the world around me seemed like a shadowy movie I was watching from an eye deep in my heart. Nothing is real, everything is reel.

I told her, as I had told others, that I was not interested in sex, and I made a drooping motion with my right forefinger. She asked my age and when I told her she said the man from "Fronds" was much older than I and he was very erect for hours and hours. Sigh!

So I upped the ante and politely told her that alas I found sex *mucho aburrido*. She insisted we need not have sex per se, but she would caress me lovingly in a way that would give me intense pleasure. So then I pulled all the stops and told her that intense pleasure would have been of great interest to me ten years ago but now I find other pleasures more intense, such as working on my stamp collection.

By this time Chichi had gone to post the letter and Marisolita had to go to the washroom. So I went to the bartender and paid the bill for all our drinks and *cigarros*. When I turned around Chichi had returned to his seat and I told him the bill had been paid and I shook his hand, said *mucho gusto*, and went to my room. For the next while my phone rang repeatedly. At first it rang thirty-seven times. Then a few minutes later it rang again but only twelve times. And then eight. And then five. And then one lonely ring, a dying gasp, and everything was *silencio y finito*.

I must add that Chichi and Marisolita were very excellent people in spite of, or maybe because of, their rather unprestigious and lowly calling as workers in the sex trade. I was very impressed with her sense of dedication and her very intriguing methods of trying to get me interested. No Canadian hooker would ever try so hard, unless the fellow was a clergyman of high standing, or a professional hockey player.

And look at Chichi! He was concentrated and purposeful. I didn't get to check out his translation all that carefully, but it looked to me as if he knew what he was doing. Mr. J—— H—— will know the letter is not from Marcel Proust, but he'll be able to figure it out if he tries.

So yes they were bright, dedicated, inventive, intelligent – and although Chichi was a bit dour he was a good man and Marisolita had a sly sense of bawdy humour. And they really did look like a pretty little teacher thrilled to be alive and a big dumb student doing lessons out of class. She will possibly remember me as the man who got away in spite of all her attempts. She also had an excellent way of making me almost feel that she wanted me because she genuinely liked me – and she laughed gleefully at my pathetic jokes such as "I have zero desiro," etc. And that I enjoy "mucho camelar mas no cama." It boggled her mind that I had not had sex with anyone all the time I'd been in Cuba. She was astonished. She kept stroking her cute little turned-up nose with an exaggerated Pinocchio gesture. She even asked if I was "normal."

I told her I thought Cuba was a very hot and sexy place – perhaps the sexiest country in the entire galaxy – but I knew in Toronto many men my age who are no longer into it, and many women too. Cuba *caliente*, Toronto *frijo*, I said, and I added that I considered myself perfectly normal but just a fellow who prefers intellectual and emotional stimulation to the perilous and frivolous excitement that lies in the lower chakras. She seemed to understand but preferred to pretend she didn't.

Marisolita had perfectly exquisite heart-shaped lips, naturally pink, but there was a nasty little scar just above her upper lip. It looked as if she'd been stabbed with a ballpoint pen. What happened? She glanced at Chichi, who was in a world of his own. "He did it."

Parque Céspedes is very different tonight. It has undergone another transformation, this time with little card tables and chairs set up for games, all the way around the outside perimeter. There's a dwarf smoking cigarettes (to show he's not a kid?) and playing checkers with a normal-sized kid about his size (who is not smoking), and they're playing with bottle caps. One side has bottle caps up, the other has bottle caps down. There's a young woman there sitting patiently by herself with a box full of dominoes but nobody wants to play with her. Maybe the idea of women playing dominoes doesn't seem quite right to the macho men of Bayamo. Or maybe she's waiting for her friends. And then there are four guys playing dominoes, with a fifth guy watching and doing a lot of excited kibitzing. Christopher P. Baker says dominoes is not a child's game in Cuba, having developed to a very subtle and complex level, but these guys were just looking at the board, looking at their own hand, and then figuring out what the others must have in their hands. It's not complicated. Chess is complicated. And there are many chess games going on, with a lot of kids half my size playing high-speed chess.

So I went over to the Royalton dining room and ordered a Bayamo Libre, after already having had one at La Bodega. On my table was an artificial rose with a fly on it. After five minutes the fly hadn't budged an inch, so I snapped my finger and it still didn't move. Aha! It's artificial too!

Two of the waitresses at the Royalton have been giving me unpleasant looks because they saw me with that disreputable woman this afternoon. Actually one of them, the older one, has now forgiven me, and she's full of smiles and pleasantries, her eyes tell me she understood exactly what was happening between me, the "teacher," and the "student" this afternoon The younger one is very miffed indeed and still keeps her nose tilted up whenever she passes by my table, and if she looks at me it's with a glare rather than a smile. She thinks I'm the scum of the earth for having wasted so much time on such low-lifes. She wonders how I could have degraded myself like that. She's the puritan and won't even give me a chance to try to win her over. Honest, I thought that nice lady was a schoolteacher! She was giving me some drawing lessons! Both waitresses were wearing little silver crosses, but one was of a more forgiving denomination than the other.

Now the puritanical lady is avoiding any kind of eye contact whatsoever with me, as if she thinks I've come down here with my filthy money to exploit women half my age at least. But the older woman is fawning over me, as if she admires me for having had a lot of fun with the "teacher" but being scrupulous enough not to follow her home for advanced lessons. Two different Cubans, two different takes on the subject.

But finally I got a smile from the younger waitress. I ordered yet another Bayamo Libre from the older nicer waitress and I could hear her in the kitchen telling the younger one to take it to me. But the younger one didn't want to. So the older one insisted. And when the younger one poutingly brought it to me she put it down with a cute little hint of a smile. She looks as if she's on the verge of forgiving me for my terrible transgression this afternoon. After all, that was six hours ago. Let's forgive and forget. And she seemed pleased when my curious eye told her that I had noticed the sexy black bra under her blouse.

BAYAMO DAYBREAK

Thursday, March 4, 2004. Way off in the barrios the roosters are crowing. Some sleepless maniac steps out of the darkness and tips over a trash can three feet from where I'm sitting. Then he starts poking through the mess to see if there's anything worth salvaging. There isn't. He sees me glaring at him and says good morning. I take the last slug of my mineral water and toss the empty bottle into the pile of garbage. He seems to get the point but comes short of looking sheepish. I'm sitting in this beautiful symmetrical park at 4 a.m., with four royal palms towering high above the Céspedes statue. As so often in Cuba, I had it all wrong – the trashcan tipper was actually a member of the early-morning street-cleaning squad. He would be joined by many others soon and they'd have this square squeaky clean.

Embarrassed, I retreat to the roof of the Hotel Royalton and discover a new world of absolute solitude. The air is very still, but it's almost cool enough for a sweater. This is a nicely maintained red-tiled roof, neat and charmingly laid out, with sixty empty hardback chairs tightly arranged in a symmetrical oval, with one chair removed so people can get in and out of the oval with ease, and this little passageway is conveniently close to the bar, which is not in operation at this hour. Also the roof provides views of a sky just beginning to pale from blue black to sky blue, with little birds chirping in the trees and the only roosters crowing are crowing faintly from a mile away.

From here I can look down at the park and see the messy pile of garbage has now been swept into a neat pile but it is still on the side-walk. A man and woman, both very corpulent Afro-Cubans, were coming out of their room, and climbing down to the lobby, as I was climbing up to the roof. Now when I lean over the retaining wall I can see them standing on the sidewalk. Finally a large black car pulls up, with one tail light missing, and the black couple silently gets in the back seat, while a skinny white woman silently and unsmilingly gets out of the back seat and climbs into the front. Everyone is careful to close the doors with as little noise as possible. The car takes off, but slowly, as if the driver just didn't want to make a noise at such an early hour. Or maybe they were sneaking out without paying.

My car is also down there, parked in front of the hotel entrance. It's been there for forty-eight hours now. Even when all the festivi-ties were going on they just worked their way around it. They even put a little portable fence around it, maybe to prevent kids from sitting on the roof. Maybe they saw an angry tourist once and didn't want to repeat that experience.

Now a whole team of sweepers is out sweeping, each wearing a khaki vest with the word COMUNALES in big yellow block letters. A well-fed blond lady goes serenely by on her bicycle with a long white skirt and a maroon T-shirt. Five minutes later she rides back with a package under her arm and as she passes she glances at her watch. There's also a splendid view of the cathedral, and especially of the bells, which have not once rung all the time I've been here. Maybe Cuban churches don't like to call attention to themselves in an officially atheist and pro-choice state. But I'm told that all the churches in Cuba toll their bells like mad on Christmas, ever since 1998 when the public observance of Christmas was reinstituted, in honour of the papal visit that year.

Directly across from me, and to one side of the *parque*, is a four-storey office building. This early, there are already three people working away at their desks. One man is doing paperwork. A woman is looking at her computer screen, and just as she turns the computer off, all the lights on lampposts around the *parque* go off as well, an odd coincidence to start the new day.

A small two-seater plane has taken off from the Carlos M. Céspedes Airport and is flying south over Bayamo, still climbing, but painfully. It's heading straight toward Kingston, Jamaica, in the first light of morning, but the engine doesn't sound very good. It's misfiring badly. It sounds exactly like a misfiring 500 cc motorcycle engine. Good luck, amigos.

After the ceremonial festivities yesterday there was some live music in the square, a bandstand was set up, with a little band backing a singer who was very macho with tight jeans, transparent T-shirt, and lots of hairy chest muscles. As soon as his name was announced, hundreds of schoolchildren appeared out of nowhere and came running from all directions up to the bandstand to get a good look at this Revolutionary pop star. He sang some tender Cuban ballads, the music very slow and with great heartfelt crescendos and diminuendos of despair. The kids adored him. What kind of a cretin would drop bombs on a country like this?

There are worse things than being a Cuban streetsweeper. These sweepers are perfectly ordinary Bayamese citizens having a good time. Nobody's working too hard, everybody knows what he or she is doing. It's an everyday opera of interesting chit-chat, gossip, repartee, laughter, and socializing. No rush, no anxiety, everything moves at the speed of nature. And the place is getting shiny clean all over again, as if by magic. And yes, the fellow who tipped the first can over turns out to be the foreman of the sweeping group, and he keeps a close but friendly eye on his flock, and yet he was doing almost as much work as everyone else. No one is doing too much or too little. Everyone's perfectly happy.

On the third floor of the office building an Afro-Cuban office worker opens the window, steps out onto the balustraded balcony, and leans over to watch the ballet of the streetsweepers just as I am doing. She's wearing a black skirt just above her dimpled knees and a white blouse, and she looks as if she's almost ready for a good day's work helping to keep the Revolution humming sweetly in a sour world. It's the Coreos de Cuba building, i.e., the post office.

Every minute that passes there are more people wandering around down there, just as at daybreak anywhere in the known world. From my field of vision, including swivelling my head from side to side, I can see about forty people. Off in the distance a mournful train whistle rises slowly in the morning air. It's the seven o'clock special to Havana. If you want to see a beautiful Latin American city of *la belle époque*, check out Bayamo. I'm tempted to find myself a little apartment and stay here forever or until they kick me out. No matter how long I lived here I'd never understand Bayamo, but it would be an interesting daily challenge trying to reach a state bordering on understanding.

A tractor goes by pulling a cart in which are standing an old *campesino* couple, man and woman, straw hats, a cart that could hold forty people standing in a pinch, and maybe soon will be. A very slim and attractive older woman, about sixty, sizzles by with a decidedly youthful aura about her, amplified by her purple miniskirt, white bobby sox, black suede shoes, and a shockingly black silk top with silky red straps over her shoulders. She looks serious too and is determined to get wherever she's going. Which is to work, no doubt. Or maybe home from work, who knows? Here comes an Afro-Cuban mama with white shoes, a green-and-red parrotlike bandana, a pair of lime green Bermuda shorts, and a very nice jacket. And a large shoulder bag filled with paperwork.

And now it has become light enough to see, from the Royalton rooftop, the faint blue jagged Sierra Maestra way off to the south. Closer at hand, the garbage has been cleaned up and put in bags, and now someone has to bring a cart around to pick up the bags and the brooms.

Even the cops are nice in Bayamo. As I came out of La Bodega last night an officer of the law smilingly pointed to my money belt, suggesting I should pull my shirt over it, which of course I immediately did, being prudent and quick of mind. He wasn't suggesting I was in danger of being robbed, but that I was in danger of causing envy among the poor townfolk. There are thieves everywhere, but it's hard to imagine one in Bayamo, it doesn't seem that kind of city at all. If two cars collided on the main street I don't think there'd be a fight: the drivers would jump out and shake hands.

People are already sitting on the long benches surrounding the square, waiting for something to happen but hoping it doesn't. Five women are standing there with brooms, just chatting. A child is talking merrily to a dog and trying to grab its tail. The dog barks. A fellow kickstarts his motorcycle, then just sits there, looking around, waiting for the little engine to warm up before taking off. One of the women, with red hair, white skin, and blue shorts down to her knees, resumes sweeping but the other four keep chatting. The sun is coming up and the high peaks of the Sierra Maestra are becoming sharply defined.

There are some German tourists in the hotel, and two big tourist buses out front. They came in late last night. The bus driver is the first one up. He unlocks the bus, goes in, makes sure everything is okay. Now he starts the engine and takes off for a little ride all by himself.

Action: A man is holding a bag open and a woman is dumping garbage from the receptacle into the bag. But the man isn't holding the bag open widely enough, so a third woman tries to help him, while a fourth sweeps up the garbage that has spilled – and all four wear those little vests with COMUNALES on the back. People are greeting each other, shaking hands, kissing, wishing each other a good day. Here comes a man in a dirty shirt carrying a table over his head. A man who seems to be the boss of Coreos de Cuba, with shiny black hair and a nice pair of trousers and shiny black shoes, comes over and starts shaking hands with all the sweepers. Then he sits down on the bench with the sweeper boss in the red shirt and they have an earnest talk. Another guy, in a straw hat and a pair of overalls and a sleeveless red T-shirt, has put his can of paint down on the bench and has sat down himself; it looks as if he has a bit of painting to do today, and he's going to get his brand-new running shoes splattered with paint if he's not careful. A lonesome smoker strolling by stops to get a light from the painter, and they chat for a few minutes, with the smoker doing a lot of coughing. There are two dogs on the roof across the way. They are as close to the edge as can be even though it's four storeys straight down, with no retaining wall. The big dog woofs, the little dog yaps, as they both look down at some sweepers directly below them.

And over on the east side of the park there's a circle of six people standing there chatting pleasantly with plenty of arm gestures – five police officers, tall and skinny in light brown shirts and dark brown trousers, and a fashionable young woman with a bag over her shoulder. Now the painter in the overalls is reading a newspaper, and the smoker, an older man, is reading it over his shoulder. It's last week's *Rebelde*. And they're talking about what they're reading as they read it. Then the painter stands up, folds the paper, puts it in his pocket. Will he continue standing there, walk away, or sit down again? The older man is wiggling his knees in anticipation. And the painter sits down again.

The little circle of cops is breaking up. Three of them are walking across the park toward the hotel, then they turn around and look at the two other cops who have opted to stay put and continue their chat with the fashionable woman. These are very benign cops; they smile, they don't have guns, they have brown baseball caps, with brown epaulettes on their shirts, they're all in shades of brown, they're not paranoid, and they don't stop you for questioning just for being black.

Parque Céspedes has two main statues. One is of the aforementioned Perucho Figueredo, who was one of many ordinary amateur musicians in Bayamo until he rose to the occasion and in a fit of inspiration dashed off the words and music for the Cuban national anthem. Little did he know that some day a Cuba Libre would be a refreshing drink on a hot day. On the reverse side of the base of the statue is a plaque commemorating the great Bayamo fire of 1869, which was started by Bayamese patriots in order to drive out the Spanish troops. The plaque shows the church in flames (the same church that, all patched up, I can see from here), and a couple of neighbouring houses also in flame, including the Céspedes house, which has been restored beautifully and is now a charming museum, situated right next to the Royalton.

Much taller and more elaborate is the other statue, showing Céspedes himself urging people to enter into battle with the foe, with a naked woman in chains huddling at his feet, a white man and a black man with machetes in their raised hands, a man gonging a bell, a woman wearing a long gown with a naked baby in her arms, and another man holding his hand up and looking the other way. Also there's a firing squad about to shoot an anguished blindfolded man (representing Céspedes's son Oscar), and there's a man with sword raised ready to bring it down and shout, "Fire!" It's very dramatic and full of action. Céspedes was a great hero, no stranger to prisons, and he did many famous things such as freeing the slaves and proclaiming the Cuban Declaration of Independence (which led to the horrendous Ten Years War). These stirring images on his statue commemorate his signing of a decree granting freedom to the slaves, on December 27, 1870. Earlier that year his son Oscar, who had been captured by the Spanish forces, faced the firing squad because Céspedes refused to negotiate for his son's freedom.

In the Royalton lobby, the Germans are getting ready for a long-distance bicycle ride from Bayamo to Manzanillo. Everything is well organized. They are all dressed in that deliberate, carefully chosen style beloved of tourists, but this gang was especially fashionable, with muted colours, no primaries, and no two alike, as if planned in advance. They are very tense and stiff, but maybe that's just a touch of culture shock. They keep bumping into tables and chairs and pretending they didn't, or pretending that it didn't hurt. I'm sure they'll be fine as soon as they get on their bicycles, which still have to be put together because they've been shipped from Germany in pieces to lessen the bulk cost. But they've got all the tools to put those pieces back together in a flash.

Thank you, Cachita, for providing me with an opportunity to apologize to that poor guy who washed my car. For slamming the door in his face, my apology was accepted with graceful unconditionality. *De nada, de nada.* He looked very splendid this morning in his blue security guard uniform. He's the security guard for the hotel. He thought the Germans were Canadians and I was German. He had a soft musical voice and he had that very handsome Lorca look, a worried, apple-shaped face with a broad forehead, sensitive, definitely no stranger to tears.

This morning I saw my shining car again, and remembered how stricken he'd looked when I snarled at him. And there he was in his uniform studying the Germans as they put the pieces of their bicycles together. Along with my apology I gave him another dollar. He was a bit embarrassed, but for the sake of his family he could hardly refuse to accept it. Apparently it's not in the Cuban temper to be angry about being awakened from the deepest sleep.

But then again he may not have been the one who actually washed the car. I had asked the bartender if he knew of anyone and he said to leave it to him. So I figured that the security guard said he'd do it. But maybe he had a kid do it, paid the kid two pesos, sent the kid home, then came up to bang on my door for the two dollars. Interesting conspiracy theory, but I reject it. The car was too clean for that. I'm discovering over and over again a certain fundamental sense of kindness and honesty in Cuba and am now looking for it and expecting it wherever I go.

But when people bang on your door in the middle of the night in Cuba you can be sure they want money. Don't make my mistake. Just say to them, *Vuelto más adelante* – "Come back later" – and they'll leave you in peace. Hemingway had a more crucial piece of advice to offer tourists with toothaches: all you have to say is, *Este diente lastima pero no lo deseo tiré* – "This tooth hurts but I do not want it pulled."

It's a chartered tour, all arranged in Munich. The Germans flew to Holguín, and by contrast with the Cubans they are graceless. I suppose I am too, but I don't feel that way, and I've had some time to get acclimatized. Every German muscle seems to be stressed. Their anxious eyes are constantly shifting, as if on guard for sneak attacks. You can tell they're not Cubans. Their heads don't seem connected to their bodies. If they're having any fun there's no indication of it. If they're enjoying themselves you would never know it from their faces, or the way they whisper to each other with their hands covering their mouths like baseball players. They're so nervous they're causing me to be nervous about not being nervous enough. They're paying a lot of money for something they don't appear to be enjoying but they're going to remember it as long as memory lasts. And they're going to remember it fondly even though they know they didn't enjoy it at the time. We can all relate to that. Only one of them is a woman, very attractive despite her extreme nervousness, a lovely women with an unpleasant look on her face, and iron self-control in every step she takes. These aren't Teutonic stereotypes, these are human observations uncontaminated by preconceptions. She came out of the hotel and started to walk toward the square, looked as if she was going to examine the statues, but then changed her mind and came back, possibly because she felt self-conscious about the bench-sitters. These Germans seem to adhere to the don't-make-eye-contact-with-the-natives school of bourgeois travel. Can that be fun?

There again is the sweet octogenarian who approached the two guys reading the *Rebelde* in the *parque* earlier. He is elegantly dressed for Bayamo, he looks as if he might be visiting from Miami Beach in his lightweight pale blue suit. He is eighty-five if he's a day, he has a fine white moustache carefully trimmed, and he's wearing a ball cap that says, No. 1 Grampa, which reminds me we're back in Granma Province.

This is the same group of Germans who were sitting in soft black leather sofas and armchairs in the lobby last night, seven men and a woman, and they each had a mimeographed history of Bayamo in their hands, in English. The Cuban tour guide, also in English, was sitting on a hardback chair and reading the history aloud for them and fielding questions. They are all youngish, forty maximum, and fit of course, but they seem so old and grey. They don't seem to notice that they're not standing or sitting comfortably and that they are not watching where they're going.

In the Casa de la Cultura, on the east side of Parque Céspedes, I'm looking at a display of paintings by young painters and listening to a well-amplified tape of mournful Cuban songs from *la belle époque*. One artist has done a whole series of intricate collages, but then he's covered them with double-gauge crinkly plastic so you can't really see them. It's frustrating and annoying. He seems to be saying, My mind is mine alone and I have no desire to share it with you. Maybe this is a silent protest about some aspect of Fidelismo. Another collagist is more comfortable with depicting a normal-sized, rosy-cheeked Yankee businesswoman about to dig into a hamburger the size of a horse. And there's a picture of a guy with no face, but he's holding up a fork with something hanging from it, and sure enough it's his face. The most disturbing collage shows a girl who looks as if she is very happily jumping on a trampoline, but owing to cut and paste there is no trampoline under her, and she is suspended several storeys in the air, as if she is falling to her death from a high building, but with a perfectly joyous look on her face.

I hope the Germans don't come in here, because there's a ghastly painting of a large passenger ship in flames and going down at sea, with people screaming and leaping for their lives, and in the foreground is a German U-Boat with a number 31 on the side and a Nazi captain chuckling with malevolent glee. His men fire at the people as they beg to be rescued from the sea. And here's one by a fellow named Frank, showing Earth surrounded by numerous planets and moons and galaxies, and right in the centre of Earth is a Cuba taking up almost the entire half of the world, with just a little room for each of the other continents, and it has a giant royal palm three thousand miles high and firmly rooted in Cuba.

A young fellow named Arnel Mohaina has done an excellent

painting of the old Bayamo church and he's captured something seemingly so obvious and yet I'd looked and hadn't noticed it. The bell tower looks like a scary human face, a face that seems to be looking out over Bayamo and reacting in horror to what it sees around it. The nose is the clock, there are bell openings in perfect position for the eyes and the mouth, and the tower itself gives the proper proportion to increase the scariness. The artist didn't have to exaggerate. It was all right there for him. But another painter has drawn the same church from the same angle, with very fine pen and ink, and the bell tower is there in the same proportion, but it doesn't look like a face. It's as if this other artist no more noticed the face than I did.

What gets me about these paintings is that they are so ambitious and yet rendered with such confidence. This is a splendid tribute to an educational system for all, in which artistic ventures are not only encouraged, but somehow are made to seem supremely important, not trivialized out of fear as they always seem to have been where I come from, and more so now than ever. These artists have no problem understanding the vital importance of art, a concept Canadian painters seem to be losing, through attrition, and lack of appreciation. There is also in this gallery a sense of the enormous voraciousness of art. You can throw anything into its craw – ideas, things, events, whatever – and solid gold comes out.

But my favourite painting is by Fidel Castro Naranjo, twelve years old. Watch for him, folks, he's going to be a great painter some day. It's a painting of a large factory, a warehouse, some workers' apartment buildings, and a river with an island in it, and there are a few trees and a few garbage receptacles on the island, plus a walkway all the way around, and a boat tied up. Sounds dull, but his style has transformed it because it is so free and effortless, and full of colour, and the whole composition is quite stunning. He has all the right instincts. The factory and warehouse have yellow walls and red roofs, blue smoke is coming out of the smokestacks, one apartment building is pink and one is green, and green mountains loom in the distance.

The friendly fellow who seems to be the curator of the exhibition is sitting there, and he has been listening to the music and carefully watching my reactions as I sail past the paintings. He disagrees entirely with my taste, for he puritanically prefers the darker work, the more laboured pieces. He won't budge an inch from his position, as he takes me around and shows me the poorly conceived paintings he most admires. I forgot to ask him if he was one of the painters. Egad, what if that wretched painting he liked so much was one of his? But both of us were very courteous in our differing opinions. I kept telling him I could see his point. Which was true.

There is also an exhibit of professional painters, but not much to report. The work is a little too clever, imitative, derivative, a basic fundamental absence of joy and freedom, and overly grand in scope – as if I were to shelve these modest little travel books and decide to write the next *War and Peace*. It's not easy to be a painter or a poet in Cuba, especially with Fidel constantly egging artists on to pay allegiance to the Revolution first, their own vision second, and knowing that if you are judged overly counter-revolutionary you might as well pack it in. But as long as El Comandante is such a great admirer of the works of his pint-sized buddy Gabriel García Márquez, things can't be all that bad.

I had an ice-cream cone for breakfast! The only way I could avoid the crowds was to be there when the Tropicrema opened at nine o'clock. My verdict? I'd prefer not to say. I've been spoiled rotten at the Coppelia. Back at the hotel, when the cyclists mount their bikes, they accidentally hit the back wheel with their leg, and they lack poise in the saddle. Their faces are slathered with sunblock. One cyclist, about twenty-five, is constantly wringing his hands. He's been up for a couple of hours, and even last night he was wringing his hands, in the most obsequious manner, and when he walks he leans strangely to the left. Maybe he's "left" behind a whole lot of troubles at the office, and at home. Maybe in capitalist countries he leans to the right.

These people are fanatic cyclists. They are very well organized, and maybe the fun for them is in the organization of the trip, and the danger of having to lose face if something that you were responsible for goes wrong. There's a Cuban motorcyclist who will be leading the eight cyclists, and her boyfriend will be sitting behind her and holding a spare bicycle wheel in his hand. A Cuban male bus driver will be following behind, but I can't tell you why they don't stow the spare bicycle wheel in the bus. I spoke with one of the cyclists. He was very nervous and could hardly speak, no matter how much I encouraged him. He showed me the map and I told him it looked like a great trip, and they'd be soaking up a lot of Cuban atmosphere and history. He nodded enthusiastically.

It turns out they have made arrangements with the Cuban Cycling Association, and now seven or eight Cubans have shown up with their bicycles. The Cubans are much more youthful, if no younger, and it's amazing how much more elegant and graceful they are getting on and off their bicycles, etc. The Germans seem grotesque by comparison, inwardly twisted out of shape, and they stand there staring off into space with ugly looks on their handsome faces. But the Cubans are like flowers, delicate and graceful, like creatures from paradise.

The tallest fellow in the German group is about six-feet-four, and he seems to be more connected to what he's doing than the others. He's actually looking around, checking out the city a bit, not so afraid of eye contact and maybe even chatting and joking with the Cubans. But he's the only one, and I get the feeling he might be a Turkish German, he does not have the typically pink and blond German colouring. Sounds as if I'm doing a bit of racial profiling, but I'm quite carefully just writing down what I see.

Everybody grimaces for a last-minute group photo. And there they go! They're off! With no fanfare, no bugle blasts, no horn honking, no cheers – they just head off in complete silence on the long lonely road to Manzanillo. Honest, there should have been a little band.

Just as I was saying bye-bye to Bayamo, a rich brassy Las Vegas–type tourist showed up and started shouting at a little old man trying to sell him a cone of peanuts: "No, no, get away. Don't want it, don't need it!" It was obvious he didn't realize what this fellow was offering, beautifully wrapped cones full of red unsalted Spanish peanuts, small, fresh, and delicious. So I told him, and suggested he give the guy a peso and try one. So then he started shouting at me, "I don't have a peso, I don't have any pesos!" But I could see that something I'd said had registered, and when I drove away and looked through the rear-view mirror he had given the vendor a dollar bill and had received a whole armful of cones of peanuts in return.

I called Enmo last night and she said, "We were thinking maybe you forgot to call me." She went on and on about what a wonderful time she had. She was so happy I couldn't resist asking if she wanted to do another day trip. We're only eighty miles apart. She's a good guide and interpreter. She helps me to understand what is going on. She is very shy of giving opinions, but she's good with background information if she's certain of her ground.

ALL DAVIDS ARE BROTHERS

Friday, March 5, 2004. On the approach to Holguín, the road becomes an excellent four-lane highway divided by a boulevard planted with flowering shrubs seemingly chosen for their durability under adverse conditions. As I was admiring these tough shrubs, the heavy traffic approaching the big city suddenly came to a halt and stayed halted – both ways. It was a police roadblock. Three police officers quietly standing there was all it took to stop four lanes of traffic for two hours. They weren't searching the cars. It was all very benign. The motorists around me didn't know what was going on and didn't care. I casually informed the guy next to me in a beautiful old white Mercedes-Benz 350 that his left rear tire was three-quarters flat and you should have seen the speed with which he got out his spare and changed the wheel. His trunk was well organized, and his tools nicely arranged. He had all the proper tools – not the toy tools that come with a rental car.

I wandered ahead to ask the cops what was going on. They weren't too sure, they were just following orders and didn't ask questions. But since we were in the vicinity of the Frank País International Airport, they thought it may have something to do with a *visitante importante*. Surely we weren't sitting here frying in the fiery sun because García Márquez was flying in to have a game of dominoes with Fidel? They really weren't sure. But all the time we sat there, not one plane was seen to land or take off. The peace and quiet was awesome on a jampacked *autopista*. Nobody was wringing their hands or pacing up and down. A harmonious serenity was in the air. Hummingbirds were flicking among the shrubs. People seemed almost happy to have a break in the driving, a pause to reassess whether they really wanted to go where they were trying to get. After an hour of this silence, the guy in the Mercedes-Benz, who was in the slow lane, got me to back up a bit and the guy in front of me to move forward a bit – then he drove in between us, mounted the high curb of the median, got stuck, gunned the engine, squealed the tires, then drove over three flowering bushes, came down on the other side, and took off.

Soon other cars were doing the same. They had decided they didn't really need to go where they were going after all, and being forcibly immobilized without even given the courtesy of an explanation violated their socialist instincts.

And wow! Are they going to do it? Yes they are! A bus jammed with at least a hundred schoolkids, like too many monkeys in too small a cage, performed the same trick, up and over, with the kids squealing away as if this was a carnival ride. And soon everybody was either climbing the median or contemplating doing so. It was amazing how resilient those flowering shrubs were. The vehicle would pass over them, and they'd spring back up without even a sepal or a petal out of place. Some smart committee had selected the hardiest shrubs for this median. This sort of situation had been foreseen.

Enmo was expecting me, but I was running late and would soon be running much later. Holguín in my absence has not become an easier city to navigate. I knew exactly how to get to the main plaza. From there I knew exactly how to get to Enmo's place. I could have parked the car and got there on foot easily. Or better still I could have parked it in some hotel lot on the highway and taken a taxi to her place. But for some inexplicable reason I was determined to get there by car or not at all. It seemed important to figure out why everyone, not just me, was having such a problem. And so I drove around and around the city for a couple of hours. I'd spiral in very close to my destination and then inexplicably I'd be spiralled far

away out into the barrios or even out into the lonesome hills overlooking the city without knowing how to get back. Every few blocks
I'd stop for directions. In fact everybody was stopping for directions.
Even the bicycle taxis were most times completely lost but trying to
pretend they weren't.

By the time I got to Enmo's, I'd overextended myself. She greeted
me at the gate, introduced me to her dogs, then reintroduced me to
her mother. Her white-haired grandmother was also there and
proudly told me she was "eighty-one-and-a-half-going-on-eighty-two
and my husband died ten years ago." Was she considering remarry-
ing at all? She gave me a big toothless smile. "Mi no loco!" But then
I collapsed in my armchair. I couldn't take the chit-chat. Are you all
right? said Enmo. I seemed to be in a previously unknown state of collapse, like a four-minute miler staggering and collapsing at the finish
line. Do you want coffee? I thought about it. No, the coffee would
make me feel worse. A big glass of red wine would have been perfect,
but this was a teetotalling house. So I asked for the coffee.

I could barely speak and my thoughts were stalled like the traffic
at the airport. The girls insisted on whipping up a meal for me. I staggered out to the car and brought in a fresh whole pineapple bought
at some roadside en route. Mirian got out her pineapple slicer and we
all dug in. Then she presented me with a plate full of cerdo frijo,
sliced tomatoes, and cabbage salad.

Gradually my senses returned to their nest, accompanied by a
great fatigue. I was dozing off in my chair while reading the big
family Bible. Psalm 23 is excellent in Spanish, and it suited the
moment perfectly. The Bible with its very fine onion-skin paper was
on a little table of its own between two windows with the shutters
almost always open. The pages would flutter in the breeze so at any
given moment you would have a seemingly random page selected for
your reading pleasure and inspiration.

Finally I felt as if I'd been enough trouble. I could drive to the
Hotel Pernik but no farther. Mirian and Enmo insisted on accompanying me to prevent a recurrence of my inability to get anywhere in
this town, so to speak. They directed me almost flawlessly, and they
navigated me through a part of town I hadn't even noticed during

my earlier lost wanderings. They were nice about it, but they refused to believe that Holguín was a difficult city to navigate.

When we got to the hotel they refused my offer of cab fare home. They wouldn't hear of it. Strange how in Cuba I'm besieged by the extremes of being unable to pay for kind services pleasantly rendered, and having to dish out cold cash for services neither required nor requested.

After a gin and tonic at the Hotel Pernik Cyber Café, my energy returns. My brother Jack has sent me an e-mail informing me of the deaths of two great Canadian painters, Tony Onley in a plane crash and Guido Molinari of lung cancer. But there were no vacancies at the Hotel Pernik, so I slithered down the road to the Villa El Bosque. Eduardo, who doubled as bellboy and front-desk clerk, soon was eagerly trying out his English on me. His vocabulary was impressive, but his grammar and pronunciation needed a lot of work.

This hotel has a pleasant tropical border blur when it comes to the categories of indoors and outdoors. There's an outdoor karaoke bar with a very good singer whose breasts, like a pair of white cockatoos, were teetering on the verge of flying from the half-open cage of her very low-cut dress. Nobody could take their eyes off her for a second, since a wardrobe malfunction seemed imminent. Then out came two male comedians, whose fast-paced repartee, with wigs and dresses, and sudden gender reversals, required no translation. One of the guys was big and fat and the other short and skinny, but together they were 100 per cent obscene. The crowd was full of families with kids, and nobody was rushing to put their hands over the kids' ears. In fact, the kids were getting the jokes before the parents were.

On the way back to my room to catch up on my note-taking and sleep I ran into a little mariachi band looking very down in the dumps. The karaoke speakers were blasting out canned Cuban music, and these guys, who were hidden in a corner of a porch outside the main dining room and with no audience whatsoever, were very quietly playing along with the karaoke music, and they looked so depressed I sensed a great injustice was being perpetrated that bodes poorly for the future of Cuban music. These musicians were being locked out in favour of canned and pirated recorded music both domestic and from other countries. When they saw me go by, then do a double-take, then stop with a look of astonishment on my face, they leapt to their feet and began to serenade me with *mucho gusto*. It was wonderful. There was David (with Indian features) on Cuban guitar. When he asked my name his jaw dropped. He gave me a hug and said, "All Davids are brothers!" He said he had two little boys at home, and they both have their own pint-sized Cuban guitars. To me, anything acoustic, with six strings, particularly in three pairs, is a Cuban guitar.

We all started dancing gaily and effortlessly, even some of the restaurant staff gathering around to applaud and laugh. But, strangely, the tourists in the restaurant and the Cubans at the karaoke bar preferred to ignore the live music. We were having too much fun for their taste. There seemed to be a few metaphorically still-lively women in their thirties or forties who were with old men who wanted nothing better than to drag them back to their room, though I sensed the women would have preferred to be free to stick around, have fun with us, and let the old guys get back to their room all on their own.

As for the band, they liked it when I declared it highly unfair that they should be relegated to a lonely corner, while the karaoke operator was making a good dollar for his "work." Well, he had to lug around the speakers and adjust the controls now and then, or pretend to. These were three of the thousands of brilliant musicians in Cuba and elsewhere who will live and die without ever seeing a hint of a recording contract, or very seldom even get a paying gig. And the hotel owners would rather pay a karaoke dealer to play recorded music than to actually hire live musicians. It's not only unfair, it's short-sighted, and it's counter-productive, and it may even be counter-revolutionary. But we are living through a period where there is a very pronounced *fin de siècle* attitude about everything. Worse than *fin de siècle*, more like a *fin du monde* mindset – not just culturally but in every way. Take the money and run.

As for the "important visitor" at the airport, nobody can tell me what that was all about. Not even Eduardo. Not even David. Not even the two gay comedians. And not even the floozy with the two cockatoos. Will we ever find out? Stay tuned.

After sitting up in bed and jotting down some notes for an hour or two in my room, the power went off, so my power went off too and I fell asleep, but when the power jolted back on, I was suddenly wide awake and resumed taking notes. This happened several times. Just as I began to feel sleepy again, at dawn, workmen showed up under my window and started hammering. So I checked out, got in the car, and the battery had died overnight. Managed to get the car started with the help of a little push from a competitor in the car-rental racket who kept saying he should not be doing this because he was from a different company. Then out on the road once again to Camagüey, where there was a Panautos agency, and where I would be able to get a battery replacement. But first, as soon as I got onto the *autopista*, I pulled the car over for a moment to check the map or something, and as an act of unconscious self-sabotage I turned off the key. With a dollar bill I managed to flag down a man and woman on a scooter: they gave me a push, enough to start rolling down the hill backwards, jammed it into gear, and the car started. But they wouldn't take my dollar bill. I had to beg them. I said, "Please?" and put on my little Lolita look, tenderly slipping the dollar into the fellow's breast pocket. He smiled sweetly, and accepted it.

After getting the second push I picked up a hitchhiker who had cleverly positioned himself at a level crossing that caused traffic to slow to a crawl. He ran alongside me with his head in my open window, and with such a funny look on his face I had to stop for him. He turned out to be a pretty good young fellow, about twenty-six, and he helped to keep me awake, and he helped me with the car as well. He was asking me so many questions about my life in Canada I didn't have a chance to ask him anything about his life in Cuba.

He said his father is an engineer, high up in the Ministry of Industry, who gets to approve and review projects, assign staff, have long lunches, etc. He's highly respected because he does good work. He even gets sent abroad now and then, most recently to Mexico for a conference on Latin American development. Mexico is the only country he mentioned, but that's something.

Jannier lives with his mother and his sister, somewhere in this general area. But he's not often home. He's got a nice personality, he's naturally likable, outgoing, smart, but he never stops talking. If you're a little tired, as I was at the time, you sort of wish he'd shut up for a while. But maybe he knew I'd doze off and crash the car if he shut up. Therefore he went on and on about how it's generally understood in Cuba, and he agrees, as does his father, that every marriage should split up after fifteen years. By that time a man has his friends and the woman has her friends, so they don't really need to be under the same roof, or even to be in touch with each other constantly.

He claims to know every town in every province of Cuba, and when I asked if he knows all eleven million Cubans as well he said that in the remoter parts of the island province of Juventad there were still a few he hasn't met yet. He says he supports his mother and his sister by travelling from one end of Cuba to the other, making friends, buying things cheap, and selling them dear, mostly portable things of great value such as rare parts for old cars or motorcycles. He goes to one province where there's a surplus of squiggle-jiggles, and he buys a box full, and then he goes to a province where there's a shortage of squiggle-jiggles and he makes a killing. It's not the sort of thing Fidel might approve of, and Che would be disappointed that this far into the Revolution people still have to operate that way to make things work, especially when they have to hitchhike everywhere they go, and stay over at an uncle's place. But it's not the sort of thing my friend would be thrown in jail for, except maybe for the occasional short stretch.

He mostly deals in car parts, bicycle parts, motorcycle parts, and he likes to pick up unusual things that nobody would think they need until they see it and then can't live without it, like toilet seats maybe. He talks to people and finds out what they need, what they're short of, or he helps them figure out what little part they need to get their motorcycle on the road again, and he remembers all these talks. Then he might return in a week or two with the very thing they've been wanting, and everybody's overjoyed. Not only do they pay him, they invite him to dinner and a sleepover.

I asked him where his bag was and he said he was just going into Camagüey to make a delivery and he'd stay over at his uncle's place. He pulled a shiny chrome gadget out of his pocket. It seemed to be the sort of thing that would be easy to rig up at a machine shop. But he insisted it was extremely rare, it broke easily, and there was a certain kind of motorcycle that couldn't run without it.

It was a strange conversation because he wanted to listen to stories about Canada, but I was too tired to tell him any more, and he picked up the slack by telling me about his life. He was excited about what he was doing, but you could tell he didn't want to be doing it when he was thirty. He was ready to make a significant shift when the time came. But he had no sense of what it would be.

I told him about the flat battery, the slow leak in the tire, the malfunctioning jack. Forgot to mention the broken radio and the bad shocks. Jannier didn't think it was the battery that was flat, there was something wrong with the ignition switch – and he knew where he could get a new one for me easily, and he'd even help me install it. Look, I said, the clock and all the digital displays are screwed up, that's not caused by an ignition switch, it's caused by a flat battery. So then he reached over and peeped the horn.

"Yes, but the horn is working," he said.

"Maybe a horn doesn't require as much power," I said.

"But a horn," he said, "must certainly draw more power than these tiny lights."

I said, "You are most certainly right, but these lights are still on. If they were a horn they'd be honking, but it is just that they can no longer register the correct numbers."

He tried the horn again for a bit longer and it faded out. "You too are most certainly right," he said. "The horn in fact does not sound the way a healthy horn should sound."

We pulled into a tourist restaurant up from the road on the side of a hill so we could get the car started easily. But he showed me how well he knew Cuba by taking me on a climb above and behind the proud tourist diner to a humble peso restaurant. It's not unheard of in Cuba for two restaurants – one high-priced, one low-priced – to share the same kitchen. It's the sort of two-price system one might expect to see in semi-touristy parts of any poor country, or even the poorer provinces of a rich country. Cubans in the back, tourists in front. It is a bit offensive from a human point of view, although if you make the stretch it's certainly defensible from an economic point of view.

Cocaine has its appeal to many, but for a quick pick-me-up there's nothing like icy-cold agua mineral con gas, the more you can get down the better. What a lifesaver on a hot day. Jannier had a pork sandwich, but sparkling spring water was all I needed.

The wonderful thing was that when we pulled into the Cuba Taxi garage in Camagüey, they confirmed that yes indeed they were part of the same company that owned my car, Panautos, and they would be glad to exchange a better battery for my battered battery. Jannier is truly a famous and well-loved guy, everybody at Cuba Taxi knew him and welcomed us with open arms. There was a woman with flashing dark eyes who, though with happy smiles, seemed a bit out of place in a greasy garage, with seven or eight guys. I pictured her as giving tango lessons on weekends. We were all standing in a semi-circle, watching as the designated workman pulled out my battery and replaced it with the one he had just removed from another car. Several of us had clipboards, and there were even notes being jotted down. And, in one of those imperishable Cuban moments, when I flicked on the ignition and the car roared to life, everybody jumped for joy and threw their arms around each other. No kidding! The tango queen naturally wanted to throw her arms around the gringo or, even better, Jannier, but she was prevented from doing so by the piggish embraces of her boring old Cuba Taxi colleagues. When we calmed down, I shook hands with every single one of them and thanked them profusely.

Jannier mentioned there was a baseball game in Sancti Spíritus tonight, with Havana. He said if I felt up to it he'd love to come along and I wouldn't even have to drive him back. I wanted to go, but I just felt it would be foolish because although I didn't feel sleepy just now, I could be overcome with sleep at any moment.

He was a sort of medieval character, a travelling tinker – but much better educated and much healthier. More of him to come.

Camagüey is not the city I remember from two weeks ago. I had a hard time finding the park where I met the two Canadians, and when I did it seemed much smaller, and the surrounding buildings more imposing. Things kept going wrong. I began to think I shouldn't stay the night. Also it seemed impossible to find a patch of shade at this time of day. It was very hot. I developed a severe burn on my left arm – the same arm I'd had out as I drove all day because of the flat battery and having to keep the air conditioning off.

A young *mosca* who was very persistent and obnoxious, but always just interesting enough to make me resist telling him to buzz off, started chasing me on his bicycle, frantically offering his various services. Like many overly energetic persons he didn't know what he was doing. For instance, I just wanted a hotel, but he insisted on taking me to all these *casa particulares*. Unfortunately for him, they were all booked up with Cubans on longer stays. They wanted to take me, a guy with U.S. dollars, but it wouldn't be right to kick out a Cuban with pesos to make way for a Canadian with dollars, now would it? So my friend kept taking me to all the wrong places. He yelled at them and told them they were crazy for not throwing out a poor Cuban to make way for a rich Canadian. And I soon had no idea how to get back to where my car was parked.

But I finally got back on the road, having failed to find a place to stay in Camagüey. And now I'm sitting in that same crummy hotel in Ciego de Ávila. Maybe I came back here because I was too tired to look for another place, or maybe I needed more punishment. The night clerk was begging me not to eat in the hotel restaurant. He didn't have to convince me, it wasn't very good before, and I wasn't going to try that again.

But I did pop into the restaurant for a moment and there was Gina. She looked at me and remembered me instantly. She approached me ever so slowly, didn't want to be too fast, she was such a fascinating mixture of womanly grace and girlish awkwardness, and she silently presented her cheek for a nice little kiss. When I gave her one she presented her other cheek for another nice little kiss, and when she switched cheeks she accidentally brushed my cold lips with her hot ones.

But the fellow insisting the food here is no good was perfectly right. There was a lot of steam rising from a lot of vats, but the grub reminded me of the descriptions of what Che and his men had to eat in the final days in Bolivia.

Maybe it was a scam, and to be sure he'd get a kickback from the *paladares*, he wasn't telling me the food here was bad out of the kindness of his heart, but he was in his own way doing the right thing. He was the whistleblower. Pretending the restaurant was good was not helping the Cuban tourist industry. The more people he tells not to eat here, the sooner the hotel people will realize improvements have to be made.

I walked through the restaurant to a bar at the back, a U-shaped bar with about twelve stools. The bar was a bit too large for the room it was in, and it was also exceedingly darksome even for a dark bar. It was definitely a bar in the Cuban-only style, but the bartender wasn't about to accept pesos for my Cuba Libre. Not only was he too smart for that, he spoke excellent English. He had real Coca-Cola, at a premium, so it was no wonder he didn't want to mess with pesos, as if Coke was somehow better than the local cola manufacturers, or in some magical way worthier of being purchased, as if Valium were better than diazepam.

Not only was this place poorly lit, but the walls, the ceiling, and the bar were all painted black. So I snapped open the can, which was unusually cold, so cold the Coke wouldn't pour. It was frozen solid. It'd been sitting in the freezer for eons waiting for a tourist and was perfectly preserved. I tried to eject some Coke like a ketchup bottle, but it didn't work; so when I gave it a squeeze it splattered all over the counter. At first the bartender had a look on his face that said when you have liquid gold don't spill a drop. But he brought his rag over and asked if I wanted ice with my drink. Haw haw!

At first I was the only one there, but then a black man and his wife came in and ordered Coke. They were smarter than me. When they noticed it was super cold and wouldn't pour they calmly let it sit and thaw out – no problemo. Then three other black people came in, but they didn't want anything just yet.

The bartender looked like a movie star of the 1930s, with pure white skin, black curly hair, red lips, and he wanted to know what part of Canada I was from. He said he had a daughter up in Canada, and I wondered if it was a romance between a Canadian tourist and him or was it something more serious. So to spare him embarrassment I simply asked if he was troubled by that at all, and he said no he was perfectly happy. Now I wish I'd asked for details.

Meanwhile, back in the lobby, the small but very comfortable leather sofas that the staff sleep on at night were just now completely occupied by very respectable family-oriented Cubans. They had no luggage, they weren't staying at the hotel, they were just sitting there stiffly in the soft chairs, in complete silence, surreptitiously eyeballing the tourists, picturing themselves in a tourist's shoes, and wondering if they would be acting the same way if they had seemingly unlimited sources of U.S. funds. It was pure entertainment and an exercise for the imagination. Mostly the same people as when I was here before. It was a nice place to sit on a hot night. There are doormen diligently refusing entry to other Cubans, but that was probably because they knew they wanted to sit on the leather chairs and they were all occupied. Try again tomorrow. Come early if you want to stay late.

But this time there were some crazy screamers upstairs. Beautiful women were running through the halls in their underwear and scaring each other by screaming fearsome pussycat meows and tiger growls at the top of their lungs, pretending they had escaped from the zoo, and they were having fun leaping out and pouncing on each other in the dark corridors. And there was a rather oafish thick-headed person behind the front desk. He hadn't been here on my previous visit, for I would have remembered him for sure, with the odd grunting sounds he persisted in making, whether talking to me or his colleagues. He insisted on carrying my bag upstairs. I didn't want him to. He kept insisting. We had a tug of war. He won. The cat people had taken possession of the elevator, so he snorted and panted all the way up the stairs. He waited at the door with his hand out. I reluctantly pulled out some money and he pointed at it and said, "Dollar! Dollar!" Earlier he had shouted, "Passport! Passport! Passport!" in my good ear three times before I had finished reaching in my pocket and getting the passport out of my wallet. I managed to shove it under his nose before he could yell "Passport" a fourth time.

When I came back down, the place had filled up with beautiful Cuban women dressed in very tiny miniskirts and bottomless cleavage, and the same desk clerk who had been telling me how bad the food was here took me to one side and pleaded with me whisperingly to try the food at this *paladares* he insisted was the best in the world. I hadn't been to a *paladares*, so it made sense to check it out, if it was the best in the world. But I couldn't possibly go until I had a shower, and there was no water in my room. The desk clerk introduced me to the little guy in charge of water, and he offered him, I suspect, a cut of the *paladares* commission if he could have my shower running in thirty minutes. After thirty minutes there was still no water and the little guy said ten more minutes. And sure enough in another twenty minutes some water started trickling out thinly and I managed to have a bit of a shower, though I was unable to shave after the shower owing to a sudden resurgence of total waterlessness.

On my way out I passed the plumber-in-chief, shook his hand, thanked him profusely for getting the water started just for me. He beamed radiantly. Cubans love to have their hand shook and they love to be thanked for their efforts. A good handshake, a look in the eye, a wink, and a *muchas graçias* often elicits a stronger response than a tip. When you hold out your hand to a Cuban it's a wonderful thing. It's not something they expect from tourists, and it's a sign of sympathy, understanding, solidarity, trust, and maybe even a cautious sort of love. When you do a double handshake, taking their hand in two of yours, that definitely adds to the atmosphere of sincerity, and they positively purr with pleasure. They also respond well to a high-five. And when you take the time to kiss a Cuban woman on both cheeks, she's liable to kiss you on the lips and be your friend for as long as you want.

After a long walk, longer and much more confusing than the map would indicate, I was just about to give up when I found the nice little house with the plastic flamingo on the door. I had to sit in the front room for an hour staring at the artificial flowers in ceramic vases on the tables and floors, along with knick-knacks, doodads, and whatnots here and there, and the framed family photos on the wall. One frame contained eight very cool action shots of a boy about ten years old all dressed up for the big game and proudly wielding a brand new Slugger baseball bat.

There were two fairly large tables in one small dining room – one with six people dining and the other with four. They all seemed to be youthful Cubans, dressed in their best clothes, and they'd be getting the peso rate. The table for six looked like well-heeled high-school graduates on a triple date. When the other four showed signs of being finished, the owner of the *paladares* took my order. Cabbage salad was very good, he said. No seafood. Chicken very good. Pork. Biftek. So I had two beers, and when he brought the biftek, cabbage salad, French fries, and papaya there was enough for ten men. He'd obviously been used to tourists with monstrous appetites. I didn't eat one-tenth of the food and it came to ten dollars.

So they've done a fair job of setting up a little alternate eatery, though the food was blander than bland, and it left me bloated after a few bites. Nothing on the table stimulated my appetite. I don't think this would be considered a proper *paladares*. Christopher P. Baker says if there's no printed menu, then it's a bad sign and you should up and walk out, but I couldn't do that. Ten years ago some such innovative entrepreneurs found themselves in jail. But now the *paladares* have been reluctantly accepted, as a competitive thorn in the side of the state restaurants, forcing them to try harder to please their patrons. The *paladares* are accepted but not liked by Fidel and the Fidelistas, who refuse to eat at them, so we're told. These places are seen as counter-revolutionary, and the people who run them are indulging in personal enrichment, a no-no in a socialist state, but the *paladares* are, like all thorns in the side, essentially useful in the larger scheme of things.

Now I'm back in my room and I have no idea how long I've been without sleep. Havana and Sancti Spíritus were playing in extra innings when I got home, so it was exciting baseball, but I still fell asleep before the final run. For some reason I had forgotten how noisy this room overlooking the street was, even in the middle of the night. It's the same room as last time and it feels as if I've been coming here off and on all my life. The room overlooks the same narrow street, the street where all the Holguín night people hang out, and all night long it's hollering and honking, squealing and shrieking, incessant revving of engines, the rolling of empty fifty-gallon drums down the street, and every now and then an emergency vehicle will blast by with its siren going, on its way to another bloody emergency somewhere, or maybe just a simple case of food poisoning at some out-of-the-way *paladares*. This is the only spot in Cuba where I have heard sirens, and there were two the last night I was here and four tonight already. Just when you're about to slip into deep sleep – another siren.

Also getting in the way of slumber was my barbecued left arm, which was tingling in the most worrisome fashion, from shoulder to knuckle. To be truthful, it was really sore, beyond pink, well done. Luckily I'd been an ardent reader of tropical adventure books as a boy, and remembered how quickly gangrene could set in, and with what unpleasant results. So I slathered the arm with Polysporin. It was the right thing to do. My arm saluted me. So then I took a full relaxing tab, rather than my normal half, and fell almost immediately into the deepest sleep.

Slept for about two hours, then the all-night screaming and screeching in this strange little street reached a crescendo and I was awakened, but it was a good awakening, because it saved me from a horrible dream that had something to do with the large chunk of biftek I'd managed to get down. It wasn't a very good cut and it was entirely lacking in taste, but I slathered it with Cuban ketchup (much like Worcestershire sauce) and foolishly ate too much of it.

In my dream, there was a crazy woman who was very angry with me. She had electrical cords coming out of her head, and they were all waving around. If one of those cords touched me I'd be fried. I wanted to turn and run, but bravely stood my ground as she approached. The scene shifted and I found myself on an underground train, but stretched out and strapped tightly to the undercarriage as the train hurtled at top speed around the bend and back again. Again, there were all these electrical cords that were wiggling around. If one touched me I'd be dead, but I couldn't move. It was the most horrible nightmare I've experienced. I'm sure it had plenty to do with the fact that I had eaten beef for the first time in years.

And then who should visit me under the subway train but my Vancouver friend George Bowering. He sized up the situation and told me I didn't have to worry about those cables. He grabbed one to show me they're harmless. See? It won't kill you. But you have to know what time it's okay to grab it. If you grab it at the wrong time, it will kill you. But if you grab it at the right time, it will be harmless. And there is even a certain time to grab it and it will set you free. He tried to explain how you could tell when the time was right, but at that point he stopped making sense.

WILDFIRES AT SUNSET

Saturday, March 6, 2004. Jannier was most impressive yesterday on political issues, such as when I asked him what he thought of the Volverán issue, Los Cinqo Innocentes, and what he thought about the Cuban drug laws.

He said it's amazing that in the United States you can actually be given life in prison for opposing terrorism – if the terrorism you're opposing is against Cuba. He said it seems odd that it has now become a crime to warn human beings that they are about to be killed. He also said it makes him sick to his stomach to realize that anyone in the United States could come to Cuba at any time and kill all the people he wanted, and if he could get back to the United States without being caught he would not be prosecuted there. So it's not only okay to kill Cubans, it's a crime to try to stop them from being killed.

As for dope, he said as far as he knows there is no marijuana anywhere on the island. Except what grows wild. He said he heard of a guy who got ten years for having a bag of pot he found growing wild. He also said his father believes from a personal experience he had in Mexico that pot is extremely powerful stuff, but he thought it would be impossible to allow popular use of marijuana in Cuba, and it was important for Fidel to "nip in the bud" any potential outbreak of pot smoking because it would just be the end of the Revolution. He thought it would be seen as counter-revolutionary because of its tendency for potheads to spend more time thinking their own thoughts and less time thinking Fidel's thoughts. People would have a greater tendency to think for themselves.

Not without sadness, I dropped Jannier off at his uncle's place outside of Camagüey. His uncle lived in some kind of walled block community. There were several sections of flats, each about four or five storeys high – grey, dark, gloomy. There was a big stone wall around it, with a locked iron fence. If it sounds like a prison, I should add there were no bars visible on the windows. Jannier asked some-body at the gate if his uncle was home. Then he came back and said, Yes, it's all right, I'm going to stay here. He didn't seem to want to say much about the place, and I didn't want to ask. He would tell me if he wanted to. He would know that I'd be interested.

And then I presented him with a brand-new five-dollar bill. His whole body stiffened as if struck by lightning and his eyes just popped out of his head. It was amazing. He couldn't believe it. He'd already told me that he wouldn't accept any money off me, but then he added, "I'm not going to charge you a cent, but if you want to make me a gift, that's okay." He figured the free ride was plenty. But he didn't figure on a guy like me. I had a whole pocket full of fives. Why not give him one? If it destroys his Revolutionary sentiments, if it detours him into a life of sin, causing him to abandon his mother and sister, nobody could possibly blame me for that.

But I have a feeling he will hang on to that five till he gets home, then give it to his mom. That's my reading of Jannier.

I woke up this morning seized by a strong desire to return to Havana forthwith, but first I had to watch Fidel on TV. He is getting old. His eyes are baggy and so is his dark blue suit, which he wears with a white shirt and a dark blue tie with white polka dots. He has no spring in his step. It's all play-acting for him these days. You could see him occasionally suppressing a yawn. The Vietnamese have great suits but lousy haircuts, the Cubans have great haircuts but not so good suits. Solution? Send barbers to Vietnam in exchange for tailors to Cuba.

Yes, that's what caused the roadblock on the *autopista* yesterday.

The top leaders of the Vietnamese government were flying into a quiet airport to be greeted by the top leaders of the Cuban government who were in the airport waiting for them. So it was a perfectly legitimate precaution to close down the highway, thereby lowering the chances of somebody eviscerating the Cuban and Vietnamese governments with one bomb. What a mess a few guys with AK-47s could have made if they opened fire just as the Vietnamese and Cubans were throwing their arms around each other.

I've had breakfast, waited on by my little sweetheart Gina, and told her I'd be sure to drop back in next time I'm in Cuba. I've phoned my sad friend Enmo and told her where I was and why. She understood perfectly, thanked me for my friendship, and hoped to see me again sometime somewhere. I'm well rested and the car is driving well. There's a shady place for coffee on the Carretera Central, near the small town of Jicotea (est. pop. 1,400). There's a baseball game on a small-screen TV above the bar. I can't seem to get a good angle on it without glare. An outfielder has a similar problem, drops a sacrifice fly, and a Havana run scores, with the Havana manager jumping up and down.

At the next stool sits a tall, fair-skinned Afro-Cuban about thirty-five, a very distinguished Buddha who looks as if his face will be as serene twenty years from now. He works for a series of tourist hotels on Cayo Coco, owned by, in part, the famous former Canadian hockey star Serge Savard, who visits Cayo Coco a lot, and not just to check out his investments. They've become good friends.

Today his job is to escort a large group of Havana Club employees on a tour of this area. There are about three little Havana Club buses full of them. Next to the coffee shop is a tourist *finca*, where the Havana Club contingent go around looking at the old-style thatched farmhouses and study how different kinds of fruit trees are grafted and grown. Now and then at Havana Club and most other state enterprises, groups of employees who have been doing good work get a free trip like this with their immediate families, and it must be thrilling for them. Maybe some of them are bartenders who have done a good job of promoting Havana Club products. But to be truthful (as always!), they don't look as if they're having any fun. The tour leader, the fellow I was chatting with, was the only one who seemed at all happy to be there. He said he was particularly happy because he got a day off work in order to do this, and "quite frankly it's a nice little break." He said he had many friends in Toronto, mostly in the tourist business, and everybody keeps in close contact.

We also talked about the Vietnamese delegation. He thought it was just a friendly visit, he didn't think there was anything special to it. Just keeping up friendly relations is the best way to operate if you want to live in a friendly world. There were about fifty people, they just decided to come over and say hello to Fidel, do some goose-stepping, make a few congratulatory remarks, cement the friendship, exchange a few Revolutionary medals. I said Fidel was looking older than he did on TV just a few weeks ago even. My friend said, Yes, he's almost seventy-eight and that's particularly old for a guy who lived such a dangerous and action-packed life as he has. Like most Cubans, he restrained himself and spoke politely about the United States and its Cuban policy. We made a quick list of what we saw were the respective virtues in leadership style exhibited by Presidents Bush and Castro, and I'm sorry, George, but the latter won the day hands down. As soon as the Havana Club gang heard we were talking about Bush and Castro they fell silent, their ears perked up, and they inched closer. Everybody's a quasi-journalist, secretly looking for a scoop. And something that seems dull today could be very interesting tomorrow. And then, with all eyes on us, and perhaps as a spoof of the visit of the Vietnamese delegation, the tour leader ceremoniously pinned a Havana Club button on my Old Navy sweatshirt – just below the left clavicle.

An old Austin-Healey went by, a relic left behind by a California playboy who brought it down to race in Cuba in 1952, during the era of organized sports-car races for small purses on dirt tracks. He totalled it on the track and didn't consider it worth shipping home. That's my fantasy. Some patient and dedicated Cuban claimed it and over the years restored it to peak form. Willy Nelson's "On the Road Again" could be the official anthem of the Cuban motoring fraternity. Whoever brought that car here fifty years ago or so is probably dead, but the car seems very much alive.

Sad news! Enmo on the phone said she finally had her interview and there was nothing for her just now. She would try again in a couple of months. She could not talk about it more than that, but she was frustrated. She would have been a good fit in any of the top hotels in Cuba. She was a highly respectable person, and not the type one would feel comfortable pumping for information. But somehow I think it may have had something to do with her religious beliefs, and her sister being in Florida may have been a factor. Maybe in the past Enmo has been supportive of some of the more extreme anti-abortionists. Probably she doesn't even know for sure why she is being stonewalled, and does not wish to speculate about it out loud. She doesn't seem to be the type to be carried away by her religious beliefs, but maybe she has been annoying tourists by talking about the evils of abortion. She certainly did not betray her feelings about such sensitive topics to me during our time together. Not a word about it.

I briefly mentioned Enmo to my Cayo Coco comrade, careful not to bring up any issues about religion or political attitudes, and he jotted down her name and promised to find out what the problem was, if there was one. And I emphasized to him that Enmo did not offer any special theories about why she was not being hired; in fact, she didn't even suggest there were any such reasons beyond the fact that the hotels in her area currently had too many employees for too few guests.

Also, you wouldn't notice this if you hadn't seen her with her mother and grandmother, but there is a certain heaviness in Enmo's eye. She's a wonderful person, but something is not quite right. She's not comfortable in her skin somehow. She's witty and spontaneous, but something is holding her back from having the same sort of absolute happiness and untrammelled joie de vivre one sees not only in most Cubans but specifically in her very happy and carefree mother and grandmother. As for her romantic side, all she offered was that she did have a passionate romance a few years ago, but it didn't last long and after her lover abruptly changed his mind about loving her forever she was furious for a long time. Apparently the fury was much more furious than the fun was fun, and she doesn't want any part of that sort of thing any more. It made perfect sense to me, so I wasn't going to be foolish enough to try to change her mind. In fact I'm of pretty well the same mind on that subject, and when I told her that she seemed very pleased. In fact, I think for a little while I became her missing father. And now I've gone missing again. In retrospect I see her as a person in a slightly depressed state who is forcing herself to seem happy, and she'll be better when she gets back on the job.

Eat eggs when in Cuba. The chicken may taste as if it has been frozen and thawed out too many times before it reaches the table. But the eggs are yummy and maybe even medicinal. They know how to fry an egg in this country. The eggs are small, but no matter how they cook them they're good. This morning, both eggs were piping hot, though one was slightly overcooked and one was slightly under-cooked – what a yummy combination! – and both were from free-range chickens.

So I shall, along with Fidel, avoid the private restaurants from now on – the *paladares* – and will concentrate on nothing but those sweet, healthy little huevos fritos, pescado, moros y cristianos – and Havana Club.

A giant garbage truck with thirty skinny *campesinos* standing up high in the back is slowly chugging up a hill. I can't see what's coming so I'm just about to slow down to the slow speed of the truck, but just before I do an alert *campesino*, standing straight up in the back of the truck, can see much farther into the distance and can see the road on the other side of the hill is clear. So he waves me on.

Wasn't that kind! Because of that poor agricultural worker's keen eye and good heart, I didn't even have to take my foot off the gas.

And as soon as I'm over the hill, so to speak, I have to slow down because we're heading into Sancti Spíritus, which a billboard proclaims as A Dignified and Respectable City of the Provinces Offering Many Interesting Experiences. But my desire to return to Sancti Spíritus has turned to dust. Havana is calling. It's time for the bypass to the fastest highway in all of Cuba – A1, the *autopista*. It's time to let this albatross of a vehicle fly home. Havana, here we come!

With that, a tall beanpole of a cop jumps out from the shady grassy median under an overpass and flags me down. This looks like trouble. So I slam on the brakes really hard. He politely asks where I'm going and if I could accommodate two *campesinos*. He gestured to indicate they were sheltering under the bridge. But there weren't any *campesinos* under the bridge. All I could see was one other cop. And as friendly as this cop seemed to be, and the other one probably would be as well, do I really want to have to take two cops all the way to Havana, even if they do call themselves *campesinos*?

This sounded a little fishy, so I thought fast and told them I wasn't actually going to Havana tonight, in fact I'm very weary and am looking for a place to stay for the night. Then tomorrow I will continue on to Havana, and these fake *campesinos* will probably be there by then. And besides they wouldn't want to get into the car with a guy as tired as I am. He could see I felt badly, so he patted me on the shoulder and said okay, thank you very much anyway, and he shook my hand so that I would feel better.

The sun is beginning to set west of the Río Manacas. Soon it will become huge and bright red as it did yesterday at about this time. People at the side of the road have beautiful pink, white, and blue birthday cakes for sale. There's a hysteria about birthday cakes in Cuba. Everywhere you go there are birthday cakes being transported, sold, bought, taken home, but I've never seen anyone actually eating one. They're always extra large and perfectly square. No circular or rectangular cakes are allowed, that just wouldn't be Cube-ah. Last night as the sun was setting the moon was rising at 180 degrees. So there could have been an eclipse last night. Haven't heard a thing, but lunar eclipses don't get much press these days, and I haven't been reading the Cuban papers, all two of them, or any other papers since leaving Havana. Which is another reason to get back to Havana. News.

There have been fires along here, very large ones, out of control, still steaming in places, and now here are the egrets again, discovering anew that grubs taste better when cooked.

And now there are great dense clouds of smoke hanging low on the highway. Fire for a mile, all along the highway, horrible-tasting smoke, and there are other fires raging off in the distance, with burnt-out sections between them. The fires are devouring what little patches of forest are left in Cuba, then burning up the grass, and then igniting new patches of dry forest, with blackened royal palms, each stripped of its leaves, and topped with a candlelike flame far above the surrounding inferno.

Now a range of pyramid-shaped mountains appears on the horizon, with the red sun setting, and we're out of the smoke and flames. Those palm trees on the slopes of pointy hills, outlined like windmills against the sky, might be burned to a crisp by the morning, but right now they're as alive as anything can be, silhouetted against the setting sun.

Through all this fiery landscape there has been no sign of human activity, and an amazing lack of traffic, in either direction, except for some cows at the side of the road. It's as if I have this vast, beautiful burning landscape with pyramids and fabulous setting sun all to myself. All this is mine, for the moment.

The sun is sinking fast. It's slipping behind a thick bank of cloud that has just moved in off the sea. As the day wanes, and we're out of the fires, and we get farther north, the climate gets cooler. And now the sun has come out from behind that cloud bank and it is fiery orange, with a crescent of blistering red superimposed on the orange. The road is heading directly into the setting sun, with myriad reflections shining in the pavement, but it's not glaringly bright, it's not blinding. It looks like a planet, like that big fat gasbag Jupiter, it doesn't look at all like a ball of flame right now, it doesn't look like the sun. It looks as if we are on a different planet, in a different solar system, and that orange ball the size of a beach umbrella is a giant neighbouring planet reflecting the sunlight, and it is inhabited by people just like us, but more peaceful. It doesn't look like the sun, nor does it look like the moon.

Now the sun has set behind some hills, and it looks as if the forests climbing to the summit of each hill are actually on fire, or perhaps they are merely reflecting the sun's fire. And there are some very nasty fires on a much larger mountain to the south – definitely not reflections from the fiery sun. From here there are numerous little fires all over the hilly landscape. Perhaps they were ignited by lightning, or maybe the fires have been slowly climbing the slopes from little settlements, where someone has flicked a cigarette. Also this must be a well-known area for sunset viewing, because here's a very large billboard showing a big round sun on it, and the words "Our Revolution Is Strong Like the SOL," and the O in SOL is a big orange round sun with sunbeams radiating out from it.

It's hard not to snicker when a police cruiser runs out of gas. This one has pulled well off the road, as far as possible, so the fewest number of people will see him and laugh. Another cruiser has come up, and the two cops are now shamefacedly pouring gas into the tank, keeping an eye out for wayward sparks from the distant fires. Now would be a good time to hold up a gas station. You'd be gone before the cops could get their caps screwed back on.

Yesterday Jannier and I saw some smaller fires with firefighters in attendance, and fire trucks. But all along this stretch I haven't seen anything like that. No sign of any emergency vehicles except for the cop out of gas. "*Bomberos!*" exclaimed Jannier. "What's the English word for *bomberos?*" I told him – firefighters. He looked disappointed, as if it wasn't a real word, not in league with *bomberos* at all. He also wanted to know what the difference was between flip-flops and sandals.

But you'd think there'd be firefighters everywhere along here, and firebombing planes spraying those nasty flames as if they were so many out of control weeds. But maybe some number-cruncher at the ministry responsible for fire control has figured out that this will be a bad year for fires, and all in all it would be less of a drain on the reserve funds to let them burn themselves out rather than fight them.

The full moon is rising, it's the second night of fullness, and it's very bright around the edge, and a bit dimmer toward the middle. If you drew a straight line from the centre of the setting sun to the centre of the rising moon, that line would go right through your heart, so if there is no lunar eclipse in a few hours it will be a close call.

And now the sky is full of stars that almost look as if they are breathing up there, slowly dimming then getting bright again, over and over. And when there are little clouds, the stars shine right through them. I wonder how Van Gogh would paint these stars, which seem like ice continually melting and continually freezing at the same time, or what William Blake would say about a moon like that, innocent of the slightest taint of doubt.

Poor Blake and Van Gogh, they never got to see Cuba.

There was a slight curve in the road and just for a split second my lights illuminated a *campesino* at midnight, in utter darkness, cutting sugar cane, with a machete so new and shiny it flashed for a moment in the headlights. He was getting some harvesting done before the fire did it for him.

And a moment later I was entering Tailfin City.

HEAVENLY HAVANA

Sunday, March 7, 2004. Havana isn't really strange, it's not as if it's on a different planet, but driving slowly through Vedado in the moonlight last night, with rows and rows of stately royal palms, and one fabulous Spanish palace after another, it felt a lot like another planet. Somewhere in this vast galaxy there must be a planet with a city in it that resembles Havana, though its roads will probably be more smoothly paved and it won't be full of old Cadillacs.

It was well after midnight at an ancient stone ferry terminal on Havana Bay, the Terminal Sierra Maestra, where the car-rental agents have their desks and chairs and telephones, in one large room on the ground floor. At the front entrance, I parked the car in the same spot where it was when I got it. Three guys were standing around and when I asked which one was the boss all three started whistling as loud as they could and shouting, Jorge! Jorge!

Out of the shadows appeared a short dark-skinned Afro-Cuban with an old rough X-shaped scar an inch above his right eye. First off he told me to pull the car inside the terminal building. So I did. I explained that I was bringing it back early because I was tired of driving, all the more so because the car wasn't suitable for the sort of roads I was encountering.

Jorge in a friendly manner wanted to know where I'd been. He'd never visited the cities in the east, but he loves Pinar del Río and

Viñales west of Havana. I said my friend A. had been down there ten years ago, but it was a bus tour so she didn't see anything more interesting than a cigar factory, a cliffside mural showing the entire history of the world from amoeba to Fidel, and some semi-submerged caves through which you were expected to row a boat. Jorge said those bus tours were famous for avoiding the real Cuba.

And then, back to business, he thought for a minute and said I was going to have to bring the car back out, and park it outside, and I'd have to pay for the parking. That seemed odd, but I didn't want to argue so I said oh all right, and I pulled it outside and parked it where I had parked it first. And he said that'll be three dollars for the night.

This was two o'clock this morning. So I paid him, grabbed my bag, and was ready to leave to find a hotel when he said it would be better if I took the car with me, and bring it back in the morning, and he'd give me back my three dollars. The last thing I wanted to do was drive that car another inch, I was that sick of it, so I looked disappointed. But instead of making a fuss I turned and said to him, By the way, how did you get to speak such excellent English?

He was very pleased. He said he studied hard, he said at night he's a security guard for this building, but in the day he teaches the English language to Cuban children. He said he was always a very dedicated student and he studied English hard for five years, spoke English with everybody he could – "and now here I am." He seemed to expand with pleasure from head to toe.

And I said, Well, that's just amazing, you're obviously a highly intelligent man, combined with such dedication, and I shook his hand and looked deeply into his eyes. This may seem condescending on the page, but I don't think it sounded that way in person, and he certainly didn't take it that way, because he suddenly flip-flopped again, and he said it would be all right after all for me to leave the car here. Arf arf!

Most people react reasonably well to flattery, if it's done right; others, perhaps people with above-average self-esteem, catch on quick, feel manipulated, and don't like it. He liked it fine. It didn't occur to him I was being anything but sincere, and he was right, paradoxically. So I got to kiss that car goodbye. And I think he ended up with the three dollars. More security guards should double as parking-lot attendants. It's a natural fit. You'd feel secure that your car would be there when you got back, though I didn't care if mine would be there because I wasn't coming back.

My heavy canvas bag got progressively heavier as I took off across the cobblestone Plaza de San Francisco, and along Calle Oficios, looking for a place to stay. I knew it was absurdly late to be doing so, but I felt absolutely confident. When I turned onto Calle Obispo, there were three fellows and three girls, who seemed to be coming home from a wedding, or a high-school graduation party, and they were making fun of me because I must have looked funny walking with such a heavy bag, so fast, and in such a straight line, as if I knew where I was going, and couldn't wait to get there. They apparently took me to be a Russian left over from the 1980s, so they kept saying things like, "Russky, Russky, why don't you go home? Russky, come here, Russky." The guys were showing off to the girls. And the girls would giggle. It was embarrassing, and my bag was increasingly heavy, and I would look over my shoulder now and then and smile good-naturedly at them, and finally they shut up. Cabbies were pleading with me to let them drive me somewhere, anywhere, they felt sorry for me. But it was as if I knew where I was going even though I wasn't conscious of knowing, and I didn't want anyone to stop me. I went past the Floridita, where the bronze Hemingway would be the only one standing at this hour, and I didn't even look in. I kept walking walking walking with my eyes straight ahead. I crossed the Prado, and went by the somnolent Hotel Inglaterra where D.H. Lawrence and Frieda spent a night or two, on their way from England to Mexico just a few years before Fidel was born. And all of a sudden I came to the Hotel Lido slightly south and west of the point where the Malecón and the Prado entwine.

Honest, I had no idea this was where I was going. It was like a miracle. I looked through the glass front into the lobby and the doorman leapt to his feet and unlocked the front door. He let me in and directed me to the night clerk. I booked in, and asked if the bar was still open. She pointed me in the direction. There was a bartender and two guys watching late-night TV at the back of the lobby, and the bartender gave me the most wonderful Cuba Libre, with just a perfect little splash of Cuban cola. And then I asked if I could take a couple of Cristals to my room. He said certainly and asked if I would like the caps off. I said sure, and he took the caps off, slightly, actually he just loosened them, expertly, so I could flip them off with my thumb when I needed to. A Canadian man and wife, very stiff and nervous, came in, sat at a table, and said, "Could we have an ashtray, please?" The bartender didn't have a clue what they were talking about, so I took one from the bar and put it on their table, and then they lit up, forgetting that all they had to do was light up and the bartender would automatically have brought an ashtray to their table. I went up to my room, with my two beers, and nobody trying to wrest my bag away from me like that oaf in Ciego de Ávila.

The room and the price were comparable with everywhere I'd been farther east. And I have a whole channel devoted to wild black-and-white Popeye cartoons from the 1940s, many featuring Betty Boop and her rivalry with Olive Oyl, and that nasty, vicious bully Pluto. The shower was clean, the towels were expertly folded in the form of a pair of swans with their necks around each other, one pair for each bed, and there was even a toilet seat on the toilet.

In the morning I headed back to where I had come from last night, the Terminal Sierra Maestra. But I shouldn't have dawdled because by the time I got there, Manolo, the guy I was supposed to settle up with, had vanished. Someone said he'd gone for the day, and when I looked disappointed, another person said Manolo hadn't gone for the day, he'd be back in an hour. So I sat there, at the Panautos desk, in a vast old stone room empty except for a cannon, some cannonballs, and another car-rental desk, where the Cubacar agent was sitting.

Manolo could make himself understood in English, but the Cubacar guy was Eloy, an Afro-Cuban as dark-skinned as Jorge, and like Jorge he spoke fluent English. The way things are going in Cuba, English will eventually be thought of as the black people's language. Eloy kept saying, Lookit, he's still got his stuff there (a bag sitting on top of a locked safe), so there's no way he won't be back by five o'clock.

Outside the much-photographed eighteenth-century Church of San Francisco de Paula (now an ecclesiastical museum) stands a bronze life-sized statue of a crazy old tinker man, who looked a lot like Jesus, except he was dressed in relatively modern style, and had a string of things he was trying to sell. It was impressive to see a statue of a poor man outside a church, standing alone in the Plazuela de Paula. This statue commemorates the man who was called Havana's most picturesque character, Lopez Lledin (1890–1985). He was a bellboy in his youth, but he went permanently out of his mind when thrown in jail on fake charges of jewel theft. Upon being released he became a homeless vagabond, who inspired many legends, and who became known as the Cabellero de Paris.

This representation of him is said to be faithful in every way, and the sculptor, José Villa, has a reputation for lifelike accuracy in his more-famous representations of such subjects as Ernest Hemingway and John Lennon, in Havana, and a statue of the great Mexican comedian Germán Valdés (Tin Tan), in Ciudad Juárez, Mexico.

As I was admiring the statue a tiny old lady, who might have been quite the cutie in the Caballero's day, asked for some money. I gave her all the coins in my pocket and she seemed very thrilled. When you do something like that in Cuba, people notice. They will embrace you, or look at you solemnly as if you may be an angel in disguise.

Back at the ferry terminal, nobody has a clue where Manolo is, but it was nice and cool in there, and the silence was also pleasant.

"Soy contenido," I said to Eloy.

"Bueno," he replied.

We both looked at the safe at the same time to make sure Manolo's stuff was still there.

"He won't be going home without that," said Eloy.

He wanted me to take the car over to Vedado where I could settle up with Nelson at the twenty-four-hour Panautos. I told him I couldn't do that because the car was not a pleasure to drive, the shocks did not work, nor did the radio. And I would hate to be in an accident now after all that careful driving I've been doing. I'd had a couple of drinks by then anyway. I had received the car from Manolo, and I wanted to deliver it back into his hands.

And just when I thought he was never going to show up, and just as Eloy was saying for the third time, he has to show up, he hasn't closed up his strongbox yet, then all of a sudden Manolo showed up. No apologies were needed or given. He simply threw his arms around me, with an ear-to-ear smile, and said, "Mí amigo! Mí papa! Mí daddi!" Then he went out to check the car, making sure there was no more damage than I had signed for two weeks ago. Sure enough, there's a tiny piece of metal off the hood ornament. The car had been full of dings when we checked it out before, we couldn't possibly have listed all the scratches and dents, and now he's busy charging me for the ones that we didn't record because he insists they must be new dents and scratches.

Then he noticed that the car aerial had been snapped off. Of course! And it must have happened about the time I was at Varadero Beach, because up to that point I was getting excellent reception from Florida. And then I couldn't get anything after that until last night upon returning to Havana, when all of a sudden the radio came on with no warning in the middle of Rod Stewart, a great fave of mine, singing "Have I Told You Lately," followed by Betty Carter singing an almost-out-of-control "East of the Sun," then Shirley Bassey's fabulous version of "This Masquerade," and a strange song I'd never heard before called "I Learned to Do the Boogie-Woogie When I Was Only a Child," sung by a girl who sounded as if she was about twelve. Sorry, I missed her name.

Also I missed out on a ton of Jamaican and Haitian music because some slimy malcontent mindlessly snapped my aerial. But why hadn't I been clever enough to buy a radio somewhere, or rig up some kind of metal attachment to the stub of the aerial? Perhaps subconsciously I didn't want a radio to complicate things and get in the way of the job at hand. Odd that Manolo charged me more to replace the aerial than I would have had to pay to buy a whole new radio.

Manolo found some other previously unchecked and unreported scratches and gouges and charged me for them even though I know I didn't cause them. I didn't hit anything and I wasn't hit by any-thing, not even a flying stone. A driver knows these things, espe-cially such a slow and cautious driver as I have been on this trip. And why would they have given me a car so obviously unsuited for the sort of expedition I was undertaking, especially since I described to them in full what I would be doing and where I was going?

Poor Manolo didn't know what to say. He was a bit upset about the sharpness of my complaints. He had done his best and wanted to remain on good terms. He wanted to be my friend. He wanted me to call him first thing on my next visit to Cuba.

So finally Eloy, who had been eavesdropping while doing some paperwork at the Cubacar desk, said something that shut me up, because I knew the truth of what he said: "We Cubans, we have a lot of problems, but we never play tricks."

I suddenly felt perfectly okay about paying the amount Manolo said I owed. Better the poor Cubans nickel and dime the rich Canadians than the other way around. I told Eloy he should remem-ber that line, the one about the tricks, that is, because it was very effective. He said he had always found it effective in the past.

I've already mentioned this place was an old stone ferry terminal with ancient cannons and cannonballs here and there. On the way out, as I passed directly in front of the muzzle of one cannon, I yelled out "BANG!," clutched my heart, and fell to the floor. Just for a second everybody thought I was dead. Now there'd be hell to pay. The last thing they were expecting was an old cannon to go off. And the second last, some foreigner pretending the cannon had gone off. But then everybody started laughing, and I jumped to my feet and bowed graciously. What a guy. Shameless. A stranger to embarrassment.

But I was feeling on top of the world because car-free equals care-free, a secret I've known for twenty years, but keep forgetting. I hopped into a cab to the Hotel Lido, where I had myself a delicious two-hour late-afternoon nap.

In the evening a bunch of students from Holy Cross University in Massachusetts appeared at the bar of the Hotel Ambos Mundos. One handsome young fellow told me they were all President Bush supporters, and were full of confidence that the ongoing U.S. invasion of Iraq would make the world a safer place. They were on a study tour of Havana and they had a special permit from their professor, which enabled them to travel freely in Cuba without earning the wrath of the U.S. State Department.

We chatted amiably as we wandered around the lobby and stopped to gaze at the framed photos of Hemingway and Fidel. The Holy Cross student vaguely knew of Hemingway from T-shirt images, but had read absolutely nothing of his. He listened carefully and seemed impressed when I briefly described the story of *The Old Man and the Sea*. But alas! he seemed to drift away when he found out it was mandatory reading for all Cuban schoolkids.

At La Floridita I ordered a gin and tonic with no ice, and José Villa's new bronze statue of Hemingway wouldn't take its eyes off me till I drained the glass. Hemingway looks arrogant and supercilious in the statue, but his eyes are gazing at everybody in the entire bar, and all at the same time. Everybody says the same tired old thing: his eyes follow me around the room. But it's true! I'm having a déjà vu over something I've never seen before! But it's as if this statue is filling the exact spot Hemingway left when he died, which is José Villa's sculptural intent in all his work, although as far as is known John Lennon never visited Havana.

La Cuna del Daiquiri/The Cradle of the Daiquiri, boasts the bilingual sign, in the form of a line of tin letters screwed into the wooden base of the large cabinet behind the bar, and then painted over a plum colour. But the "f" in "of" was missing, and it was missing ten years ago, recalls A., who seems to be whispering in my ear. And just then it occurs to me that given the look on the face of Hemingway's statue, he could be looking up and down the bar saying to himself, "Look at these ignorant bastards, not one of them has noticed that missing 'f.'"

And I'm saying right back to him, "Yes, but I bet you, oh great genius, didn't notice the interesting coincidence that the only letter missing just happens to be the first letter in the name of this famous bar." I think Hemingway appreciated people who stood up to his insults, and he was basically insulting people all the time because he wanted to see if they had what it took to stand up to him, and if you did stand up to him you would be friends for life, and if you didn't stand up to him he would write about you in such a way you would want to shoot yourself when you read it.

With his right elbow on the bar, and his left hand on his hip with his elbow sticking out behind him, and looking at his fellow drinkers with friendly contempt, Hemingway had a way of looking nastier when he was smiling than when he was frowning, and the sculptor brings it all back perfectly. Everybody's saying to himself, "That's exactly the way he was," as if they'd been on the scene here in Havana in 1955.

And you look around and see numerous people having serious boozy conversations, and most of them are neither looking at the statue nor thinking about Hemingway, but the statue of Hemingway is looking at them, smirking at them, and you can't help thinking that he might be thinking bad thoughts about them too, in order perhaps to make himself feel better. For when you feel as lousy as Hemingway did in the last decade of your life, booze is definitely not enough.

So I brazenly walked up to this bronze statue of the guy I've been reading and thinking about constantly since latching on to *For Whom the Bell Tolls* at age eleven.

I looked him right in the eye. It was just like talking to Hemingway. He even had a sort of spiritual glow around him as if alive. This is the way people speak of Che Guevara in the hours immediately following his death. While, oddly enough, Che's statue in Santa Clara, as well as all graven images of him around Cuba, seem limp and lifeless. José Villa needs to do one, perhaps in front of the Hotel Havana Libre where Che used to play chess. Maybe a statue of him sitting at a table playing chess. And maybe another one standing on ground level, in the park in Santa Clara, with his rifle in his hand, calling on his men to fire on the hotel.

Papa H.'s head was as big as mine, and I have a pretty big head. And his body was much bigger. I looked him right in the face, nose to nose, and I said, "Why did you have to go and kill yourself?" It was just like being in his presence. I'll always feel as if I've met Hemingway now after having seen that statue.

Unfortunately he had no answer for the only question I wanted to ask him.

So I ordered another gin and tonic and, in honour of Hemingway, mixed in a couple of shakes of Angostura bitters, which was how he liked his gin and tonics before he discovered (or invented, if you wish) the daiquiri.

The bar was filling up, with an alarming percentage of male drinkers. The guy on the stool to my right introduced himself as a "bartender from Bratislava." And then on his right all the way down the bar were six or seven other guys. He pointed at them and said, "These guys are too, we're all bartenders from Bratislava." They had been selected to take part in a competition for the world's greatest bartender, in the utterly fabulous Hotel Naçional. They're only here for a week, but they were so happy to be here, and they all spoke seven or eight languages ranging from Slovakian, Russian, Czech, and English (all excellent) all the way down to Spanish (not so good), and they've all read Hemingway, in various translations, whatever is handy. In fact they knew a lot about Hemingway and had studied him at school. I didn't ask if it was at bartender's school, but that would be very fitting.

What did they think of the bartenders at La Floridita? They said they were in awe. In fact, they were here to watch them in action because of their terrific reputation. "These daiquiris are beyond perfection," they said. "These guys really know what they're doing."

The bartenders at La Floridita, unlike the Bratislava boys, were all
close to retirement age, but you wouldn't dare ask if they remembered Hemingway. When I first asked for a gin and tonic they
seemed a bit startled. It threw them. They hadn't been asked for a
gin and tonic since the Triumph of the Revolution. So one of them,
in complete silence and with great dignity, dusts off a bottle from the
back of the shelf and pours me a half-inch in a martini glass. I tasted
it. It was gin. He smiled and showed me the bottle. It said on it
ginebra – another word for my Spanish vocabulary (but every time I
learn a new one I forget an old one). It means gin, but it also means
bedlam or confusion, strangely enough, and it is a girl's name as well,
the equivalent of Guinevere. I told him it was excellent gin. He was
pleased and poured me a long one. They seldom get asked for gin
here, obviously. It was great with a dozen drops of Angostura.

A band came in – a singer, who also had little castanets she
bashed together rhythmically, and a female conga drummer, and a
white guy on guitar, and a really good black violinist who played
Latino torch songs with enormous brio. Frankly, the violinist was
much more interesting than the singer, who seemed to be having a
bad night and, I later heard, was on the verge of changing careers.

An earlier band comprised a flute player who also sang, a percussionist who also sang, a pianist, and a string bass player. A lot of the
Cuban bands have string bass players, which are certainly classier
and more sonorous than bass guitars. People who couldn't get in
because the place was full were putting their arms through the
wrought-iron windows and clapping at the end of each song.

A tourist yelled out a stereotypically tourist request, "La Rumba,"
and the musicians rolled their eyes and played something else. The
next break, some smartass (not me, honest) held out a dollar and
with a grand flourish tossed it into the guitar case, looked the leader
in the eye, and said, "La Rumba." That time they played "La Rumba,"
but not with much spirit.

I kept checking out a married couple, only about thirty-five but already packing on the pounds, and they were sitting solemnly at a table, drinking mojitos, and passing a cigar back and forth. He would take a puff, then she would take a puff. The interesting part about it was that everybody, and I mean everybody, was interested in everybody. Everybody was checking everybody else out. You don't have that in a lot of places in the world, and it's even not that common in Cuba. I think it was the Hemingway spirit, and the fact that Hemingway's statue was there, and in the statue he had assumed a pose and a look that indicated that was exactly what he was doing. He was checking everybody out, which is what he would have been doing anyway, if he had been alive, and not too drunk. And it was as if he was alive, to be truthful, and just slightly tipsy. So if a person of Papa H.'s authority can do it, that sort of gives a *carta blanca* to everybody else.

Can you believe it? The woman who waited on me next door at Il Gentiluomo where I dined a few hours earlier was now busy sweeping the floor in La Floridita. Apparently there is a passageway between the two restaurants. And it would appear they use the same kitchen, except that they tend to have different menus, and very much different prices, and you know which one will be the most expensive.

On the way home I got caught short passing by the Club des Arabes on the Prado and asked if I could pop in for a minute. "Four dollars," they said. But I just have to have a pee. "Five dollars."

Then I became surrounded by all these ladies of the night, who were pointing at me and saying grab him, don't let him get away, and making all kinds of merry suggestions about various things we could do if I had the dough, and they knew damn well I did. I was just wearing an old pair of jeans and T-shirt, and my shoes were falling off my feet, but they instinctively knew, perhaps because of my pink face, that I had a credit card and lots of U.S. cash.

Without paying much attention to them I was thinking that they seem to be into the joy of the thing, unlike the poor sex trade workers in Toronto who sometimes seem not even to know how to spell fun, never mind joy. In a weird sort of way, it seems that Cuban hookers are better off than their Canadian counterparts. For one thing they can pop in and out of the neighbourhood *polyclinico* as often as they want for friendly, lecture-free checkups. For another thing, Havana is happy and Toronto is *triste*.

And just then the tortured sad-eyed face of a woman about sixteen going on sixty drifted out of the shadows like a ghost, and she accosted me by standing in my way, without actually touching me. We both stopped and looked full into each other's eyes, and in a perfectly haunting iambic pentameter line (a metrical form we often instinctively adopt in moments of intense passion or utter desperation), and in a raspy voice, with a look of acute anguish on her face, she said, "S**ky f**ky all night, twenty dollars." I turned away and she disappeared into the darkness.

SAD-EYED SEÑORITAS
OF EL MORRO

Monday, March 8, 2004. Maybe those young fellows in handcuffs being lead to prison last week had been accused of "ambiguity" or "anti-historical attitudes," as was the recently deceased poet Heberto Padilla in the late 1960s. Or maybe they were accused of "disseminating an imperialist-type reality," as was playwright Antón Arrufat in the same period. They couldn't have been accused of homosexuality, because that particular view of reality hasn't been a crime since 1988. I'm sure also that those silly-sounding crimes from the 1960s are no longer in effect, except in the minds of those who had to do the time for them.

But as of August 2003, poet and independent journalist Raúl Rivero Castañeda, pushing sixty, had lost close to sixty pounds while serving the first few months of a twenty-year sentence in the Canaleta prison in Ciego de Ávila for the seemingly ridiculous crimes of "undermining the independence and unity of the state," "collaborating with the United States," and "spreading anti-socialist sentiment" – plus one charge of treason. Rivero was arrested in March of 2002 and was accused of writing "biased" articles in the foreign press, meeting with U.S. diplomats, and working with Reporters Without Borders, which was described on a Revolutionary Cuban Web site as a "French terrorist organization used by the U.S. government."

Rivero has an oddly sarcastic, bitter, humourless but hot-blooded writing style. Many of his essays, in which he portrays Cubans as living in the midst of a propaganda machine, are available on the Internet (as is his poetry). He published a piece in the Argentinian newspaper *La Naçion*, in 2001, denying that he was in the pay of U.S. interests (though many of his anti-Fidel articles have appeared in major U.S. papers), and stating that the only crime he is guilty of is "writing without being dictated to." He is also supportive of the U.S. trade embargo, at least to the degree that he maintains it's Fidel rather than the embargo that is the main problem affecting Cuba.

His name seems to have been hijacked by those calling for an invasion of Cuba, so it might be better for Cuba if he were given his freedom. There's a good case for keeping him in jail and a good case for releasing him. But forty years in prison doesn't sound right for a poet opposed to the system. How could any poet worth his tropes not be opposed to the system? I don't know, I just don't know.

All I know for sure is I'm hereby recommending the scrapping of the ubiquitous bubble cars, which are used by Havana taxi drivers who lack the energy to pedal a bicycle taxi, or want more speed than a bicycle taxi can afford, but can't afford the luxury of a four-wheel automobile. The bubble car is a motorcycle surrounded by a comical plastic bubble the colour and shape of a partially peeled grapefruit, and it will seat three passengers in a pinch. Sounds like fun, but being a bubble-car driver must be the world's unhealthiest job, next to being a packer in a dynamite plant or a French cabinet minister trying to trim the arts budget. There's no windshield, so driver and passengers are forced to breathe thick clouds of black exhaust gushing out of the vehicles in front of them. And there always seems to be a vehicle directly in front of them belching out black clouds of poison. Every day at a job like that would cut a month off one's life expectancy.

A bubble car has whisked me off to El Morro, the Fortress, standing on a high promontory – though it doesn't seem that high when you're gazing at it from the Malecón across Havana Bay. One feels a

sense of wonder at this place, and the numerous cruelties it represents. There were four hundred Spanish soldiers garrisoned here
when Samuel de Champlain paid a visit in 1601, before he turned
his attention to his vast exploration of the Canadian wilderness. The
more recent history of El Morro is featured prominently in Reinaldo
Arenas's autobiography, *Before Night Falls*, and in the eponymous
movie version (2000) as well, where the Arenas character (played by
Spanish actor Javier Bardem) is dually titillated and tortured by U.S.
actor Johnny Depp in his dual role as transvestite prisoner and psy-
chotic prison guard.

Now there are no prisoners in El Morro, at least none I could discover. It's an enormously silent, imposing labyrinth, and when you're
the only visitor in such a place it can't help but conjure up strangely
mournful emotions that seem to seep out of the stones. El Cristo is
nearby, it shares with El Morro the same promontory, and from their
locations one has splendid views of all of Havana, including the
entire length of the sinuous serpentine Malecón, which may soon
need some sensitive reconstruction after several decades of being
smashed by hurricane waves.

This fortress was built in 1589, about the time Shakespeare began
to shape his own fortress of poetry. The king of Spain (forgive me if
you've heard this) was so aghast at how much had been spent on its
construction he facetiously grabbed a telescope and said, "We should
be able to see it from here." More than a hundred years later the
French king said something similar about the fortress of Louisbourg.
It's so sweet the way reigning monarchs, from Philip II to Louis XIV
to Fidel to George W. Bush, like to leaven their sarcasm with a scin-
tilla of humour.

While wandering solo through many silent and empty galleries,
profoundly sonorous rooms built out of great blocks of limestone that
show no signs of crumbling even after the continual shock of so many
dramatic events over the centuries, mostly involving death and
destruction, I found framed copies of ancient maps, replicas of old
rudders, and of old sails with bright red and white stripes, drawings of
old astrolabes and so on. Here there are sea monsters, or fanciful

pictures thereof, and immaculate scale drawings of various ships of the fifteenth century – the later the date of each ship the larger, speedier, and more dangerous it looks. There are many portraits of famous sea-faring contemporaries of Columbus – and several of Columbus himself looking like a chubby blond or red-haired Boy George.

As I scrutinize a painting of that dramatic event of October 11, 1492, when Columbus moored his boats in the bay and came ashore with all his men, and with naked unarmed natives timidly hiding behind each tree, a woman who wishes to offer herself as my guide to El Morro sneaks up behind me and cheerfully starts serenading me with little children's songs about the landing of the *Niña*, the *Pinta*, and the *Santa María*. I congratulate her on remembering that from grade school. She tells me it seems like yesterday.

This tiny señorita of forty drags me over to see a map pinpointing all the known pre-Columbian settlements. The red dots are the farming villages, the yellow dots fishing villages. Many of the large cities of Cuba were once Aboriginal settlements, and she had me repeating the place names with her exact pronunciation: Bare-adáro (Varadero), Labánna (l'Havana), Wan-tán-amo (Guantánamo), Bara-kúwa (Baracoa), and when she said Granma (not an Aboriginal word), I jokingly said, Are you a granma? She punched me on the chest for insinuating she was old.

All the exhibits are copies, few things in El Morro are real except for El Morro itself, and the people who work here – the guides, who double as salespeople in the gift shop, and also when required as window-washers, floor-sweepers, bookkeepers, and sometimes even plumbers. Nothing original or in any way valuable can be kept here for fear of it being damaged by the proximity to the sea and the pawing of the tourists. The maps, drawings, paintings are carefully assembled colour photocopies. The reconstructed palm-thatched Aboriginal houses are fake, and any Aboriginal looking at them would probably burst into tears. Even the pottery is fake. But nice fake. Some of the stone implements used for grinding corn might be real, though the Aboriginal shovel looks like a facsimile. The pic-tograms look real, and in their painstakingly geometric complexity closely resemble the much earlier carvings in the stones at Newgrange, far away and long ago.

The cannons and cannonballs are real. Nobody would make a fake cannonball because there are loose cannonballs everywhere you look in Cuba. Loose cannons too, no doubt. And bells, immense bells, the tolling of which in days of yore would bring the salivating slaves in from the fields for lunch. The bells and the cannonballs have found new functions in recent years, the bells for ornamental additions to inner courtyards of restaurants and historical buildings, and the cannonballs for blocking off roads to vehicular traffic. The cannonballs here are overlarge, like a ten-pin bowling ball in size (and shape of course), but not as polished, in fact not polished at all. It would be very uncomfortable to be hit by a cannonball, you would have to lie where you fell, and you would have to be very still because of your pulverized spine and other broken bones. For half a millennium, up until 1959 when Fidel took over, Cuba has had a long history of being crushed and humiliated by imperial powers. Its spine has been pulverized many times.

Although I'm the sole visitor to El Morro, there are several female guides sitting around, enjoying the lonesome ambience, contemplating the nature of time and eternity, listening to the innocent chirping of sparrows, and wishing some handsome man from a distant country might ask to be escorted through the ancient holding cells where many brave souls over the centuries starved, and bled, and suffered great tortures, and died. Sometimes without realizing it, one learns things, such as how to address a Cuban lady. Call her a señorita. The older she is the more she'll like it. Hearing herself called señora is not a big thrill for Cuban women. It's like calling a Canadian woman missus. They're likely to respond coolly. Call her señorita and she'll give you a bright attentive look. If she seems really grandmotherly, however, señorita can sound a bit facetious, but even then don't call her señora, call her *compañera* (they love that), and pronounce the word with gusto! If people would start calling all their female friends, from anywhere on earth, señorita (and maybe their male friends as well), it could start some momentum, like a stadium wave.

One little brown-skinned señorita who claimed to be thirty-one, when she found out I was from Canada, said that the Cubans have a high regard for Canada, and reminded me that Fidel was an honorary pallbearer at Trudeau's funeral. And she said that when the people of Cuba are suffering, Fidel suffers too, and when they are happy Fidel is also happy – which is undoubtedly true. And even though nobody seemed to be working very hard around El Morro on this particular day, she complained about the overriding and neverending plight of Cuba: *mucho trabajo, poco dinero*. Shyly and with much embarrassment, I offered her what I considered to be an insignificant sum of money, and she was flabbergasted. It was just a ten-peso bill.

Then she calmed down and became very sad, and she began to tell me sad stories about Cuban life, and family breakups, and friends dying trying to get to Florida, and how difficult it is to get enough food. . . .

The outer walls of El Morro are six or seven feet thick. Antique cannons sit around dreaming of past battles, of ships going down in flames with the screams of dying men. It's all so lonesome, brooding, melancholy and very strange. This is the archetype to which all those dungeons and fortresses in computer games owe their existence. A poet with a camera could take some wonderful pictures in El Morro on a day like today, with nobody around but the stone walls, the precipitous cobblestone walkways, perfectly curved arches leading from one level to another, the long-dormant skills of the ancient stone masons, the occasional cat sneaking up on a bird, the brilliant sun, the welcome shadows, the blue sky, the flat sea, the silent pale silver ship way out on the horizon, and the lonely guides with no one to guide.

There's also a hint of low-grade irrational anxiety in the air, as if it were possible that this entire massive fortress could suddenly sink into the sea, or an errant cannonball could rip the head off your shoulders. Or you could be arrested, put in chains, have your nose cut off, and given smaller and smaller portions of gruel until you starved to death. But I like it nevertheless, and I am not at all unhappy to be a solitary tourist from a faraway land, wandering through the multitudinous symbols of human selfishness, fiendish ingenuity, cruelty, and stupidity.

But tourists here must be careful, especially when looking out over the city, and especially when they have children with them. Many of these retaining walls are not high, and one false move could send a body to the wave-washed rocks below. Many have fallen to their deaths or been thrown from these downward-sloping ramparts, some of which are only a couple of feet high, and the waves eventually washing everything away. In *Before Night Falls*, Arenas speaks of being incarcerated in El Morro in the early 1970s during the anti-homosexual phase of the Revolution, when homosexuality was considered a bourgeois affectation. He witnessed a prisoner become crazed with desperation and throw himself off the ramparts. The poor fellow broke both his legs on the rocks below. He started pulling himself toward the sea. A compassionate guard fired at him and killed him.

A chubby smiling señorita, with cafe con leche skin, serenades me from a filigreed upper window as I stroll by meditatively. She's singing "Dos Gardenias" (a gushy romantic ballad made famous by the Buena Vista Social Club), but she has shrewdly changed the words from "Two gardenias for you" to "No gardenias for me" – and as I stop to listen and look up at her, she locks eyes with me and the song becomes more passionate. She has a beautiful voice and knows how to use it. There are a lot of guides, and it seems that I am the only one in this massive fortress who is not a full staff member. Buses pull in, the tourists get out, and they run up to the gift shop for Che T-shirts, Fidel change-purses, José Martí ashtrays, Buena Vista Social Club bottle openers, and maybe even video tapes detailing the history of El Morro. Then they run back to the bus and zoom off to the next souvenir shop. Sad but perfectly understandable that they have desire perhaps, but no time for the fulfilment of it. They'll return to Cuba some day for sure, at least in their dreams. Our ancestors had no problem living in eternity, so it's said, but the god of time, armed with a razor-sharp machete, has captured us and chopped our sense of timelessness into bits and pieces, minutes and seconds – just like the English navy destroying the old lighthouse at El Morro, as it did during the siege of Havana in 1762.

By the parking lot, there's a nice little breezy palm-shaded outdoor restaurant called Los Doce Apóstoles. Only two of the twelve are on duty today, and they're calling me over to have a look at the menu. It was a nice menu, but much to their dismay I was neither hungry nor thirsty. High season, but no visitors.

One of the two apostles has two fingers on his left hand strapped together with a splint and a heavy bandage. What happened? He rather proudly says he slammed a car door on his hand. Did you cry? He looks at me, surprised that I would ask such an intimate question. Yes, I did, he said. I cried like a baby.

Parked nearby is a white Baby Austin, a tiny British car from 1952, not much bigger than a bubble car, in fact smaller, you'd feel more cramped and claustrophobic in one of these. This one has retained the original grill, a very handsome vertical grill like a Mercedes-Benz, but where there would have been an A for Austin at the top of the grill, someone has very carefully painted the Rolling Stone emblem, with bright red lips and a bright yellow tongue.

The man who cried asked if I wanted a taxi. He made a call and a dirty old beat-up Lada appeared, with no fare box or meter, or any indication it was a taxi. The driver said it'd be four dollars. I said it was only three dollars to get here in a real taxi. He said no, four dollars. So then he drove me down the hill, stopped the car, got out, and another guy got behind the wheel and drove me down through the tunnel under Havana Bay without turning his lights on (probably didn't have lights), and let me off at a dangerous spot on the traffic circle (with the Máximo Gómez statue smack in the centre) leading into Old Havana. This was neither a licensed cab nor a licensed driver. So I cheekily gave him a bright orange three-dollar bill, expecting him to say one more, but he seemed perfectly okay with the three, and so did I without it.

Even the innocent can see a scam when it presents itself. It's not a serious scam, though, because no real taxi driver would be up there waiting for a fare. He'd be waiting all day. So these guys are performing a vital service, even if there is little demand for it even at high season, and even if it is illegal in Cuba to charge for a ride without being licensed.

Inspired by the sweet singing of "Dos Gardenias" at the Fortress, I darted dangerously across the street and into the Museo de la Musica, and immediately felt unwelcome. There seems to be a foreigners-by-invitation-only routine here, but there I was, and although nobody seemed pleased nobody made a move to usher me out. This place is considered to hold in its hand the beating heart of Cuban music, plus a really small but brilliant and optimistic little store selling Cuban recordings.

I stumbled into the cutest auditorium, with a grand piano taking up more than half the stage, and old-fashioned cinema-style seating – thirteen rows of seven seats each, so that it will hold ninety-one, with just a single very narrow aisle along one wall.

Two female guides did not wish to know how long I'd been in Cuba, but they were eager to know how many *chicas* I'd danced the boogie-woogie with since arriving in Cuba. They thought it was hilarious when I informed them I'm only attracted to nuns.

In the little shop, on the main floor, there were many photos of famous Cuban musicians on the wall. Some of the old-time musicians looked really interesting, but everybody seemed busy so I left without buying anything. In Cuba, it seems that everybody has great music in their soul – with the curious exception of Fidel, who is famous for not being able to dance or sing. But look at that chubby señorita at El Morro just now – her voice was stunningly beautiful in the silence of that huge fortress, suddenly, through the filigree-barred window where she was sitting, and reclining languorously, singing a sad song about the absence of gardenias.

The Museo de la Revoluçion with tremendous irony is housed in the magnificent old Presidential Palace where Batista lived and where he hosted fascists from all around the world, and where in 1958 an attack by student rebels intent on assassinating him was foiled. The attack was very well organized, but unforeseeable things went wrong, there was an accident on the way to the palace, gunfire broke out prematurely, and many young idealistic Revolutionaries were killed. Fidel wasn't involved at all in that one.

So I wandered around the first floor, and watched some films of parades. The still photos from the 1950s were more interesting, many photos of armed men in the heat of battle. I was wishing I could take a pill that would confer on my brain full command of the Spanish language, when an unpleasant woman in a brown shirt and a dark brown skirt came up to me and demanded that I check my shoulder bag. I understood perfectly, it was a legitimate request, I could have a camera in my bag, or something even more deadly, but I didn't want to give her the satisfaction, so I left, vowing to return another day.

The Presidential Palace is still known by that name, though Fidel wisely refused the opportunity to make it his home base. Doing so would have made him seem like just another Batista, whose unsavoury friends, such as the young Richard Nixon and certain Hollywood movie stars, would congregate here on occasion for massive pigouts while the country starved. The Presidential Palace is still a symbol of the opulence of power in a poor country, and to have it filled with photos of unwashed bearded rebels and other ragtags is an irony of juxtaposition.

Iglesia del Santo Ángel Custodio is the name of the magnificent old cathedral across the street from Batista's former digs. I'm standing at the Lourdes altar, with a life-sized Nuestra Señora de Lourdes flanked by Jesús Nazarino on her left and el Niño Jesús de Praga on her right. But someone has come in, a handsome fellow with a worried look on his face and great authority in his bearing. He sees me talking into my tape recorder, and indicates he wishes to kneel and pray at the very altar where I'm standing. This seems odd, since there are so many altars, and this is by no means the most impressive. And now, looking back over my shoulder, he looks like a very nice devout Cuban, kneeling silently and sending up a message to

Our Lady of Lourdes to protect him and his loved ones from excessive suffering in this uncertain life.

The praying man is now my friend! And he wasn't a Cuban at all, he was a tourist. I said adios to the cathedral and started strolling down the steep and cobblestoned Calle Compostela – and suddenly a man overtook me. He was wearing a form-fitting undershirt and skin-tight jeans, a man in his prime and in great physical shape. He was full of charm and enthusiasm. He harboured no doubts about himself. If he had, he wouldn't have been so radiant. He sensed I'd been here a while, and might have some tourist tips for him. Also, being a cop, he had a natural desire to know why I was talking into my tape recorder. But like a good cop he betrayed no suspicion when he asked, it was just a friendly question.

He was a French tourist, a Mauritian named Christophe who lives and works in Paris. He has a touch of food poisoning. Maybe that's why he'd been praying. But it's probably just the tourist tummy, and he'll soon be fine. He's right now in the toilet of a dark but friendly little peso bar in the shadow of the baroque seventeenth-century towers of Santo Ángel. He bought me a beer and I bought him a cigar. When we paid up, several poor Cubans who were watching the transaction turned to look at each other and cock their eyebrows, as if to say these guys must be fabulously wealthy.

Between visits to the john he tells me his thirty-eight-year-old brother quit his government job as an ichythologist to write sci-fi novels. He has now finished his first one, and it's doing so well he's already started another. Christophe himself works as a secret police officer with the French government, and he is very much enjoying this little holiday in Havana, walking around so casually, without having to carry a gun. He's only in Cuba for four days, and feels lucky to have got away because he's been working around the clock, dealing with a serious assassination threat against the minister of culture. As elsewhere, the government is slashing arts-funding budgets. Unlike elsewhere, artists are so furious they're calling for blood.

It's hard to imagine what he's like at home, but in the heavenly Havana milieu Christophe comes across as an extremely fine person, and wildly enthusiastic about everyone he meets and everything he sees. He likes to make an impression, he likes to be remembered, and he even shows me pictures of his children. He likes to stand in the sun and be observed, while on the job he would likely prefer to lurk in the shadows and observe.

MAGIC IS WHAT
YOU IMAGINE!

Tuesday, March 9, 2004. After the magician had gone through his amazing routine last night, Christophe's friend Isabella remarked that "Magic is what you imagine." At first that didn't seem helpful in understanding magic or the imagination. She said it after I said something even more meaningless: "And they say there is no magic." It's the sort of puerile thing baffled people say after some spectacular trick. We knew these were tricks, very skilfully done, but the smiling Afro-Cuban somehow managed to convince us, almost, that he was causing the laws of physics to vanish and be replaced by the laws of his own subjectivity. He wasn't manipulating the laws of the universe in order to make coins appear where they couldn't possibly be. He didn't levitate, and he didn't cause the moon to open its mouth and say, Howdy, Isabella. But it was as if he could have, if he had wanted to.

What he did do was cause knots in a soft white cord five feet long to disappear by passing his hand over them. With another hypnotic gesture, this Cuban Mandrake/Lothar all-in-one made the cord turn into five cords each one foot long. And then back again, all with a detached smile on his face. He went on for about twenty minutes without a pause, without a word, with all four members of his audience desperately trying to see the trickery behind the facade of the miraculous.

The poor bartender earlier yesterday was brimming over with happiness at having two tourists there, delighted to be getting even such a small amount of U.S. funds. He was selling loose cigarettes to the locals. People would come in with a peso in their hand and he'd count out five cigarettes. He also had an open box of cigars and man oh man were they good, the best one-dollar cigar imaginable. The smoke was as thick and rich as warm liquid chocolate and it coated your entire respiratory track with a glowingly intense pleasure. They weren't anything famous, just cheap no-name Cuban cigars, and yet they seemed on a level with your Cohibas and your Romeo y Julietas. Christophe said he usually preferred cigars from Mauritius, but given the price these would do.

Christophe was enthralling everyone with his tiny Minolta digital camera. In the bar he took a picture of the bartender and then showed him the picture instantly, not printed, but viewable inside the camera, like a tiny bartender inside a tiny bar. And he'd press a button to show all the pictures he'd already taken, then zoom in on any one of them.

So the word got out and several people came into the bar wanting to get their pictures taken. Radio Bemba, as they call this sort of thing in Cuba, where word-of-mouth news often seems to travel faster than radio signals. They didn't have to ask twice. Just a hint would be enough to cause Christophe to leap into action and take all the pictures they required. They didn't care that they couldn't take the shot home with them. It was enough just to be part of the cutting edge of global technology for a moment. Whole crowds were surrounding him, and jockeying to see the little guys inside the camera. When he got tired of it he just slipped the camera into his pocket and the people would politely disperse. Just like magic!

Christophe had found a private apartment for $25 a night and it was spacious enough for himself and his two friends. He said he was astonished at his own luck: he had ordered this camera, and he knew he had a few days off, so he decided to go to Cuba with his friend Marcel. It was a miracle that his camera arrived just as he was about to step into his taxi to the airport for his flight from Orly to Varadero. Such miraculous timing inspired him to use the camera as much as possible.

Christophe was sharing the apartment with Marcel – a relatively new friend of his – and Isabella, a Paris TV producer of Corsican origin whom Christophe and Marcel met for the first time two days ago. Marcel and Isabella didn't have Christophe's dynamic flat-out energies, and although they loved him they found him impossible to keep up with. Christophe invited me into the flat, where the other two were having a nap, and they sleepily shook my hand as he woke them up and introduced us. Isabella looked very cynical, as Christophe described the show she produced as the best Paris TV show of all time. It covered all aspects of the cinema, and was extremely popular. Marcel was the manager (and owner, insisted Christophe) of a fabulously expensive restaurant in Paris. He sleepily told me about his chefs with the big white hats and how he's quietly trying to devise ways of getting them to sample less of the product. Tasting is fine, but the way they were overindulging was making them fat and him skinny.

Isabella was a short woman approaching forty with blond hair, soft fair features, and beautiful eyes. Christophe noticed me admiring her eyes, and said she was just a producer behind the scenes, and never was on-camera, and with those eyes wasn't it a shame. She said she has no desire to be on-screen because she knew she would hate being famous. She'd hate to be gawked at on the street by people who had seen her on the tube. She said some people love it, but she would hate it. She said if you're famous you can't become anonymous, you're stuck with it, but if you're anonymous you can always become famous, or at least give it a try. She said fame was like money, you spend your whole life amassing it but no matter how much you amass it's never enough to satisfy you.

Christophe and Marcel had known each other for six months. Isabella was on the same flight, heading to Varadero on her own for some solitary seaside rest and relaxation. They met and hit it off on the bus from the airport to the beach hotel. She said she knew they were destined to be friends forever, but she just wished Christophe would slow down a bit, it was so exhausting trying to keep up with him. She complained unsmilingly, without irony, as a woman might complain about some bad habits that she has to endure with her husband, yet they'll never part.

So Isabella would have preferred to stay in Varadero, and Marcel would have as well, but Christophe insisted they head down to Cárdenas, where they rented scooters. Christophe wrecked his and hurt his shoulder, and there was a nasty bruise on his lower left arm. A slight separation for sure, he said. It was very painful, especially when coupled with his tourist tummy. But it wasn't slowing down this extraordinarily dynamic person, because he immediately insisted the three of them head for Havana. Marcel was as laid-back as anyone I'd ever known. Isabella kept complaining that she couldn't keep up with the pace Christophe was setting.

As a security officer with the French government, Christophe said there were so many critically important things going on in Paris, including mass protests by the artists, it was necessary for him to get away for a few days, and try to see things with more perspective. He'd been deeply involved, and working around the clock. Folk burnt out need a vacation, says Ezra Pound. But only Marcel and Isabella seem at all burnt out.

Christophe is involved with some top-level security tasks. He comes in close contact with all kinds of interesting figures such as Yasser Arafat, with whom he speaks in English because Yasser speaks no French. Beyond that all he wished to say about him was that he was a very kind person. Also he's worked closely with Bill Clinton, whom he admires and he felt it was awful that Bill had to suffer so much simply for being a human being. George W. Bush was causing all kinds of problems at the federal level in France because he'll be at a meeting and suddenly he'll get angry for no reason at all. Everybody in the French government considers him a madman. He's really crazy, he's dyslexic, he has no manners, he can't concentrate, and every time he opens his mouth he says something inappropriate. At meetings he gets angry at perceived but non-existent slights. He wants France to become just like the United States, and when he is told that that is just not possible he blows up. Any differences between

France and the United States are intolerable to him and he cannot accept them. Everybody in government is on the verge of resigning, because they can't stand being in the same room as poor George.

These three adopted me into their little high-power Parisian circle of TV production, restaurant management, and top-level security. They knew about my book and said I should have no qualms about repeating anything they told me. This was before I'd decided to go on a first-name basis throughout, and in many cases changing the first name, just to be on the safe side. Christophe has no qualms about revelling in the intensely erotic sensuality of Havana and has already had at least one interesting fling. We didn't have to beg for the details. Christophe and a Cárdenas woman were going at it so furiously the bed broke. He thought that was hilarious. And that didn't cause them to miss a beat, they just continued on, at such a high decibel level that the woman's female friend barged in to see if her friend was being murdered. And she stayed to watch. Which only inspired them to even greater efforts.

Christophe is a little guy, fast and strong. From what he said I'd expect him to be handy with his weapon of choice, a 9mm Glock. He'd been a French army officer before switching to the police.

We gave the magician four dollars and he was very happy about that, then he proceeded to the bar to enthrall the more serious drinkers up there. He performed very subtle and beguiling feats of magic – indefatigable – twenty minutes without the slightest error – no commercial breaks – and left the four of us having no idea how he did any of the tricks even though we were deeply concentrating, and trying to see through his legerdemain.

One trick, he puts a card – say the nine of diamonds – inside an empty glass, turns the glass around, pulls the card out, and it's the ten of spades – when we could see very clearly, or thought we could, that he had only put one card in that glass. And he would just turn it and it would be a different card. Strange thing is, we didn't get his name.

It was sort of an anonymous thing. He didn't seem to be interested in promoting himself in any way. He had no card to offer. He didn't want anyone to think he was trying to get a free one-way trip to Canada or France. He had the modesty of the highly secure person with an amazing set of skills and artistry that couldn't be beat and would always ensure a little bit of money in his pocket. What more can life bring you?

I had the feeling it might have been a family trade, passed on from father to son, handed down for a few generations perhaps, and always evolving. Maybe his father had worked the posh hotels in the Batista era. I did ask if he had started as a child and he indicated he was doing these tricks at a very early age, putting his hand way down to knee level. But that was all the information we were able to get. If one becomes dedicated to a certain trade or art or set of interests at an early age, one does tend to become very good at it, without even really trying. It's sort of like something he's been doing every day of his life since birth practically. Just keeps evolving and in that way he never loses interest. People like that often don't make much money but that somehow is not a reason to quit.

Christophe was such a spontaneous person, and with such a quick mind, he'd be quite capable of shooting first and asking questions later. He also mentioned that he is a painter, so when we finished with the magician, and when we finished our drinks, I suggested that it might be interesting to visit the Museo Naçional de Bellas Artes. I touted it with sincere enthusiasm, and said it contained the essential distillation of the heart and soul of Cuba. Their ears perked up, and off we went.

But they didn't get into the paintings the way I thought they would. Maybe my buildup shouldn't have been so strong. They just didn't have the sort of commitment to really see the paintings somehow. It didn't measure up to the Louvre, I suppose. They didn't say much, except for Isabella, who was very outspoken about her problems with some of the work. They seem like "copies," she kept saying, meaning imitations, of other "paintings," meaning painting styles. She would look at one painting and say, "Picasso," then at another and say, "Magritte," and so on. Isabella saw it as imitation, the sign of the second rate. I saw it as homage, the sign of the first rate. Maybe she was right, maybe I was just looking at the paintings from a Cuban point of view, while she was looking at them from a global point of view.

The painting from the 1960s, showing the multiple images of Che, and by the same painter with the multiple images of José Martí – I didn't even bother thinking of them as being inspired by Andy Warhol, because it was so obvious, and it detracted not a whit from the work. But she just instantly dismissed them with a stern countenance as being "imitative," and refused to spend any time looking at them.

I said that everybody was painting like Picasso in those days, and she kind of accepted that. But she was openly dismissive, and I saw silent hints in the faces of the others that they agreed with her, but were too polite to tell me I was wrong about this museum. Mind you, some of the paintings she really liked. All three were astonished by the painting of the previously mentioned *The Great Fascist*, the bull on the platform with blood drooling from his mouth. I said it seemed to me to be rather astonishing that such a painting should be in the national museum because it is a wee bit reminiscent of Fidel, wouldn't you say? And they said, Not reminiscent, it is Fidel. "It even looks like him," said Christophe. It never occurred to them it might be meant to represent Mussolini, and they had no problem seeing it as Fidel. "No doubt about it." And the three of them spent a lot of time together, silently looking at that painting, lost in their private thoughts about the bloody history of the twentieth century, and perhaps among other things reassessing their notions of artistic freedom in Cuba. They may have been thinking that the painting is an emblem of the courage of the Cuban people, the artist's courage in painting such a picture, the courage required for the museum to hang it, and the courage of Fidel to allow it to be shown.

Fidel was shrewd enough and detached enough to take the hit like a man, and allow it to continue to hang as a symbol of artistic freedom in Cuba. He must see the painting as another side of himself, the side

of him that lays the law down all over the land, who has had anti-
abortionists jailed, priests and drug smugglers shot, and so on.

When the four of us were leaving the art museum, the ever-
effervescent Christophe began jumping up and down enthusiastically. "A Sea Fury!" he shouted. "A Sea Fury!" He tended to get fired
up about anything to do with the Cold War, the Cuban Missile
Crisis, and the Vietnam War. The Sea Fury was an airplane on
display across the street by the *Granma* memorial, as part of a display
of large outdoor historical relics of the Cuban Revolution. He spent
ten minutes touching the Sea Fury all over, talking to it, admiring it,
while Isabella spoke to Marcel and me about the paintings, how she
liked some of them.

When Christophe returned he raved about what he had seen and
what he had heard. He wasn't at all concerned about the bullet-
riddled Fast Delivery truck on display, the one in which numerous
armed students were killed while trying to smash their way into the
palace and assassinate Batista. For some odd reason he only wanted
to talk about the Sea Fury – how they're so rare, and how he'd never
seen one before – and he made the rest of us feel a bit inferior for not
being similarly enthusiastic about it. Fidel employed seventeen
British Second World War Sea Furies in defending Cuba in the Bay
of Pigs invasion in 1961. They performed beautifully. This particular
plane, piloted by Maj. Enrique Carrera, strafed and sank the *Houston*,
the main CIA supply ship.

He was also enthused about part of a U2 on display. The spy
plane was shot down on October 26, 1962, while taking aerial sur-
veillance photographs of Russian missiles planted in Cuba by Nikita
Khrushchev. President Kennedy succeeded in keeping the U2 incident under wraps. It wasn't reported in the papers. The United States
decided it would be prudent not to request the return of the pilot's
body, and he was eventually buried in Cuba. His name was Maj.
Rudolph Anderson Jr. of the United States Air Force.

The four of us strolled over to Il Gentiluomo on Calle Obispo. My friends were interested when I said they could get a perfectly grilled pescado for eight dollars. First they wanted to go into La Floridita for a drink and to bask in the golden aura of the statue of Hemingway. But we were turned away at the door because Christophe was deemed to be inappropriately attired – wearing a tight sleeveless undershirt only, showing off his perfect body. He looked like a sex machine. He took a silk scarf from around Isabella's neck, wrapped it around his neck, and said, "Is this better?" The Floridita doormen were not amused. No, they said, you still can't come in. So still wearing the scarf he asked if he could just go in and take a quick picture of the statue, and they happily allowed him to do that. So he took some pictures of Hemingway and off we went to the other restaurant, which had a more liberal dress policy.

Isabella, as if to make up for not liking the paintings, went into ecstasies over the pescado of the day, which was tuna steak an inch thick, and Christophe and Marcel shared with us the pizza, which was excellent, in exchange for tastes of our tuna. There was hardly anyone in there, and I was very pleased to have guided three Parisians to a restaurant they found so much to their liking. I jokingly said to the maitre d', "This is a lot better than La Floridita," and he laughed and said, "This is La Floridita!" This was just the Italian arm of La Floridita, with a less-expensive menu for Cubans and impecunious tourists.

Marcel the sleepy skinny restaurateur liked his pizza so much he ordered another one, but we had to help him finish it off. We also split an excellent bottle of Spanish red wine, chosen by Marcel. The maitre d' was very impressed with the choice. And the whole bill came to fifty-two dollars.

Meanwhile, poor Isabella was getting very sleepy. She'd been working hard for the past year and she just thought she needed to lie on the beach and empty her mind for a week or two. It was her fate to meet these two guys on the bus. She was dragging herself along after them. She loved her two new French friends and they loved her, and she was glad she'd met them, but that didn't stop her from being tired.

For a Corsican, Isabella was very light-skinned, and she is peeling already. After the meal she put cream on her face, while the two guys slapped me on the back and told me I was an excellent guide. We went strolling down Calle Obispo, getting ready to call it a night, and Christophe noticed a very attractive Cuban woman sitting alone at an almost empty bar. There were two guys at one end of the bar, and she was at the other end, looking down in the dumps. Well, this would never do. Christophe saw her and immediately bolted into the bar with no hesitation whatsoever and sat down next to her. I clandestinely watched through the open window as her melancholy evaporated and her frown turned upside down. She was leaving no doubt that she fully welcomed this intrusion into her privacy. Christophe came out a few minutes later with a sly little smile on his face.

"Well, what happened?"

He said, "We made plans to meet later and go dancing, and after that who knows what."

Christophe had earlier taken some photos of kids on the Prado practising the sport of fencing, with their coach. They were serious. They knew this was an Olympic sport. Just as Christophe was about to take a picture, one of the kids had his face mask knocked right off by his opponent, and that's about the worse thing that can happen in this sport, judging by the look on the kid's face. He was an Afro-Cuban, about twelve, and he was so disappointed with himself, shocked and humiliated, he was doing all he could to keep from crying. It would have been a great picture, but it was cool that Christophe decided not to take it. He just looked at me and shrugged.

Finally, back to the present, I tear myself away from the TV and drag myself out to the street. The first thing that happens is I get involved once again in the "milk for my baby" scam. This is the first time I've actually been caught on it. I've just lost five dollars on a bizarre scam, but I still don't completely understand it. Marcel got approached yesterday, and it never occurred to him it was a scam. He said it was problems with the ration books, and he was happy to help out. It's always Afro-Cuban males, who tell you they need milk for their baby. But they won't take the money, they insist you come to the store with them and buy the milk for them.

What can you say and what can you do when someone tells you his baby is dying from lack of milk? The first time I just knew it was a scam, but this time, because of Marcel's attitude toward it, I became curious to see what would develop if I went along with it. What developed was I lost my five dollars. The fellow came up to me at the sea end of the Prado; I had asked him for directions, and he asked me the normal questions you get asked by touts everywhere: Where you from? Canada. Quebec, eh? Yeah. Oh, I know somebody who lives in Quebec. Blah blah blah. All the things touts get taught to say. Hotel or *casa*? Hotel? What hotel are you in? And finally he'll say, very politely, with a worried look on his face: Could you help me, sir? I need some milk for my baby.

So he takes me into the store where they sell milk. And the woman has a big plastic bag full of milk waiting there for him in the cooler. And she gives me a look as if to say, Oh aren't you the big sucker today. She obviously knows this guy very well. He says, Could you give her the five dollars, sir? I pulled out a five-peso note and the woman looks very alarmed and starts screaming, No no no no. And he says, impatiently, No, it has to be five U.S. dollars. Wait a minute, five U.S. dollars, you could practically buy the whole cow for that.

All of a sudden it hit me. What they're doing is a kickback scheme. It's just like the cars up at the fortress, not real taxis, so they can't go cruising, but they have to wait till you ask them. Nobody could prove that I hadn't just asked him for a ride, and so on. So it's a ubiquitous scam, and it's just a way of making money for the store. The storekeepers, who are usually white, will get some black guy down on his luck (black for sympathy and to make the story more plausible) to accost tourists and ask for money for the baby. So I gave her the five, she hands the milk to the fellow, I leave, the fellow hands the milk back to the storekeeper, and she gives him his cut. A dollar? Two-fifty? I don't know.

There is no baby involved, because there is no shortage of milk for babies in Cuba. That's one thing there is never any shortage of. No rations for babies as far as I know. This is the first scam I've knowingly been part of in Cuba, though there have been several semi-scams.

I did give her the five dollars, I couldn't very well not do so at that stage, it just would have been wrong. I wasn't 100 per cent sure it was a scam at that point, but I was 90 per cent sure. I could very easily have just walked out, so she was lucky she got the five dollars. But I did plunk down the five dollars rather abruptly, and they could tell I was a bit miffed. The fellow grabbed the milk and took off, saying in the most sarcastic tone, It was very nice meeting you, sir.

So I went next door for coffee. The waitress was very young-pretty-smart, so I was surprised when she said she'd never heard of the "milk for my baby" scam. I watched her eyes carefully and I don't think she was lying. She'd genuinely never heard of the scam. Maybe because it's never been played on her, being a Cuban. But she did say that particular store is for U.S. funds only. They won't take pesos for anything there. So that surprised me, and maybe I'm wrong, maybe it's not a scam.

And so I sat there reading the paper and drinking my coffee, and keeping an eye open for the young fellow to sneak back with the bag of milk so he can get his rebate. But he never came. I was there half an hour and he didn't return. Maybe he was hiding behind a tree waiting for me to vacate the area. I don't know, but now I'm even more confused, and I don't know if it's a scam or not. But the wait-ress insisted that babies were provided plenty of milk free from the state, up to the age of six, shortages of milk for babies are impossible, and she very seriously told me that when people want to talk to me on the street – and she had a very distasteful look on her face – I should just ignore them, she said.

Also, she said that if you had to ask tourists for help with milk for your baby, then for sure you'd be a lot more anxious than these guys were. None of this laid-back cool-cat "where you from" nonsense. Next time I'll ask to see the poor starving baby before I get generous.

I spent several hours in the Museo de la Reveluçion. It's a powerful experience, no matter what your politics may be. It's one of those dedicated museums where you can enter knowing nothing about the subject and leave feeling as if you're a leading expert.

For instance, I used to think the March 13, 1957, attempted assassination of Batista just involved the little red Fast Delivery truck stuffed with forty-two heavily armed students, but it was much bigger than that. Carlos Gutierrez Menoyo was the leader, and it appears that he was a bitter rival of Fidel Castro. They both wanted the top job, and they both knew Batista was vulnerable. Carlos was no kid, he'd already fought in the Spanish Civil War and later in France during the Second World War. The little display on the wall of the Museo lists him as an "anti-fascist combatant."

Carlos had become leader of the university Revolutionaries about the time that Fidel was establishing himself in the Sierra Maestra mountains. The photo shows a powerful man of great intelligence and ambition. A very tough-looking no-nonsense guy, tall and thin, with a narrow face, square jaw, deep penetrating eyes, and a pencil moustache. Fidel was greatly annoyed when Carlos and the "Revolutionary Directorate" he led, mostly composed of university students in Havana, refused to support the *Granma* landing. Fidel accused the Revolutionary Directorate of treachery and cowardice.

Carlos was getting fed information from the Presidential Palace about Batista's schedule, all the details. And a bold and highly detailed plan of attack was worked out. At three o'clock on the afternoon of March 13, 1957, two cars and a van full of well-armed students arrived at the Presidential Palace and started firing. They burst into the building and raced up the stairs. But Batista wasn't in his office where he was expected to be. Chaos ensued, and the presidential guard launched a counter-attack that lasted for hours. Some of the students escaped but most were killed inside the palace.

Meanwhile Carlos and his smaller group had taken over the radio station and were announcing that the palace was occupied and Batista was dead. Carlos didn't live to find out that he had been mistaken on both counts. He and his group left the station to head back to the university, which they planned as their headquarters for a new government. But halfway there, an accident ensued. Carlos's car was in collision with a police vehicle. Carlos lost his cool, jumped from his car, and started firing his machine gun. The police officers returned fire and he was killed. Fidel had no rival. The game was his to win.

Today, behind the palace, one can see on display the Fast Delivery truck, complete with the original bullet holes. Also on display is the *Granma*, which Carlos and his Revolutionary Directorate maybe should have been there for when they knew it was about to land.

Also on display in the museum are numerous highly dramatic photos from the trials of some of Batista's men in the Revolutionary Court of Justice. Some of these photos are hard to look at. One shows a livid Inés Leal, a very proud and beautiful woman, angrily pointing her finger at former Capt. Jesús Sosa Blanco, as being responsible for the assassination of her husband and eight members of the Argote family. Another shows María Arman García pointing her finger in a similar fashion at former police officer Silvino Junco for having murdered her husband, Hector Molina Real.

There are also some tremendous photos from the Bay of Pigs invasion, showing captured U.S. soldiers, the U.S. supply ship *Houston* in flames out in the bay, and so on. One learns that the Bay of Pigs was the first imperialist defeat ever in Latin America, and that between 1971 and 1980 CIA agents introduced into Cuba the pig fever virus. More than a million pigs died.

I strongly recommend a visit to the Presidential Palace. It was very crowded when I was there, but there were only a handful of non-Cubans. Most of the visitors seemed to be from distant parts of Cuba and this was their first chance to tour the museum. To me, it's one of the great museums of the world, and if I heard that someone was flying to Havana simply to spend a day or two visiting the museum, I wouldn't at all think that was crazy.

People who come to La Floridita to snap a picture of the José Villa statue of Ernest Hemingway may not realize it right away, but when they get home they'll see stuck to the wall above Hemingway's head an ad for "Restaurant-Bar La Floridita – Havana Cuba." In every picture, hundreds a day during the heavy tourist season, free ads for La Floridita get e-mailed around the world. Some women will pose by snuggling right up to him and putting their arm through his, because he's got his bronze hand on his bronze hip, with his bronze elbow sticking out, so it's a very welcome place for a woman to slide her arm. And his bronze eyes of course keep moving, and flashing.

Most of the married women want their husbands to take a picture of them in front of Hemingway, and most do. But sometimes a man won't wish to, he will wish to be in the picture too, as if jealous of having his wife alone with Hemingway, even in a photo. So they will ask someone else to take the picture with them. And the woman always looks a bit disappointed, and a bit peeved for having married such a jerk.

One very prim-looking German lady posed beside the statue for a photo, and she began gently stroking his very pronounced crotch area, with the most innocent look on her face. Hope that one turns out well.

Eight Chinese guys in a row have had their pictures taken next to Hemingway, and every single one picks up Hemingway's daiquiri and pretends to be drinking it. The first one did it, so all the others had to do it. Except for the last guy. He didn't pick up the daiquiri, instead he looked up into Hemingway's eyes as the camera flashed.

Every morning the bartender places a fresh daiquiri in front of the statue. He jokingly says he thinks Hemingway would prefer a single daiquiri to a single rose. But these bartenders aren't stupid, for when you look carefully you see there is no booze in the daiquiri glass, it's just full of crushed glass, to make it look like crushed ice, with a couple of straws sticking up. The glass will last all day without melting, and Hemingway will stand there all day and all night without getting any tipsier.

There is definitely something magical about this statue. People are wandering around in Hemingway T-shirts, there are photos of Hemingway on the wall, we are located on Calle Obispo, which was Hemingway's favourite street in the world, but nothing is as much like Hemingway as that statue. Hats off to José Villa! Magic is what you imagine, sir!

At the Hotel Lido, I went up to the rooftop restaurant, to see if they served food all day or it was just breakfast. Sure enough they had a dinner menu. I had the three-dollar grilled pescado special. It was right up there with the eight-dollar pescado at Il Gentiluomo. For an extra $1.75 they will even pour half a pound of melted cheese over it, should that be to your taste.

It's quite the wintry breeze up here, and the Cubans are feeling shivery and uncomfortable. The waitress offered to put me in a protected corner so I wouldn't feel so cold, but I don't feel cold at all, I feel very refreshed after a blazing hot and still day. So I told her we Canadians don't feel the cold. It doesn't bother us at all. She rolled her eyes, to show she couldn't imagine living in a cold country, what a nightmare that would be, to be cold all the time.

They haven't had coffee in this restaurant for two days now. Most of the tourists were just laughing it off, but it disturbs me. So I finally ask the waitress what's the problem. She says, "Cafetera rota" – which I thought meant cafeteria broken. I looked confused, so she said, "Follow me, please." Turned out *cafetera* means coffee maker. She took me into the kitchen, and there she pointed with a rueful smile at a once-proud and very elaborate industrial-size coffee maker. It was blasted, blackened, and beyond repair. It looked as if it had been struck by lightning, or by an awesome power surge, or maybe it had been shot by Hemingway. Various broken springs, dials, and miscellaneous ragged chunks of metal and plastic looked as if they had been swept into a corner next to it. It looked as wrecked as some of those once grand old buildings along the Malecón. Whatever happened, they had put in a request for a new one, but with all the paperwork you can't expect it to arrive immediately.

When I left I gave her a dollar and said, "Pera la cafetera rota, señorita." She understood perfectly, but had to explain it to her coworkers. They thought that was the most thoughtful thing any tourist had ever done in the history of tourism, or at least since the coffee maker broke down. Someone pulled out an empty little box from a drawer and put the dollar in there. They'd get a new coffee maker fast if the word got out that the tourists are making contributions toward the cost of one.

MIMI'S GIFT

Wednesday, March 10, 2004. A crowded rush-hour commuter train has been blown up in Madrid. The TV shows bodies all over the place. Oh my God, what a mess. The Spanish ambassador to the United States is saying it's "a terrible blow for European democracy" and so on. Immediately upon waking up after a good night's sleep it's not a good idea to flick on the TV. Best to have a shower first, get dressed, get acclimatized, have some coffee. The cutest sparrow is sitting on the ledge of this rooftop restaurant, and he's enjoying a sunny but cool and breezy morning. Now he's on the floor doing one two three little hops, then he stops and looks around, then three more little hops. Then he spots a crumb and eats it. Then he goes by a whole pile of crumbs and doesn't even notice it. Now he sees one crumb all by itself, looks like a piece of cheese, and he beaks it up and gobbles it down, oh good good good. He has an evil look around the eyes, but that would be just to scare off the sparrow hawks.

Be generous, says Christopher P. Baker. That's the best part of Baker's book, when he's telling tourists to be generous.

The pure physical grace of the Cubans is more pronounced than anything visible in the numerous scenes of Havana life in the movie *Memories of Underdevelopment* from forty years ago or *I Am Cuba*, from the same period. It might have something to do with the never-ending chain of poverty, or with the notion that it's never going to get any better so let's dance sort of attitude. But maybe it's simply that this is the unconscious direction the Cubans are moving in: all nations evolve, but each in a different way, and the Cubans are evolving into a people of tremendous physical grace. This might be the birth of the "new man" promised by such local Marxists as Fidel and Che – although Fidel, and Che if he were alive, might not recognize it as such. The Cubans do not have the freedoms that Canadians, for instance, take for granted, or so the story goes. Maybe the lack of certain freedoms gives vent to a sort of gracefulness, a paradoxical freedom from stress, for we in the "developed" countries sometimes feel crushed by all our wonderful freedoms. In fact we are so free that we spend all our spare time worrying what we should do with all this freedom, and we end up doing nothing. When you're spending night and day wondering if you are exercising your freedoms in the best possible way, your own sense of grace and movement may easily suffer, and many other things as well, such as gusto for life, the ability to think rationally, and so on – only to be replaced with anxiety, guilt, and murderous impulses. It's a different kind of life here in Cuba, and it would be a mistake to say that the principal problem is lack of freedom.

One very elegant Canadian couple, when I was going up the stairs to the cafeteria, they were moving out, and they had an exquisite double set of fine leather luggage, about twelve pieces in all, six for each of them. The woman had them arranged next to the elevator, the button of which she was leaning into as she not so patiently waited for her husband to get his luggage together and out there next to hers. As I zipped by I said to her, smilingly, "Going somewhere?" and she looked at me, suddenly relaxed, and broke out laughing. "Looks that way," she said. I was pleased that she laughed because it must be awful being able to afford all that expensive luggage, and whatever is in them, and have to stay in such a cheap hotel. Then I could hear her nosy husband stick his head out and say, "What did he say?" She said, "He was talking to me, dear."

Barbaríta cleans my room every morning. On my freshly made bed she places a pair of clean towels folded, rolled, and twisted to resemble a pair of swans. She also makes powerful kissing sounds when she sees me, sounds that would seem offensive in Canada but are friendly as a howdy-do in Cuba. She knows that if I'm there when she is, she gets a dollar tip, but if I've gone already I always forget to leave a tip. So she's at my room early. She's Afro-Cuban, close to forty. She seems to have never suffered, her face is as unlined as a child's, life for her has been one nice thing after another. Her pale green maid's uniform is always unbuttoned daringly from neck to deepest cleavage. Yesterday she had a collection of three or four naughty compact discs on her maid's dolly. She tried to sell me a reggae CD featuring a naked dancing white woman on the cover. She seemed astonished that I didn't go for it.

The big restoration projects along the Malecón and throughout Havana Vieja seem to have stalled lately. Right now there are a large number of beautiful old buildings halfway renovated, and in many cases the facades are being salvaged because the rest of the building was too far gone. The facade will be just standing alone, propped up with girders. Occasionally you see some serious work going on, but the work only goes in fits and starts.

It's very cold in the other Museo de Bellas Artes, the one that houses the international collection rather than the Cuban collection. It's a ravishingly designed nineteenth-century Renaissance palace, and looming massively through the west windows is the great golden dome of the Capitolio, which is said in Washington to have been a blatant copy of the U.S. Capitol building.

It's odd to enter a gallery in a tropical country, and immediately start shivering. The first painting doesn't help: It's a frigid winter scene in the far north, Niagara Falls, in 1858, with a lighthouse sitting on an ice-covered rock at the far end of the falls. The lighthouse is caked with ice, there are icicles hanging from it like tears from a snowman. There is a wooden walkway along the lip of the Falls leading from the shore to the lighthouse, and the walkway is also of course covered with ice. Hard to imagine anyone walking along that walkway. Also it seems like a stupid place for a lighthouse. There's something highly suspect about this painting.

Regis-François Gignoux was a Frenchman who wandered through the United States in the nineteenth century and is famous for his paintings of Indians and battle scenes. He apparently did two highly unusual paintings of Niagara Falls in the winter, one I remember being frightened by in childhood, and this one that is new to me, and which is frightening me now. They have to be on the shortest list of his greatest works. But why would he have put that lighthouse there at the brow of the Falls? And who would willingly walk that scary walkway along the edge of the great abyss? I'm sure Gignoux visited Niagara Falls, but this painting, and the other one, were done at his studio in New York, and his aim obviously was to be inspired by his subject rather than faithful to it. He must have had fun fooling people.

Gignoux's other Niagara Falls painting in winter hangs, with pathetic irony, in the Senate Wing of the U.S. Capitol building, and shows the old Table Rock on the edge of the Falls, two years before it collapsed and broke apart at the foot of the Falls. In this work too he uses odd distortions to increase the dramatic effect.

The Cuban paintings are much warmer and more interesting for the most part. Here's a view of the Prado, looking north from the roof of this very palace it would seem. It's dated 1895 – with many more boats out in the sea than there are today. There's only one steamer, but dozens of sailboats and numerous little dots representing canoes. Another picture, like a Norman Rockwell but not as sentimental, shows a black waiter sitting on the floor with one plate smashed and two intact, and he is glaring up at another young black fellow who is laughing merrily, presumably having just tripped the first guy.

I'm taking more time over this highly detailed and realistic bird's-eye view of a backyard bullfight gone bad. There have been some problems, people are very excited and leaping from their benches; the picador has been knocked off his horse, and it looks as if he's been badly gored. Another fellow who has also been gored is lying on the ground dead and covered with blood. The horse is lying on the ground, the bull is trying to trample it to death, and a little boy is trying to get the bull to back off the horse by pulling with all his weight on the bull's tail. Someone is trying to spear the bull through the neck. Three horses in all are lying on the ground with their intestines spilling out – one is dead, one about to die, and one is just sitting there propped up on his forelegs, wide awake and watching his blood gush out. Whew! All on one medium-size canvas.

There is also a small gallery devoted to paintings of the Virgin Mary baring her breast and squirting milk into St. Fernando's mouth. This seems to be a distinctive motif among nineteenth-century Latin American painters, and maybe earlier. St. Fernando is climbing Calvary, and he is carrying the cross, the hammer, the ladder, the INRI sign, all the implements of Christ's crucifixion. But he's not too busy to take the time to open his mouth to drink from a two-foot arc of milk pouring from Mary's breast, and splashing off his lower lip! And sitting on Mary's lap is the infant Jesus, quietly observing the preparations for his own crucifixion to come.

Meanwhile a black gallery guard with no neck and the meanest look on his face apprehended me and insisted I put my camera in my pocket. I tried to tell him it wasn't a camera, but he wouldn't listen. So I put my tape recorder in my inside pocket, then continued to record little comments by whipping my jacket open and pressing the record button while he watched grouchily from a distance, like an angry bull with red eyes, pawing the floor with his hooves.

Having convinced myself that English is a dying language in Cuba, at least among the white people, I came across several people, employees of the museum, who were spending their abundant downtime frantically studying that greatest of all languages, as most of us like to think of our mother tongue. The first woman, in a gallery on the second floor, was very dark-skinned, but with Spanish features, and her undeniable beauty was marred by a serious skin problem, which I managed to ignore by focusing on her deep dark eyes. She was a warm and pleasant young woman, she had a very sensitive and delicate face, with a flat nose and extremely tiny nostrils, and seemed generally disposed toward brightness and beauty. When I walked into the gallery I thought I heard someone singing, so I looked around, and there she was, sitting on a bench, reading a book giving words and simple phrases in four or five European languages. She was trying to say the words out loud, singing them, but it was a very cheap book, and there was no pronunciation guide, if you can believe it.

She was trying to learn English words without having a clue how to pronounce them. But soon she was pointing to words and phrases, I'd give the proper pronunciation, and she'd repeat it perfectly the first time. She said she has been studying hard because it's a boring job and she has all this time on her hands. She works five eight-hour shifts a week, often without any people coming through, even at peak tourist times, such as the famous spring break, which was now, and she makes the equivalent of thirteen U.S. dollars a month, same as Mariano. She and her colleagues sit around studying languages all day long.

She hailed from some sad village in Granma Province, and she said it was very difficult to find another job, because all the interesting jobs had been taken already by the time she rolled into the capital. Her eyes flashed when I told her that Cuban people in general don't seem to have much in the way of options. She laughingly tightened her lips, kissed the tip of her forefinger, and said, "I'm not saying a thing!" I told her it must seem at times like being in a quagmire, but that doesn't mean you can't enjoy your life, because it's still a terrific country. She didn't say a thing.

The woman tending the spacious and well-stocked gift shop was similarly bored out of her skull. She was tickled pink to have a visitor. She straightaway asked if I knew anything about Cuban music. I had a feel for it, but I was no expert. So she slipped a CD into the stereo, and played some fairly staid music, nothing that would tempt us to dance. We couldn't have that, could we? That furious bull downstairs just might decide to charge up the stairs and throw us both out on the street. She asked if there was anything I'd like to hear, they have everything by everybody who's anybody in all the fourteen provinces.

So I asked for something by the classical guitarist Leo Brouwer. His international reputation had reached my ears, but his music hadn't and I was curious. So she put on a CD called *From Bach to the Beatles*, and I listened carefully to several Bach songs and several Beatles songs before saying enough already. She asked if I knew about the Buena Vista Social Club, and she sadly related that some of the members have died, and they're folding up now. She played a few of her favourite songs, but they didn't get to me the way I expected. She must have suddenly got an inspiration, because she played some Lecuona piano music, and I loved it immediately. This was Cuban music, even if some of the songs were old Spanish classics, he gave them a strangely Cuban spin. So I bought it – plus, without even sampling it, José María Vitier's twelve-part mass, *Misa Cubana a la Virgen de la Caridad de El Cobre*, in honour of my visit to El Cobre.

Maybe it's not as grand as the Presidential Palace, but the swirling staircases of this building are exquisitely designed to make you forget, in the most pleasant manner, what floor you're on and what floor you're trying to get to. Everything is just perfect. I find myself standing or sitting and staring at nothing and everything. There's a coffee shop adjacent to the gift shop, and it's large and empty of people. It does have good coffee though, and the fellow behind the bar was making some for me. First customer of the day – except for staff members. As in every city, no matter how crowded and noisy things become you can always find a quiet and uncrowded spot when you need one. He insisted this place is nowhere near the architectural marvel that the Presidential Palace is, but to me the Presidential Palace is much heavier and darker, maybe even clunkier.

Best not to go into this in great detail, but there were several very flirtatious encounters in this building with attractive female guides. In Canada, women no longer flock about me, if they ever did, but here the babes love me like crazy. One was actually holding my hand as the two of us looked at a seventeenth-century Spanish painting by Alexandro DeLoarto. It was called *El Manna del Cielo*, and showed several people solemnly picking up all these strange little floating white things falling from the sky. We looked at each other and smiled.

And when I tore myself away, she held up her hand to be kissed. Mid-kiss there was a bit of a cough and we both turned and noticed the bull-necked red-eyed security guard from the first floor. He was watching us from behind a marble pillar and had a fiendish look on his face. I had the strongest feeling there would soon be a directive on guides being overly friendly with single male tourists.

The Palacio de los Capitanes Generales (also known as the Museo de la Ciudad, or the City Museum) is a repository for relics from the Havana of a century ago: fragments of statues and remarkable old crosses from churches that have been turned into banks; corner-stones, dedication stones, marker stones, and dozens of stone lions from long-demolished buildings. There's a charming series of four marble drinking fountains long ago rescued from a block being torn down, the four chubby little deities with no water gushing from their open mouths.

There are many interesting old pictures and maps of Havana down through the centuries, some nineteenth-century engravings showing rows of splendid buildings hugging the seafront, but no seawall yet, no Malecón. Somehow these relics make Havana seem more real, while not taking anything away from its dream quality. In fact the dream becomes deeper, takes on further dimensions.

There's an interesting painting showing the death of Gen. Antonio Maceo. The setting is a grassy field with a dense grove of tall palm trees behind it. Maceo looks dead already, his men are holding him up, trying to ease his pain although they know it's a lost cause, and one sympathetic *campesino* in the background is holding his gun in his left hand, and has his right hand over his heart, which is exactly where Antonio Maceo took his fatal wound, according to the paint-ing. But real life is not so tidy. After being wounded twenty times in previous battles, the Bronze Titan, as Antonio was called, took two bullets on this day, one in the chin (and out the back of the neck) and the other in the stomach (after passing through the body of General Máximo Gómez's son Panchito and then through a horse).

As I drank in this painting, a guide approached me and said that Antonio was a handsome, well-groomed, and very small Afro-Cuban, with an excellent moustache and beard, a fastidious dresser, and gentle with people when not on the battlefield. Also at one period when Antonio, after much deliberation, had finally decided to free a female spy his men had captured, he was told that she had already been executed, by his no-nonsense brother José.

Antonio was only fifty-one when he died, and Cubans still regard him as the greatest general of all time. Not only was Maceo an Afro-Cuban, all his men were too, though most of them towered over him in size. My guide also showed me his eyeglasses, and the saddle that he used through all his campaigns, though not always on the same horse.

She also said Antonio, unlike many of the other generals, had refused to make peace with the colonial armies until slavery was abolished. He insisted that only a coward asks for his rights, a real man must take them.

She became warmer and friendlier when she found out I knew a little bit about Cuban history, and actually remembered having seen the magnificent and imposing statue of Antonio Maceo in Santiago de Cuba. It doesn't take much for a tourist to impress a Cuban, especially one who although in her forties still looked smashing in a miniskirt and fishnet stockings. She showed me a picture of Manuel de Céspedes, and when I told her (before she told me) that he was from Bayamo and had designed the first Cuban flag, had honoured his country above the life of his son, and had his beautiful house burned down for strategic reasons, she gasped with astonishment. By now she realized I wasn't on a single-male sex tour, and she became all smiles, and close contact, and even a bit of feline purring. She proceeded to show me all the old satin and velvet flags of all the countries of the Western Hemisphere – with the notable exception of the United States, that flag having been found missing, so she said, after a very heavy tourist day a few years back, and was never recovered. I loved the way she pronounced Bolivia, and made me think how interesting it would be to attend (with her, if possible) a football game between Libya and Boo-Libya. Then she draped the Canadian flag over her shoulder and stroked it so lovingly I knew it was time to say adios.

As I was leaving, a tourist came in the front door with a terribly bored look on her face, stood between the two main columns at the entrance, snapped a picture, yawned, and walked out to rejoin her tour group. When she gets home her picture will show an inner courtyard with a luxuriant garden full of brilliant flowers, tall palm trees, numerous exotic birds all squawking away, forty-four gothic arches arranged on three two-storey walls, and about fifty-two granite columns.

Perhaps this is silly, but I still do not wish to identify the beautiful government building where Mimi and I had a friendly encounter on my third day in Cuba – the building outside of which I waited for her in vain on the evening of my fourth day. But I popped into the same building this afternoon and there she was. Many tourists had come and gone in the past three weeks, but she hadn't forgotten me. We definitely didn't shout and embrace, we spoke politely, quietly, and kept our distance. We were happy to see each other again, she slipped me her address and invited me for coffee. We could go for a "petite promenade." She'd be looking for me at eight o'clock.

On the way over to Mimi's place I was walking along a very dark street and all of a sudden my feet wouldn't move, like a fast freeze in a movie. It was exactly as if somebody had tossed a lariat on the pavement and the moment I stepped inside it he gave it a yank. But it turned out not to be a lariat but a circular strip of soft metal, a band of steel not much bigger than the fan belt of a Humvee, and by the strangest fluke one foot went inside it and then the other did as well, so I had to stop dead or take a serious tumble. This seemed so strange it was like a dreadful omen, and something told me I should turn around and forget all about visiting my friend. But it would have been very ungentlemanly of me to have chickened out now. I'd never forgive myself for my cowardice. Besides, it was perhaps ominous in a good way. After all, it was amazing I didn't fall to the ground and break my head open.

She came running down from her second-floor apartment wrapped in a white towel and with her hair all wet. She took me upstairs by the hand and I sat at the kitchen table while she got dressed. She kept apologizing for the mess of the place, but it was a big apartment and I kept seeing it as it might have been thirty years ago, before things started falling apart. She has a nineteen-year-old son who has been drafted into the army for a year or two. I met two of her son's friends, two guys also nineteen, and they were very sweet, lovely, charming, well-mannered, honest young fellows. Very nice guys. They had just popped in to say hello and see if there's any news from her son.

So we went for our petite promenade, but she had a cold coming on, and I was hungry, and she hadn't eaten, so we had to get to a restaurant fast. We went over to Il Gentiluomo, but there was a private party going on and we couldn't get in. So we walked a bit down Obispo to another pizza joint. We ordered a pizza and a couple of beers. They took an awful long time to bring the beer, the two bartenders just ignored our order and kept talking. And when the pizza came, it was inedible. It was smothered in what looked like ketchup, and there were little melted globs of cheese here and there floating in the ketchup. It tasted even worse than it sounded, but I couldn't figure out which tasted worse, the ketchup or the cheese. Mimi, who hadn't taken a bite yet, said the cheese was actually a concoction of bread and cheese – sort of a cheesy breadball. So I told her I couldn't eat it, and she refused even a taste. We paid our bill in full – seven dollars – and walked out, with two withering backward glances at the waiter and bartender who were not at all concerned.

We went over to La Floridita. She refused anything more expensive than the cheese sandwich, the cheapest item on the menu. I had the tuna sandwich. She kept switching from English to Spanish to French around and around in circles, and I got a bit overloaded. I couldn't concentrate any more, and I know I was missing a lot of interesting stuff.

But I recovered when we got back to her apartment. We talked for hours. She did tell me her salary was three hundred pesos a month, and out of that comes twenty-seven pesos for lunch each working day, whether she has lunch or not. Although Mariano claimed that he didn't have to pay any rent, or water, or power, Mimi said she had to pay thirty pesos each month for the rent, two pesos per month for the water, and twenty-two pesos a month for the power. So with the mandatory lunch she has 219 pesos to throw around, which is the equivalent of US$8.11 a month. But she turned to me and said, "I'm not desperate for anything. Life has not smiled on me, but I'm not desperate."

She also noted, with no pleasure whatsoever, that when we were in La Floridita, everybody was smiling at me but they were not smiling at her. I said it might be because she was dark-skinned, and there might still be some racial prejudice in Havana. But she denied that strongly, no way could she accept that. She was simply astonished that salespeople and waiters were actually smiling at me. They knew that she was Cuban and I was Canadian and I had the dollars and she had the pesos, and therefore people instinctively bestow their smiles on the person with the greatest amount of ready cash. She hadn't noticed that before, that her fellow Cubans could be so crass, and it was a little knife twisting in her heart. We tourists are doing a lot to benefit Cuba, we are the biggest cash cow the Cubans have, and maybe the smiles are smiles of gratitude – but why couldn't she have had a smile bestowed on her now and then?

So we sat for half an hour in her favourite park, mine also, the Plaza de Armas, with the Hotel Isabella on the east and the Museo Ciudad on the west. What a charming spot, especially with such a warm friendly companion to help me admire and thrill to certain particularly beautiful sightlines, angles, corners, juxtapositions, certain patches of shadow and starlight, or a glance of moonlight penetrating a dark alley, or the little halos of lamplight underfoot along the pavement, and now and then a glimpse of the moonlit alabaster El Cristo high on its promontory on the other side of Havana Bay.

Now and then we would notice a police officer watching us from a distance, or from behind a bush, as if they were simply curious about someone who seemed to be a tourist hitching up with an older black woman when there are so many young exciting ones around for the taking. I suppose Mimi would seem more like a dark-skinned Indian than an Afro-Cuban, but she told me right off the bat that she thinks of herself as a black woman right down to the inner core of her being. Even though she looked more like a dark Mexican

Indian than anything else, she identified totally with her negritude. She showed me pictures of her son, her late father, her brother, and her long-gone husband – all of whom were 100 per cent African in appearance. She may have been more spiritually connected with her paternal negritude than her maternal aztecitude – but she definitely thinks of herself as an Indian as well. She said she hurts very badly when she hears sad stories about life on the Native reserves in Canada.

And as we walked in the moonlight, she would keep shivering with pleasure as she beheld certain seldom-observed sightlines, or exquisitely odd little nighttime tableaus, and she would stop suddenly and say, "Oh, look at that, isn't that wonderful," and so on, as if her lack of opportunity to travel to other countries has turned her into a tourist in her own backyard.

The sun doesn't shine on her, but she is a great lover of Havana, and she is not in despair. And when you are a great lover of anything under the sun, it doesn't matter if the sun shines on you or not. She is a great lover of Havana, and that's enough for anyone to be in love with.

I walked her home, she brewed up some coffee, and when I left at 2:30 a.m. she presented me with a gift. She wanted me to have a hand-crafted Aztec goddess about eight inches tall. It's from the Quetzalcóatl pantheon, a rather stout little Chicomecóatl, a corn goddess of great antiquity, who has gone through many forms. In this form she has a long nose, sad eyes, and a chubby face, so that she actually looks like Mimi. She is standing with great presence, dressed in an elaborate headdress, a splendid robe. She seems very serene and full of understanding of the importance of her role as an archetype for Aztec women down through the centuries. She's almost geometrically symmetrical, she is a pleasure to look at, and she radiates serenity.

TWO ENGLISHMEN
IN HAVANA

Thursday, March 11, 2004. Mimi said she used to be married to a little guy who drank a lot, but she got rid of him. Why? She looked up and said, Because he was a little guy who drank a lot. She said he was even smaller than she was, and she was only about five-foot-two. She also said her mother had recently had a large skin cancer completely cured by laser surgery. You couldn't even see where it used to be. Her mother's original tongue was Náhuatl, the language of the Aztecs, but her Spanish was fluent.

We found out we were both solitary creatures. She had been worrying about tales she'd been told regarding the alleged tendency of solitude to speed up the aging process. I suggested surely not if you like it. If it's right for you it would have to slow down the aging process rather than speed it up. If you were a solitary soul and liked it, being with people would be more likely to speed up the aging process. She enthusiastically thanked me for saying that and said she'd never worry about being alone again. She said she was forty-nine, and I said see? You only look about thirty-five. So she didn't have to worry about her aging process.

That wretched restaurant last night had me confused this morning. I woke up wondering if they had got mixed up and gave us the peso pizza for tourist dollars. Since I was a Canadian and Mimi a Cuban, obviously I had a taste for peso people and therefore would also have a taste for peso pizza. Would I have been given a different menu, or a different pizza, with special ingredients for the tourists, if I had come in by myself, or with another Canadian? It was hard to say.

But then, I'd had peso pizza before, at the baseball game at Santa Clara, bought and paid for by Orestes, and it was fine. So I didn't understand it, and if Mimi had any opinions on the subject she didn't offer them. But she definitely did not think it was deliberate at all on the part of the restaurant staff. She maintained it had absolutely nothing to do with us. We were not the target. In fact, she grabbed my arm and pointed dramatically to the little apartments above the stores along Calle Obispo, and her voice took on a fiery quality.

She said, See those windows? The people who work in these restaurants and these stores along this street, they all live in those apartments up there, in very crowded conditions. They don't have time to be prejudiced in any way. They can't afford it.

Earlier that day I'd bought, in a dollar store on the Prado, for forty-one dollars, a cheap digital watch to replace the one I'd lost. It was black and yellow, to match my nylon Hamilton Tiger-Cats jacket. When I showed her the rather gaudy watch, she looked at it in astonishment and said, "You paid forty dollars for that piece of shit?"

I laughed and said the watch I lost was also a plastic digital watch, I bought it sixteen years ago for forty dollars, and it was very much like this one, and it kept perfect time for sixteen years, and wherever it is now it's probably still keeping perfect time. So I got my forty dollars' worth out of that.

Then she started beating her breast and tearing her hair out. "Oh, I'm so sorry," she wailed. "How could I have said such a thing?" She was a fiery woman! Such seriousness! I used to think I had the lowest self-esteem rating in the world, but lately I've been noticing that almost everybody is in the same boat. Some hide it better than others. It seems I'm naturally drawn to those who don't hide it well.

Also I was a bit mad at myself for not having waited until I could ask her if she could get me one cheaper at a peso store.

Not much happening today, but let me offer two short, sad stories about Englishmen in Havana. The first was in a little coffee shop on the lower west side of the Prado, where I had a pair of delicious hot huevos fritos with Tabasco sauce this morning, owing to waking up too late for the hotel rooftop with the *cafetera rota*. I always feel better after a couple of eggs in the morning, at least in Cuba. I can't imagine having cholesterol problems if you eat a pair of these eggs every morning. Cuban eggs seem to be anti-cholesterol, giant delicious cholesterol-fighting pills.

It must have been obvious I was enjoying my eggs because there was a table of Germans in the corner and one of them called out to the waitress, in English, "I'll have what he's having. Eggs? Eggs?" Then in came two very beautiful, tall, graceful Afro-Cuban women, followed by a very tall, skinny, aristocratic Englishman more than three times their age, dressed very tastefully, everything carefully chosen for carefree travel in tropical countries. The women with their café au lait skin sat down and they seemed to have a lot to discuss, and they seemed to be brimming with intelligence and excitement at being together. The taller wore a white turban, a white silk suit, white shoes, and a string of white pearls around her neck. Smashing! This is the outfit favoured by initiates into the mystical core of the Santería belief system. They have to wear white for a full year. Mimi told me last night when we passed several women dressed that way.

And the other woman was just dressed like an ordinary *habanera calle chica*, but equally beautiful in her own way.

The Englishman was of a breed that is almost extinct, having been largely wiped out in two world wars. He still had that "stiff upper lip" mentality. But he lacked the calm, cool, collected patience of the Cubans as we shall soon see. He was one scrappy guy.

The women were excitedly yacking back and forth in inscrutable Spanish, rolling their eyes, squealing with laughter, drawing pictures in the air with their hands, hugging each other, and generally having a wonderful conversation. But the Englishman was not thrilled about this. He sat down and just glared at them. You could sense his blood pressure rising as he got more and more miffed. Soon he'd blow up like a *cafetera rota*. And he did. He all of a sudden rudely interrupted them and started talking angrily at them. He was trying to keep his voice down and I didn't catch what he was saying, and the women hardly paid any attention to him, they just kept talking to each other, which made him even angrier and caused him to explode once again, at a higher level, and he leapt to his feet and started yelling, so that everyone in the place could hear him.

"You can keep on talking to yourselves if you want," he screamed, "but you can pay the bill too." With that he stormed toward the door, but then he inexplicably turned around and walked back to the table. This could be a mistake. Would there be reconciliation or escalation? Neither, he just sat down, they continued talking to each other as if nothing had happened. Still his anachronistic English superiority couldn't accept not being the centre of attention. You could see him getting angry again, but before he could explode he just got up and walked out.

When I left, this perfect English aristocrat was standing under the laurel trees on the Prado, where Calle Colón intersects, and staring northward toward the Capitolio. He had the look of a man who knew where he was but didn't know where the heck he wanted to go. It was as if his day had been spoiled and it was all the fault of those ungrateful bitches. I couldn't resist saying with a little smile, "Don't let them get you down." He looked at me and said, "I'm easy."

The second Englishman looked a bit like actor Michael Caine except he was very short, sheepish, and seemed about to burst into tears. He walked into the Hotel Lido as I was standing at the counter annoying the flashy manageress about something. Just as the Englishman came in, a tall and dignified Cuban man in a business suit was leaving the hotel. The Englishman stopped him and said, "I owe you a tremendous apology. I wonder if you could spare me five minutes." The Cuban fellow said, "No, I can't" – and he left.

This was a terrible blow to the Englishman, who had already been whipping himself to death, so I felt sorry for him, and being interested in getting the story, I said, pleasantly, "I can spare you five minutes if you wish." He looked at me as if he thought that was kind of me, and his lips were moving, and he was trying to say something, but the words just wouldn't come out somehow. I felt so sorry for him. He was having a terrible attack of culture shock, or so it seemed. His self-esteem had hit rock bottom.

Then he turned to the iron-fisted manageress, the most obese and impatient Afro-Cuban woman imaginable. She was covered in gold necklaces and rings, and he tried to say something to her, but the words still wouldn't come out. I never did find out what the story was, dammit. Then an attractive young German couple went to the front desk and said to the manageress, with shy and nervous smiles on their faces, very slowly, "Sorry, but we accidentally left our key in the room? And we'd like to have a new one? A new key, that is? So we can get back in?" With the glummest look, the manageress handed them another key, and said, "Bring it back – right away! Instantly!" I burst out laughing, which caused the manageress to give me a withering look, but it eased the pain of the German couple. They turned to me and the woman said, "It's very embarrassing." I told her not to be. I said, "You wouldn't be human if you didn't leave your keys in the room now and then." They liked that and it made them feel better. "Thank you very much," they said. When you're newly married, as they seemed to be, such things can be mortifying, but when you're newly divorced losing a key is nothing.

So then I decided to check my mail on the single little computer at the back of the lobby by the bar. The bartender, a nice guy named Máximo, seems to be sleeplessly manning that bar around the clock and with never a day off. It's not a busy bar, but he never sits down. When there's nothing going on he stands there watching the overhead TV. I gave him six dollars in advance, and I sat down at the computer, and it was so slow, that I would issue a command, and then wait and wait until it timed out. This happened over and over again, so finally I gave up and asked Máximo for my money back.

Well! He'd never heard of such a thing. He'd been my friend up to that point, ever since I first checked in. But no more. No matter how I tried to explain to him what that problem was, he obviously thought I was trying to cheat him. I thought he was a mensch, but he thought I was a crook and a liar. He finally offered three dollars back because I'd been on the computer half an hour, but I insisted on the six dollars because I'd wasted that half-hour unsuccessfully trying to get the computer to work.

So he told a female hotel employee about the problem, they spent about fifteen minutes talking it over, then she got on the phone and a male employee came down and spent fifteen minutes talking to Máximo. Then Máximo went over to the big fat woman covered in gold, and spent fifteen minutes telling her about it, then she got on the phone and spent half an hour talking to someone in the upper levels of the Ministry of Tourism about this big issue – and then finally she hung up and called Máximo over and told him to give me my six dollars back. Strangely, in all that time, nobody thought to have a look at the computer.

So from then on whenever Máximo saw me coming, he'd come out from behind the bar and turn the computer off. As if to say, "This computer is off limits to you, chum."

One of those rare beings, a desperate, homeless down-and-out Cuban, a white man about thirty-five with stinking clothes and badly in need of fumigation, a bath, a barbershop, a massage, a month at Varadero Beach, and maybe a well-paid job in the government, has shown up at the corner of Agramonte and Neptuno, by Parque Centro, and is impatiently pawing through a pair of overloaded industrial-size garbage bins, looking for something of value, and tossing everything else out on the street, causing passersby to look at him with disgust. Oh, he's an ugly fellow for sure, with a deadly disposition and a vicious look on his face. I'm watching from a distance and can't hear what is being said, but I have the odd feeling that this wretch might be a non-Cuban, some tough case who came down on a sex holiday a few years ago, lost his wallet, decided to stay, but then everything started to go wrong and now look at him, a perfect example of premature psychopathological paranoid dementia with possible homicidal tendencies and serious dandruff.

Meanwhile, a black police officer, tall and skinny as a rake as they all seem to be, wanders serenely by and of course does a hilarious double-take and orders this wretch to stop making such a mess. So the messy wretch gets angry and takes a pretty vicious swing at the cop, who neatly ducks the punch. The grungy guy turns and goes back to his task of going through the garbage and tossing it on the street, though a fraction more carefully than before. The cop was armed with a gun and a billy club, but he just shrugged it off and let him be, continued watching him, but without getting angry, exercising perfect restraint – a refreshing change from police procedures in most other big cities of the world, where in a case like that there'd be instantly mindless retaliation of some sort or another.

So here I am walking along Calle Obispo, it's getting late already, and I'm being accosted by bright and beautiful young women offering the world for a few dollars, and handsome dark young men in flashy tropical shirts wanting me to come in and drink with them. I'm looking for that fetid pizza restaurant Mimi and I were in last night but I can't find it, it seems to have disappeared.

Then at midnight, under a dim lamppost at the dark southwest corner of Plaza de Armas, a handsome little white fellow about forty was standing there strumming on his guitar. His name was Rolf and he just got back from a couple of years in California. He didn't like the politics there. He was bummed out, homesick, and depressed. Now he's back where he belongs and feels on top of the world. He sang and played "Hotel California" all the way through, just for me. He said he meets a lot of Canadians in Havana, and they almost always turn out to be from the United States. He tells them don't be ashamed, nobody blamed the ordinary Germans for Hitler. Just then a lone male tourist came by wearing an Oberlin College (U.S.A.) sweatshirt and a Sioux Lookout (Canada) baseball cap, obviously hedging his bets. He gave us a quick glance and kept going.

My guitarist friend was getting ready to join other musicians at a

late-night bar around the corner. But he didn't seem in a rush, so I
asked if he knew "Dos Gardenias." He sang it brilliantly, with great
tenderness and passion, all four verses, with some really good guitar
work, on a dark empty street to an audience of one. He didn't even
mind me taping him. When he finished he smiled, accepted my
modest tip, and rushed off.

Thanks, Rolf – forty years old, happy guy, handsome, a gentleman
of sensible height (about five-foot-seven), a great singer. He seemed
very connected between himself and his country, especially after
having been away, and he seemed pleased with the world around
him, as if it might have taken a long stay in California to make him
see clearly how much more interesting Cuba and the Cubans really
is and are. In fact, when we first started talking he began telling me
the history and date of construction of all the ancient buildings that
surrounded us. He didn't learn any English in California, but being
there must have tempered his Spanish, because I seemed to understand every word he said, as if in a dream, as long as I didn't concentrate too hard.

He got me thinking there must be a lot more Cubans in the
United States who are terribly homesick, but don't want to admit
they made a mistake in leaving. They had jumped from the barbe-
cue into the furnace, or whatever the old saying is.

Calle Obispo seems like a very long street at first, but the more often
you walk it the shorter it becomes. Eventually it will disappear. A
little mariachi band turned up in the park, and I sat to drink in the
sounds. There were four young black women sitting together on a
bench opposite, and one of them looked right at me, stuck her
tongue out and wiggled it. So I returned the favour, stuck my tongue
out and wiggled it back at her. She shook her head frowningly, said
no no no, shook her finger at me, and said not you, him – then
pointed at some guy standing behind me. He was a Finnish tourist
with a video camera, and he was shooting everything that moved,
including the girl with the tantalizing tongue. So I shrugged my
shoulders, and she laughed.

ANOTHER DREAM FOR CUBA

Friday, March 12, 2004. At the Museo de la Ciudad I'd gazed at an old painting showing a grand stretch of Havana, from an elevated viewpoint out in the Straits of Florida, and with British warships sailing past El Morro and into the bay. The ships are in the foreground, and the entire city is spread out behind them. Strangely, the painter seems to have exaggerated the hills to the south of Havana, unless the last 150 years of hurricanes have ground them down considerably.

The dream from which I awoke at 7:17 this morning placed me in that ancient Havana, not much larger than today's Havana Vieja, and with little donkey paths leading up the high grassy hills as depicted in the painting. I feel compelled to describe the dream, as I have described others, and as I would describe anything that caught my interest on this trip.

Somewhere in Havana I met two people, a man and a woman. The woman was Isabella the Corsican (from Day Twenty-five), and the man was Fraser Hughes, an old Scottish friend of my youth. Fraser is now a professional music critic, and Isabella a professional cinéaste (as well as amateur art critic). How odd to see them paired up in a dream! But these were two people with a strong critical intelligence. The strong critical intelligence I should be applying to Cuba? Maybe.

The two of them persuaded me to travel to a certain place way up in the hills above Havana. They refused to tell me why at this point, but they insisted so strongly I couldn't say no. There was no traffic, few buildings, just a few huts and narrow pathways leading up to the high ground. Yet I found a bicycle, anachronistically, and rode effortlessly along the paths up into the hills, then knocked on the door of a big old southern Ontario-style brick farmhouse. The door opened. I was ushered in and presented to none other than Fraser and Isabella, who had somehow got there before me.

They asked if I would be interested in the task of building some earthworks, a stone wall and a flower garden around the house. I was given all the basic information on what was required and was told to do whatever I wanted within that framework. They wanted me to start work immediately. I believed them when they said there would be great benefits if I performed this job properly, but I'm not sure what the benefits were, or who would be benefited. Yet I was certain I wanted to do it. I didn't even think of saying no.

So I was working alone on the wall, and the earthworks, and the planting of flowers – all at the same time. But gradually I became confused, and couldn't remember what I was supposed to be doing. I doubted! Suddenly there was an earthquake: the earth opened up and swallowed all my work, my tools, my materials, my plans. But there was no other damage. The house had not been damaged.

Fraser and Isabella came rushing out, and they were very upset. They thought it was somehow my fault, and they decided it wouldn't be a good idea to continue on, because obviously the gods had turned against this project. But maybe if I were to leave my bicycle here and roller-skate back down to Old Havana, then I could skate back up the next day, and it would be okay to try to start over again and see what happens. Such a strong show of dedication to sacred rituals would somehow placate the gods, and finally the same all-important benefits would accrue, plus bonuses.

The dog from the house in the hills was running right along with me as I skated back down to the city. The dog's friendliness was a sign that I would successfully return and give the earthworks project another shot. But it was not to be: after a while I became tired and had to stop at the side of the road. It was easy to climb the hill but getting down is hard work. The dog jumped into my arms and started licking my face – then, with no warning, it bit me on the finger so hard that blood spurted out in a long powerful arc. The dog started licking the blood as it fell in puddles on the ground. I put my head down and fell asleep.

I don't know what it all means, but there's nothing in it that sounded like an urgent warning about anything. So I'll just give this dream back to Cuba, with good wishes, for Cuba gave it to me in the first place.

Today when I went up to the rooftop for breakfast, after having missed yesterday, the staff remembered my donation toward a new coffee maker. They repaid me with the largest breakfast imaginable – with big thick slices of fresh tomato and raw onion, and three of their delicious dry rolls, and though I usually get two small eggs today they presented me with three extra-large ones perfectly cooked. And plenty of coffee. I'd finish one cup and another would be placed on my table. Even the kitchen staff was coming out and blowing kisses. This is absolutely nuts. Somehow they managed to get their coffee maker replaced, but surely it took more than my one-dollar contribution. And the serious young waiter, new on the job, who has been slow to learn the basics of tending table, actually relaxed a bit and allowed himself a smile.

But this young fellow, the little guy with the stern but handsome face and the stiff-legged manner of walking, still almost always takes the plate to the wrong table, and he's been here for a week already. The would-be diner will say that's not what I ordered. Then the young fellow will look very perplexed, as if he had been certain this sort of thing would never happen again. The diner will then say but I will take it anyway. Then the waiter will look even more baffled, not understanding why the diner would take it if it wasn't what he'd ordered. Then the maitre d' comes running over and says no, don't take it, it belongs to the lady at table 8.

On my way out, I passed four attractive youngish women sitting at a table. One of the women was a dark-haired beauty with braces on her teeth, though she was at least thirty. As the others chatted she was flipping through a mint copy of Christopher P. Baker's book, same as mine. So I introduced myself and politely asked if she were enjoying it. Her name was Montse. She said yes, it's heavy to tote around but it is filled with almost too much detail. She said the four of them were from Spain, but they were working as schoolteachers in San Antonio, Texas. I looked surprised, and they laughed. I expressed my sympathies for the horrible explosion on the Madrid commuter train yesterday. Montse looked very sad and said, Oh yes, we weren't there of course, but we've been watching it on TV, and monitoring it very closely. And then for some foolish reason I started to cry. Tears popped out and ran down my cheeks. I couldn't have been more embarrassed if my pants had fallen down. It was like a pair of little volcanoes erupting, with no warning. So I said adios and scurried away.

It was a day off for Mimi so we went for our petite promenade du jour. She walked closely in step with me, so I had to put my arm around her. It was very pleasant. It's odd that she has been trying so hard for years to learn English, and it has always been a struggle for her. But when she began studying French she found it equally hard but she was more motivated, because it appealed to her somehow, French was in some way more suited to her personality, and she found herself thinking about it all the time even when she wasn't studying it, so it was as if she was learning it with little effort. She didn't have that experience with English.

If only her lengthy, fast-paced narratives in three languages were easier to understand. I would have a certain understanding of something she said – for instance, that her father had fought at the Bay of Pigs, sinking ships and blasting fighter planes out of the sky. But then it turned out she hadn't said that at all. With her rapidly switching from English to Spanish to French, one minute I was certain she was telling me that her father had been a close personal friend of

Fidel, and that Che taught her to play chess, and the next minute she would deny having said that.

What was it like when the Russians suddenly left Cuba? She said she was unhappy, she knew something terrible had happened, and she couldn't understand why it had to be. It was very difficult for her, and sometimes when she was studying she would just start crying. "I had a lot of Russian friends, boys and girls, since high school, we all lived together in my building," she said. Her three closest Russian girlfriends were Navia, Nastia, and Skip. "They were very good girls." And overnight they were gone.

Fidel was quoted a while back by the recently deceased Arthur Miller as telling him that the Russians left because Fidel wanted them to help him in liberating various other Latin American countries from the yoke of U.S. domination. The Russians weren't all that keen on this idea, because they feared a nuclear war would break out. Clever Russians. But Mimi said that couldn't have been the reason, because if it had been someone would have told her.

She agreed that Havana is a warm, sexy vibrant city full of music now, but during the Special Period she and everyone she knew were in deep depression, there were no smiles. People were walking around like zombies. Was that a difficult time for her personally? She said it was terrible, and she was desperate and uncomfortable. She felt as though she were walking in quicksand. She said there is a law against selling a child's virginity now, but things were so desperate during that terrible period, such things were done. In fact a friend of hers sold her daughter's virginity for US$150 to a rich man from another country. He didn't take her back to his country, but he slept with her that night, and enjoyed taking her virginity. The girl is now married and has children of her own.

Mimi is, of course, like any Cuban, worried about another U.S. invasion. For what it was worth I told her that I thought there was no reason to be afraid. She was dubious, she wanted to know why. I told her it was because the whole world loves Cuba, and is concerned about its welfare. Cuba is the most famous country in the world, everybody in the world admires Fidel and everybody loves Cuba, except for the people in the U.S. government. And if the United

States were to attack Cuba, they would be branded as war criminals, they would be universally despised and disgraced. Everybody loves Fidel except for George Bush and his friends. I thought it was important to deliver that message for some reason, so I stopped every few words to make sure she was getting it.

Nevertheless, I told her I thought I had seen some people building a bomb shelter. Could that be right? "Yes," she said, "it would be that. I know this has been going on, because the new U.S. government is so thirsty for blood."

When she began to realize that I had such positive feelings about Cuba she was surprised. She wasn't used to that sort of talk from tourists. She always sensed that the tourists she met in her work were always very negative about her home and native land. She became very excited and said, "I love you, if you love Cuba, I love you." I told her I was not talking this way so the Cubans will love me, but because I believe it. I told her that I always admired Fidel, even when others didn't, and lately my admiration has been growing to the point where I now think of Fidel as a great genius. He will soon be dead, but I am sure the Revolution will continue on without him. I have more appreciation for Fidel today than ever before. And when people speak badly about him, they sometimes, to my ear, seem to be twisting the truth, putting an ugly spin on beautiful things, or to be repeating the lies of others as if true. The people who admire Fidel, for instance, will always be prepared to offer sources for their factual information.

She thought that when sympathetic foreigners come to Cuba they think of the country as something strange, something rare, because not always can they understand how the Cubans were able to withstand the blockade and the imperialistic arrogance, the slander and hatred, and continue on being happy, industrious human beings.

I said that if the human race is evolving, and a new breed of men and women is appearing anywhere in the world, that place would have to be Cuba. And if you asked that question pretty well anybody would say the same thing, especially if they had visited Cuba.

I wanted to give Mimi a gift. I didn't have anything to compare with the beautiful Aztec goddess. The best possible thing I could think of was money. But Cubans are often difficult to give money to. Would she accept it? I counted out a modest 150 pesos – to her it would be half a month's salary, to me it's a pizza. She refused to take it. I explained why I was giving it to her. She wouldn't take it. So I began to think I should not press it any further, because it was offending her Revolutionary principles, or maybe just her human principles, and it was as if I was being stubborn and overbearing by continuing to insist that she take it. In fact, I asked her if this was offending her Revolutionary principles and she laughed hysterically. So I think I had her there, it was true, and she was laughing because she knew that was true, that I had guessed correctly, though she hated to hear me use such a phrase so stale and pompous. I could have accidentally on purpose left the money behind, but that would have been giving her a problem of my own.

So I'm still stuck with these pesos. I do hand them out to people who are obviously destitute but aren't so obviously pestering me for a handout. I'm still hoping some miraculous idea will pop into my mind, satisfying my desire to give Mimi something she would value as much as I valued her goddess, and her goodness.

And when Mimi told me that she loved me it was a Revolutionary thing to say, because she didn't love me because she wanted anything from me, or because she wanted to romance me. Rather she loved me for no other reason than that I loved Cuba, because she was moved by what I said about Cuba, and because I somehow made her feel better, prouder, about being a Cuban. And when I told her about the Cuban craze going on right now in Japan, so I've heard, in terms of music, culture, history, and so on, she hadn't heard of that, and that too made her feel proud of her poor country. It also reminded her that when she was a child she wanted to live in a Japanese house.

But most of all she loved me simply because I told her that Cuba is the most famous country in the world, everybody loves Cuba and wants it to prosper, and Fidel is everybody's favourite world leader.

Earlier today I stopped to chat with a fellow who was sitting in the open door of a house on Calle Tejadillo hawking bananas. It wasn't his house, it was a friend's house. He lived out in the large suburban community of Regla. He wanted to visit his friend, so he brought as many bananas as he could handle and was now offering them for sale.

His name was Yasser Aly. He reminded me of Jannier very much in his outgoing personality and enthusiastic manner of speaking – also in his sense of useful private enterprise. Both were young men with a lot of integrity. Neither was at all bitter about anything as far as I could see, but Yasser Aly did find it odd that he was unable to get a job, and was also unable to get a satisfactory explanation for being continually told no dice. Same situation as Enmo. He wanted to be a marine engineer, but when he applied at the school they kept turning him down without explanation.

He said, "I used to chase tourists for money. You know: Amigo! Where you from? Are you staying in a *casa* or a hotel?" But as he grew older he grew tired of it. Maybe that sort of background got in the way of him getting into the marine engineering course.

He had also sometimes worked at escorting groups of foreigners on tours of the city, pointing out all the sights. He did that every day for a whole season. He made twenty dollars a day, but the police caught him, and he was forced to quit. He said it wasn't that he didn't have a licence, for such a thing is usually overlooked. It was because he was doing it too much on his own, in some kind of unauthorized manner he didn't understand, rather than through the channels, and with all the requisite paperwork. We're into a murky area of Cuban politics for sure. They seemed to be accusing him of taking shortcuts because he didn't have the patience to read the fine print or to figure out all that detail. And so he was forced to quit. In Canada someone in a situation like that would just phone a lawyer.

So now he's been desperately trying to get a job with his excellent English but with no luck. He thinks he has a mark against his name for being more interested in enriching himself than enriching the state. It's hard to defend yourself against a rap like that. Just a little private enterprise can do you in, though many are able to leap the barriers.

I told him about my experiences with the "milk for my baby" routine, and he said it was a complete and utter scam, and that's all there was to it. This was the first he had heard of this scam, but he had no doubt it was a scam. Every baby in Cuba gets a litre of milk a day, free, he said, until the age of four at least. I asked him if he thought that the fellow would have split the five dollars with the woman who ran the store, and that the milk would go right back into the cooler. He was affirmative on both counts. I felt like phoning Fidel and telling him about it and giving him the name of the store. Yasser Aly did have some admiration for the nature of the scam, playing as it did so cleverly on the average tourist's desire to help the poor people of Cuba, and their natural suspicion that perhaps the right-wing line on Cuba may be right, and that Fidel may be deliberately bleeding the soul out of the Cuban people for his own personal enrichment. They will go home and tell their friends, "I actually met a very nice man who was desperate to get some milk for his baby. So I marched him right to the store and bought him a three-quart plastic bag full. He was so grateful! You should have seen him run home with that bag."

Yasser Aly was the only one who could answer my silly question about how Cuba got its name. He said when the Spanish first arrived, the natives were talking about "kooba," "koova," or "koowa" all the time, because that was the name of a certain fruit they were very fond of, and that the Spanish were fond of too. He couldn't remember what we call it today. Maybe it was pineapple. That's my choice. Or maybe coconut. As soon as he told me that, I remembered I had read it somewhere a long time ago. So it must be true. The Spanish would say to the natives, "What is your name for this place?" The natives would think they were saying, "What is your name for this fruit?" So they would hand the Spanish more fruit and say "kooba, koova, koowa."

MY LEFT EARLOBE

Saturday, March 13, 2004. A falling leaf can hit you and cause damage. Not as much damage as the brick that hit that fellow in Sancti Spíritus maybe – but one leaf from a laurel tree on the Prado, with unerring accuracy, whacked me on the left earlobe very hard late last night, and drew blood. Glad I was watching my step instead of stargazing or I might have lost an eye. I actually noticed the leaf pass my eyes before scoring a bull's eye on my earlobe, and it stung like a bee. I had to show my left ear to Barbarita this morning because she wanted to know where the blood on my pillow was coming from.

When my friend A. was here ten years ago, she visited the seventeenth-century San Felipe Neri church and convent, at Aguiar and Obrapia Streets in Havana Vieja. She took some mysterious and moody photographs of the interior of the church, with people kneeling at the altar, and the beautiful interior courtyard, with people sitting on benches and drinking in the silence. She met a man who had just been appointed head of a restoration project, with headquarters at the church. He had a team of three students who were halfway through restoring some old silver candlesticks. She asked if I'd pop in to see how the restoration was coming along. I can report it's coming along brilliantly, but it's no longer a church, it's a secular concert hall. He must have known that's what they were planning to do when he had his interview with A., but he didn't have the heart to tell her because she likes churches.

This may be distressing to Catholics, but more people are attending the concerts than ever attended mass. In fact, most of the concerts are of religious music, and the concert hall has an ecclesiastical feel to it. By some miracle of the arts of restoration and renovation, the hall retains an eighteenth-century atmosphere; the old religious paintings have been saved, and restored, and are placed lovingly on the fresh new walls. The orchestra plays where the altar was, there is no sign of an altar now, and the chorus sings on the balcony behind and above the audience.

I'm being given a tour by Marita, a charming woman of thirty-three, happy to be able to practise her English on me. We have the usual small talk – but I am getting better at it, and enjoying it more. She is happy to describe the transformation from church to concert hall – in English, and insisting that I correct the slightest error. We were on the second floor and she said, "Come, I have my affairs on the first floor." I didn't know whether to correct her on that one or not, so I just laughed.

Her "affairs" turned out to be a table loaded down with compact discs and books for sale. The books are by the official historian of Havana, Dr. Eusebio Leal Spengler, author of an excellent guide to Havana Vieja, which A. bought when she was here, and which she solemnly presented to me when I left on this trip. The maps are particularly beautiful. So I was thrilled to see that Dr. Spengler as he is known, is still at it, and has more recently written many other books about Havana, highly detailed histories of certain distinguished buildings and neighbourhoods.

Marita said Dr. Spengler spends most of his time wandering around Havana Vieja and he pops into the concert hall at least twice a week. I should keep my eye open for him, she said. He's a great guy to talk to. He's my age, my height, and it's amazing how much alike we look.

So I decided to go looking for a guy that looked like me, and when I found him I would say, "Dr. Spengler, I presume." But it wasn't to be. I asked around, met many people who told me pretty well what

Marita had told me, but I couldn't find him. I think he was told someone was looking for him and he went into hiding. Maybe he'd spoken to a tourist once before and never again.

Marita did say if I didn't find him, I should come to the concert hall tomorrow at 7 or 8 p.m., he'd be here for sure. Her face just lit up with pleasure. She seemed to relish seeing the two of us together, and she thought it was important that we meet. In fact she gave me a throwaway map of Havana Vieja, and marked where his office was, at the corner of Mercaderes and Empedrado, just off the Plaza de la Catedral.

I was making my way slowly, serenely, in the general direction of Dr. Spengler's office, when I ran into the four friendly Spanish ladies from Texas. They were sitting in a row on the long east bench of the beautiful Plaza de Armas. We all exchanged names this time. Montse, Rosaria, María, and Reisa teach Spanish to Hispanic children. Sounds crazy, but the Hispanic population in Texas is growing more quickly than the number of Spanish teachers, so they are importing teachers from other countries. Each of them teaches at a different school.

We sat in the park and talked. They are going to rent a car and go down to Pinar del Río. I warned them about the dangers of driving and that the roads are much worse than advertised. But that didn't bother them.

Montse said she was interested in exploring the Santería religion, but the others weren't interested and I didn't want to tell her that I wasn't interested either, but I think she could tell. There was a band in the park, a large Sentería musical group. Several women dressed all in white (and some not) had begun to dance wildly, with swirling skirts. The highly percussive music was beyond critique. I couldn't resist jumping to my feet, transformed into a madman as if by a little Sentería miracle, and one of the dancers, not one of the ones in white, beckoned me enticingly. Who says tough guys don't dance? I caught the rhythm, or it caught me, and these old bones were whirling and twirling like mad. I could hear kids screaming: Look at that gringo go! My partner, black as shoe polish but shining with pleasure, gave me a big kiss on both cheeks, and then an even bigger one on both lips. She had blue-and-green stripes of paint on her cheekbones, and she was wearing a swirling red-and-green ankle-length dress. Whew! That was one big fat steaming wet kiss, but when she did that I was so shocked, from head to toe, that I lost the beat and had to retire. It was like a knockout blow. She took the juice out of me, dear reader. One kiss did it! And when I turned around everyone in the park, including Montse and her friends, were laughing and applauding. I'm usually a bad dancer, but felt I'd done a good job for an older gentleman, perhaps under the spell of some Senterían goddess named Euterpe.

The shoe store was very well stocked, but it was also very busy. My size and preferred style was forthcoming, but the shoe pinched. It seems that each size came in just one width. Without checking they said they didn't have anything wider. They were so busy they didn't have the time to waste on someone who was hard to please. They were practically throwing shoes at people, and if the shoe didn't fit, don't wear it.

But a lot of money was changing hands and that's the main thing. People need money, so that nobody will step on their toes, and people need shoes for the same reason.

When I catch up with Mimi she looks at me with alarm and says, Why is your face all red? She must have remembered it as white from two days ago. I said it's called sunburn, everybody gets it but only fair-skinned turnips like me turn red. She looked closely to make sure I wasn't fooling her, then said, "Oh!"

She also mused, meaningfully and pointedly, about how it often happens that writers come here and go around telling everybody how much they love Cuba and then go home and write horrible stuff about the country. I didn't ask for any examples of who that would be, but surely she wasn't suggesting anything. I've definitely heard those complaints before, particularly in Ireland. And I might even have been accused, by the people who live in the area written about, of that kind of duplicity, because we all tend to hate any travel book written about our hometown, or the place where we have chosen to live. We hate the writer for noticing stuff we've never noticed, and we hate him for writing about stuff that we would have preferred he hadn't noticed.

Mimi told me she has a brother who lives in Florida. I asked her what he does. She said, "He's a black Mexican, he doesn't do anything." She sounded bitter, but I didn't pursue her on it because I didn't want either of us to be bitter just then. It would have been too obvious to point out that she herself is a black Mexican, and she does lots. I felt as if I didn't want to get into all that with her. She earlier had made a statement to the effect that she's not on very good terms with her mother because she won't forgive Mimi for having married a black man. And at that time I did say the obvious, that Mimi's mother married a black man, and it was a good marriage, and he was a good man. But she didn't reply, and it would be best not to pry. Given the language difficulties, it's not easy to determine how profoundly we might have been misinterpreting and misunderstanding each other.

A group of about 150 people were trying to get exit permits, at the foot of the Prado the other day. They were dressed in their best business suits, carried little suitcases, and looked very grim. They were milling around, not meeting anyone's eyes. They looked uniformly grey, but that may have been the shadows from a large grey building or two nearby. There was a sign on a high wooden fence saying EMI-GRAÇION. Maybe some of them were the very people who used to criticize other Cubans for wanting out. Now they wanted out. It's no longer considered proper to call those who wish to leave *gusanos* (worms), as they were back in the days shortly after the Revolution when bloody machete battles were breaking out between the people who wanted to leave and the ones who wanted to stay. Now the very people who used to call others *gusanos* are applying for exit visas. If that's true, no wonder they look a bit grey. We all make mistakes. Life's a gamble. They were reading notices on the wall, waiting for their name to come up, so they could get their visa to wherever it is they so desperately want to get to. Everyone was dead solemn. Nobody was smiling. Nobody was talking.

A GHOST IN THE AIR

Sunday, March 14, 2004. There was no way of getting out of a very claustrophobic situation in my dream. Many Cubans undoubtedly have that dream. They manage to live with it, but in this dream I was unable to. Some of the things were obvious. There was an older woman I was working for. She was issuing me instructions on the telephone, but I couldn't understand anything she had said even though she was speaking perfect English. It was a cellphone, and I didn't know how to hang up, so I put it in the glove compartment. Why couldn't I understand someone speaking my own language? Why couldn't I use a simple cellphone? There seemed to be a ghost in the air.

Everything being hopeless, I decided to commit suicide. I watched from a distance, as one is said to do at the moment of death, as I galloped by on a black horse and into a black tunnel. I somehow timed the pace of the horse so that with each gallop I'd bounce up in the air and hit my head on one of the wooden crossbeams positioned at regular intervals along the stone ceiling. I had become my own guardian angel and was trying to destroy myself, from a distance.

At breakfast this morning, the four Spanish señoritas were there. We sat at the same table, we all talked at once, and there was picture taking and the exchanging of addresses. Amund Schliemann, from Oslo, was there, at the next table, and he courteously offered to take our pictures. Montse told me not to be concerned about their driving, they'd be fine on their trip to Pinar del Río. After all, they were used to Spanish roads. They had listened wide-eyed to all the pitfalls I'd experienced, and they were certain they were ready for anything.

There is María, who smokes a lot, and Reisa – "like Gorbachev's wife" – the serious dancer with a lean and long muscular body, and there is Rosaria, who is a bit older, from Morocco originally, with red hair and a Norwegian look about her. Montse Quibus is the one I first spoke with, and she has been the friendliest of the four. María is the cynical one, the independent thinker; she seems to be saying, Oh how did we get mixed up with this guy, but then she got chatting along with the rest of us, it just took her a bit longer. Rosaria is shy, a keen listener, friendly but with not much to say, maybe because she's a year or two older, and is the mother of the group in a way. She seems to be a special friend of Reisa.

When the women left, I stayed on and talked to Amund for a while. Amund is an engineer in Oslo, and a native of that city, but he got his engineering degree at South Dakota State University. He's thirty-five and is on a little tour that he thinks will change his life. He's been to Jamaica, Guatemala, Mexico, has two weeks in Cuba, then back to Oslo. He sees big changes happening in the world, and wants to make a change himself. He says that "capitalism is putting on an increasingly ugly face," or "capitalism used to look like Santa Claus but now it looks like Satan's Claws." He also says there's no reason why the socialist countries like Cuba, Vietnam, China, and so on can't get along with all the other countries of the world. Really, there's not all that much difference. It's not exactly apples and oranges, it's more like Macs and Spies. And it's nonsense that they should be in such aggressive competition. He was a very kind, well-spoken gentleman, a very attractive fellow, with fluffy blond sideburns and a long braid, blond and beaded.

While the six of us were having breakfast, a fighter plane flew over very low and then four helicopters zoomed far out over the sea and over the horizon on the far side of El Morro, in the direction of Miami Beach. We could hear gunfire from far beyond the suburbs to the south of here, at some military training ground that won't likely be on the map.

In the leafy inner courtyard at the lovely La Mina Restaurant on Calle Obispo, across from the Plaza de Armas, one of the peacocks is showing off, a real lot, even by peacock standards – a beautiful spread of feathers among the chickens, whose bright brown feathers and golden beaks seem dull by contrast. It doesn't seem to bother the hens that a great star of featherdom is in their midst. All those feathers and no fly. And this grand peacock is pacing with slow, silent grandeur, looking as if he has been trained to spread his tailfeathers in just that way, facing the customers, every five minutes or so. I'd like to be a peacock for about five minutes just to experience spreading my tailfeathers. A bunch of gringo spring-breakers are mingling about, taking pictures of this fabled beast, from the front of course. He's a peacock, and he wants those colours up front where they can be seen when the peahen he is pursuing gives him a backwards glance, then stops dead in her tracks, overcome with desire.

A grossly obese black tourist has been eating non-stop for at least thirty minutes, and is now on her third elaborate dessert. She's eating like a tourist who has decided to go on a diet the minute she gets back home, or maybe she wishes to stuff herself to death so she won't have to go home. But then she slows down and it appears that . . . yes, she has finally worked up the energy to fish her camera out of her bag. She swivels her chair a bit, then – snap takes a picture of the peacock, from the rear end, and without raising her rear end from her chair. I suppose that's better than getting up and walking around to face the bloody thing head on. Mind you, we've all seen that famous photo by Michael Ondaatje of the Sphinx from the rear, instantly recognizable as the Sphinx but nonetheless strangely disorienting. The peacock is not like that. It may have a beautiful tail to spread from the front, but from the rear it definitely lacks charm.

Of course we're all like that: sometimes we're taken aback, and other times we're affronted! Except for the Sphinx.

So there I was quietly drinking coffee, eating ice cream, and listening to an interesting band of older musicians, with the cutest girl in a pink jumpsuit on flute. There was a big fat Englishman with a little Cuban *chica* and oh man was he ever a loudmouth. And there was a second Englishman who seemed to have his very pretty daughter with him. They looked rather upper crust, in that hereditary English way, but they were laughing enthusiastically at all these vulgar jokes the first Englishman was making about his *chica*, and about why he likes to come to Cuba. He says he lives in Ipswich but he comes to Cuba every two weeks. Who could blame you, said the second Englishman, batting his eyes at the *chica*. He and his daughter or niece, who was eighteen maximum and very proper, were laughing their heads off at these idiot jokes that I won't repeat. So the flute player came around soliciting tips from diners, and the fat vulgar Englishman stood up, ostentatiously took a large bunch of loose U.S. dollars out of his pocket, and threw them at the band. It didn't bother the band members; they all got down on their hands and knees and picked up the money, put it in the box, then came over to thank the bloke and chat with him.

Later, at the Ambos Mundos, a single male tourist comes in sporting a new cast from wrist to shoulder. It seems as if he's fallen on the street the first day of his holiday. He's a tall thin fellow, maybe French, and he looks and acts a bit like Monsieur Hulot. He has an oversized leather money belt, which he is trying to put on over his head, but it has become stuck, and it has come down in such a way that it's keeping his two arms squeezed tightly against his body, and he can't quite move, and he doesn't seem to know why, or what to do about it. The stress of being in a foreign country plus having broken his arm must have short-circuited his brain momentarily. Not only does he not see any humour in the situation, but it also appears that he doesn't know he's become trapped by his own money belt. He leaves the bar abruptly, like everything's perfectly okay, and walks off down Calle Obispo like that, with both arms squeezed against his body, a parody of a soldier at attention. I would have offered to help him, but I didn't want to embarrass him, or to have him think I was trying to steal his money. He was hoping that nobody would notice and laugh at him. He must be very uncomfortable, for anybody could go up to him, unzip the belt, and casually take out all his dough and traveller's cheques. Being tied up already, what could he do? Nothing! In books like this, people swim by, we have no idea where they are going or if they'll get there.

On the Prado today there were about fifty artists showing their paintings. Some of the art was touristy, some of it was a copy of things we've all seen a zillion times, and some of it was interesting. But nobody was buying. Nobody was complaining that some of the work was quite erotic, even pornographic, supposedly for the alleged sex tourists. The only embarrassing thing was that there were fifty painters, each with at least ten works on display, and during the half-hour I was there I was the only one looking at the work.

Something exceedingly strange was about to happen, as a result of the arcane law of acausality, or, if you prefer, possibly through the agency of omniscient spirit guides on the astral plane pulling strings in order to manipulate events on earth. In the string of little incidents that separates two hours ago from this moment, something out of place has turned up, something so odd it blows the boredom of ordinary life right out of the water. Or you could just think of it as the spirit of Cuba, leading me all the way back to my childhood, and then back to the future again.

I was in my room resting up a bit, with the TV on, and was amazed to see that the Spanish election had resulted in a socialist government. It was expected the popular government would win in a landslide, but then the crowded commuter train was blown up, and the government mishandled it so badly, immediately accusing the Basque separatists, and then only later finding out they were not to blame. To misaccuse the Basques was something the Spanish people could not abide, and they switched their vote to the socialists. Then a snippet came on saying that it was obvious to Fidel from the start that it wasn't the Basque separatists, that it was the Muslim funda-mentalists who had engineered the train wreck.

After being engrossed in the coverage of the carnage, I tried to have a little nap but couldn't. If I had slept for an hour, the acausally amazing event wouldn't have happened. Sure, an even more amazing event might have happened – but what was about to happen was a five-star event, and there are no six-star events that I know about for sure these days.

Tired, I turned out the light, put my head down, and by all rights should have fallen asleep, but something was urging me to get up and do something, to go to see Dr. Spengler perhaps, because Marita had told me he would be at the San Felipe concert hall between seven and eight. So I went out, and to make sure I wouldn't be too late I hailed a bicycle taxi at the corner of Consulado and Animas Streets, and asked the young fellow to take me to the corner of Obrapia and Aigular, where the concert hall was located. We turned south on to the Prado, past Calle Virtudes, past Calle Neptuno, past the posh new Hotel Parque Centrale, built with Dutch money, past the old Hotel Inglaterra, past the Grand Teatro that houses the Teatro Federico García Lorca (where, when A. was here, she caught premier Cuban ballerina Rosario Suaraz in *Coppelia*), then turned left, at Calle San Martin (also known as San José), and across Agramonte (also known as Zulueta), then right at Avenida de Belgica (also known as Monserrate), then left at Calle Lamparilla, then right at Calle Villegas . . . and eventually, at the corner of Calles Obrapia and Habana, the driver was going very slowly over a great crack in the road, and to my right was a little old bar. There was no sign, but in Dr. Spengler's book it's referred to as El Gallo. It was a very dark and stark bar, small and with no decor at all, and a black-skinned bar-tender was behind the bar staring off into space. He had the dazed look of a bartender who hasn't had a customer in days, so I thought I'd pop in later and have a quiet drink, and buy one for him too.

At the San Felipe concert hall there was a reconditioned Lada parked out front, and a police officer was writing out a ticket. I tried the door to the former church, but it was locked. I started hammering, and the officer looked up and said no no no, it's closed. I said I was supposed to meet Dr. Spengler here. He brightened up, and said tomorrow, tomorrow. I figured I must have misunderstood Marita, as I may have misunderstood a zillion things over the past month, so I walked back sadly to El Gallo, looking forward to consoling my disappointment with a refreshing drink on a warm night.

I tiptoed into the bar and gave a little cough. The bartender jerked his head up from his slumber. I asked for a Cristal. He didn't know what I meant. I said, Cuba's top beer, Cristal. So I tried pronouncing it in different ways: Kreeth Tall? Kreeth Toll? Kristle? Krithtle? Kreettle? Christall? Nothing worked. He either didn't get it or it wasn't there for him to get. And there wasn't any beer on the back counter for me to point to.

You never saw two more frustrated guys. So I said I'd just have whatever sort of beer he wanted to give me. And he said he was very sorry but they didn't have any beer. So I said that's okay, give me a gin and tonic. He said we have neither gin nor tonic. I said okay then what do you have? He said mohito. This is a mohito bar. I apologized and said I did not care for mohitos, they bring back bad memories, and besides a real man does not drink what the tourists drink. And I told him I hoped he got some business soon. Then I noticed he was napping on his feet again.

More details are required here because we're still on countdown to the amazing event, and everything leading up to it is part of its unfolding. I began walking rapidly along Calle Habana, then turned left onto Obispo, heading toward Il Gentiluomo at such a rate of speed crowds were parting for me. Again, I have no idea why I was in such a hurry. The place was crowded, and there was only one table available, so I sat at the bar and tried again to order a Cristal. But it was forever coming, and whenever a waiter would get a beer out of the fridge I'd think oh here it comes, but then he'd go right past me and put it on somebody else's table. This seemed odd.

Then a large group of people, who had been taking up three tables behind me, got up and left. When the waitress had finished clearing the tables, I asked if it was okay if I took a table now. It was more than okay, and she instantly came over and took my order, which was the pescado and Cristal special. And then she brought the beer and said the fish would be there momentarily. Invisible at the bar, but he looms large at the table.

As I was sitting there with my Cristal, I noticed some other tables had left and new people had come in, and I noticed a single man, a tourist, at the third table away from me. He was wearing a black-on-white polka-dot shirt. The waiter poured him a glass of red wine, and the tourist noticed there was just a bit left in the bottle, maybe half a glass, so he told the waiter just leave it on the table. And then, before he actually took his first sip of the wine, he seemed to notice, with a bit of a double-take, that it did not look like red wine, it looked like rosé, or rosado. With me observing from such a distance, he picked up the wine, checked the label, violently slammed the bottle down, and made an angrily sarcastic gesture at the waiter, got up in a huff, and stormed out of the restaurant. He'd asked for red wine but had been brought rosado – a high crime and misdemeanour, in his mind. If not a crime against humanity.

I'm thinking, What a fool. He's missing out on a great meal, because of his irritability and pigheadedness, and he lost the chance to enjoy the pleasure of teaching the waiter the difference between rosado and red wine. Whatever that may be. And to make a fuss like that in a humble restaurant, with rock-bottom prices, in a country that is being starved to death by the rest of the world made me hope he'll be suitably annoyed with himself in the morning. He couldn't expect the joint to have an extensive variety of the finest wines to choose from.

Actually the fellow might have thought he was being cheated. It was a habit of the restaurant to have a bottle of good red wine on each table, and once someone sits down to dine he can either ask for the wine to be opened, ask for another kind of wine, or whatever. So this fellow just wanted a glass, and so asked for one, expecting it to be like the wine on the table, or in that ballpark. Perfectly understandable, for those preoccupied with other things besides the details of the moment. Quite possibly the only wine that was open was the rosado, and it could be argued that rosado is a red wine, and that he got what he asked for.

If this fellow hadn't been so irritable, and had swallowed his anger and stayed on for the feast, then I wouldn't have wandered over to his now-vacant table to check the situation out. My pescado was still being prepared, so I took my Cristal with me and looked at the wine. Sure enough, it said rosado, Spanish rosé. The waiter said, It's good wine, why don't you sit down here? [I'm getting goosebumps typing this out.]

So I sat down, finished my beer, and began sipping the rosado, which was fine. And at the next table there was another single male tourist, I hadn't noticed him come in, but he was just sitting there staring at the menu. At this point I wasn't sure he was a tourist, he looked like a very benign and thoughtful businessman of some sort, someone who likes to be alone at the end of the day to sort things out.

So as he continued staring at the menu, my steaming pescado arrived. And as it arrived the fellow at the next table was eyeballing it. I tilted the plate up a bit, making sure the food didn't start sliding, so he could have a clear look at it, and he looked at it, then he looked me in the eye, and he said, "Looks good." And so he ordered it too and he thanked me very much. And I said, very uncharacteristically, You can join me if you wish. He said, Thank you very much, and he came over and sat down, and we started chatting.

He was a man of my age, with very beautiful eyes, we had great eye contact. He was the kind of guy you just wanted to have eye contact with all the time. Often when I have eye contact with a male I become shy and find it hard to concentrate on the chit-chat. But this was unusual for me to have such constant friendly eye contact with anyone, immediately, at first meeting.

He began telling me about a project he was working on. He was getting close to retirement age but was obviously active, in good shape, with all his wits about him, thinking all the time. He had spent his earlier years in marketing and communication projects, working for various companies, and how to get the most out of the largest number of customers. He told me he was working on a book now, because he felt he had a lot to say about what is wrong with marketing practices and how they could be improved for the benefit of everyone. Like Amund, he felt capitalism was showing its ugly face in recent times. The working title of his book was "Quantum Ideas." His working subtitle could have been something along the lines of "systems for co-operative endeavour." He was interested in new ways of doing things, and he was concerned in general about businesses and governments stumbling about blindly and continually screwing up in the most counterproductive way imaginable. For instance, the intense rivalry between the United States and Cuba seemed entirely counterproductive to both sides.

For starters he thought it would be preferable for customers to be thought of as clients, which would lessen the emphasis of getting as much money out of the customer as possible and increasing the emphasis on learning how to share with clients ideas on how to improve the service. "Clients" would lead to a more mutually enriching experience. In other words, he was developing working principles that would lead to better and more humane ways of doing things, and showing that sharp business practices are harmful to everyone.

So he was writing a series of essays on this. At one point I asked where he was from and he said, Vancouver, Canada. I said I thought you were a Canadian, because I am too, I'm from Toronto. He said he thought I was a Canadian too, and I told him I was very glad. We agreed that the world is gradually becoming able to tell a Canadian's nationality at first guess. We divulged our ages and it turned out he was nine months older. I asked if he had always lived in Vancouver. He said no, he had been born in Hamilton, Ontario. And not only was he my age, but he was born in the same general neighbourhood as I was.

We looked at each other. We had exchanged names earlier, but his didn't register.

I said, "What was your name again?"

He said, "Roger Chilton."

My hair stood on end. Chills went up and down my spine.

I said, "Oh my God, Roger Chilton! I can see it now, you *are* Roger Chilton. I thought you were dead."

He said, "Oh, you *are* that David McFadden. I was wondering but I figured there were lots of David McFaddens around. So I didn't say anything. But I see now that you are David McFadden. . . ."

And I repeated myself, "But I was under the impression you were dead. About fifteen years ago somebody told me you had died, of brain cancer."

"No, I never had cancer and I never died."

"Well, isn't that strange? I went through a period of mourning for you."

We were never intimate friends, but we had spent a very wild and boozy late adolescence together, as part of a gang of five or six other fellows, all a bit older than I was. The jazz age had hit southern Ontario, and we were always rushing off to nearby Toronto or Buffalo to hear our favourite bands live and in person.

So it was all so very exciting to meet an old friend you haven't seen in all those long, strange bittersweet years, and it was more of a shock to me than to him because he had never heard any news of my death, and I had thought of him often over the years, and always felt sad that such a fine person died so young and undergoing such slow torture to the end. And here he was suddenly resurrected in the paradise of Havana, among the Cubans, and their flowers, and their music, and their joy.

We talked about the others, what they're doing now. He knew that Ron was living in small-town California with his high-school sweetheart with whom he has spent all these years together, and had taken an early retirement, reading and rereading the classics of world literature. I was pretty sure that John was still teaching in the music department at McMaster University, and that Brian was in Victoria and took an early retirement as a high-school music teacher.

Roger was pleased that I remembered certain events that he had, and in almost exactly the same little details. I remembered the time he and Ron had driven to New York, and they had been involved in an accident on the New York State Thruway, on the way home. All the details, as reported to me, had stuck in my mind all these years, and Roger confirmed them: Roger was driving and the force of the crash caused Ron to fly through the front window headfirst. But he was scarcely injured at all because he had been sleeping, with his brown suede jacket over his head.

Roger was always a more serious thinker than the rest of us. His mind always seemed to be working out problems we had no access to. He's even more like that now, I'd guess. He's calm and quiet, and he wasn't getting excited about all this, but he did express a bit of amazement that I even remembered that Ron's jacket was brown and suede. We performed several confirmation checks on our ancient memories and pronounced them dead-on for the most part. I remembered so much, and he confirmed everything.

We spent the rest of the evening reminiscing and philosophizing. We went to various pubs, the final one being the posh hotel he was staying at, the Hotel Parque Central, newly built but employing many Cuban design traditions. We talked at the bar till two in the morning and solemnly promised we'd never get out of contact again.

This meeting was a double miracle for me, because I couldn't stop thinking about how it wouldn't have happened if so many links in the chain hadn't been forged at exactly the same time and place and in exactly the same manner, if the same little mistakes hadn't been made, and it made everything feel haunted, and strange. Also the fact that I had long thought that Roger had passed away at an early age. In my overworked imagination, fired up by the atmospherics of the Cuban night, I had just witnessed a resurrection from the dead.

Roger was pleased, but it wasn't as much a resurrection for him. For one thing, he's never been that shockable, and he hadn't heard any reports of my death, of course, nor of his own. And I was the younger fellow in that circle. I was only nine months younger, but that's a lot when you're eighteen. Mel, Ron, John, Brian, Al were all older, more mature and sophisticated, and I was eager to learn from them. So they would naturally make a bigger impression on me than I on them, and I had stronger memories of them than they had of me.

Roger had only been in Cuba for a week, he'd always wanted to visit Havana and had been looking for the right time. He finally said to hell with it, he wasn't going to wait till he had the time to do it, he was just going to do it right now, take the time off and go. So he came down for one week. And was flying back tomorrow morning.

If that man hadn't lost his temper and stormed out of the restaurant, I'd have finished my meal and left the place without having said a word to Roger, walking right past his table, and maybe continuing to believe for the rest of my life that he had died in his thirties. Further, I had sat in three different spots. I was so slow getting served at first. Dr. Spengler hadn't been where I thought he would be. El Gallo didn't serve beer. I was very tired but something told me to get up and go somewhere. And on and on. All these little fateful events seemed to have an intelligence of their own, and were somehow intent on engineering this meeting between us. Fate was sly and secretive, but it had its compassionate side as well, at times, and it whispers in our ear without us knowing it, as in the foregoing dream, and it had conspired, in a moment of generosity, to cause two old friends to become reacquainted.

And it would appear that when you think some old friend is dead, he or she is not really dead, they're just in Havana, Cuba, waiting for you to show up.

Roger had seemed pleased that I had such vivid memories of so long ago, but to his credit he was more interested in talking about the quantum ideas he was involved in, also about Cuba and how it related to these ideas. At one point I went to the bar, and when I returned he said, "Yeah, I can see you're David McFadden from the way you walk. We don't really change that much, do we?"

I said, "No, and I can see your face as it was then and as it is now, in a sort of double vision, and I can see exactly where you have changed and where you haven't." I also told him he expressed himself in ways I remember, and he was always, in our group, the quietest one, the one who would be most likely to switch the conversation back to ideas, the life of the mind. I told him that he was the least mundane of the group. "We were more frivolous than you, goofier. You were more reserved. You were the intellectual, the philosopher. And you still are."

He said, "Yes, we don't change very much from our childhood to old age, and life is pretty much what we dream it to be."

One other odd thing: our friendship had flourished during the time of the Cuban Revolution. When Fidel and Che were heading toward Havana, we cool cats were excitedly making plans to go to see Count Basie at Kleinhans Music Hall, Miles Davis at the Town Casino, Cannonball Adderley at The House of Hambourg. And it turns out that we were both touring the Museo de la Revoluçion on the same afternoon, and if we had been more observant, and the place hadn't been so crowded, we might have bumped into each other then. Out of all the people I could have accidentally met here, it couldn't have been anyone any better. It was as if the fates were really trying to get us to meet.

THE DEATH OF HEMINGWAY

Monday, March 15, 2004. When Amund from Oslo landed at José Martí Airport Thursday night he was the only passenger to be detained. He was held for an hour, and every piece of his luggage was open, unfolded, shaken, and sniffed. They even unzipped his diary and skimmed through the pages. They were polite, but he figured it was because of his hippie hair that they wasted all that time in a futile search for drugs. And as soon as he got into town he was offered marijuana and cocaine, again because of his hair no doubt, but he is neither a toker nor a snorter, so both the good guys and the bad guys were wasting their time on him. He was living proof you can't tell a book from its cover, front or back. Some ancient Roman probably wrote a play about a fellow like Amund. The strangest thing is that he has never yet been offered a *chica* in Cuba. I tell him all they ever offer me is *chicas*. What gives? Shrewd of the Cubans to have figured out that the younger guys desire drugs and the older guys desire sex. But guys like Amund and me, we don't fit the mould, for we desire nothing.

Amund's first day in Jamaica, however, a fellow on the street offered him drugs. "And I declined." Did he want a woman? "No thank you." To be ready for next time, he came up with a "white lie, that's not entirely untrue, that I have this girl at home in Norway, and that I'd rather not be unfaithful to her. And they accepted that, surprisingly." He said he knew that one is supposed to leave his home at home when one visits Jamaica. Only then can one get accustomed to the Jamaican way.

He got in trouble in Kingston when he took a picture of the entrance to Nelson Mandela Park, where two police officers were standing. They were upset because so many of them get killed in the line of duty each year. They seemed to think that he might show the photos to some gangster who would then shoot them. "They were speaking to me politely, but I felt a bit intimidated." It was scary waiting for the cops to be convinced he was just an innocent tourist. They told him don't ever take a photo of a police officer again. If you want to take a picture of a park, address the officer and ask him if he will mind moving out of the way for a minute, and they will.

"But I was a bit shaky after that. They could easily have jailed me, confiscated my camera, my film, fined me, given me a lot of trouble." The strange thing about it was that he had been with two Jamaicans, a man and a woman, who were showing him the sights of Kingston, and who had suggested he take the photo. They didn't say anything about asking the police to move. And when the police were grilling him, his guides did nothing to intervene. "I still haven't figured out why they told me that." I couldn't figure it out either. Maybe they were just being prudent, not wanting to make things worse for Amund.

"Proud people, proud of their island the way it is," he said when I asked for his basic impression of Jamaica. He thought there was a noticeable level of bitterness directed toward the white tourists, though. He'd accidentally heard some comments about the colour of his skin. He thought it was because of past injustices perpetrated by the white race on the poor Jamaicans over four hundred years of slavery, brutal colonization, repression, then having to fight their way back to independence.

At first he had to learn how to say no gracefully to their kind offers of women and drugs and various other things they wanted to sell him. Once he learned, things got easier. As a person from a country that is about 98 per cent white, he admitted to finding Jamaicans a bit frightening. "They sort of keep their image, they look scary, but once you speak to them, they lighten up, and actually they're quite friendly and warm." He divided the people he met into those who were "genuinely warm people," and people who were "quite bitter, and not that friendly toward tourists." He felt there was considerable envy if not resentment of the wealth of the tourists. "Once they realized they weren't going to get my money they were warm and friendly, and lots of jokes and smiling. And if you greeted a Jamaican his face would break up in a smile."

In Cuba, however, he felt that his greetings were not being responded to. "When I say *buenos dias, buenos tardes, buenos noches* to the Cubans I see no smile, I only see a hard face. I don't know what it is. The first time I saw genuine happiness was in Havana Vieja yesterday when I was listening to Cuban music in the park. They were dancing and cheering and making fun. If it wasn't for the earth their smile would go all the way around."

I thought it might have something to do with the spring break, for when there are too many tourists it gets tiring. I'd noticed the change this week. There was much more friendliness before the spring break. It seemed odd to think that the Cubans should break into happy smiles just because of being greeted by a tourist. Especially in tourist season.

Amund wasn't convinced. Maybe he was "greeting" the Cubans in a way that seemed condescending and frivolous. Monsieur Hulot was one to go around offering unsolicited greetings to the natives in the south of France, but nobody ever greeted him back. Amund said he felt his greetings were simply a polite way of expressing his pleasure about being a guest in their country. How odd that I was seeing Cuba as a joyful country, while he so far sees it as hostile. Also that the *chicas* leave him alone but are always after me.

"That's what makes travel tales so interesting," he said. "The strange subjectivity that comes from trying to interpret one giant ink blot."

We were still sitting in the open-air rooftop restaurant, quietly observing the amusing behaviour of the previously noted little male waiter. He was being particularly interesting today. With a tray full of hot breakfasts in one hand, he would stop, take a note out of his pocket, read it, put it back in his pocket, then take it out, and read it again. We looked the other way and pretended to be sharing a laugh at something down in the street.

Amund said that in Oaxaca, he found that people wanted to greet him, but they expected him to make the first move. "When I'd greet them there'd be a big smile on their face. And it was like – well, they were just smiling. And that makes me feel so good, because to me it's all about happiness, and I'm looking for signs, even though I know the answer, that happiness is not necessarily what we have in the western world. Happiness goes far beyond that. And there is that kind of happiness, that's my impression, in both Mexico and Guatemala, I also think in Jamaica, but I'm not so sure about Cuba. So having been here for only three-four days now, I hope they are, but I haven't seen as many smiles as I've seen in both Guatemala and Mexico, and Jamaica too."

I suggested that might be a sign of a superior educational system. The Cubans carry too much of the burden of history, the men and women of Cuba know too much, they have long memories, they definitely do not carry the burden of a national inferiority complex, and it amazes me that they are so friendly considering everything. Their spontaneous friendliness and lack of obvious resentment is amazing. They may simply grunt when you greet them in passing, but if you have something real to say to them they've got all the time in the world for you.

I don't know if I'd worn him out or won him over, but he said, "That's right, that's right. But I'm happy about being here, because this is one of the experiences I really wanted to have. One of the things I was most looking forward to, was to come here to Cuba and see how things are. I'm fascinated by how the system works, though I don't know how it works here." I told him my impression is that nobody does, not even Fidel.

He said he'd spent several hours yesterday in the Museo de la Revoluçion and followed the history from the first Spaniards coming to Cuba all the way up to the 1960s. "And then I was full, I couldn't take any more in. There's a lot going on here for sure."

Which of the four countries would he be most likely to return to? "That's interesting. Even though I was shocked, and intimidated, and uncomfortable with the situation in Jamaica the first four days, I would say it's the country I'm most likely to return to." He thought that was because he was so pleased and proud to have made the transition from being extremely awkward and fearful in Kingston, to learning how to cope, to finding the Jamaican way, so to speak. He was thrilled to end up being able to relax totally with the Jamaicans. I suspect, however, that soon he will be able to relax that way, and more so, with the Cubans. Let's hope it happens before he leaves Cuba in three weeks, with a week in Havana, then two weeks visiting Pinar del Río, Viñales, Cienfuegos, and Trinidad.

Amund went with a fellow named Lammy to see Bob Marley's tomb, and up there in the mountains the people were friendlier and less aggressive. "They were poor, but there were no signs of deprivation. A lot of Rastafarians were smoking their joints all the time. I couldn't really tell whether they were happy or what it was, but they certainly seemed satisfied in some way. Everything is mellow, everything is chilled out. Nobody's stressed in Jamaica. It's soon come, soon come, that may be ten minutes, that may be an hour. And that's a thing you have to get used to in Jamaica. It's not like that in Norway. In Jamaica it's all about knowing that you are the tourist, you don't set the agenda. If you try, you're arrogant. I think that's where many tourists fail, in their attitude toward the locals, they think they are the superior ones, they have no humility. They think of themselves as coming from some western civilized prosperous country and then everybody should jump when they holler."

When he was boarding a plane in Cozumel he heard a woman say, "'Oh my gawd, you know where I can buy a can of Coke for regular money?' And she held up two dollars. And it's like I was just about to tell her, man you're in Mexico, the regular money is pesos. But it was like, okay, I shouldn't say that. But it was such an arrogant and ignorant comment. But they're not all like that. I met quite a few backpackers in Mexico and they were reflective, intellectual, pissed off with the system. I asked if they had been harassed on their travels because of being from the United States, and they said yes. And that is so sad, that should not be, that makes me more ignorant and arrogant than they are for harassing them." He was surprised when I told him that sort of thing definitely does not exist in Cuba. Everybody says the same thing, it's not the U.S. tourists they dislike, it's their government.

In his travels so far he had met no tourists from the southern states, only from the states that border with Canada. Why would that be? I suggested maybe because Cuba makes it convenient for them because of daily flights from Vancouver, Montreal, and Toronto. Also the northern part of the United States is more liberal because of proximity to Canada. They read our papers, watch our TV, listen to the CBC, and they hear different viewpoints and fresh attitudes, and they become more liberal, and more likely to think for themselves and to harbour strong desires to go to forbidden places. I always think of Canada as the conscience of the United States.

"Just as Norway is the conscience of Europe!" Amund said he'd been to Canada just the once. During his time at college in North Dakota (the conscience of South Dakota?), in 1994, during the spring break, he and some fellow students drove up to Saskatoon, Saskatchewan. "We drank beer for three days and chilled out. That was that. But on this trip so far, I've met so many Canadians, and they seem so friendly and open, and just comfortable to be around. I have the idea that the western part of Canada is beautiful, everybody tells me British Columbia is so fertile, so green, so mountainous, so close to the Pacific. But I also met quite a few Ontarians who said the Ontario area is beautiful as well. So I guess there are a lot of things to see in Canada too. But travelling the way I'm travelling now, you suddenly realize oh there's so many things to see, oh, so many."

He also said he met six Torontonians in Jamaica, non-Jamaican Torontonians, and they spent the last four or five days of Amund's stay together in Negril. He didn't speak about Toronto with any Jamaicans, but these fellows told him that the big city is cosmopolitan and there are several hundred thousand Jamaicans living there. "These people I stayed with had nothing but praise for the Jamaicans living in Toronto. They say the police try to blame them for all the crime, but only the police believe that. The Toronto Jamaicans are the most friendly, decent, honest people. They have a lot of Jamaican friends, and these guys have been spending two weeks in Jamaica every year for fifteen years. They just love it. They have not a bad word about the Jamaicans at all, they behave themselves, and I think they're being stereotyped."

I told Amund the long version of the story about meeting my old high-school friend last night. When we got to the rosado cock-up preamble, he was incensed. "Nothing, no degree of ignorance, could justify the rudeness and anger of that man, even if it was his first day in Cuba. That's the gringo attitude you see everywhere, the one that says they should be happy for me coming here, after all I'm superior, make them speak English. Maybe the waiter didn't know it was rosé. People are allowed to make mistakes. It could always be sorted out. We're only human. But then again I shouldn't be too hard on the tourist, because it's only human for him to react badly as well. It's interesting – me personally, I'm not like that. I would have sat there, scratched my head, figured there must be some mistake, and called the waiter over. And maybe on another day this tourist would have acted more decently."

He thought that was the whole story, so I said, "But that had to happen, don't you see? If it hadn't been for that incident, this miracle would not have happened."

Amund's eyes brightened. "Ohh!" he sighed in suspense and anticipation. He liked miracles.

So when I told him how that led to chatting with the nice fellow at the next table, and he turned out to be a friend of mine I thought had died twenty years ago, he was almost as stunned by it all as I was. "Oh man!" said Amund. "How weird is that!"

"Weird's the word. And that was his last night in Cuba. He's thirty thousand feet in the air as we speak, rushing away from us at a thousand miles an hour."

Amund: I'm not a religious person at all, but . . . there's something with destiny, I can't really put my finger on any particular situations, but I've had those experiences that happened only because of other things that didn't have anything to do with it, except put you in the time and place where something astounding happens. And it leaves you saying why, why did that happen? Things that just happen because of some other things that you would not expect, and this leads to this and this leads to that. There's so many things happening that I can't really explain and yet I do not believe in any God or any divine beings, I have not been able to recognize anything that has something to do with something divine. Maybe destiny is something connected to something divine, I don't know. I have those things once in a while, and it makes you think. Was this coincidence, was this destiny, or what was it? I don't know.

Dave: We have an instinct for fatalism and predestination that all the sophistication of the modern age won't wash away. But I did have a premonition that I would meet somebody I knew in Cuba, because Canadians go to Cuba a lot. Like I wanted to be prepared and not drop dead with shock if I hear someone calling out my name. But that would have been different. That wouldn't have been as interesting as this somehow. For instance, think how easy it would have been, even after meeting and chatting with Roger, to have gone our own ways without having recognized each other from the past. And even when he told me his name the first time, it didn't register.

Amund: Yes. It is those moments you will memorize, or should I say remember, for the rest of your days.

Dave: At one point he told me something he remembered about me, and which I had completely forgotten, but when he told me it was as if a grapefruit had grown out of my head all of a sudden. And I think the same sort of thing was happening to him. But he was much more quiet about it.

I told Amund I'd been thinking of going to the zoo this afternoon. He wanted to come along. I was delighted to have such an excellent companion. He said he feels he knows the Havana Vieja area well enough after strolling around it for three days. Shall we share a taxi?

Then halfway to the zoo we mutually changed our minds, and ordered the cabbie to turn around and head to the Hemingway house, Finca Vigía, at San Francisco de Paula. He didn't need any directions. As he made a U-turn, Amund was telling me that on the way in from the airport he told his cabbie he was anxious to improve his Spanish on this visit. The cabbie told him you've come to the wrong place. This is Cuban we speak here.

The second half of *Islands in the Stream* largely revolves around this place where we are now, the Finca Vigía, and about Calle Obispo, walking up and down along that street, and drinking at La Floridita and the other bars. The book is right up there with the best writing Hemingway ever did, outside of the best of the short stories, includ-ing the early Nick Adams stories. How wonderful if all his writing were this good, and how wonderful that so much of it is. But the bad stuff ranges from less good to more boring to unreadable. And many if not all assessments of what is good and bad in Hemingway will continue to change with every new reading.

Amund is drinking all this in. He enjoys my literary opinions. He has heard a lot about Hemingway, and is interested in everything about him, but has read nothing of him or about him. I'm whisper-ing vital factoids and downright rumours in his ear as we climb the road to this grand literary shrine. It is high on a hill, with views of distant Havana Bay, Havana, and the Straits of Florida way off through the warm mist. It looks like the sort of place that could always attract a cool breeze, but oddly enough not today. Everything is still and uncomfortable. For some reason I'm not happy. The place irritates me. It's not at all what I expected. I've always felt a certain way about the place whenever I've read descriptions of it. But now that I'm here, I can't fault the descriptions of the place, but the atmosphere is different than I imagined, and sort of twisted. It's like looking at a finger bone in a gold case and trying to imagine the saint.

Hemingway loved Cuba for sure, but it's impossible to imagine him happy in this house. It's not something he would talk about in his books, and I suppose I'll have to read his letters from this period. But no, this is not Hemingway. The place in Key West is more Hemingway. Also one suspects that in some strange way Hemingway, without realizing it, had bad luck with high altitudes. His stories about the Italian and Swiss Alps are never pleasant, he was always crashing planes into mountains in Africa, he couldn't possibly have liked living here so high above everything, and he was so unhappy in the mountains of Idaho he shot himself. He was only happy in low-lying places, like Paris, Toronto, Upper Michigan, Key West, Cozimar, Habana Vieja. I think a diviner would not have been pleased with the underground currents below the Finca Vigía. I felt something dark drawing the energy out of me a mile a minute. I didn't say anything to Amund, though I think he felt it too. Even though we were privileged to be allowed to wander throughout the building wherever we wanted, there was no pleasure in seeing the soggy old books in their sagging old shelves, and old-fashioned record albums displaying an advanced ear for classical music (Rachmaninoff and Ravel) and a retrograde one for jazz (more Bix Beiderbecke than Basie), the mildewed old *Life Magazines*, and the wretched oil paintings of Hemingway that look as if they were copied from photographs, or maybe from photos of original paintings of other photos, and the bullfight posters that look like descendants of the ones that would have been on the wall when Il Papa was here.

The animals whose heads are on the wall, or whose hides are on the couch or on the floor, look better than the other stuff. The place was cluttered, the furniture didn't match the layout, there was no elegance about the place, it was clunky, graceless. It felt damper than it should have felt. There was a rot in it that it couldn't shake. It was too remote, unlike his earlier digs in Key West that had been closer to downtown, his favourite bars a five-minute walk.

We were surprised to be getting inside the sacred sanctuary. I think we paid a bit extra, plus Amund might have paid an extra dollar to take photos. I think one of the señoritas at the door wanted five dollars to take photos, and when Amund went to pay it the other one cautioned her to just charge him one dollar. Can't be sure. Cuba: so different, so much the same.

The furniture here is not in Hemingway's grand style and has not held up well. The beds seem to have been lifted from a clearance sale at a derelict hotel. Some of the books on the shelves are old library books. Either his valuable books have been squirrelled away and replaced with junk, or Hemingway was too cheap to pay his library fine. There are many paperbacks from the 1950s, and here's a curved candle with a handwritten notice saying that it has bent over "into the form of a tusk."

The view over Havana would have been smoggier than in Hemingway's day. No wonder we had such a hard time breathing on the way up here in that old beat-up Lada with diesel exhaust gushing through the floorboards. But it would take more than one Lada to ruin this landscape. It would be pretty at night. Trees have been removed to give views from the tower. Amund had the eyes of a hawk. I was saying we should be able to see the Plaza de la Revoluçion, and he helped me by locating the Capitolio, just beyond the radio tower, then you go "one and a half knuckles" to the left of that, and there it is. Down there, it's an hour's walk from the Capitolio, up here it's a thumb's width. And, for nights when he couldn't get away, here is Hemingway's telescope. Or is it?

There is a stuffed lion here more depressing than the one in Cárdenas. "Look at the eyes," says Amund. "They look like tennis balls painted green, and with black dots for pupils."

In Hemingway's military library hangs a pretty good painting of the great man kneeling next to a dead leopard. Papa seems only marginally happier than the leopard. There are maybe a hundred books in this room, with titles such as *Instructions to Young Sportsmen in All That Regulates to Guns and Shooting*, *Hitler and His Admirals*, *Memoirs*

of Ulysses S. Grant, History of the Art of War in the Middle Ages, and it
strikes me that this is the stuff he'd have been reading, in this spot,
in the period leading up to 1942 when his anthology of war writing
was published, *Men at War,* which was one of my greatest reading
experiences in my early teens. Amund excitedly leaps upon a
Norwegian edition of a novel written by Hemingway. The title trans-
lates as "The One Against the Many." I suggest it may be *To Have
and Have Not.* He's dubious.

There are windows all around, and it must have been pleasantly cool
up here, in the tower, on a hot day, spying on his neighbours, and
reading books, and writing a line or two now and then, with the
giant palm fronds brushing the windows as they sway in the breezes.
Hemingway was a great admirer of the royal palm, and there is a
regal row of six of them in immediate view of this window, growing
out of the foot of this hill, but looking down at the top of the tower.
One of the guides was telling us all about Hemingway's final days in
Idaho, which she thought was in Canada, an understandable mistake.
Amund wanted to know why Hemingway was so discouraged and so
depressed after leaving Havana. I gave him a list of the reasons that
make sense to me, given that few kill themselves for just one reason,
but the one Amund thought made most sense was that Idaho must
seem terribly grey and gloomy after twenty years in Cuba.

After a while I got bored with playing the what-is-original and
what-isn't game. It's been forty-five years since Hemingway left this
house. The sad empty austere grey swimming pool here is much
larger and deeper than the one at Key West, but not as playfully
colourful. It also has a sombre, faded art deco closing-day theatrical
look, with the stairs leading down into it being curved and concentric like the steps in a Busby Berkeley musical after the show is over
and all the film's been shot. And there must have been a lot of film
shot at parties around this pool. Where is all this film now? And an
old authentic 1930ish clunker of a wood-and-steel chaise longue
wide enough for two. Lugging that chaise longue around would be a
big job for the servants.

Then there is the actual *Pilar* (similar to the *Granma* but half its size). During the Second World War, Hemingway used this cabin cruiser for other things besides fishing. For instance, he had it fixed up with a machine gun and used it to patrol the Caribbean for German U-boats. It's to his credit that none was found: it's thought that the Germans heard what Hemingway was up to and stayed out of that area. Amund was interested in whatever we could dredge up in connection with what we were seeing. He claimed to know beans about boats, but was impressed by this one. "Look at the woodwork, and all the hinges and shackles. I know when I see a beautiful thing. To me this is beautiful, because of the curves, and the lines, the bow of the boat, the straight line going down to the sea, and the end or the aft."

This boat had been built in Key West, and in the film version of *To Have and Have Not*, with Bogie and Bacall, the boat they use is similar, but it looks smaller in the film – but then again boats always look smaller when they're in the water. Amund knew all the stories about Bogie and Bacall, but had never seen them together in a movie.

Did Hemingway install that high swivel-chair? Amund laughed at the holes in the arms of the chair to keep a drink steady. I said, You can't expect Hemingway to go out looking for U-boats without being half-pissed. Amund said, That makes sense though because if he was going out looking for German submarines he'd have to be high up, to see above the horizon. I said, That's true, you could see miles farther at sea by just climbing a few steps. Amund said, It seems to be in pretty good shape though, the boat. Even though it may need a paint job in some places. It seems pretty well preserved, and I guess the climate here is pretty dry. I said, It's in better shape than a lot of things in Cuba for sure. And I also said, I've read all his books, some of them many times, but I've only read about one and a half of the biographies. He said, I don't know, reading a lot of biographies can screw up your mind, I think. He meant in terms of trying to sort out all the differing opinions about some little event in Hemingway's life could turn into a big time-sink. He said, You should keep in mind your own opinions. I said, I'm glad I saw this. Amund said, Oh yeah, absolutely.

Hemingway referred to the great fortress guarding Havana as the Morro, and he was caught in a storm just off the Morro on one occasion, if his fiction can be trusted. He says to his cat, Boise, in *Islands in the Stream*, "I wish you could have seen us come into the mouth of the harbour, with the sea breaking over the Morro. You'd have been spooked, boy."

We all know where the *Pilar* is, but nobody knows what happened to Hemingway's shiny black 1955 Chrysler New Yorker. When he left Cuba he gave that car to some army colonel who had done him a good turn. The colonel later became fed up with Fidel and fled for Florida, without the car. Before he fled, he hid the car somewhere, but nobody knows where he hid it.

Unfortunately the cabbie, Luis, who had driven us up to the Finca in his smelly old Lada, waited for us although we had pleaded with him not to. We were hoping to get a nicer cab. But now he is taking us back to the Hotel Lido, with horrible black smoke coming up through the floorboards. There is no sign that it is bothering Luis, but both Amund and I feel sick. We have headaches. We can't wait to get back to the hotel. And have a nap. We are so exhausted by the exhaust. In retrospect the hazardous effects of the trip up may have coloured the visit to the Finca, and ill-disposed both Amund and me toward appreciating the ghostly relics and artifacts. It was as if the intense pleasure a lifelong Hemingway fan would have taken in visiting the Finca had been stolen away by airborne poisons. Our second dose is more immediate and more debilitating. Luis refuses to give any distance to the vehicle ahead, usually a slow-moving one belching out tons of diesel exhaust to add to our woes in the back seat.

I told Amund that another irony of meeting Roger in Havana is that the last time we saw each other, many of these cars were brand new, or not so old. Fate has an archaeology all its own. Amund said, "It's not every day you meet someone you haven't seen in forty years."

After all those fumes we staggered to our rooms for an afternoon nap, mine being interrupted at an early stage by a call from Mimi. She invited me to go with her to the Alliance Française, to meet her there. She was attending some kind of function there, and the French ambassador would be in attendance. It was over by the Plaza de la Revoluçion. I said I'd love to come except I had to continue my nap owing to diesel-fume poisoning. So we arranged to meet at the Parque Central at 8 p.m.

The north wing and the south wing of that park are dark, but the spectacular extra-large José Martí statue, dating from 1905, is brightly illuminated. There are some steps leading up to the base of the statue, and you can walk around it. So I innocently decided I'd go up there and sit on the retaining wall/balustrade sort of thing. That way I could see her from a long way off. No need to lurk in the shadows. It didn't occur to me it might be unwise to try to share the spotlight with José Martí. I'm not proud of how I handled what ensued, but feel compelled to record it truthfully.

I didn't think anyone else could see me because I was up high, and who looks up high these days? All the nocturnal parklike activity was happening below me, and outside the umbra of the spotlights. About forty black guys were having a powerful discussion, but I could not catch the drift. They were oratorically overriding each other with such enthusiasm, all talking at top speed and top volume at the same time, hoping something they say will register with the others, or will otherwise cancel out someone else's brilliant syllogism. The bunch of them became one organism, and this giant amoeba kept drifting all over the park, like one slow-moving hurricane, while the waving of their hands and the passion of their voices were engaged at top speed. The excitement was at a fever pitch, but there was no hostility whatsoever. It's hard to get in a fight in Cuba, there is a great tolerance for differences of opinion. I kept thinking this is Fidel's battle of ideas going on, and me with the serenity of a bird's-eye view. They all were tall powerful men with a lot to say and nobody outside the group was paying the slightest attention to them. So concentrated were they on the issue at hand they seemed not to realize that they were moving, as a unit, slowly, out from the shadows of the leafy southern end of the park into the heavy illumination of the Martí statue, so close I had to pull my dangling feet up out of the way. Then, slowly, they went back again into the shadows, still outshouting each other, so I dangled my legs again. Then an old fellow came by and gave me a quizzical look. I gave him a quizzical look right back. Then he gave me another quizzical look, even more quizzical than the first, and walked off.

Then a security guard came by and insisted I come down. Later I would wonder why I was so stubborn, but at the time it made perfect sense to refuse. He insisted he would call the police if I didn't go with the flow and get down right away. I told him I would make a compromise. I would stand up rather than sit on the wall with legs dangling.

So I went over to the west side of the grand marble base of this statue and stood there, figuring Mimi would see me even better that way and maybe the security guard would leave me in peace. But then he returned with a fiercer look on his face and ordered me out of the park. I told him he was the worst excuse for a Cuban I'd seen in weeks. He abruptly turned and walked away.

So then I got thinking, Maybe I'm being culturally insensitive. Maybe this is a sacred shrine and I'm desecrating it, like the *Satanic Verses*, and maybe there will be a fatwa put on my head. So I reluctantly got down to the ground level, and just stood there, on the west side of the base of the statue. I didn't want to go sit on the benches because they were in the shadows and Mimi might have had a problem finding me.

And then I was suddenly confronted by a large Afro-Cuban cop, who, with a deep voice and anguished face, pleaded with me to come to my senses and be like everybody else, keep a respectful distance from the statue, even if you do not in your heart recognize the genius of José Martí, at least please do not offend others by being so disrespectful. Suddenly I became grown up again, my absurd stubbornness left me, I apologized, shook his hand, looked in his eye, we both smiled, and I walked off just as Mimi was hopping off the *camella* from the Alliance Française.

I told her what happened. She said, Are you crazy? You were sitting up there? No wonder they were so upset. You just don't do that in Cuba.

A photographer and his assistant were setting up a tripod to take photos of the statue. Maybe they had complained, and that was why

I was ordered off. I later found out that a similar event occurred in this exact same spot, on March 11, 1949, and it escalated into an international situation. Some drunken U.S. navy sailors urinated on the base of the statue and one managed to get to the top and sit on José's head. An infuriated crowd gathered. The sailors were saved by the police in the nick of time. The Cubans were outraged that no charges were laid, and that the sailors were simply escorted back to their ship. Fidel's great biographer, Tad Szulc, claims this incident gave Cuban anti-Americanism a big boost, and served to show that Fidel was anti-American that far back, ten years before the Revolution. Fidel was one of the leaders of the student protest the next day, but the police riot squads attacked the students with "extraordinary brutality," in the words of Szulc. Fidel was beaten with truncheons. His men delivered statements to the papers, charging that it was a shame for Cuba to have a police chief who refused to arrest the sailors who were desecrating the monument, and instead attacked the patriotic students who were defending Cuba's honour.

THE WORLD IS
A HANDKERCHIEF

Tuesday, March 16, 2004. I phoned down to the desk and said when I was out last night somebody came into my room and stole the towels. Oh, that's normal, said the desk clerk. She would have some towels sent up very soon. And she also said that a "message" had come in from the Spanish ladies. Please read it to me, I said. No, it's not that kind of message. It's just that they want to see you. She must have been about to buzz my room when I buzzed her.

So I came down, and there they were, sitting in the car, parked at the entrance, waiting for me. All four of them got out, with four slams of four doors, and surrounded me on the narrow sidewalk. They'd had a wonderful trip to Pinar del Río. They said it was as they remember rural Spain, in their childhood memories: at every inter-section there would be numerous hitchhikers. Montse said, "Every chance we got we'd pick up a hitchhiker and she would sit between us in the back seat. One of them told us she was going to the prison to visit her husband. We said oh my, what did he do? She said he killed a cow. He got six years in jail for killing a cow."

Reisa jumped in. "Oh no, he didn't kill the cow. He witnessed the killing of the cow. He got six years in prison just for witnessing the killing of the cow – and not telling anybody."

"Not telling the authorities," said Montse.

I knew it was illegal to kill a cow. Or even a chicken. But six years?

"She told us," said Montse, "that she heard it was going to be reduced to three years. So she was going to the prison to tell him the good news."

Is this what it's come down to? Does Fidel really want to create a nation of snitches? What will Mimi have to say about this?

The señoritas wanted to know how my meeting went with Dr. Spengler. I said someone must have had the time mixed up, because he wasn't there. But it was a good thing, because otherwise I wouldn't have met an old friend of mine from forty years ago whom I thought was dead. Montse responded with glee and said, "You know, we have a saying in Spanish: The world is a handkerchief. Do you have that in English?" I didn't think so. "Yes, the world is a handkerchief. You open it up, you never know what you're going to find. No, that's just my naughty paraphrase. You open it up and you might find something you lost twenty years ago."

So now they were off to Trinidad de Cuba. They were chiding me for worrying so much about them, but you could tell they were pleased. I said I was glad my advice wasn't necessary.

Montse: Oh, no! Your advice was helpful.

Reisa: Because of you we were more careful than we would have been.

María: And we didn't trust the maps as much as we would have.

Montse: And we didn't drive at night.

Reisa: And we didn't take any roads unless we were sure where they were leading to.

María: And what shape they were in.

Rosaria: Without your help we might not have returned by now.

They expressed regret that I was going to be flying out Friday morning because they wouldn't be getting back till Friday afternoon from Trinidad de Cuba. So I wished them a wonderful time, and kissed the hand of each of them, and kissed them each on the cheek.

Montse looked me in the eye and said, "You are a good advertisement for your country. The Canadians are so civilized, such gentlemen."

Last night, at the Alliance Française, Mimi had also had a nice compliment. After she had forgiven me for being overly familiar with José Martí, she told me how thrilled she was to be in the company of the French *ambassadrice*, and she felt as if she was on a higher plane now. Moreover, *l'ambassadrice* complimented her on her excellent French, isn't that wonderful? And a French poet gave her a copy of his book. And inscribed it, with warm regards. She showed me the book, a modestly produced edition of a hundred poems, one on each page, and each poem was six short lines long – five lines, then a line space, followed by a final line. The poet seemed to be working on each poem as a jeweller cleans each facet of a diamond, and the poems evoked the landscape, with its burning horizons and ruined castles, its pain, its ugliness, as a symbol of the anguish of being human.

Mimi looked splendid in her bright red lipstick, with her dark-chocolate face, and her bare arms a lighter softer chocolate, because she tends to keep her arms covered when in the sun, but not so her face. She's nice to be with and she explains things to me. For instance, she told me I was lucky I hadn't been thrown in jail over that José Martí kerfuffle.

Being with Mimi on such a beautiful night in Habana Vieja was a badge of honour for me, because you could tell at a glance she was a highly intelligent woman with a great sense of humour, a pointy nose and receding chin, and when she wore her glasses she looked scholarly, and when she didn't she looked bright and attractive. For a male gringo to be strutting around with a Cuban woman in his own age bracket is quite rare, apparently, and a bit unsettling, at least in the more touristy parts of town. I had a bite to eat at the Gentiluomo, and Mimi, having pigged out at the reception, had a beer and a few Hollywoods. When she ran out and I offered her a Popular, she removed the tip. Her voice was raspy, almost as if it would certainly be painful to speak, but she insisted it wasn't. Sometimes things that sound painful aren't painful at all.

Sitting at the bar of the Ambos Mundos, to which we had strolled, was a very large fat tourist about sixty-five, knee to knee with a blond Cuban girl about eighteen, who was gleefully stroking his thighs, and slipping her hands up under his shirt and tickling his ribs and causing him to get red in the face. He whispered things in her ear and she replied, while giggling fiendishly: "Oh! I'd love to do that to you!" There were two empty stools to their right and then there was a lone intellectual Canadian woman wearing horn-rimmed glasses with thick black frames. She was about thirty-five, no lipstick or makeup, round-faced and wearing a grey business suit over a white silk blouse, and with a silver cross around her neck, intently studying her Cuban guidebook. And there were two empty stools to the left, then there was a man wearing a sweat-stained bright red Team Canada baseball cap (looking a lot like the one I lost) and watching the soccer game on television.

We finished our drinks and strolled down toward the Hotel Isabella. I had often admired a beautiful flowering tree in a little gated park there, and it turned out to be Mimi's favourite tree of all time. "That's the *flamboyant*," she said. That seemed a perfect name for such a graceful tree, almost throbbing with passion, enthralled with its own beauty, with blossoms halfway between lipstick violet and lipstick red, with delicate leaves that look almost fernlike, and with great green plants ululating at the base of the tree and tickling their way up its trunk. Next to the *flamboyant* was a gnomelike statue of Sancho Panza and his donkey.

Being with Mimi made Havana look lovelier because she loves it so much and understands it so well. Sometimes I would point out some exquisite view and she would say, "Oh yes, I loves that too, I see that often." She wished I'd choose something she hadn't noticed; for just about everything she pointed out was something I hadn't noticed. You couldn't ask for more from the most highly paid guide.

We kept looking for special images as if we were cinematographers, blessedly unencumbered by all the equipment that has to accompany the making of a movie. My most companionable companion found many more exquisitely subtle little images than the martyrs of photography would be likely to, and enjoyed them more. All we had to do was wander and watch, with nothing separating the eyeball from its object. We wandered around the winding little streets north of O'Reilly, around the Catedral Colón, and I knew I would later think back on this petite promenade and remember it as one of the most romantic and friendliest strolls since the Second World War, even if we were about to separate, perhaps forever.

She was going overboard in making it clear she wasn't interested in my money, and she wasn't interested in using me as a ticket out of the country. She refused my pesos, and even when I asked her to get us ice cream she brought back just one, for me, and I couldn't force her to take even one little lick. She also demonstrated her faith in Fidel, and in the principles of the Revolution, by her shivers of pleasure whenever I would say something nice about him.

Again I asked how her mother could have been so annoyed that Mimi had married a black man – especially when she had married a black man herself. Mimi had a hard time expressing it, but it seemed that her mother considered her very special, and if she met a white man it would give her more of a chance to develop in the world and find the proper place for her own talents instead of being submerged, marginalized, optioned off somehow. So it was a keen disappointment to her mother, especially when the fellow in fact turned out to be a little man who drank a lot.

That's what Cuba's like, I said. The big men stay sober and run the country and the little men drink a lot. She laughed and acknowledged that was probably an accurate description of Cuba. Or of any country.

There is always sadness. Without sadness, something is not quite right. One must have sadness, as a sign that he or she is making the proper sacrifices one must make in order to honour one's own existence in the universe. But this is a profoundly sad evening for me. I'm sad that I'm leaving Cuba and Mimi both. With Cuba I'm close to tears four days before I have to leave, while with other countries, it was at the most a tear or two on the final day. What gives? Maybe I'm crying for the Cubans and the spectacular sacrifices they've had to make in order to live in a country where everyone gets the basics for a decent life and lives in a fairly steady rate of harmony with just the right amount of irritants to test one's mettle.

On Calle O'Reilly, you can stick your head in a window and buy a loose cigar for a dollar, and you'll see a lot of guys walking along with conga drums, guitars, bongos – if you want to hear music just find a guy with a guitar and follow him.

There are so many *amputados* on clogged O'Reilly, with slow-moving cars pushing people onto the narrow sidewalks, they're in danger of bumping into each other with their wheelchairs.

And just off Calle O'Reilly, by a little urban renewal area, there's a large yellow garbage bin, and someone has spent several hours painting on it, very professionally, with blue and red lettering on white, an oft-repeated message from Fidel reminding Cubans that they are engaged in building a new civilization: "Un mondo mejor es posible." But surely a better world is not possible if it entails having everyone spying on their neighbours and snitching on them. Surely that can't be true. That's not what Fidel had in mind. How could this be rationalized?

When we got back to Mimi's place, I told her about the cow killing, and about the man who was convicted of the crime of witnessing the slaughter but not reporting it. Six years.

"Of course," she said. "Do you understand why? Because we have not a lot of cows." She said the few they do have are reserved for sick children. And maybe it was a dairy cow, producing free milk for children all over Cuba. But to throw someone in jail for not having blown the whistle on a cow-killer? She said she realizes it sounds like a very strange situation, but the government owns all those animals and only the government can kill them and distribute them in the way they want to. You can have goats all over your front lawn but you can't kill them, you have to let the government trucks pick them up, freeze them, and distribute them, and you get your goat when it's time for you to get it. She thought these problems were insoluble in a socialist state just as there are many insoluble problems in a capitalist state. If everyone were allowed to kill a cow any time he wanted, it would result in a very awkward situation, it would open the floodgates for a whole new form of private enterprise and be a terrible threat to the sovereignty of the socialist state. Plus they might run out of cows. So that is why there is no choice but to jail people who don't report the private slaughter of public livestock.

She got up and drank copiously from the rain barrel in a corner of her kitchen. Then she said she was hungry. I said I was too. She said I was just like her father, because, as he used to say, if you're hungry, I'm hungry, if you're tired I'm tired, if you're thirsty I'm thirsty. I told her she was cute. She said, What's cute? Cuba is apparently innocent of that word. I said you can be pretty, but maybe you're not cute. But if you're cute, that's better than being pretty, and you don't have to be pretty. She said, "Oooh, thank you. If I said something amusing, you might say that was cute?" Yes, I said, and I told her that cute means pretty, but a pretty girl can be stupid while a cute girl is almost always very intelligent. She took that as a compliment right up there with the one from *l'ambassadrice française*.

Mimi had been trying to understand how I could be rich in Cuba but poor in Canada. She asked me, "What is the opposite of expensive?" I said cheap. She said, "Yes, Cuba is a cheap country, isn't it?" I said yes, to get a Cuban cigar for one dollar is something that can only occur in Cuba.

This afternoon, at the Lido rooftop restaurant, while writing out these events, and more, from last night, I drank three beers. Then on my way up to my room for a nap I met Amund. He was going to a nightclub nearby that was featuring live music starting soon. It was a nightclub all right, wonderfully spacious, as if it had been converted from a great 1920s cinema palace. We arrived about four-thirty for a five o'clock start. At five-thirty we heard the start had been postponed to six-thirty. It was cold! We wished we'd brought a sweater or two, but we felt close to the moment when the music and the temperature would be red hot. And then at six-thirty the curtain did open, and a wailing wall of Cuban cacophony burst forth. And everyone leapt to their feet whistling and screaming. There were five vocalist/dancers on the front line, and behind them were eight musicians – two trumpets, a tenor saxophone, five percussionists, a stand-up electric bass. And it was pretty well no costumes, all street clothes, no emcee, no conductor, no announcer – just a solid monolithic wall of music.

Pretty soon there were some fabulous dancers on the floor. But the music wasn't really catching fire. The band would perform a piece, up there on the remote stage, in the icy-cold ballroom, and they would go for about ten minutes, then stop for applause, then start up for another ten or fifteen minutes. But the music was very monotonous and repetitive, it never varied in tempo, or tone, or decibel level, there was no rise and fall, and all the musicians drowned each other out. I'm sure there was a lot of talent up there, but it wasn't discernible, because everybody was dancing and playing and singing at once and non-stop: there were no solos, or maybe there were a few but they got drowned out.

Also there was none of the kind of rhythmic quality one requires for dance music, and relies on with Cuban music. It was like a giant noise band with a somewhat Creole flavour. Hate to say it, but these Cubans needed a leader! Well, there was a leader, but all he did was tell them when to start and when to stop. To get them to stop, he'd hold his arm up till the proper moment, then pull it hard. To get them to start he would just hold his arm up, then shake it. There was no serious difference between the new song and the one just abandoned.

Amund shared my discomfort. At one point twelve Italians came in. We knew they were Italians because Amund had met them earlier. Oh oh, here come the Italians, he said. And man, did they ever have a bad sense of rhythm. They were dancing really badly, but they didn't give a damn. It was the cold in part, because just about everyone in this club had been out in the heat most of the day, and was now half-frozen, and that's good neither for music nor dance. Also any band that big had to have a leader. And some concept of what they're doing.

So Amund said, No, it's not working for me either, let's wait till the end of this song then go. Well, the song was just interminable. Never have I wished so hard for a song to end, while at the same time hoping for the music to spring to life all of a sudden. But it was finally over, and we got up, and when we got out it was pouring rain. It had looked like rain before but it was still hot and humid. Now it was cold and wet.

A few hours later I'm ringing Mimi's doorbell to see if she is in and she is. We talked non-stop. It felt perfect to be here. And now and then she would say, "Oh, I love you," and she would kiss me on the cheek.

She answered the question about the cow, once again, in pretty well the same way, and I'll let the reader be the judge on that one. I'm flip-flopping on whether the sentence of six years was understandable, never mind fair. But then she added that this cow would not have been an ordinary cow. This would have been a cow specially bred, with beef so good it's reserved for use in certain medical therapies.

She said someone would have decided to kill a cow, and asked for people to throw in money for shares of the meat. That's the way it happens. Usually they don't get caught. But this time somebody snitched. And maybe the man who was in jail had been arrested and given such a lengthy term because he steadfastly refused to name any names, to say who organized the killing or who performed the death blow. So now when his term is over he will be able to return to his own neighbourhood without worrying about being attacked for having snitched. And the person who did kill the cow will have to suffer knowing his friend was doing big time in the big house on his behalf. There wouldn't be any more slaughter of cows in that neighbourhood in a hurry.

It began to sound plausible. I felt at peace. And even if I don't understand it, I feel better knowing that my friend Mimi understands

it and approves of it. That's the way it is when we visit other countries. We have to turn off our minds from time to time in order to get
some perspective.

Tomorrow was a day off for Mimi. I asked if she would like to go
to the zoo. She broke out in the biggest smile. She hadn't been since
her father was alive. I thought it must be a good zoo if she likes it
because she's very sensitive about animals and people. And I suggested we bring my Norwegian friend. I described him. Yes, she wants
to meet him for sure. I think he'll be into it. Three on Thursday.

It's 1:12 a.m. It must have been shortly after midnight that I walked
home, and there were many people on the street, chit-chatting in
groups, just standing there, or sitting on concrete benches with
drooping flowers in their hair, and calling to each other across the
Prado. Mimi says that I am the only man who ever touched her
mind. Maybe she means lately. I'm sure her father touched her mind.
In fact, she added that I am the only man who has treated her with
the kindness her father treated her with. Geez, does that ever make
me feel good. But then again, it makes me feel not so good, for it is
a pity that she has not been properly appreciated by other males,
principally the little guy who drank a lot.

SEA OF SADNESS

Wednesday, March 17, 2004. On the way to the zoo we passed a vast necropolis, on a broad hilltop, with many splendid mortuary monuments. Mimi confessed she hadn't visited her father's grave in a long time. I could see why not. There were no trees, no shade. It was hot as hell in there.

The zoo resembled the cemetery except there were cages instead of monuments, and there were trees, and shade. At the crocodile pit, Mimi sentimentally recalled that her son "was afraid of crocodiles when he was a little boy – *but now he is in the army!*"

One crocodile was lying so still he looked dead, and I said so, causing Mimi to grasp my arm and start a loud lament for the departed soul of the beast. But then it blinked, causing her to recover quickly, and not without embarrassment. She said she had over-reacted because the crocodile was very young and must have been looking for his mother. Young? It was ten feet long! She said that was small for crocodiles. Let's see if we can find some larger ones.

All we could find were smaller ones. "There's one – two, three, four," she said. She had a good eye. They camouflage themselves very well. But these were truly babies.

She said she visited this zoo with her father "when my son was little. And once when I was very little too. A long time ago." She looked sad.

"What do you call these birds?"

"Flamingos," I said. She said the Uruguayan people have a good story about the "history of these birds." They call them "serpent birds" because their necks can twist and turn any way they want. They got their name because they were considered very ugly. There was a big party, and these birds decided to attend wearing something that would make them more attractive. They did not like being considered ugly, so they found some sleeping serpents and wore them over their shoulders. But the others at the party were not impressed, they still made fun of the birds for being ugly. And so the serpents woke up and poisoned all the nasty people, but they didn't harm the birds at all. And now the flamingos are still called "serpent birds" in Uruguay, but the people have changed their mind and think that they are beautiful. But in actual fact they are just as ugly as they ever were.

Mimi wanted to know if the story was funny. I said it was more than funny, it was an excellent story, with a lot of psychological depth, and I thanked her for it. Where did she hear it? She said when her son was a little boy he came home with the story one day. The teacher had told it to the class.

Meanwhile the flamingos seemed to be cohabiting very well on an island with a number of ducks, except that whenever the serene and ugly/beautiful flamingos sleepwalk too close to the small ugly ducks, the ducks snap at them and force them to back off.

Mimi said that the ducks don't mind visitors as long as they don't get too close. How did she know that the ducks weren't the visitors? She pointed at an unoccupied island in another pond farther along. That was where the flamingos lived, she said. They were just paying a friendly call.

These flamingos were orange and white, rather than pink. I've never thought of them as ugly before today. Odd-looking for sure. But Hemingway considered them ugly. He would have been poisoned had he been at that party. In *Islands in the Stream* they're sailing around Cayo Contrabando, and Hemingway alter-ego Thomas Hudson is standing on the flying bridge, looking for U-boats, with one hand on his machine gun and a icy-cold drink in the other. Suddenly a flock of flamingos flies over the water. Thomas Hudson calmly calls them "ugly in detail and yet perversely beautiful." And he says, "They must be a very old bird from the earliest times."

She was only eleven months old and had an enormous cage, all to herself. The cage was shaped like a bell jar, and she was sitting silently on the highest perch, just a few feet down from the pointy top, about three human storeys high, as high as a Saskatchewan grain elevator. She seemed to be focusing hard on whatever could be seen out there, predominantly a solid wall of rich green trees separating the zoo from a row of residential buildings.

"This is an Andean condor, one of the first to be born in jail," said Mimi.

"In captivity?" I said.

"Oh, I'm sorry, in captivity."

"Much the same thing. And birds aren't born, they're hatched." She didn't know the word *hatched*.

Mimi said that Chinese scientists came all the way to Cuba to see this condor. "And this is her up there!" She was a very youthful specimen, not a year old, but she looked serious, and intelligent beyond her months. She definitely was not in a playful mood, nor was she hungry, nor was she sleepy. She just wanted to stare, way off in the distance, from the tower of her captivity. Maybe she was waiting for her parents to return.

"There's only one? She must be very lonely," I said.

"I think she feels very sad too," said Mimi, "and probably she will die soon because she is alone."

"Maybe the Chinese will send her a partner."

And a zebra. And many burros. And what other animals have we seen so far? A big fat rhino with very grey skin, very sad. How can I tell it's sad? Because it has its head in the corner and won't look at anyone. Not that there's anyone to look at. Oh, here he comes, he's turning around now. He's very slow on his feet, each of which bears three toes. Bonjour, monsieur. He's very slow to think. He has nothing to do except stand around. He knows something's wrong but he's not quite sure what it is. Mimi notes he's losing weight, he has many wrinkles around his stomach. There he goes. Now he's really trotting around. Poor boy. Free to stand in the corner or trot around.

Mimi says the first time she was at the zoo she was six years old. In fact, they lived nearby. She remembers that there were more animals then. But there was only one lion. They could hear the growling and roaring of the lion continuously. "We were afraid all the time. Our father had to get us a different house. That was a long time ago."

It is well known that the Havana Zoo has many dedicated and caring people behind it, but there is no money in the budget for zoos, as is the case, of course, more or less, everywhere. The animals are so bored that if a leaf falls from a tree and lands in their enclosure it's a big event.

The gorillas are in good shape, but the four lions didn't move all the time we were there. Christopher P. Black says they regularly have sex – thirty times a day. But today they must have already consummated their daily quota. That's right, get the hard work over with early, then you can relax. The various little monkeys and baboons were also trying to make the best life they could out of a bad situation. Unlike many people we know.

Mimi mourned the decrease in the number of animals, and said that when they died they don't get replaced, and when offspring are born they sell them to other zoos. So it's a fairly big zoo with not many animals in it and many of the enclosures are empty.

Later, at the Hotel Isabella, I was checking my e-mail, and sent off a little note to my friend George Bowering, Canada's award-winning poet. He hates it when I get to go to places he's never been, such as Cuba. For the twentieth time he tells me how envious he is. This is so I won't feel badly when he wins yet another award.

There were a number of messages, so I sent a line to each saying I'd be home tomorrow, just to show I was thinking of them while in Cuba. Mimi was reading over my shoulder. When we got to George's note, she said he's funny, and I said oh yes he's famous for being funny. She asked if she could write something to him herself. So I wrote to George that my friend Mimi was going to say a word, and she wrote, "I love David very much because he love Cuba. And we needs people like David, because we are struggling for our survival."

So that'll give George a little something to think about. Or maybe a lot. Who knows?

On our several petites promenades we saw many beautiful sights. I'd forgotten how a little romance in the air can reconfigure the landscape. We would stop. We would stare. We would shiver. We would gape. We would hold hands. That's not what you do when you look at a photograph. You don't stop and shiver in astonishment. And your heart doesn't go boing boing boing. Not usually. Maybe sometimes.

EPILOGUE

I've had my last breakfast on the rooftop of the Hotel Lido. The young fellow learning to be a waiter, and who had a little beard just like mine, did not give me the ritual fake look of sadness or sympathy that one would expect, but I gave him a dollar anyway. An Englishman saw me forking out the cash and yelled over from his table, Isn't the price of the breakfast included? I said, Yes, but the people here respond well to tips. He said, Pardon? I laughed.

He came over and said that he had a problem with tipping, because when he and the missus were coming in they had some sandwiches left over from the flight, buns and ham, butter and mustard. And it had been all confiscated. He couldn't stop imagining, with great bitterness, those airport employees sitting in the back room and having a great time wolfing down the food he had paid good money for yesterday in Sheffield.

I told him, jokingly, that although it's well known that there's a law against bringing food into Cuba, it's also well known that the customs people only apply the law just before lunchtime. He turned to his much younger wife and said, "Hear that, dear? He agrees with me." She rolled her eyes sullenly.

Then he asked if it was safe to walk the streets at night. His wife was watching us. She was not a young trophy wife as much as a prematurely dowdy wife, about twenty-five going on sixty. She looked about twice as smart as he did, and half his age. I told him as long as he held on tight to his wife's hand they'd both be fine. He laughed. Even she laughed.

It's amazing how irritated I've been the last few days. Everything was bothering me, especially the mariachi bands, not the good ones, but the ones who relentlessly chase the tourists from the time they get off their bus till the time they get back on. They practically have to slam the bus doors on their fingers. These are the holidayers from Varadero who sign up for an all-day bus tour to relieve the tedium. But these mariachi bands should be banned, they just keep playing the same bloody song over and over again. And it's so nauseating to see them grovelling, following the tourists around like gulls following the ferry, but with less grace, even though the tourists completely ignore them, especially when they hold their hats out for tips. But who can blame the tourists for that? It's so undignified for the Cubans and so irritating to everyone else.

A thousand mariachi bands, one song. You know the one. "Guantanamera." Fine song, based on a poem by José Martí. But the finest song will drive you around the bend real fast if it's played over and over by a bad band.

Even Mimi was irritating me a bit, through no fault of her own. Why does she have to keep asking why my face is red? And surely it's not that hard to understand that I like being in the shade whenever possible. And surely she doesn't have to pull me out of the way when a car is coming down the street. I can see if I've got enough room.

A horrible thing happened at work the other day. A colleague received a call that her father and brother had been killed in a car accident. That's all that Mimi knew about it. She couldn't tell me any details. The girl, strangely, shrugged off all attempts to get her to go home, she insisted on remaining at her post until her shift was over. She just cried and cried all day long. Why didn't she go home? Mimi, for once, had no idea.

Finally I managed to convince Mimi that it would be okay to accept my large roll of pesos. Here's what happened: She insisted on making a meal for me and wouldn't take no for an answer. I thought it was going to be a disaster for some reason. I was so irritable I got prejudiced. But it was rice, black beans, and some kind of vegetable-protein product that she fried very lightly in little patties. It was a great meal, and I brought some icy-cold beer.

After dinner I tried again to give her the pesos. No way. So I pulled out my trump card. I suggested she present this money as a little gift to the woman whose father and brother were killed in the accident. Just tell her it's for additional funeral expenses. She went for the idea in a big way. I think it was the word *additional* that won her over. So finally I was able to make good use of all those pesos I was unable to spend in Havana, though they are still appreciated in Camagüey and Santiago de Cuba.

When one spends thirty-three days wandering in any country anywhere, one's impressions will change from day to day. So in a true travel journal we must be prepared for inconsistencies, reversals, perceptual error, and corrections. When I told the Spanish ladies that, they said it sounds like the kind of book they'd like to read.

Again, everything is irritating me. Especially the overwhelming fact of my ignorance about this country, that there are so many important things I know nothing about. So many streets I haven't walked along. So many observations I failed to make. For instance every peanut vendor, every flower seller, and the bicycle taxis, each one trying to be a little bit different in the way they do business or the way they holler their high-pitched come-on. Each one made individual by some ingenious knack on the part of the owner, like the fellow who found a hubcap so he fastened it very beautifully as a decorative item on the back of his bicycle taxi so you can spot him at a moment. He may not have a car but at least he's got a hubcap. Or another fellow, a bicycle taxi driver with a box on the back with his dog in it, and that dog never seems to be without a fresh bone. Or an excited little boy with a puppy in his hands, trying to sell it.

Or all these wonderful buildings I've never seen before, on strange old streets I still haven't walked along, so many parks I haven't sat in, and my airport taxi passes an old building, now used as a *polyclinico*, and renamed Edificio Nguyen Van Troi, in honour of the great Vietnamese hero who was killed in 1964.

How stupid, counterproductive, and foolishly expensive it was of me to have rented a car on this trip. I thought it would give me more freedom and more time for fruitful contemplation, but it just made me feel more isolated. Also I should have gone to more baseball games; a game in Havana would have been nice. It even pangs me I didn't go to the peanut factory, or the cigar factory, or to the Occidental Provinces.

My irritability might be a portion of a larger irritability that is mysteriously affecting a lot of people on this particular day. For instance, a girl who is hitchhiking hops out of one car at a stoplight. She has a fed-up, intolerant look on her face. She immediately hops into another car.

Even my driver seems to be suffering. If the driver ahead of him takes one split second too long before taking off when the light turns green, my guy will clench the steering wheel so hard his knuckles will turn white, and he'll be on the verge of slamming his fist down hard on the horn.

I didn't spend enough time on the Malecón or even in Havana Vieja. I should have taken Mimi to the Coppelia for ice cream instead of to the zoo. She loves the sun, and she has no tolerance for my attachment to the shade. But she seems to be getting too much of the sun, for she's darker than she should be, and she has a kind of discolouration on the back of her neck that looks as if it could develop into the cancer her mother had. Not that I'm a dermatologist. Also I shouldn't have tried to change her mind about the degree of racism in Cuba. She refused the notion that things had improved in the past ten years, because there was never any racism in Cuba in her entire lifetime, as far as she could see. But on occasion she will say something that indicates a contrary opinion also lurks in a corner of her large mind.

Barbaríta saw me going and looked sufficiently sad for me to remember to give her a tip. She said, "One dollar, you go, that is all?" I reminded her I'd given her a dollar every day. You'd think we were married with kids. She stopped pouting and gave me a smile.

People on bicycles nonchalantly ride the wrong way in the fast lane of the expressway while eating a sandwich. Thick black clouds of diesel exhaust everywhere. But the "milk for my baby" mystery has been resolved, at least to my satisfaction.

In the departure lounge of José Martí Airport, every non-perishable item offered for sale has CUBA stamped on it, and every garbage bin has LUCKY STRIKE stamped on it. And there are flags hanging from the ceiling from every country in the world – again, except the United States And there's a whole bank of clocks showing the time in different cities, but no clocks show the times in U.S. cities.

I felt sad about leaving, then I felt irritated, now I don't feel anything. But I laugh when I hear a mother telling her twelve-year-old boy, "It's okay to call a smart person an idiot, but it's not nice to call an idiot an idiot."

Lucky I have a window seat, so I can hide my hot, silent, non-sobbing tears as the plane lifts off. Up at the Finca Vigía, in its days of glory, Marlene Dietrich, Ava Gardner, Spencer Tracy, Gary Cooper, and Errol Flynn frolicked in that large grey pool with the Busby Berkeley steps. All those people are gone, so why can't I be gone? I have to learn to accept my fate like a man, I can't become a Cuban.

I'm looking down at what I'm being wrenched away from, and it is hurting my heart and causing me to mourn how incomplete my visit somehow seems to have been, although the very nature of my modus operandi practically guarantees sudden departures and elliptical behaviour, just as it feeds on surprising bolts from the blue, and the odd tricks one's spirit guide will play if one pays close enough attention to things of that nature. It's also sad that I couldn't stop thinking of my book, not for a minute. Torturing myself about it too.

And there was the sadness for not having visited Cienfuegos, for not having spent more time in Santiago, Bayamo, or for not having visited the English school in Baracoa, and for not having explored Havana more thoroughly. Sadness at not having headed up to the extreme north coast, the Romany Archipelago that Hemingway writes so well about. Innumerable sadnesses hung from the roof of my mind like bats from a cave.

I thought thirty-three days would be enough. Maybe for the book, but not for the author.

SUGGESTED READING

Anderson, Jon Lee. *Che Guevara: A Revolutionary Life.* New York: Grove Press, 1997.

Arenas, Reinaldo. *Before Night Falls.* Toronto: Viking-Penguin Books Canada, 1993.

Cabrera Alvarez, Guillermo. ed. *Memories of Che.* Secaucus, N.J.: L. Stuart, 1987.

Cardenal, Ernesto. *In Cuba.* New York: New Directions, 1974.

Castro, Fidel. *Che: A Memoir.* Sydney: Ocean Books, 1994.

———. *History Will Absolve Me.* Secaucus, N.J.: L. Stuart, 1984.

Carpentier, Alejo. *The Chase.* New York: Farrar, Straus and Giroux; Collins, 1989.

———. *Concierto Barroco.* Tulsa, Okla.: Council Oak Books, 1988.

Cirules, Enrique. *Ernest Hemingway in the Romano Archipelago.* Havana: Editiones Unión, 1999.

Didion, Joan. *Miami.* Toronto: Lester & Orpen Dennys, 1987.

Fernández, Alina. *Castro's Daughter.* New York: St. Martin's Press, 1998.

Galeano, Eduardo. *Upside Down: A Primer for the Looking-Glass World.* New York: Picador, 2001.

Gébler, Carlo. *Driving Through Cuba.* London: Hamish Hamilton, 1988.

Greene, Graham. *Our Man in Havana.* London: Heinemann, 1958.

Guevara, Che. *Bolivian Diary*. London: Pimlico, 2000.

——. *Motorcycle Diaries*. Mississauga, Ont.: Penguin, 1996.

Hébert, Jacques, and Pierre Elliott Trudeau. *Two Innocents in Red China*. Toronto: Oxford University Press, 1968.

Hemingway, Ernest. *Islands in the Stream*. New York: Scribner's, 1970.

Hijuelos, Oscar. *The Mambo Kings Play Songs of Love*. New York: Farrar, Straus and Giroux, 1989.

Hinckle, Warren, and William Turner. *Deadly Secrets*. New York: Thunder's Mouth Press, 1992.

Michener, James. *Six Days in Havana*. Toronto: McClelland & Stewart, 1989.

Saldana, Roldofo. *Fertile Ground: Che Guevara & Bolivia*. College Park, Ga.: Pathfinder, 2001.

Smith, Wayne S. *The Closest of Enemies: A Personal and Diplomatic Account of U.S.-Cuban Relations since 1957*. New York: W.W. Norton, 1987.

Sullivan, Rosemary. *Cuba: Grace Under Pressure*. Toronto: McArthur & Company, 2003.

Szulc, Tad. *Fidel: A Critical Portrait*. New York: Morrow, 1986.

Taibo II, Paco Ignacio. *Guevara, Also Known as Che*. New York: St. Martin's Press, 1997.